**Rand McNally**

# Traveler's World Atlas & Guide

**Rand McNally & Company**
Chicago · New York · San Francisco

# Quick Reference Contents

© 1993 Rand McNally & Company
All rights reserved.
Printed in the United States of America

Library of Congress Cataloging-in-Publication Data
Rand McNally & Company
    Traveler's world atlas and guide.
        p.   cm.
    Includes index.
    ISBN 0-528-83497-5
    1. Atlases.   I. Title.
G1021.R487   1992  < G&M >
912—dc20                          92-24032
                                             CIP
                                             MAP

# Contents

# 4 Contents

## Guide to Selected Cities (cont'd)

## World Travel Maps 81

## World Comparisons 145

## Country Profiles 214

**6**

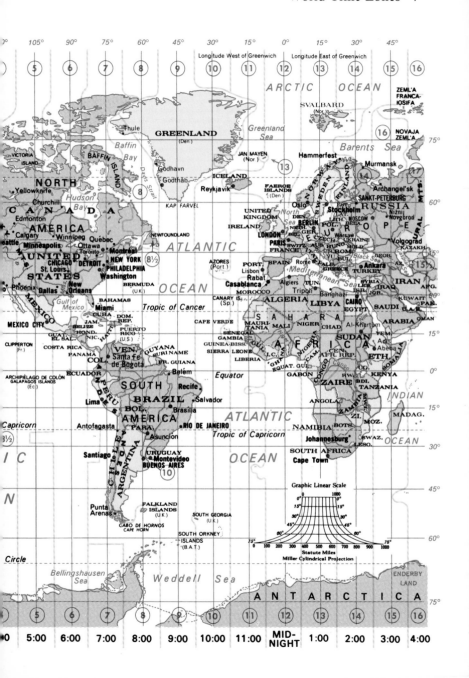

# Air Distances Between World Cities
*Given in statute miles*

| | Apia, Western Samoa | Azores Islands | Beijing, China | Berlin, Germany | Bombay, India | Buenos Aires, Argentina | Calcutta, India | Cape Town, South Africa | Cape Verde Islands | Chicago, U.S.A. | Darwin, Australia | Denver, U.S.A. | Gibraltar | Hong Kong |
|---|---|---|---|---|---|---|---|---|---|---|---|---|---|---|
| Apia | | 9644 | 5903 | 9743 | 8154 | 6931 | 7183 | 9064 | 10246 | 6557 | 3843 | 5653 | 10676 | 5591 |
| Azores Islands | 9644 | | 6565 | 2185 | 5967 | 5417 | 6549 | 5854 | 1499 | 3093 | 10209 | 3991 | 1249 | 7572 |
| Beijing | 5903 | 6565 | | 4567 | 2964 | 11974 | 2024 | 8045 | 7763 | 6592 | 3728 | 6348 | 6009 | 1226 |
| Berlin | 9743 | 2185 | 4567 | | 3910 | 7376 | 4376 | 5977 | 3194 | 4402 | 8036 | 5077 | 1453 | 5500 |
| Bombay | 8154 | 5967 | 2964 | 3910 | | 9273 | 1041 | 5134 | 6297 | 8054 | 4503 | 8383 | 4814 | 2673 |
| Buenos Aires | 6931 | 5417 | 11974 | 7376 | 9273 | | 10242 | 4270 | 4208 | 5596 | 9127 | 5928 | 5963 | 11463 |
| Calcutta | 7183 | 6549 | 2024 | 4376 | 1041 | 10242 | | 6026 | 7148 | 7981 | 3744 | 8050 | 5521 | 1534 |
| Cape Town | 9064 | 5854 | 8045 | 5977 | 5134 | 4270 | 6026 | | 4509 | 8449 | 6947 | 9327 | 5076 | 7372 |
| Cape Verde Is. | 10246 | 1499 | 7763 | 3194 | 6297 | 4208 | 7148 | 4509 | | 4066 | 10664 | 4975 | 1762 | 8539 |
| Chicago | 6557 | 3093 | 6592 | 4402 | 8054 | 5596 | 7981 | 8449 | 4066 | | 9346 | 920 | 4258 | 7790 |
| Darwin | 3843 | 10209 | 3728 | 8036 | 4503 | 9127 | 3744 | 6947 | 10664 | 9346 | | 8557 | 9265 | 2642 |
| Denver | 5653 | 3991 | 6348 | 5077 | 8383 | 5928 | 8050 | 9327 | 4975 | 920 | 8557 | | 5122 | 7465 |
| Gibraltar | 10676 | 1249 | 6009 | 1453 | 4814 | 5963 | 5521 | 5076 | 1762 | 4258 | 9265 | 5122 | | 6828 |
| Hong Kong | 5591 | 7572 | 1226 | 5500 | 2673 | 11463 | 1534 | 7372 | 8539 | 7790 | 2642 | 7465 | 6828 | |
| Honolulu | 2604 | 7180 | 5067 | 7305 | 8020 | 7558 | 7037 | 11532 | 8311 | 4244 | 5355 | 3338 | 8075 | 5537 |
| Istanbul | 10175 | 2975 | 4379 | 1078 | 2991 | 7568 | 3646 | 5219 | 3507 | 5476 | 7390 | 6154 | 1874 | 4980 |
| Juneau | 5415 | 4526 | 4522 | 4560 | 6866 | 7759 | 6326 | 10330 | 5911 | 2305 | 7105 | 1831 | 5273 | 5634 |
| London | 9789 | 1527 | 5054 | 574 | 4462 | 6918 | 4954 | 6005 | 2731 | 3950 | 8598 | 4688 | 1094 | 5981 |
| Los Angeles | 4828 | 4794 | 6250 | 5782 | 8701 | 6118 | 8148 | 9969 | 5772 | 1745 | 7835 | 831 | 5936 | 7240 |
| Manila | 4993 | 8250 | 1770 | 6128 | 3148 | 11042 | 2189 | 7525 | 9221 | 8128 | 1979 | 7661 | 7483 | 693 |
| Melbourne | 3113 | 12101 | 5667 | 9919 | 6097 | 7234 | 5547 | 6412 | 10856 | 9668 | 1964 | 8759 | 10798 | 4607 |
| Mexico City | 5449 | 4385 | 7733 | 6037 | 9722 | 4633 | 9495 | 8511 | 4857 | 1673 | 9081 | 1434 | 5629 | 8776 |
| Moscow | 9116 | 3165 | 3597 | 996 | 3131 | 8375 | 3447 | 6294 | 3982 | 4984 | 7046 | 5485 | 2413 | 4439 |
| New Orleans | 6085 | 3524 | 7314 | 5116 | 8865 | 4916 | 8803 | 8316 | 4194 | 833 | 9545 | 1082 | 4757 | 8480 |
| New York | 7242 | 2422 | 6823 | 3961 | 7794 | 5297 | 7921 | 7801 | 3355 | 713 | 9959 | 1631 | 3627 | 8051 |
| Nome | 5438 | 4954 | 3428 | 4342 | 5901 | 8848 | 5271 | 10097 | 6438 | 3314 | 6235 | 2925 | 5398 | 4547 |
| Oslo | 9247 | 2234 | 4360 | 515 | 4130 | 7613 | 4459 | 6494 | 3444 | 4040 | 8022 | 4653 | 1791 | 5337 |
| Panamá | 6514 | 3778 | 8906 | 5849 | 9742 | 3381 | 10114 | 7014 | 3734 | 2325 | 10352 | 2636 | 4926 | 10084 |
| Paris | 9990 | 1659 | 5101 | 542 | 4359 | 6877 | 4889 | 3841 | 2666 | 4133 | 8575 | 4885 | 964 | 5956 |
| Port Said | 10485 | 3391 | 4584 | 1747 | 2659 | 7362 | 3506 | 4590 | 3672 | 6103 | 7159 | 6819 | 2179 | 4975 |
| Quebec | 7406 | 2240 | 6423 | 3583 | 7371 | 5680 | 7481 | 7857 | 3355 | 878 | 9724 | 1752 | 3383 | 8650 |
| Reykjavik | 8678 | 1777 | 4903 | 1479 | 5191 | 7099 | 5409 | 7111 | 3248 | 2954 | 8631 | 3596 | 2047 | 6031 |
| Rio de Janeiro | 8120 | 4428 | 10768 | 6144 | 8257 | 1218 | 9376 | 3769 | 3040 | 5296 | 9960 | 5871 | 4775 | 10995 |
| Rome | 10475 | 2125 | 5047 | 734 | 3843 | 6929 | 4496 | 5249 | 2772 | 4808 | 8190 | 5561 | 1034 | 5768 |
| San Francisco | 4786 | 4872 | 5902 | 5657 | 8392 | 6474 | 7809 | 10241 | 5921 | 1858 | 7637 | 949 | 5936 | 6894 |
| Seattle | 5222 | 4501 | 5396 | 5041 | 7741 | 6913 | 7224 | 10199 | 5714 | 1737 | 7619 | 1021 | 5462 | 6471 |
| Shanghai | 5399 | 7229 | 662 | 5215 | 3133 | 12197 | 2112 | 8059 | 8443 | 7053 | 3142 | 6698 | 6646 | 772 |
| Singapore | 5850 | 8326 | 2774 | 6166 | 2429 | 9864 | 1791 | 6016 | 8700 | 9365 | 2075 | 9063 | 7231 | 1652 |
| Tokyo | 4656 | 7247 | 1307 | 5538 | 4188 | 11400 | 3186 | 9071 | 8589 | 6303 | 3367 | 5795 | 6988 | 1796 |
| Valparaíso | 6267 | 5678 | 11774 | 7795 | 10037 | 761 | 10993 | 4998 | 4649 | 5268 | 8961 | 5452 | 6408 | 11607 |
| Vienna | 10010 | 2291 | 4639 | 328 | 3718 | 7368 | 4259 | 5671 | 3147 | 4694 | 7974 | 5383 | 1386 | 5429 |
| Washington, D.C. | 7066 | 2667 | 6922 | 4167 | 7988 | 5216 | 8088 | 7894 | 3486 | 597 | 9923 | 1494 | 3822 | 8148 |
| Wellington | 2062 | 11269 | 6698 | 11265 | 7677 | 6260 | 7042 | 7019 | 10363 | 8349 | 3310 | 7516 | 12060 | 5853 |
| Winnipeg | 6283 | 3389 | 5907 | 4286 | 7644 | 6297 | 7424 | 9054 | 4556 | 714 | 8684 | 798 | 4435 | 7096 |
| Zanzibar | 9892 | 5323 | 5803 | 4309 | 2855 | 6421 | 3859 | 2346 | 4635 | 8358 | 6409 | 9221 | 4103 | 5414 |

| Honolulu, Hawaii, U.S.A. | Istanbul, Turkey | Juneau, Alaska, U.S.A. | London, United Kingdom | Los Angeles, U.S.A. | Manila, Philippines | Melbourne, Australia | Mexico City, Mexico | Moscow, Russia | New Orleans, U.S.A. | New York, U.S.A. | Nome, Alaska, U.S.A. | Oslo, Norway | Panamá, Panama | Paris, France | Port Said, Egypt | Quebec, Canada |
|---|---|---|---|---|---|---|---|---|---|---|---|---|---|---|---|---|
| 2604 | 10175 | 5415 | 9789 | 4828 | 4993 | 3113 | 5449 | 9116 | 6085 | 7242 | 5438 | 9247 | 6514 | 9990 | 10485 | 7406 |
| 7180 | 2975 | 4526 | 1527 | 4794 | 8250 | 12101 | 4385 | 3165 | 3524 | 2422 | 4954 | 2234 | 3778 | 1659 | 3391 | 2240 |
| 5067 | 4379 | 4522 | 5054 | 6250 | 1770 | 5667 | 7733 | 3597 | 7314 | 6823 | 3428 | 4360 | 8906 | 5101 | 4584 | 6423 |
| 7305 | 1078 | 4560 | 574 | 5782 | 6128 | 9919 | 6037 | 996 | 5116 | 3961 | 4342 | 515 | 5849 | 542 | 1747 | 3583 |
| 8020 | 2991 | 6866 | 4462 | 8701 | 3148 | 6097 | 9722 | 3131 | 8865 | 7794 | 5901 | 4130 | 9742 | 4359 | 2659 | 7371 |
| 7558 | 7568 | 7759 | 6918 | 6118 | 11042 | 7234 | 4633 | 8375 | 4916 | 5297 | 8848 | 7613 | 3381 | 6877 | 7362 | 5680 |
| 7037 | 3646 | 6326 | 4954 | 8148 | 2189 | 5547 | 9495 | 3447 | 8803 | 7921 | 5271 | 4459 | 10114 | 4889 | 3506 | 7481 |
| 11532 | 5219 | 10330 | 6005 | 9969 | 7525 | 6412 | 8511 | 6294 | 8316 | 7801 | 10107 | 6494 | 7014 | 5841 | 4590 | 7857 |
| 8311 | 3507 | 5911 | 2731 | 9221 | 10856 | 4857 | 3982 |  | 4194 | 3355 | 6438 | 3444 | 3734 | 2666 | 3672 | 3355 |
| 4244 | 5476 | 2305 | 3950 | 1745 | 8128 | 9668 | 1673 | 4984 | 833 | 713 | 3314 | 4040 | 2325 | 4133 | 6103 | 878 |
| 5355 | 7390 | 7105 | 8598 | 7835 | 1979 | 1964 | 9081 | 7046 | 9545 | 9959 | 6235 | 8022 | 10352 | 8575 | 7159 | 9724 |
| 3338 | 6154 | 1831 | 4688 | 831 | 7661 | 8759 | 1434 | 5485 | 1082 | 1631 | 2925 | 4653 | 2636 | 4885 | 6819 | 1732 |
| 8075 | 1874 | 5273 | 1094 | 5936 | 7483 | 10798 | 5629 | 2413 | 4757 | 3627 | 5398 | 1791 | 4926 | 964 | 2179 | 3383 |
| 5537 | 4980 | 5634 | 5981 | 7240 | 693 | 4607 | 8776 | 4439 | 8480 | 8051 | 4547 | 5337 | 10084 | 5956 | 4975 | 7650 |
| 8104 |  |  |  |  |  |  |  |  |  |  |  |  |  |  |  |  |
| 2815 | 5498 |  |  |  |  |  |  |  |  |  |  |  |  |  |  |  |
| 7226 | 1551 | 4418 |  |  |  |  |  |  |  |  |  |  |  |  |  |  |
| 2557 | 6843 | 1842 | 5439 |  |  |  |  |  |  |  |  |  |  |  |  |  |
| 5296 | 5659 | 5869 | 6667 | 7269 |  |  |  |  |  |  |  |  |  |  |  |  |
| 5513 | 9088 | 8035 | 10501 | 7931 | 3941 |  |  |  |  |  |  |  |  |  |  |  |
| 3781 | 7102 | 3219 | 5541 | 1542 | 8829 | 8422 |  |  |  |  |  |  |  |  |  |  |
| 7033 | 1088 | 4534 | 1549 | 6068 | 5130 | 8963 | 6688 |  |  |  |  |  |  |  |  |  |
| 4207 | 6171 | 2905 | 4627 | 1673 | 8724 | 9275 | 934 | 5756 |  |  |  |  |  |  |  |  |
| 4959 | 5009 | 2854 | 3459 | 2451 | 8493 | 10355 | 2085 | 4662 | 1171 |  |  |  |  |  |  |  |
| 3004 | 5101 | 1094 | 4381 | 2876 | 4817 | 7558 | 4309 | 4036 | 3937 | 3769 |  |  |  |  |  |  |
| 6784 | 1518 | 4045 | 714 | 5325 | 6016 | 9926 | 5706 | 1016 | 4795 | 3672 | 3836 |  |  |  |  |  |
| 5245 | 6750 | 4460 | 5278 | 3001 | 10283 | 9022 | 1495 | 6711 | 1603 | 2231 | 5541 | 5691 |  |  |  |  |
| 7434 | 1401 | 4628 | 213 | 5601 | 6673 | 10396 | 5706 | 1541 | 4788 | 3622 | 4574 | 832 | 5382 |  |  |  |
| 8738 | 693 | 6215 | 2154 | 7528 | 5619 | 8658 | 7671 | 1710 | 6756 | 5590 | 5745 | 2211 | 7146 | 1975 |  |  |
| 5000 | 4644 | 2660 | 3101 | 2579 | 8124 | 10497 | 2454 | 4242 | 1534 | 439 | 3489 | 3263 | 2659 | 3235 | 5250 |  |
| 6084 | 2558 | 3268 | 1171 | 4306 | 6651 | 10544 | 4622 | 2056 | 3711 | 2576 | 3366 | 1083 | 4706 | 1380 | 3227 | 2189 |
| 8190 | 6395 | 7598 | 5772 | 6296 | 11254 | 8186 | 4770 | 7179 | 4796 | 4820 | 8586 | 6482 | 3294 | 5703 | 6244 | 5125 |
| 8022 | 854 | 5247 | 887 | 6326 | 6457 | 9934 | 6353 | 1474 | 5439 | 4273 | 5082 | 1243 | 5903 | 682 | 1317 | 3943 |
| 2392 | 6700 | 1525 | 5355 | 347 | 6963 | 7854 | 1885 | 5868 | 1926 | 2571 | 2547 | 5181 | 3322 | 5441 | 7394 | 2642 |
| 2678 | 6063 | 899 | 4782 | 959 | 6641 | 8186 | 2337 | 5199 | 2101 | 2408 | 1976 | 4591 | 3651 | 4993 | 6759 | 2353 |
| 4934 | 4959 | 4869 | 5710 | 6477 | 1152 | 5005 | 8039 | 4235 | 7720 | 7357 | 3784 | 5020 | 9324 | 5752 | 5132 | 6981 |
| 6710 | 5373 | 7235 | 6744 | 8767 | 1479 | 3761 | 10307 | 5238 | 10082 | 9630 | 6148 | 6246 | 11687 | 6671 | 5088 | 9097 |
| 3850 | 5556 | 4011 | 5938 | 5470 | 1863 | 5089 | 7035 | 4650 | 6858 | 6735 | 2983 | 5221 | 8423 | 6033 | 5842 | 6417 |
| 6793 | 8172 | 7271 | 7263 | 5527 | 10930 | 6998 | 4053 | 8792 | 4514 | 5094 | 8360 | 7914 | 2943 | 7251 | 8088 | 5504 |
| 7626 | 783 | 4895 | 772 | 6108 | 6120 | 9792 | 6306 | 1044 | 5385 | 4224 | 4657 | 850 | 6026 | 644 | 1429 | 3858 |
| 4829 | 5216 | 2834 | 3665 | 2300 | 8560 | 10173 | 1878 | 4883 | 966 | 205 | 3792 | 3870 | 2080 | 3828 | 5796 | 610 |
| 4708 | 10663 | 7475 | 11682 | 6714 | 5162 | 1595 | 6899 | 10279 | 7794 | 8946 | 7383 | 10974 | 7433 | 11791 | 10249 | 9228 |
| 3806 | 5361 | 1597 | 3918 | 1525 | 7414 | 9319 | 2097 | 4687 | 1418 | 1281 | 2599 | 3854 | 2998 | 4118 | 6032 | 1199 |
| 10869 | 3312 | 8795 | 4604 | 10021 | 5763 | 6802 | 9484 | 4270 | 8754 | 7698 | 8209 | 4803 | 8245 | 4396 | 2729 | 7443 |

| Reykjavik, Iceland | Rio de Janeiro, Brazil | Rome, Italy | San Francisco, U.S.A. | Seattle, U.S.A. | Shanghai, China | Singapore, Singapore | Tokyo, Japan | Valparaíso, Chile | Vienna, Austria | Washington, D.C., U.S.A. | Wellington, New Zealand | Winnipeg, Canada | Zanzibar, Tanzania | |
|---|---|---|---|---|---|---|---|---|---|---|---|---|---|---|
| 8678 | 8120 | 10475 | 4786 | 5222 | 5399 | 5850 | 4656 | 6267 | 10010 | 7066 | 2062 | 6283 | 9892 | Apia |
| 1777 | 4428 | 2125 | 4872 | 4501 | 7229 | 8326 | 7247 | 5678 | 2291 | 2667 | 11269 | 3389 | 5323 | Azores Islands |
| 4903 | 10768 | 5047 | 5902 | 5396 | 662 | 2774 | 1307 | 11774 | 4639 | 6922 | 6698 | 5907 | 5803 | Beijing |
| 1479 | 6114 | 734 | 5657 | 5041 | 5215 | 6166 | 5538 | 7795 | 328 | 4167 | 11265 | 4285 | 4309 | Berlin |
| 5191 | 8257 | 3843 | 8392 | 7741 | 3133 | 2429 | 4188 | 10037 | 3718 | 7988 | 7677 | 7644 | 2855 | Bombay |
| 7099 | 1218 | 6929 | 6474 | 6913 | 12197 | 9864 | 11400 | 761 | 7368 | 5216 | 6260 | 6297 | 6421 | Buenos Aires |
| 5409 | 9376 | 4496 | 7809 | 7224 | 2112 | 1791 | 3186 | 10993 | 4259 | 8088 | 7042 | 7424 | 3859 | Calcutta |
| 7111 | 3769 | 5249 | 10241 | 10199 | 8059 | 6016 | 9071 | 4998 | 5671 | 7894 | 7019 | 9054 | 2346 | Cape Town |
| 3248 | 3040 | 2772 | 5921 | 5714 | 8443 | 8700 | 8589 | 4649 | 3147 | 3486 | 10363 | 4556 | 4635 | Cape Verde Is. |
| 2954 | 5296 | 4808 | 1858 | 1737 | 7053 | 9365 | 6303 | 5268 | 4694 | 597 | 8349 | 714 | 8358 | Chicago |
| 8631 | 9960 | 8190 | 7637 | 7619 | 3142 | 2075 | 3367 | 8961 | 7974 | 9923 | 3310 | 8684 | 6409 | Darwin |
| 3596 | 5871 | 5561 | 949 | 1021 | 6698 | 9063 | 5795 | 5452 | 5383 | 1494 | 7516 | 798 | 9921 | Denver |
| 2047 | 4775 | 1034 | 5936 | 5462 | 6646 | 7231 | 6988 | 6408 | 1386 | 3822 | 12060 | 4435 | 4103 | Gibraltar |
| 6031 | 10995 | 5768 | 6894 | 6471 | 772 | 1652 | 1796 | 11607 | 5429 | 8148 | 5853 | 7096 | 5414 | Hong Kong |
| 6084 | 8190 | 8022 | 2392 | 2678 | 4934 | 6710 | 3850 | 6793 | 7626 | 4829 | 4708 | 3806 | 10869 | Honolulu |
| 2558 | 6395 | 854 | 6700 | 6063 | 4959 | 5373 | 5556 | 8172 | 783 | 5216 | 10663 | 5361 | 3312 | Istanbul |
| 3268 | 7598 | 5247 | 1525 | 899 | 4869 | 7235 | 4011 | 7271 | 4895 | 2834 | 7475 | 1597 | 8795 | Juneau |
| 1171 | 5772 | 887 | 5355 | 4782 | 5710 | 6744 | 5938 | 7263 | 772 | 3665 | 11682 | 3918 | 4604 | London |
| 4306 | 6296 | 6326 | 347 | 959 | 6477 | 8767 | 5470 | 5527 | 6108 | 2300 | 6714 | 1525 | 10021 | Los Angeles |
| 6651 | 11254 | 6457 | 6963 | 6641 | 1152 | 1479 | 1863 | 10930 | 6120 | 8560 | 5162 | 7414 | 5763 | Manila |
| 10544 | 8186 | 9934 | 7854 | 8186 | 5005 | 3761 | 5089 | 6998 | 9792 | 10173 | 1595 | 9319 | 6802 | Melbourne |
| 4622 | 4770 | 6353 | 1885 | 2337 | 8039 | 10307 | 7035 | 4053 | 6306 | 1878 | 6899 | 2097 | 9484 | Mexico City |
| 2056 | 7179 | 1474 | 5868 | 5199 | 4235 | 5238 | 4650 | 8792 | 1044 | 4883 | 10279 | 4307 | 4270 | Moscow |
| 3711 | 4796 | 5439 | 1926 | 2101 | 7720 | 10082 | 6858 | 4514 | 5385 | 966 | 7794 | 1418 | 8754 | New Orleans |
| 2576 | 4820 | 4273 | 2571 | 2408 | 7357 | 9630 | 6735 | 5094 | 4224 | 205 | 8946 | 1281 | 7698 | New York |
| 3366 | 8586 | 5082 | 2547 | 1976 | 3784 | 6148 | 2983 | 8360 | 4657 | 3792 | 7383 | 2599 | 8209 | Nome |
| 1083 | 6482 | 1243 | 5181 | 4591 | 5020 | 6246 | 5221 | 7914 | 859 | 3870 | 10974 | 3854 | 4803 | Oslo |
| 4706 | 3294 | 5903 | 3322 | 3651 | 9324 | 11687 | 8423 | 2943 | 6026 | 2080 | 7433 | 2998 | 8245 | Panamá |
| 1380 | 5703 | 682 | 5441 | 4993 | 5752 | 6671 | 6033 | 7251 | 644 | 3828 | 11791 | 4118 | 4396 | Paris |
| 3227 | 6244 | 1317 | 7394 | 6759 | 5132 | 5088 | 5842 | 8088 | 1429 | 5796 | 10249 | 6032 | 2729 | Port Said |
| 2189 | 5125 | 3943 | 2642 | 2353 | 6981 | 9097 | 6417 | 5504 | 3858 | 610 | 9228 | 1199 | 7443 | Quebec |
| | 6118 | 2044 | 4199 | 3614 | 5559 | 7160 | 5472 | 7225 | 1805 | 2800 | 10724 | 2804 | 5757 | Reykjavik |
| 6118 | | 5684 | 6619 | 6891 | 11340 | 9774 | 11535 | 1855 | 6136 | 4797 | 7349 | 6010 | 5589 | Rio de Janeiro |
| 2044 | 5684 | | 6240 | 5659 | 5677 | 6232 | 6124 | 7420 | 463 | 4435 | 11524 | 4803 | 3712 | Rome |
| 4199 | 6619 | 6240 | | 678 | 6132 | 8479 | 5131 | 5876 | 5988 | 2442 | 6739 | 1504 | 9958 | San Francisco |
| 3614 | 6891 | 5639 | 678 | | 5703 | 8057 | 4777 | 6230 | 5376 | 2329 | 7242 | 1150 | 9359 | Seattle |
| 5559 | 11340 | 5677 | 6132 | 5703 | | 2377 | 1094 | 11650 | 5270 | 7442 | 6054 | 6350 | 5971 | Shanghai |
| 7160 | 9774 | 6232 | 8479 | 8057 | 2377 | | 3304 | 10226 | 6036 | 9834 | 5292 | 8685 | 4480 | Singapore |
| 5472 | 11535 | 6124 | 5131 | 4777 | 1094 | 3304 | | 10635 | 5679 | 6769 | 5760 | 5575 | 7040 | Tokyo |
| 7225 | 1855 | 7420 | 5876 | 6230 | 11650 | 10226 | 10635 | | 7783 | 4977 | 5785 | 5931 | 7184 | Valparaíso |
| 1805 | 6136 | 463 | 5988 | 5376 | 5270 | 6036 | 5679 | 7783 | | 4429 | 11278 | 4604 | 3983 | Vienna |
| 2800 | 4797 | 4435 | 2442 | 2329 | 7442 | 9834 | 6769 | 4977 | 4429 | | 8745 | 1243 | 7884 | Washington, D.C. |
| 10724 | 7349 | 11524 | 6739 | 7242 | 6054 | 5292 | 5760 | 5785 | 11278 | 8745 | | 8230 | 8122 | Wellington |
| 2804 | 6010 | 4803 | 1504 | 1150 | 6350 | 8685 | 5575 | 5931 | 4604 | 1243 | 8230 | | 8416 | Winnipeg |
| 5757 | 5589 | 3712 | 9958 | 9359 | 5971 | 4480 | 7040 | 7184 | 3983 | 7884 | 8122 | 8416 | | Zanzibar |

# Travel Information

Entry requirements and travel advisories are subject to change. Travelers are advised to contact a travel agent, the State Department, a passport office, and/or the embassy of the destination for definitive travel information. In Islamic countries, when appearing in public, women should cover their arms, legs, and, in some places, their heads. Holidays for which a date is not given change from year to year; contact the country's embassy for exact dates.

| Country | Algeria | Argentina | Australia |
|---|---|---|---|
| **Int'l Dialing Code** | 213 | 54 | 61 |
| **City Codes** | | Buenos Aires 1, Córdoba 51, La Plata 21, Mendoza 61, Rosario 41 | Adelaide 8, Brisbane 7, Canberra 62, Melbourne 3, Sydney 2 |
| **Consulate Phone** | (202) 265-2800 | (202) 939-6400 | (202) 797-3000 |
| **Climate** | Mild, wet winters with hot, dry summers along the coast; drier with cold winters and hot summers on high plateau. | Climate ranges from hot, subtropical lowlands of the north to cold and rainy in the south. January in Buenos Aires is like Washington, D.C. in July; July is like San Francisco in January. | Arid to semiarid; temperate in the south and east; tropical in the north; most of southern Australia has warm summers and mild winters (seasons are reversed from North America). |
| **Clothing** | Lightweight clothing for summer; lightweight winter clothing for November to April. A hat and sunglasses are essential. Not all rooms are warmly heated in the winter. | Lightweight cottons are advisable for the north; woolens are needed during the winters and year-round in the extreme south. Dress is more formal than in the U.S. Shorts are not universally acceptable. | Wear lightweight clothing year round in the temperate regions during the winter; warmer clothes and an overcoat are then required. Casual clothing is usually appropriate. |
| **Entry Requirements** | Passport, visa, ticket to leave, sufficient funds; cholera and other inoculations recommended | Passport, visa | Passport, visa, ticket to leave, sufficient funds |
| **Holidays** | New Year's Day, Jan. 1; Prophet's Ascension; Ramadan and Id al-Fitr; Labor Day, May 1; Id al Adha; Independence Day, July 5; Islamic New Year; Prophet's Birthday; Anniversary of the Revolution, Nov. 1 | New Year's Day, Jan. 1; Maundy Thursday; Good Friday; Labor Day, May 1; National Day, May 25; Flag Day, June 20; Independence Day, July 9; Anniversary of San Martin's Death, Aug. 17; Columbus Day, Oct. 12; Immaculate Conception, Dec. 8; Christmas Day, Dec. 25 | New Year's Day, Jan. 1; Australia Day, late Jan.; Good Friday; Holy Saturday; Easter Monday; ANZAC Day, Apr. 25; Queen's Birthday, June; Christmas Day, Dec. 25; Boxing Day, Dec. 26 |
| **Special Notes** | There is a shortage of hotel rooms in Algiers. Tapwater is not potable; bottled water is available. | Tapwater is safe. | |

| Country | Austria | Bahamas | Barbados |
|---|---|---|---|
| **Int'l Dialing Code** | 43 | 809 | 809 |
| **City Codes** | Graz 316, Linz 732, Wien (Vienna) 222 | | |
| **Consulate Phone** | (202) 483-4474 | (202) 319-2660 | (202) 939-9200 |
| **Climate** | Cold winters with frequent rain in the lowlands and snow in the mountains; cool summers with occasional showers. | Tropical marine. | Tropical. |
| **Clothing** | Clothing needs and tastes are about the same as the northeastern United States. Bring sweaters and light woolens during possible cool spells in the summer. Many restaurants in Vienna have dress codes. | Lightweight clothing is worn year-round. Beachwear should be confined to resort areas. Daytime dress is casual, evening clothes are more formal. | Light-weight clothing is worn year-round; rainwear is needed for the rainy season. Casual clothes are usually acceptable. |
| **Entry Requirements** | Passport | Proof of citizenship, ticket to leave | Passport, ticket to leave |
| **Holidays** | New Year's Day, Jan. 1; Epiphany, Jan. 6; Easter Monday; Labor Day, May 1; Ascension Day; Whitmonday; Corpus Christi; Assumption Day, Aug. 15; National Day, Oct. 26; All Saints' Day, Nov. 1; Feast of the Immaculate Conception, Dec. 8; Christmas Day, Dec. 25; St. Stephen's Day, Dec. 26 | New Year's Day, Jan. 1; Good Friday; Easter Monday; Whitmonday; Labor Day, early June; Independence Day, July 10; Emancipation Day, early Aug.; Discovery Day, Oct. 12; Christmas Day, Dec. 25; Boxing Day, Dec. 26 | New Year's Day, Jan. 1; Good Friday; Easter Monday; Labor Day, May 1; Whitmonday; Kadooment Day, early July; United Nations Day, early Oct.; Independence Day, November 30; Christmas Day, Dec. 25; Boxing Day, Dec. 26 |
| **Special Notes** | | Hurricane season is from June to November. Water is potable but saline, and many people use bottled water. Mosquitos and sandflies may be a problem. | Hurricane season is from June to October. |

| Belgium | Bermuda | Botswana | Brazil |
|---|---|---|---|
| 32 | 809 | 267 | 55 |
| Antwerpen 3, Bruxelles 2, Gent 91, Liège 41 | | Francistown 21, Gaborone 31 | Belo Horizonte 31, Brasília 61, Rio de Janeiro 21, São Paulo 11 |
| (202) 333-6900 | (202) 462-1340 | (202) 244-4990 | (202) 745-2700 |
| Mild winters with little snow; cool summers; rainy, humid, cloudy. | Subtropical; mild, humid; gales, winds are common during the frost-free but chilly winter | Semiarid with warm winters and hot summers. | In most of the country, days range from warm to hot; rainy season from November to February; cool winters in the extreme south; seasons are reversed from North America. |
| Clothing and shoe needs in Belgium are about the same as for the Pacific Northwest. Raincoat, umbrellas, and low-heeled, thick-soled walking shoes are necessary. | Warm-weather clothing is suitable April-November; moderately heavy clothing is needed during the winter. Swimwear should be worn only on the beach. Most restaurants have evening dress codes. | Lightweight clothing is worn, with spring clothing for cool evenings and winter months. | Spring or summer clothes are appropriate year-round. |
| Passport, ticket to leave, sufficient funds | Proof of citizenship, visa (for stays of more than 21 days), ticket to leave | Passport; yellow fever and hepatitis innoculations recommended | Passport, visa; yellow fever and other innoculations recommended |
| New Year's Day, Jan. 1; Easter Monday; Labor Day, May 1; Ascension Day; Whitmonday; National Day, July 21; Assumption Day, Aug. 15; All Saints' Day, Nov. 1; Armistice Day, Nov. 11; Christmas Day, Dec. 25 | New Year's Day, Jan. 1; Good Friday; Commonwealth Day, May 24; Bermuda Day, late May; Queen's Birthday, June; Cup Match Day, late July; Labor Day, early Sept.; Remembrance Day, Nov. 11; Christmas Day, Dec. 25; Boxing Day, Dec. 26 | New Year's Day, Jan. 1; Good Friday; Easter Monday; Ascension Day; President's Day, July 16; Botswana Day, Sept. 30; Public Holiday, Oct. 1; Christmas Day, Dec. 25; Boxing Day, Dec. 26 | New Year's Day, Jan. 1; Carnival, Feb./Mar.; Good Friday; Tiradentes Day, Apr. 21; Labor Day, May 1; Corpus Christi; Independence Day, Sept. 7; Nossa Senhora de Aparecida, Oct. 12; Proclamation of the Republic, Nov. 15; Christmas Day, Dec. 25 |
| Tapwater is potable. | | Tapwater is potable in the major towns. Do not swim in lakes or rivers. | Street crime is common in Brazil's larger cities. Tapwater is not safe for consumption. Carefully prepared and thoroughly cooked foods are safe for consumption. |

| Country | Bulgaria | Canada | Chile |
|---|---|---|---|
| Int'l Dialing Code | 359 | | 56 |
| City Codes | Plovdiv 32, Sofija 2, Varna 52 | | Concepción 41, Santiago 2, Valparaíso 32 |
| Consulate Phone | (202) 387-7969 | (202) 682-1740 | (202) 785-1746 |
| Climate | Cold, damp winters with considerable snowfall; hot, dry, summers. | Varies from temperate in the south to subarctic and arctic in the north. | Climate ranges from desert in the north to cool and damp in the south; summers are dry and hot with cool nights; winters are cold and rainy. Seasons are reversed from North America. |
| Clothing | Summer clothing should include sweaters for cool evenings. Warm clothing advisable for cold winters. Formal wear is seldom required. | Lightweight clothes for summer months with a sweater for cool evenings; heavy clothing for winter months. | Sweaters are useful for cool summer nights; a jacket or coat is needed in the winter. Shorts should not be worn outside resort areas. |
| Entry Requirements | Passport | Proof of citizenship | Passport, business visa or tourist card; difficult to enter and exit by car; innoculations recommended |
| Holidays | New Year's Day, Jan. 1; Independence Day, Mar. 3; Labor Days, May 1,2; Bulgarian Culture Day, May 24; Liberation Days, Sept. 9,10; October Revolution Day, Nov. 7 | New Year's Day, Jan. 1; Good Friday; Easter Monday; Victoria Day, mid-May; Dominion Day, July 1; Civic Holiday, early Aug.; Thanksgiving, Oct. 12; Remembrance Day, Nov. 11; Christmas Day, Dec. 25; Boxing Day, Dec. 26 | New Year's Day, Jan. 1; Good Friday; Labor Day, May 1; Battle of Iquique, May 21; Corpus Christi; St. Peter's and Paul's Day; Assumption Day, Aug. 15; National Liberation Day, Sept. 11; Independence Day, Sept. 18; Day of the Army, Sept. 10; Columbus Day, Oct. 12; All Saints Day, Nov. 1; Immaculate Conception, Dec. 8; Christmas Day, Dec. 25 |
| Special Notes | Tapwater is potable in the capital. Eating in larger restaurants is advised. | | Do not eat unwashed fruits and vegetables. Tapwater is generally potable except after occasional winter floods. It is prudent to gradually accustom the body to tap water by using bottled water initially. Smog is prevalent in Santiago. |

| China (excl. Taiwan) | Colombia | Costa Rica | Czechoslovakia |
|---|---|---|---|
| 86 | 57 | 506 | 42 |
| Beijing (Peking) 1, Fuzhou 591, Guangzhou (Canton) 20, Jinan 531, Nanjing 25, Shanghai 21 | Barranquilla 5, Bogotá 1, Cali 23, Medellin 4 | | Bratislava 7, Brno 5, Ostrava 69, Praha (Prague) 2 |
| (202) 328-2517 | (202) 387-8338 | (202) 234-2945 | (202) 363-6315 |
| Extremely diverse; tropical in the south to subarctic in the north. | Tropical along the coast and eastern plains; cooler in the highlands. | Tropical; rainy season from May to November; dry season from December to April. | Cool, pleasant summers; cold, cloudy, humid winters. |
| In the north, lightweight clothing is required for the summer and heavy woolens for the harsh winters. In the south, tropical clothing is suitable for summer and spring-like clothing is worn in the winter. Clothing should be casual but conservative. | Knits and lightweight woolens are suitable in Bogota. Tropical clothing is worn in the lowlands. | Spring-weight clothing, with a sweater for cool evenings is recommended. Beachwear should be confined to resorts. | Bring rainwear and light or heavy woolens depending on the season. Casual but conservative dress is appropriate. |
| Passport, visa; innoculations recommended | Passport, business visa or tourist card | Passport, business visa or tourist card, ticket to leave, sufficient funds | Passport |
| New Year's Day, Jan. 1; Chinese New Year, Jan. or Feb.; Labor Day, May 1; National Day, Oct. 1 | New Year's Day, Jan. 1; Epiphany, Jan. 6; St. Joseph's Day, Mar. 19; Maundy Thursday; Good Friday; Labor Day, May 1; Ascension Day; Corpus Christi; Feast of the Sacred Heart; St. Peter and Paul Day; Independence Day, July 20; Battle of Boyaca, Aug. 7; Assumption Day, Aug. 15; Columbus Day, Oct. 12; All Saints' Day, Nov. 1; Independence of Cartagena, Nov. 11; Immaculate Consumption, Dec. 8; Christmas Day, Dec. 25 | New Year's Day, Jan. 1; St. Joseph's Day, Mar. 19; Maundy Thursday; Good Friday; Anniversary of the Battle of Rivas, Apr. 11; Labor Day, May 1; Corpus Christi; Annexation of Guanacaste, July 5; Our Lady of the Angels, Aug. 2; Assumption Day, Aug. 15; Independence Day, Sept. 15; Columbus Day, Oct. 12; Immaculate Conception, Dec. 8; Christmas Day, Dec. 25 | New Year's Day, Jan. 1; Easter Monday; Labor Day, May 1; Liberation Day, May 9; Christmas Day, Dec. 25; Boxing Day, Dec. 26. |
| Travel to most of Tibet and many other areas is restricted without special permission. Tours can be extremely strenuous. Use bottled water. | Because of sporadic guerrilla activity, travel in certain areas may be hazardous. Tapwater is not always safe in large cities; food should be prepared carefully. | Drinking water in major San Jose hotels and restaurants is purified; outside the capital drinking water should be purified. | Tapwater is usually safe. |

| Country | Denmark | Dominican Republic | Egypt |
|---|---|---|---|
| Int'l Dialing Code | 45 | 809 | 20 |
| City Codes | Ålborg 8, Århus 6, København (Copenhagen) 1 or 2, Odense 7 | | Al-Iskandarīyah (Alexandria) 3, Al-Qāhirah (Cairo) 2, Aswän 97, Asyūt 88 |
| Consulate Phone | (202) 234-4300 | (202) 332-6280 | (202) 232-5400 |
| Climate | Humid and overcast; mild, windy winters; cool, sunny summers. | Tropical; little temperature variation. | Desert; hot, dry summers with moderate winters. |
| Clothing | Woolen clothes are worn most of the year. Lightweight clothes may be required in the summer. | Lightweight clothing suitable for hot, humid weather is appropriate in Santo Domingo year round. Restaurants may have evening dress codes. | Lightweight summer clothing is needed for the summer; light woolens for the winter and cool evenings. Casual dress is appropriate, but revealing clothing is not appreciated. |
| Entry Requirements | Passport, ticket to leave, sufficient funds | Passport, business visa or tourist card, ticket to leave | Passport, visa, sufficient funds; innoculations recommended |
| Holidays | New Year's Day, Jan. 1; Thurs.-Mon. surrounding Easter; Prayer Day; Ascension Day; Constitution Day, June 5; Christmas Day, Dec. 25; Boxing Day, Dec. 26 | New Year's Day, Jan. 1; Epiphany, Jan. 6; Our Lady of Altagracia, Jan. 21; Duarte, Jan. 26; Independence Day, February 27, Good Friday; Labor Day, May 1; Corpus Christi, May 25; Restoration of Independence Day, Aug. 16; Our Lady of Las Mercedes, Sept. 24; Christmas Day, Dec. 25 | Union Day, Feb. 22; Ramadan; Sinai Liberation Day, April 25; Labor Day, May 1; Evacuation Day, June 18; Islamic New Year; Revolution Day, July 23; Prophet's Birthday; Armed Forces Day, Oct. 6; Suez Day, Oct. 24; Victory Day, Dec. 23 |
| Special Notes | | Hurricane season is from June to November. Tapwater is not potable. | Water in Cairo and Alexandria is generally safe, but milk should be boiled. Negotiate the fare with taxi drivers before entering the taxi. |

| Fiji | Finland | France | French Polynesia |
|---|---|---|---|
| 679 | 358 | 33 | 689 |
|  | Espoo 15, Helsinki 0, Tampere 31, Turku 21 | Bordeaux 56, Lyon 7, Marseille 91, Nice 93, Paris 1, Toulouse 61 |  |
| (202) 337-8320 | (202) 363-2430 | (202) 944-6000 | (202) 944-6087 |
| Tropical with high humidity; rainfall is abundant in Suva; little temperature variation. | Cold winters; mild summers. Helsinki's winter climate is similar to Boston's. | Cool winters and mild summers inland; mild winters and hot summers along the Mediterranean. | Tropical, but moderate. |
| Lightweight clothing is appropriate; dress is generally casual. Swimwear should not be worn in towns. | Warm outdoor clothing for winter and light woolens for summer are necessary. | Clothing needs are similar to those in Washington, D.C. | Lightweight clothing is worn throughout the year. |
| Passport, ticket to leave, sufficient funds | Passport, ticket to leave, sufficient funds | Passport | Passport, visa |
| New Year's Day, Jan. 1; Good Friday; Holy Saturday; Easter Monday; Queen's Birthday, June; Bank Holiday, early Aug.; Prophet's Birthday; Fiji Day, early Oct.; Diwali (Festival of Lights); Prince of Wales's Birthday, Nov. 14; Christmas Day, Dec. 25; Boxing Day, Dec. 26 | New Year's Day, Jan. 1; Epiphany; Good Friday; Easter; Easter Monday; May Day Eve, Apr. 30; May Day, May 1; Ascension Day; Whitsunday; Whitmonday; Midsummer's Day; All Saints' Day; Independence Day, Dec. 6, Christmas Day, Dec. 25 | New Year's Day, Jan. 1; Easter Monday; Labor Day, May 1; Ascension Day; Whitmonday; Bastille Day, July 14; Assumption Day, Aug. 15; All Saints' Day, Nov. 1; Armistice Day, Nov. 11; Christmas Day, Dec. 25 | New Year's Day, Jan. 1; Good Friday; Easter Monday; Labor Day, May 1; Ascension Day; Whitmonday; Bastille Day, July 14; All Saints' Day, Nov. 1; Armistice Day, Nov. 11; Christmas, Dec. 25, 26 |
| Drinking water is safe in all cities and major tourist resorts. | Tapwater is potable. |  |  |

| Country | Germany | Greece | Guatemala |
|---|---|---|---|
| **Int'l Dialing Code** | 49 | 30 | 502 |
| **City Codes** | Berlin 30, Bonn 228, Essen 201, Frankfurt am Main 69, Hamburg 40, München (Munich) 89 | Athínai (Athens) 1, Iráklion 81, Lárisa 41, Piraiévs 1, Thessaloníki 31 | Guatemala 2, all other cities 9 |
| **Consulate Phone** | (202) 298-4000 | (202) 939-5800 | (202) 745-4952 |
| **Climate** | Cool, cloudy, wet winters and summers; high relative humidity. | Mild, wet winters; hot, dry, summers. | Hot and humid in the lowlands; cooler in the highlands. |
| **Clothing** | Germany is cooler than much of the United States, especially in summer. Light-weight summer clothing is seldom needed. Very warm clothing is needed in the winter. | Lightweight clothing from May-September; woolens from October-April. | Spring or summer-weight clothing is needed most of the year; woolens are practical November through February. |
| **Entry Requirements** | Passport, ticket to leave, sufficient funds | Passport | Passport, business visa or tourist card, innoculations recommended |
| **Holidays** | New Year's Day, Jan. 1; Good Friday; Easter Monday; Labor Day, May 1; Ascension Day; Whitmonday; Day of Unity, June 17; Repentance Day, Nov. 16; Christmas Day, Dec. 25; Boxing Day, Dec. 26. | New Year's Day, Jan. 1; Epiphany, Jan. 6; Independence Day, Mar. 25; Good Friday; Easter Monday; Labor Day, May 1; Pentecost; Assumption Day, Aug. 15; Ochi Day, Oct. 28; Christmas Day, Dec. 25 | New Year's Day, Jan. 1; Maundy Thursday; Good Friday; Holy Saturday; Labor Day, May 1; Army Day, June 30; Assumption Day, Aug. 15; Independence Day, Sept. 15; Revolution Day, Oct. 20; All Saints' Day, Nov. 1; Christmas Eve, Dec. 24, Christmas Day, Dec. 25; New Year's Eve, Dec. 31 |
| **Special Notes** | All water and food is safe. Telecommunications in former East Germany remain poor. | Drinking water is safe in Athens and most resorts. Wash fruit before eating. | Tapwater is not potable, and fruits and vegetables should be prepared carefully. |

| Hong Kong | Hungary | India | Indonesia |
|---|---|---|---|
| 852 | 36 | 91 | 62 |
| Kowloon 3, New Territories 0, Victoria (Hong Kong) 5 | Budapest 1, Debrecen 52, Győr 96, Miskolc 46 | Bangalore 812, Bombay 22, Calcutta 33, Madras 44, New Delhi 11 | Bandung 22, Jakarta 21, Medan 61, Semarang 24, Surabaya 31 |
| (202) 462-1340 | (202) 362-6730 | (202) 939-7000 | (202) 775-5200 |
| Cool, humid winters; hot, rainy summers. | Cold, cloudy, humid winters; warm, pleasant summers. | Varies from tropical monsoon in the south to temperate in the north. Summers are very hot in most of India. | Tropical; hot, humid; more moderate in the highlands; rainy season from November to April. |
| Cottons and rainwear are advisable for the summer; warmer clothes are needed for the winter. Sports clothes are good for daytime, evening clothes are more formal. | Lightweight clothing is needed for the summer and heavy woolens for the winter. | Summer clothing is suitable year round in the south. In the north, lightweight woolens are necessary from mid-December to mid-February. Women should wear modest, loose-fitting clothing. | Light-weight cotton clothes are worn year-round, often with two changes a day. Women should dress conservatively. |
| Passport, visa (for stays of more than 1 month), ticket to leave, sufficient funds | Passport | Passport, visa, ticket to leave; innoculations recommended | Passport, visa (for stays of more than 60 days); innoculations recommended |
| New Year's Day, Jan. 1; Chinese New Year, Jan. or Feb.; Good Friday; Easter Monday; Queen's Birthday, late June; Liberation Day, Aug.; Christmas Day, Dec. 25; Boxing Day, Dec. 26 | New Year's Day, Jan. 1; National (Liberation) Day, Apr. 4; Easter Monday; Labor Day, May 1; Constitution Day, Aug. 20; October Revolution Day, Nov. 7; Christmas Day, Dec. 25; Boxing Day, Dec. 26 | Republic Day, Jan. 26; Holi; Independence Day, Aug. 15; Dashara; Mahatma Gandhi's Birthday, Oct. 2; Diwali; Christmas Day, Dec. 25 | New Year's Day, Jan. 1; Good Friday; Ramadan and Id al-Fitr; Ascension Day; Hijra; Independence Day, Aug. 17; Prophet's Birthday; Christmas Day, Dec. 25 |
| | Tapwater in Budapest is potable. Avoid unpasteurized milk and food products that lack preservatives. | Political unrest makes travel to West Bengal, Jammu and Kashmir, and the Punjab potentially dangerous. Permits are required for many restricted areas. Tapwater is unsafe throughout India. In hotels and restaurants, drink only bottled or carbonated water and avoid ice cubes. | Increasing numbers of thefts have been reported on public transportation, especially in Jakarta and Bali. Sanitation is adequate to excellent in Indonesia's international hotels, but caution should be exercised outside major cities. |

| Country | Ireland | Israel | Italy |
|---|---|---|---|
| **Int'l Dialing Code** | 353 | 972 | 39 |
| **City Codes** | Cork 21, Dublin 1, Galway 91, Limerick 61, Waterford 51 | Hefa (Haifa) 4, Ramat Gan 3, Tel Aviv-Yafo 3, Yerushalayim (Jerusalem) 2 | Firenze 55, Genova 10, Milano 2, Napoli 81, Palermo 91, Roma (Rome) 6, Venezia 41 |
| **Consulate Phone** | (202) 462-3939 | (202) 364-5500 | (202) 328-5500 |
| **Climate** | Humid and overcast; mild winters; cool summers. | Temperate; hot and dry in desert areas; cooler and more rainy in December through March. | Predominantly Mediterranean climate; alpine in the far north; hot and dry in the south. |
| **Clothing** | Medium to heavy-weight clothing is worn most of the year. | Clothing and shoe needs are about the same as for the American southwest. Dress at religious sites should be appropriately modest. | Woolens and sweaters are practical most of the year; cottons are recommended for the hot summers. |
| **Entry Requirements** | Passport, ticket to leave, sufficient funds | Passport | Passport |
| **Holidays** | New Year's Day, Jan. 1; St. Patrick's Day, Mar. 17; Good Friday; Easter Monday; Bank Holiday, early June; Bank Holiday, early August; Bank Holiday, late October; Christmas Day, Dec. 25; St. Stephen's Day, Dec. 26 | Purim; Passover; Independence Day; Yom Kippur; Rosh Hashana; Tabernacles; Hanukkah | New Year's Day, Jan. 1; Epiphany, Jan. 6; Easter Monday; Liberation Day, Apr. 25; Labor Day, May 1; Ascension Day; Anniversary of the Republic, June 2; Assumption Day, Aug. 15; All Saint's Day, Nov. 1; Immaculate Conception Day, Dec. 8; Christmas Day, Dec. 25; St. Stephen's Day, Dec. 26 |
| **Special Notes** | Tapwater is potable. | Travel to the West Bank and Gaza Strip is potentially dangerous. Tapwater is potable. All stores and banks are closed from sundown on Friday until sundown on Saturday. | Tapwater is safe. Meat, fruit, vegetables, and shellfish should be well-prepared. |

| Jamaica | Japan | Kenya | Korea, South |
|---------|-------|-------|--------------|
| 809 | 81 | 254 | 82 |
| | Kyōto 75, Nagoya 52, Naha 988, Ōsaka 6, Sapporo 11, Tōkyō 3, Yokohama 45 | Kisumu 35, Mombasa 11, Nairobi 2, Nakuru 37 | Inch'ŏn 32, Pusan 51, Sŏul 2, Taegu 53 |
| (202) 452-0660 | (202) 939-6700 | (202) 387-6101 | (202) 939-5600 |
| Tropical; hot, humid; temperatures are more moderate in the interior highlands. | Varies from tropical in the south to cool temperate in the north. | Varies from tropical along the coast to arid in the interior. Rainy seasons are from March to June and from October to December. | Temperate, with rainfall heavier in summer than winter. |
| Summer clothes are suitable year round. The evenings can be chilly, especially from November to March, and light wraps or sweaters are recommended. Dress is informal, but swimsuits should be worn only at the beach. | Lightweight clothing is worn in the summer throughout the country. Medium to heavy-weight clothing is needed for the winter. Very heavy clothing is needed for the mountains. | Light and medium weight clothing is worn most of the year. Sweaters and light raincoats are needed during the rainy season. Some restaurants have evening dress codes. | Clothing requirements are similar to those of the eastern U.S. Dress is more conservative than in the U.S. |
| Proof of citizenship, business visa, ticket to leave, sufficient funds | Passport, visa, ticket to leave | Passport, visa, ticket to leave; cholera and other innoculations recommended | Passport, visa, ticket to leave |
| New Year's Day, Jan. 1; Ash Wednesday; Good Friday; Easter Monday; Labor Day, May 23; Independence Day, early August; National Heroes' Day, late Oct.; Christmas Day, Dec. 25; Boxing Day, Dec. 26 | New Year's Dec. 28-Jan. 3; Adult's Day, Jan. 15; National Foundation Day, Feb. 11; Vernal Equinox Day, Mar. 21; Constitution Day, May 3; Children's Day, May 5; Respect for the Aged Day, Sept. 15; Autumnal Equinox Day, Sept.; Health and Sports Day, Oct. 10; Culture Day, Nov. 3; Labor Thanksgiving Day, Nov. 23; Emperor's Birthday, Dec. 23 | New Year's Day, Jan. 1; Ramadan and Id al-Fitr; Good Friday; Easter Monday; Labor Day, May 1; Madaraka Day, June 1; Kenyatta Day, Oct. 20; Independence Day, Dec. 12; Christmas Day, Dec. 25; Boxing Day, Dec. 26 | New Year, Jan. 1-3; Lunar New Year, Jan. or Feb.; Independence Day, Mar. 1; Buddha's Birthday, May; Memorial Day, June 6; Constitution Day, July 17; Liberation Day, Aug. 15; Chusok (Thanksgiving), Aug. or Sept.; Armed Forces Day, Oct. 1; Foundation Day, Oct. 3; Korean Alphabet Day, Oct. 9; Christmas Day, Dec. 25 |
| Hurricane season is from June to November. Crime is becoming a serious problem in Kingston. Municipal water supplies are potable. Fruits and vegetables are safe. | Drinking water, fruits, and vegetables are safe. | Avoid tapwater and unwashed fruits outside the capital. Anti-malarial drugs are recommended. | Outside of the major hotels, water is generally not potable. |

| Country | Luxembourg | Malaysia | Malta |
|---|---|---|---|
| **Int'l Dialing Code** | 352 | 60 | 356 |
| **City Codes** | | Ipoh 5, Johor Baharu 7, Kajang 3, Kuala Lumpur 3 | |
| **Consulate Phone** | (202) 265-4171 | (202) 328-2700 | (202) 462-3611 |
| **Climate** | Mild winters; cool summers. | Tropical; hot summers and winters; heavy summer rainfall, moderate winter rainfall. | Mild rainy winter; hot, dry summers. |
| **Clothing** | Fall and light winter clothing is worn. Some restaurants have evening dress codes. | Lightweight clothing is suitable for the tropical climate, except in the highland resort areas. | City casual dress is appropriate. Lightweight apparel for the summer and woolens for thee winter are required. |
| **Entry Requirements** | Passport, ticket to leave, sufficient funds | Passport, ticket to leave, sufficient funds | Passport |
| **Holidays** | New Year's Day, Jan. 1; Easter Monday; May Day, May 1; Ascension Day; Whitmonday; National Day, June 23; Assumption Day, Aug. 15; All Saints' Day, Nov. 1; Christmas Day, Dec. 25; St. Stephen's Day, Dec. 26 | Ramadan and Id al-Fitr; Chinese New Year, Jan. or Feb.; Labor Day, May 1; Wesak Day, May 30; Monarch's Day, June 1; Id al-Adha; National Day, Aug. 31; Prophet's Birthday; Diwali; Christmas, Dec. 25 | New Year's Day, Jan. 1; Freedom Day, Mar. 31; Good Friday; Easter Monday; Labor Day, May 1; Assumption Day, Aug. 15; Republic Day, Dec. 13; Christmas Day, Dec. 25 |
| **Special Notes** | | Tapwater in the cities is considered safe. Malaria is a problem in rural areas. | Tapwater is very saline; bottled water is necessary and available. |

| Martinique | Mauritius | Mexico | Morocco |
|---|---|---|---|
| 596 | | 52 | 212 |
| | | Acapulco 748, Cancún 988, Chihuahua 14, Ciudad de México 5, Monterrey 83, Puebla 22, Tijuana 66 | Casablanca , Fès 6, Marrakech 4, Rabat 7, Tanger 9 |
| (202) 944-6087 | (202) 244-1491 | (202) 728-1600 | (202) 462-7979 |
| Tropical. | Warm, dry winters; hot, humid summers. Seasons are reversed from those in North America. | Varies from tropical to desert; cooler at higher elevations. Guadalajara and Mexico City are pleasant year-round. Monterey, the Yucatan Peninsula, and desert areas are very hot in the summer. | Mild winters; hot summers; moderate winter rainfall along the coast; interior dry all year; wide daily temperature variations. |
| Lightweight clothing and rainwear are advisable. Some restaurants have evening dress codes. | Lightweight cottons are worn with a sweater for cooler evenings. Woolens are needed for winter months. | Wear tropical clothing in desert areas and lowlands. In Mexico City and other mountainous areas, medium-weight clothing is comfortable. Shorts are worn only on the beaches. | Wear clothing suitable for the eastern central U.S., but more conservative. Bring a jacket or sweater for cool evenings. |
| Proof of citizenship, ticket to leave | Passport, ticket to leave | Proof of citizenship, business visa or tourist card; innoculations recommended | Passport |
| New Year's Day, Jan. 1; Mardi Gras, Feb.; Good Friday; Easter Monday; Labor Day, May 1; Ascension Day; Whitmonday; Bastille Day, July 14; Schoelcher Day, July 21; Assumption Day, Aug. 15; All Saints' Day, Nov. 1; Armistice Day, Nov. 11; Christmas Day, Dec. 25 | New Year's Day, Jan. 1; Cavadee; Mahashivaratri; Independence Day, Mar. 12; Ougadi; Ramadan and Id al-Fitr; Easter Monday; Labor Day, May 1; Assumption Day, Aug. 15; Ganesh Chaturthi, Sept. 14; Diwali; All Saints' Day, Nov. 1; Christmas Day, Dec. 25; Boxing Day, Dec. 26 | New Year's Day, Jan. 1; Constitution Day, Feb. 5; Birthday of Benito Juarez, Mar. 21; Maundy Thursday; Good Friday; Holy Saturday; Labor Day, May 1; Battle of Puebla, May 5; President's Message Day, Sept. 1; Independence Day, Sept. 16; Columbus Day, Oct. 12; Revolution Aniversary, Nov. 20; Christmas Day, Dec. 25 | New Year's Day, Jan. 1; Prophet's Ascension; Ramadan and Id al-Fitr; Feast of the Throne, Mar. 3; Labor Day, May 1; Id al-Adha; Islamic New Year; Ashura; Sahara Annexation Day, Aug. 14; Prophet's Birthday; Green March Day, Nov. 6; Independence Day, Nov. 18; Christmas Day, Dec. 25 |
| Hurricane season is from June to October. Drinking water is safe. | Tapwater is potable. Avoid uncooked vegetables. | Tapwater is not safe. Cooked food is safe to eat; raw vegetables often are not. Avoid ice cubes. | When outside the large cities and resorts, carry water purification tablets or a supply of purified drinking water. Eat only carefully prepared foods. |

| Country | Netherlands | New Zealand | Nigeria |
|---|---|---|---|
| Int'l Dialing Code | 31 | 64 | 234 |
| City Codes | Amsterdam 20, Rotterdam 10, 's-Gravenhage (The Hague) 70, Utrecht 30 | Auckland 9, Christchurch 3, Dunedin 24, Hamilton 71, Wellington 4 | Lagos 1 |
| Consulate Phone | (202) 244-5300 | (202) 328-4800 | (202) 822-1500 |
| Climate | Mild winters, cool summers. | Temperate; wet, windy, cool; warm summers; mild winters; seasons are reversed from North America. | Equatorial in the south, tropical in the center, arid in the north. |
| Clothing | Clothing needs are similar to those of Seattle, Washington. Some restaurants have evening dress codes. | Warm clothing is comfortable most of the year. Raincoats are essential. | Tropical wash-and-wear clothing and rainwear are recommended. Women should dress conservatively and slacks are not commonly worn. |
| Entry Requirements | Passport, ticket to leave | Passport, ticket to leave, sufficient funds | Passport, visa, ticket to leave, yellow fever innoculation; cholera innoculation recommended |
| Holidays | New Year's Day, Jan. 1; Good Friday; Easter Monday; Queen's Birthday, Apr. 30; Ascension Day; Whitmonday; Christmas Day, Dec. 25; Boxing Day, Dec. 26 | New Year's Day, Jan. 1; New Zealand Day, Feb. 6; Good Friday; Easter Monday; Queen's Birthday, June; Labor Day, late Oct.; Christmas Day, Dec. 25; Boxing Day, Dec. 26 | New Year's Day, Jan. 1; Ramadan and Id al-Fitr; Good Friday; Easter Monday; Worker's Day, May 1; Hijra; National Day, Oct. 1; Prophet's Birthday; Christmas Day, Dec. 25; Boxing Day, Dec. 26 |
| Special Notes | Tapwater is safe. | | Tapwater is not potable. Fruits and vegetables should be carefully prepared and meats cooked until well done. Take anti-malarial pills. |

| Norway | Peru | Philippines | Poland |
|---|---|---|---|
| 47 | 51 | 63 | 48 |
| Bergen 5, Oslo 2, Stavanger 4, Trondheim 7 | Arequipa 54, Callao 14, Chiclayo 74, Cuzco 84, Lima 14, Trujillo 44 | Bacolod 34, Cebu 32, Davao 35, Iloilo 33, Manila 2 | Gdańsk 58, Katowice 32, Łódź 42, Poznań 61, Kraków 12, Warszawa (Warsaw) 22 |
| (202) 333-6000 | (202) 833-9860 | (202) 483-1414 | (202) 234-3800 |
| Temperate along coast, colder interior; rainy year-round on west coast. | Varies from tropical in the east to dry desert in the west; winters are damp; seasons are reversed from those in North America. | Hot and humid; cooler in mountainous areas. | Cold, cloudy, moderately severe winters with frequent precipitation; mild summers with frequent showers and thundershowers. |
| Lightweight clothing and light woolens are worn in the summer, and heavy clothing in the winter. | Medium-weight clothing is suitable in the winter; in summer, wear lightweight clothing. Fashions are similar to those in the U.S., but shorts should be worn only in resort areas. | Cotton and other lightweight clothing is worn all year. If traveling to the popular mountain resorts in northern Luzon, light sweaters are appropriate. Some resteraunts have evening dress codes. | Spring-weight clothing is worn in the summer and heavy clothing for the winter. Rainwear is advisable throughout the year. |
| Passport, ticket to leave, sufficient funds | Passport, business visa, ticket to leave; hepatitis innoculation recommended | Passport | Passport |
| New Year's Day, Jan. 1; Maundy Thursday; Good Friday; Easter Monday; May Day, May 1; Constitution Day, May 17; Ascension Day; Whitmonday; Christmas Day, Dec. 25; Boxing Day, Dec. 26 | New Year's Day, Jan. 1; Maundy Thursday; Good Friday; Labor Day, May 1; St. Peter and St. Paul's Day, June 29; Independence Days, July 28,29; Santa Rosa Day, Aug. 30; National Dignity Day, early Oct.; All Saints' Day, Nov. 1; Immaculate Conception, Dec. 8; December 24, Christmas Eve; Christmas Day, Dec. 25 | New Year's Day, Jan. 1; Maundy Thursday; Good Friday; Labor Day, May 1; Independence Day, June 12; Philippine-American Friendship Day, July 4; All Saint's Day, Nov. 1; Bonifacio Day, Nov. 30; Christmas Day, Dec. 25; Rizal Day, Dec. 30 | New Year's Day, Jan. 1; Easter Monday; Labor Day, May 1; Corpus Christi; National Day, July 22; All Saints' Day, Nov. 1; Christmas Day, Dec. 25; Boxing Day, Dec. 26 |
| Tapwater is potable. | Terrorism is prevalent in rural Peru, and a cholera epidemic makes fruits, vegetables and tapwater unsafe. | The Manila water supply is generally safe. Untreated or unboiled water should not be drunk outside the city. It is advisable to eat only fruits which can be peeled and to avoid fresh vegetables unless cleaned with safe water. | |

| Country | Portugal | Puerto Rico | Romania |
|---|---|---|---|
| **Int'l Dialing Code** | 351 | | 40 |
| **City Codes** | Coimbra 39, Lisboa (Lisbon) 1, Porto 2, Setúbal 65 | | Bucureşti (Bucharest) 0, Cluj-Napoca 51, Constanţa 16, Iaşi 81 |
| **Consulate Phone** | (202) 328-8610 | | (202) 232-4747 |
| **Climate** | Mild, damp winters; hot, dry summers; climate is more moderate along the coast. | Mild, little seasonal temperature variation. | Temperate; cold, cloudy winters with frequent snow and fog; sunny summers with frequent showers and thunderstorms. |
| **Clothing** | Wear summer clothing during the temperate sunny days and cool nights. Fall-weight clothing and a topcoat or warm raincoat are appropriate for winter. A rain hat or umbrella is recommended. Swimsuits should be confined to the beach. | Lightweight clothing is worn throughout the year with a sweater or jacket for cooler evenings. Some restaurants have evening dress codes. | Lightweight clothing is worn in the summer. Warm clothing is needed in the winter and throughout the year in the highlands. |
| **Entry Requirements** | Passport, visa | Proof of citizenship | Passport, visa; innoculations recommended |
| **Holidays** | New Year's Day, Jan. 1; Shrove Tuesday, Good Friday; Anniversary of the Revolution, Apr. 25; Labor Day, May 1; Portugal Day, June 10; Corpus Christi; Assumption Day, Aug. 15; Republic Day, Oct. 5; All Saints' Day, Nov. 1; Independence Day, Dec. 1; Immaculate Conception, Dec. 8; Christmas Day, Dec. 25. | New Year's Day, Jan. 1; Epiphany, Jan. 6; De Hostos' Birthday, Jan. 11; Martin Luther King's Birthday, Jan. 15; Presidents' Day, Feb.; Emancipation Day, Mar. 22; De Diego's Birthday, Apr. 16; Memorial Day, late May; Independence Day, July 4; Munoz Rivera's Birthday, July 17; Constitution Day, July 25; Barbosa's Birthday, July 27; Labor Day, early Sept.; Columbus Day, Oct.; Veteran's Day, Nov. 11; Discovery of Puerto Rico, Nov. 19; Thanksgiving, late Nov.; Christmas Day, Dec. 25 | New Year's Day, Jan. 1; Labor Day, May 1,2; Liberation Day, Aug. 23, 24 |
| **Special Notes** | Tapwater is potable year round in large cities and in outlying areas during rainy seasons. Bottled spring water is available. | Hurricane season is from June to November. | Hotel rooms are often poorly heated. Consumer goods are in short supply. |

| Russia | San Marino | Saudi Arabia | Singapore |
|---|---|---|---|
| | 39 | 966 | 65 |
| | All points 541 | Al-Madīnah 4, Ar-Ridād (Riyadh) 1, Jiddah 2, Makkah (Mecca) 2 | |
| (202) 628-7551 | | (202) 342-3800 | (202) 667-7555 |
| Mostly temperate to arctic continental; winters vary from cold in the west to frigid in Siberia; summers range from hot in the south to cool along the Arctic coast. | Mild to cool winters; warm, sunny summers. | Dry desert with hot days and cool nights. Winter months in the interior can be quite cool. | Tropical; hot, humid, rainy. |
| Clothing requirements the same as the nothern U.S., although the weather tends to be cooler. Public buildings, hotels, and homes are well heated. Hot weather occurs from June through August. | Woolens and sweaters are practical most of the year; cottons are recommended for hot summers. | Lightweight clothing is essential for the hot climate. However, during the winter months in the interior, warmer clothing is recommended. The coastal areas are more humid than the interior. Both men and women should dress conservatively. | Light cotton clothing is worn throughout the year. An umbrella is needed. Some restaurants have evening dress codes. |
| Passport, visa | Passport | Passport, visa, ticket to leave, cholera innoculation; sponsorship by a Saudi citizen or employer required | Passport, ticket to leave, sufficient funds |
| New Year's Day, Jan. 1; International Women's Day, Mar. 8; Labor Day, May 1,2; Victory Day, May 9; Constitution Day, Oct. 7 | New Year's Day, Jan. 1; Epiphany; Liberation Day, Feb. 5; Good Friday; Easter Monday; Labor Day, May 1; Ascension Day; Corpus Christi; Assumption Day, Aug. 15; National Day, Sept. 3; All Saints' Day, Nov. 1; All Souls' Day, Nov. 2; Immaculate Conception, Dec. 8., Christmas Day, Dec. 25, 26 | Ramadan and Id al-Fitr; Id al-Adha; Hijra; Prophet's Birthday | Chinese New Year, Jan. or Feb.; Ramadan and Id al-Fitr; Good Friday; Labor Day, May 1; Wesak Day, May; National Day, Aug. 9; Diwali; Christmas Day, Dec. 25 |
| Avoid tapwater, especially in St. Petersburg, and drink bottled water. Avoid cold foods, such as salads. | | Travel to Mecca and Medina is forbidden to non-Muslims. Do not photograph mosques or people at prayer. Women are not allowed to drive cars or bicycles. Alcoholic beverages are illegal. Eat and drink cautiously outside major hotels and restaurants. | |

| Country | South Africa | Spain | Sweden |
|---|---|---|---|
| Int'l Dialing Code | 27 | 34 | 46 |
| City Codes | Bloemfontein 51, Cape Town 21, Durban 31, Johannesburg 11, Pretoria 12 | Barcelona 3, Madrid 1, Sevilla 54, Valencia 6 | Göteborg 31, Malmö 40, Stockholm 8, Uppsala 18, Västerås 21 |
| Consulate Phone | (202) 232-4400 | (202) 265-0190 | (202) 944-5600 |
| Climate | Mostly semiarid; subtropical along coast; sunny days, cool nights. Seasons are reversed from those in North America. | Interior has hot, clear summers and cold winters; coast has moderate, cloudy summers and cool winters. | Temperate in the south with cold, cloudy winters and cool, partly cloudy summers; subarctic in the north |
| Clothing | Clothing suitable for central and southern California is appropriate for South Africa's mild climate. Many restaurants have evening dress codes. | Clothes suitable for the Washington, D.C., climate are recommended. Slacks are worn in public, but not shorts. Sweaters and raincoats are advisable. | Lightweight clothing is used in the summer, with heavy clothing for winter. |
| Entry Requirements | Passport, visa, ticket to leave, sufficient funds; cholera innoculation recommended | Passport; innoculations recommended | Passport, ticket to leave, sufficient funds |
| Holidays | New Year's Day, Jan. 1; Founder's Day, Apr. 6; Good Friday; Easter Monday; Ascension Day; Republic Day, May 31; Settler's Day, early Sept.; Kruger Day, Oct. 10; Day of the Covenant, Dec. 16; Christmas Day, Dec. 25; Boxing Day, Dec. 26 | New Year's Day, Jan. 1; Epiphany, Jan. 6; St. Joseph's Day, Mar. 19; Good Friday; May Day, May 1; Corpus Christi; St. John's Day, June 24; St. James' Day, July 25; Assumption Day, Aug. 15; National Day, Oct. 12; All Saints' Day, Nov. 1; Constitution Day, Dec. 6; Immaculate Conception, Dec. 8; Christmas Day, Dec. 25 | New Year's Day, Jan. 1; Good Friday; Easter Monday; Labor Day, May 1; Ascension Day; Whitmonday; Midsummer's Day, late June; All Saints' Day, early November; Christmas Day, Dec. 25; Boxing Day, Dec. 26 |
| Special Notes | The U.S. State Department warns that the political situation in South Africa is potentially dangerous. Drinking water is generally safe, but avoid bathing in lakes or streams. Anti-malarial pills are recommended in rural areas. | Drinking water in Madrid is safe. Use bottled water elsewhere. Peel all fruit. | Tapwater is potable, and dairy products pure. |

| Switzerland | Taiwan | Tanzania | Thailand |
|---|---|---|---|
| 41 | 886 | 255 | 66 |
| Basel 61, Bern 31, Genève 22, Lausanne 21, Lucerne 41, Zürich 1 | Kaohsiung 7, T'ainan 6, T'aipei 2 | Dar es Salaam 51, Dodoma 61, Mwanza 68, Tanga 53 | Chiang Mai 53, Krung Thep (Bangkok) 2, Nakhon Sawan 56, Ubon Ratchathani 45 |
| (202) 745-7900 | | (202) 939-6125 | (202) 483-7200 |
| Varies with altitude; cold, cloudy, snowy winters; cool to warm, cloudy, humid summers with occasional showers. | Chilly, damp winters; hot, humid summers; rainy season from June to August; often cloudy. | Varies from tropical along the coast to temperate in the highlands; rainy season from November to April; dry season from May to October. | Tropical; dry, cooler winters; warm, rainy, cloudy summers; southern isthmus is always hot and humid. |
| Light woolens may be worn in the summer and heavy winter clothing in the winter. | In winter, light jackets and sweaters are recommended; in summer, light-weight garments are essential. An umbrella is useful year-round. | Lightweight, tropical clothing is worn year-round, although in the cooler season, a light wrap is useful in the evenings. Conservative dress is required. Bring sunglasses and a hat. | Lightweight, washable clothing is comfortable and practical for Bankok's tropical climate. In northern Thailand, a jacket or sweater is needed during the cool season. Swimwear should be worn only on the beach. |
| Passport | Passport, visa, ticket to leave | Passport, visa, ticket to leave, cholera and yellow fever innoculations | Passport, ticket to leave; innoculations recommended |
| New Year's, Jan. 1,2; Good Friday; Easter Monday; Ascension Day; Whitmonday; Labor Day, May 1; National Day, Aug. 1; Christmas Day, Dec. 25; Boxing Day, Dec. 26 | Founding of the Republic, Jan. 1; Chinese New Year, Jan. or Feb.; Youth Day, Mar. 29; Tomb-sweeping Day, Apr. 5; Confucius's Birthday, Sept. 28; National Day, Oct. 10; Taiwan Restoration Day, Oct. 25; Chiang Kai-shek's Birthday, Oct. 31; Dr. Sun Yat-Sen's Birthday, Nov. 12; Constitution Day, Dec. 25 | Zanzibar Revolution Day, Jan. 12; CCM Day, Feb. 5; Good Friday; Easter Monday; Ramadan and Id al-Fitr; Union Day, Apr. 26; Peasants' Day, July 7; Hijra; Prophet's Birthday; Independence Day, Dec. 9; Christmas Day, Dec. 25 | New Year's Day, Jan. 1; Songkran Festival, Apr. 13; Coronation Day Anniversary, May 5; Visakhja Puja, May; Buddhist Lent, June or July; Queen's Birthday, Aug. 12; Chulalongkorn Day, Oct. 23; King's Birthday, Dec. 5; New Year's Eve, Dec. 31 |
| | Drinking water is safe at Taipei's major hotels, but when dining elsewhere, drink only hot or bottled water. High pollen counts and air pollution can contribute to asthma. | Tapwater is not potable. Water should be boiled and filtered and fruits and vegetables carefully prepared. Do not swim or paddle in lakes or streams. Anti-malarial drugs are recommended. Do not go barefoot. | Thailand has an extremely strict anti-narcotics law that provides for severe sentences, including the death penalty, for narcotics traffickers and users. Avoid tap water, raw milk, ice cream, uncooked meats, and unwashed raw fruits and vegetables. |

| Country | Trinidad and Tobago | Tunisia | Turkey |
|---|---|---|---|
| Int'l Dialing Code | 809 | 216 | 90 |
| City Codes | | Béja 8, Bizerte 2, El Kairouan 7, Sousse 3, Tunis 1 | Adana 711, Ankara 41, İstanbul 1, İzmir 51 |
| Consulate Phone | (202) 467-6490 | (202) 862-1850 | (202) 659-8200 |
| Climate | Tropical; dry season from January to May. | Temperate in the north with mild, rainy winters and hot, dry summers; desert in the south. | Mild, wet winters; hot, dry summers. Climate is more severe in the interior. |
| Clothing | Summerweight clothing is worn year round. Beachwear should be confined to the beach. Restaurants may have evening dress codes. | Wear lightweight clothes in the summer, light woolens and rainwear in the winter. Women should dress conservatively. | Summer requires lightweight clothing in the northern areas and tropical clothing in the south. Warm woolens are necessary for the winter months. |
| Entry Requirements | Passport, ticket to leave | Passport, ticket to leave, sufficient funds | Passport |
| Holidays | New Year's Day, Jan. 1; Ramadan and Id al-Fitr; Good Friday; Easter Monday; Whitmonday; Corpus Christi; Labor Day, June 19; Discovery Day, early Aug.; Independence Day, Aug. 31; Republic Day, Sept. 24; Diwali (Festival of Lights); Christmas Day, Dec. 25; Boxing Day, Dec. 26 | New Year's Day, Jan. 1; Anniversary of the Revolution, Jan. 18; Ramadan and Id al-Fitr; Independence Day, Mar. 20; Martyr's Day, Apr. 9; Labor Day, May 1; Id al-Adha; June 1, National Day; Youth Day, June 2; Islamic New Year; Ashura; Republic Day, July 25; Women's Day, Aug. 13; Prophet's Birthday; Evacuation Day, Oct. 15 | New Year's Day, Jan. 1; Ramadan and Id-al Fitr; National Sovereignty Day, Apr. 23; Spring Day, May 1; Youth Day, May 19; Constitution Day, May 27; Id al-Adha; Victory Day, Aug. 30; Republic Day, Oct. 29 |
| Special Notes | Hurricane season is from June to November. Tapwater is safe but do not drink water from an unknown source. Wash fruits and vegetables carefully. | Tunisia has no particular health hazards, but tapwater is not potable in certain seasons. | Tapwater should be avoided. |

| United Arab Emirates | United Kingdom | United States | Uruguay |
|---|---|---|---|
| 971 | 44 | 1 | 598 |
| Abū Ẓaby (Abu Dhabi) 2, Al-'Ayn 3, Ash-Shāriqah 6, Dubayy 4, 'Ujmān 6 | Belfast 232, Birmingham 21, Cardiff 222, Glasgow 41, Liverpool 51, London 71 or 81, Manchester 61 | | Canelones 332, Mercedes 532, Montevideo 2, Paysandú 722 |
| (202) 338-6500 | (202) 462-1340 | | (202) 331-1313 |
| Desert; hot and dry; cooler in the eastern mountains and during the winter. | Temperate; mild winters; cool summers; cloudy with rainfall in all seasons. | Mostly temperate, but varies from tropical to arctic; arid to semiarid in west. | Warm temperate; winters are cool, but temperature seldom drops below freezing. Seasons are reversed from those in North America. |
| Lightweight attire is necessary during the summer. From mid-October through April, spring or fall clothing is suitable. Everyone should dress modestly. | Fall and winter clothing is needed from about September through April; spring and summer clothing is useful the rest of the year. Always bring a raincoat and umbrella. Some restaurants have dress codes. | Clothing ranges from very lightweight to very heavy, depending on the region and time of year. | Seasonal clothing, as in the U.S., is recommended. Warm clothing is essential in winter. Rainwear is useful. |
| Passport, visa, ticket to leave | Passport | Passport, visa | Passport, ticket to leave |
| New Year's Day, Jan. 1; Ramadan and Id al-Fitr; Id al-Adha; Hijra; National Day, Dec. 2; Christmas Day, Dec. 25 | New Year's Day, Jan. 1; Good Friday; Easter Monday; May Day, early May; Spring Bank Holiday, late May; Summer Bank Holiday, late August; Christmas Day, Dec. 25; Boxing Day, Dec. 26 | New Year's Day, Jan. 1; Martin Luther King's Birthday, Jan. 15; Presidents' Day, late Feb.; Memorial Day, late May; Independence Day, July 4; Labor Day, early Sept.; Columbus Day, early Oct.; Veteran's Day, Nov. 11; Thanksgiving Day, late Nov.; ChristmasDay, Dec. 25 | New Year's Day, Jan. 1; Epiphany, Jan. 6; Carnival; Holy Week; Landing of the 33 Patriots, Apr. 19; Labor Day, May 1; Battle of Las Piedras, May 18; Birth of Don Jose Artigas, June 19; Constitution Day, July 18; Independence Day, Aug. 25; Columbus Day, Oct. 12; All Souls' Day, Nov. 2; Immaculate Conception, Dec. 8; Christmas Day, Dec. 25 |
| Water is potable. | Traffic moves on the left on British roads. | | Water supply is well maintained. |

| Country | Venezuela | Yugoslavia | Zimbabwe |
|---|---|---|---|
| **Int'l Dialing Code** | 58 | 38 | 263 |
| **City Codes** | Barquisimeto 51, Caracas 2, Maracaibo 61, Valencia 41 | Beograd (Belgrade 11, Sarajevo 71, Zagreb 41 | Bulawayo 9, Harare 4, Mutare 20 |
| **Consulate Phone** | (202) 342-2214 | (202) 462-6566 | (202) 332-7100 |
| **Climate** | Tropical; hot, humid; more moderate in the highlands; rainy season from may to November. | Temperate; hot, relatively dry summers with mild, rainy winters along the coast; warm summer with cold winters inland. | Tropical; moderated by altitude; rainy season from November to March. |
| **Clothing** | Spring-weight clothing is appropriate in Caracas. Elsewhere temperatures vary with altitude from tropics to freezing. Many restaurants have dress codes. Shorts should be worn only on the beach. | Lightweight clothing is worn in the summer and heavy clothing is required for the winter. | Light, summer apparel is appropriate from October to May. Fall or spring clothing is suitable the rest of the year. Some urban restaurants have evining dress codes. |
| **Entry Requirements** | Passport, business visa or tourist card, ticket to leave | Passport, visa | Passport, ticket to leave, sufficient funds, yellow fever innoculation |
| **Holidays** | New Year's Day, Jan. 1; Carnival; Maundy Thursday; Good Friday; Holy Saturday; Declaration of Independence Day, Apr. 19; Labor Day, May 1; Battle of Carabobo, June 24; Independence Day, July 5; Bolivar's Birthday, July 24; Columbus Day, Oct. 12; Christmas Eve, Dec. 24; Christmas Day, Dec. 25 | New Year, Jan. 1,2; Labor Day, May 1,2; Veterans' Day, July 4; Republic Day, Nov. 29, 30 | New Year's Day, Jan. 1; Good Friday; Easter Monday; Independence Day, Apr. 18; Worker's Day, early May; Africa Day; May 25; Heroes' Days, Aug. 11-12; Christmas Day, Dec. 25; Boxing Day, Dec. 26 |
| **Special Notes** | Tapwater should be boiled and vegetables carefully prepared. | Political instability makes travel to some areas potentially hazardous. | Sporadic violence is not uncommon; travel in rural areas is not advised. Tapwater is safe in all urban areas but not in rural regions. |

# City Maps

## Legend

For easy comparison of the major cities of the world, all the metropolitan maps are drawn at a consistent scale of 1:350,000. One inch on the map represents 5.5 miles on the earth's surface.

## Inhabited Localities

The symbol represents the number of inhabitants within the locality

| | |
|---|---|
| • | 0–10,000 |
| ○ | 10,000–25,000 |
| ◉ | 25,000–100,000 |
| ⊡ | 100,000–250,000 |
| ▣ | 250,000–1,000,000 |
| ■ | >1,000,000 |

The size of type indicates the relative economic and political importance of the locality

| | |
|---|---|
| Écommoy | **St.-Denis** |
| Trouville | |
| Lisieux | **PARIS** |

| | |
|---|---|
| Hollywood ■ | **Section of a City,** |
| Westminster | **Neighborhood** |
| Northland ■ Center | **Major Shopping Center** |

Urban Area (area of continuous industrial, commercial, and residential development)

**Major Industial Area**

**Wooded Area**

## Political Boundaries

### International
(First-order political unit)

**Demarcated, Undemarcated, and Administrative**

**Demarcation Line**

### Internal

**State, Province, etc.**
(Second-order political unit)

**County, Oblast, etc.**
(Third-order political unit)

**Okrug, Kreis, etc.**
(Fourth-order political unit)

**City or Municipality**
(may appear in combination with another boundary symbol)

## Capitals of Political Units

| | |
|---|---|
| **BUDAPEST** | **Independent Nation** |
| Recife | **State, Province, etc.** |
| White Plains | **County, Oblast, etc.** |
| Iserlohn | **Okrug, Kreis, etc.** |

## Transportation

### Road

**Primary**

BERLINER RING
**Secondary**

**Tertiary**

### Railway

CANADIAN NATIONAL **Primary**

+—+—+—+—+ **Secondary**

——————— **Rapid Transit**

### Airport

LONDON (HEATHROW) AIRPORT

### Rail or Air Terminal

■ *SÜD BAHNHOF*

**Bridge**

REICHS-BRÜCKE
**Tunnel**

*GREAT ST. BERNARD TUNNEL*

## Other Features

| | |
|---|---|
| SORBONNE ▲ | **Point of Interest** (Battlefield, museum temple, university, etc.) |
| STEPHANSDOM ♨ | **Church, Monastery** |
| UXMAL ∴ | **Ruins** |
| WINDSOR CASTLE ♥ | **Castle** |
| ♨ | **Lighthouse** |
| ASWĀN DAM \ | **Dam** |
| ◇ | **Lock** |
| Mt. Kenya 5199 △ | **Elevation Above Sea Level** |
| ★ | **Rock** |

Elevations are given in meters

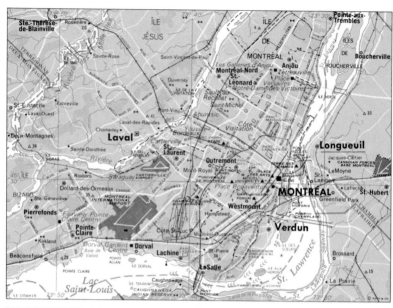

0        5        10 Miles

0        5        10 Kilometers

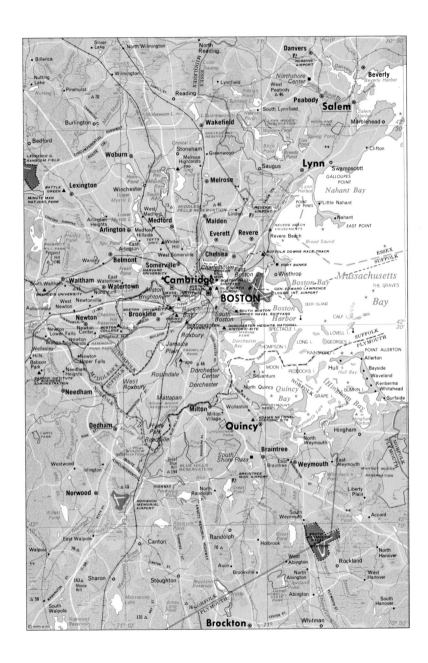

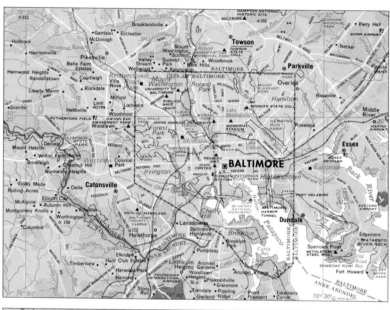

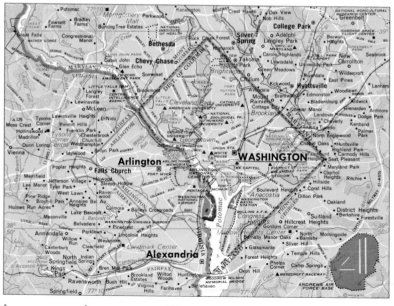

0 | 5 | 10 Miles

0 | 5 | 10 Kilometers

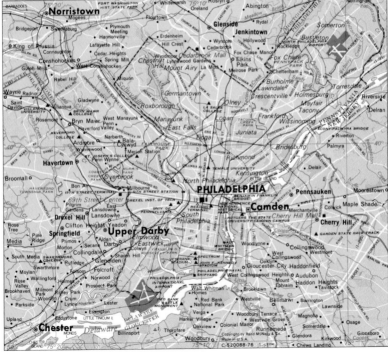

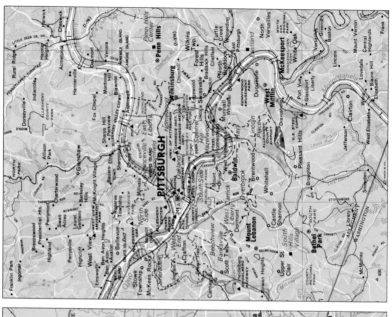

0       5       10 Miles

0       5       10 Kilometers

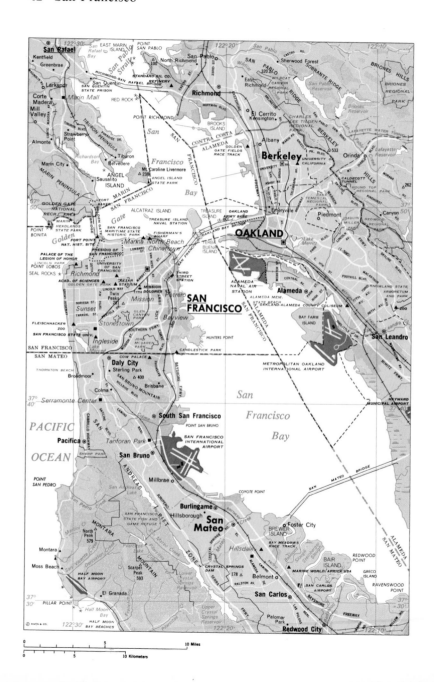

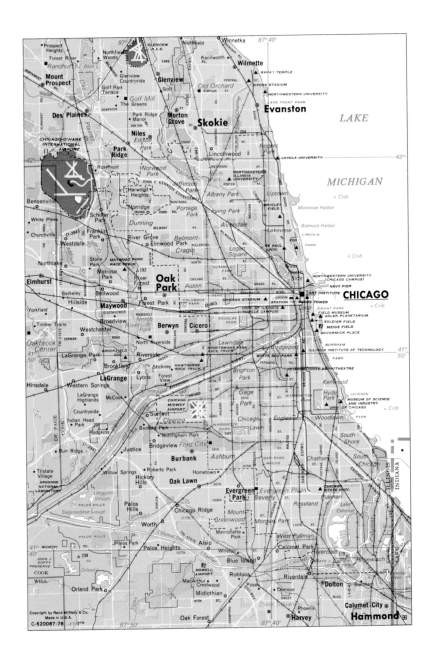

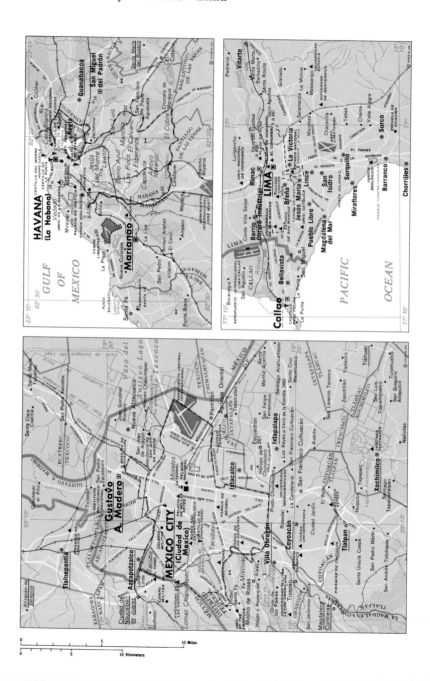

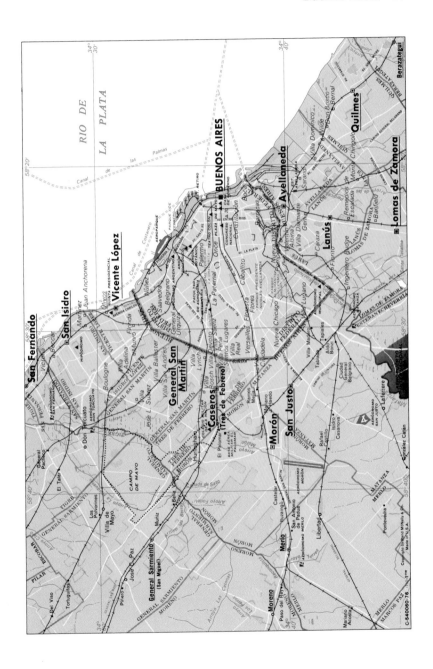

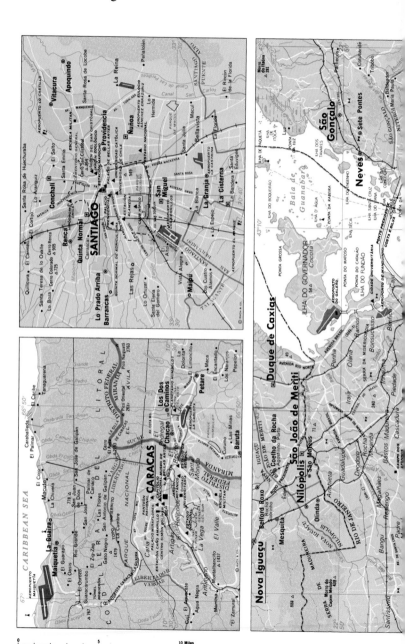

0       5         10 Miles

0       5         10 Kilometers

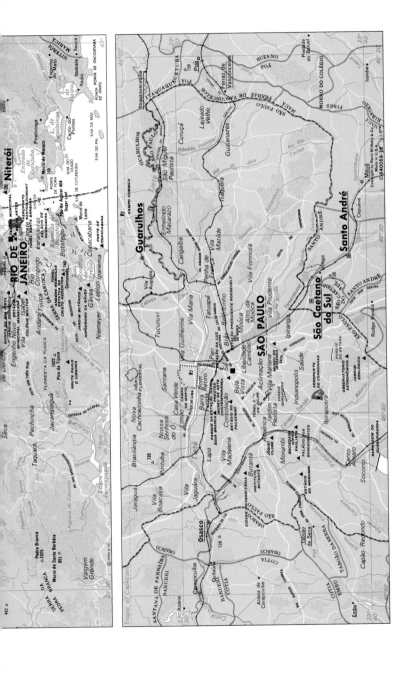

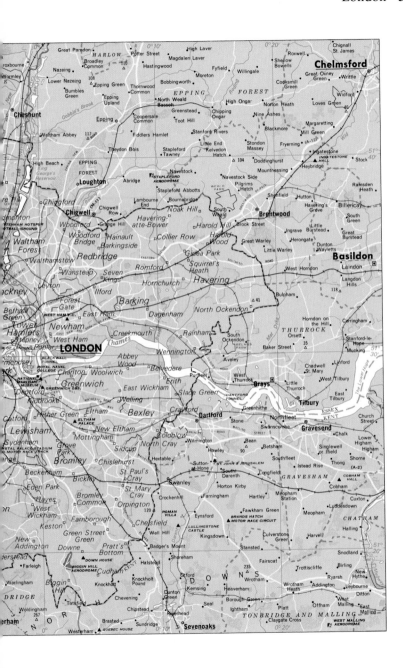

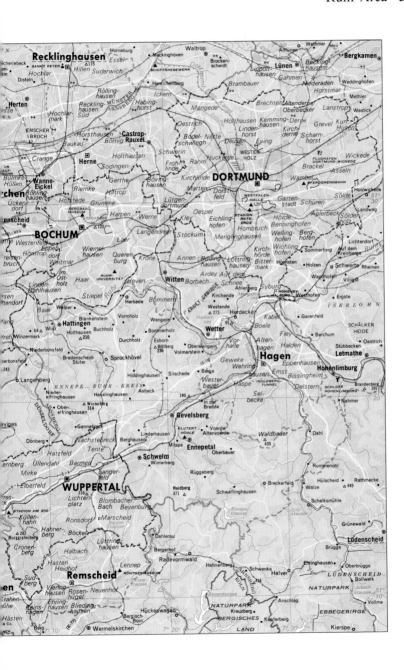

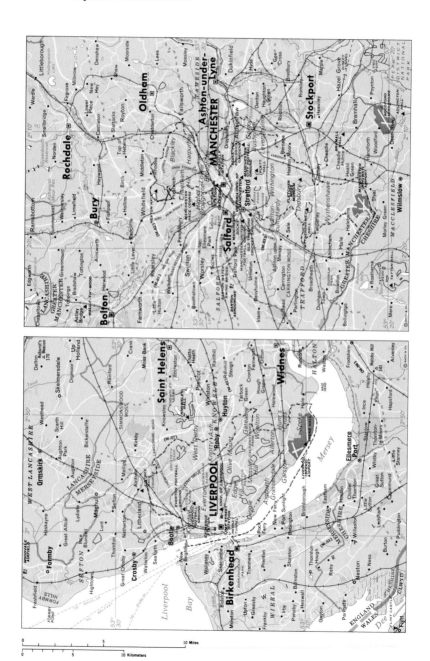

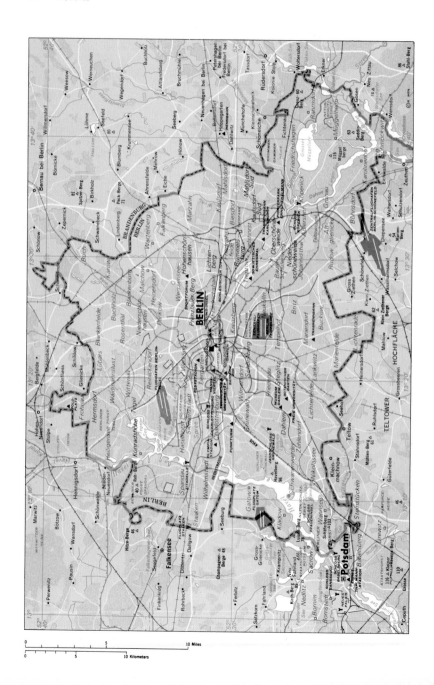

0        5        10 Miles

0        5        10 Kilometers

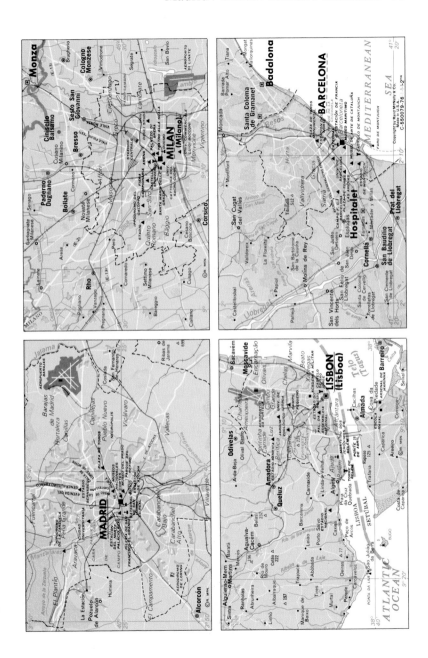

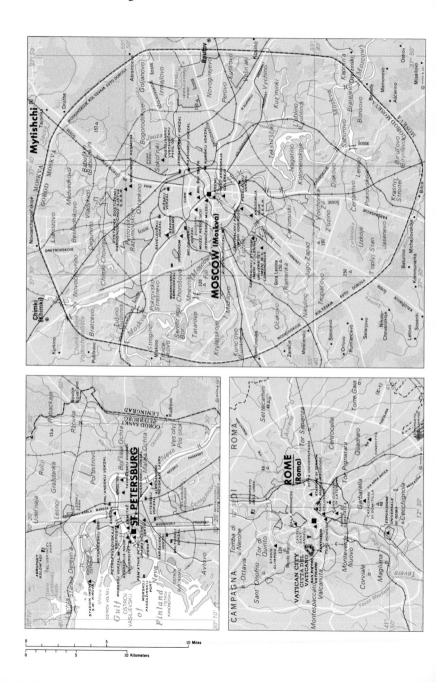

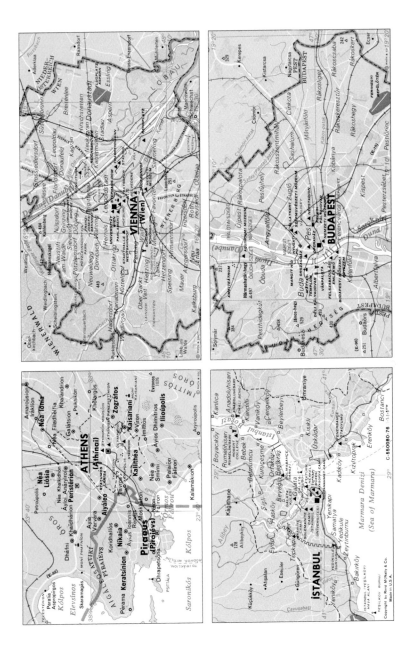

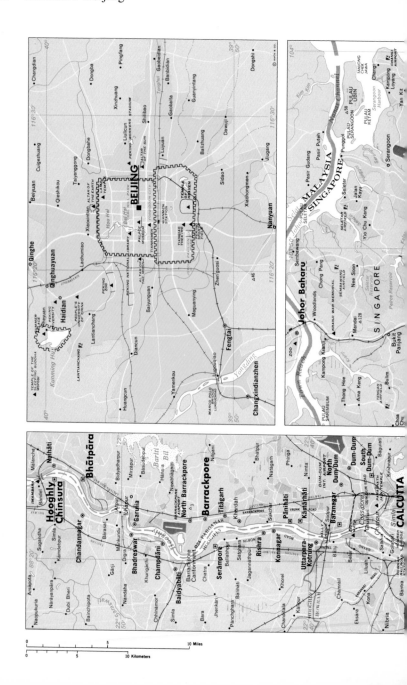

0 ____ 5 ____ 10 Miles
0 ____ 5 ____ 10 Kilometers

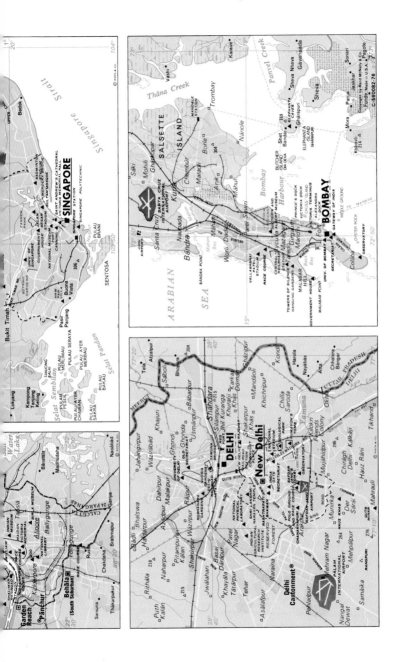

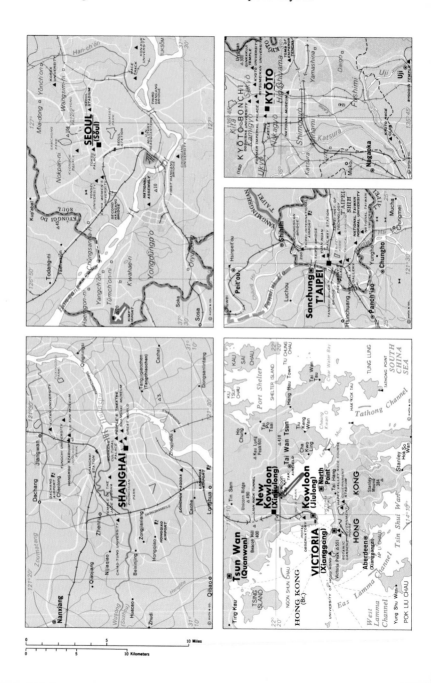

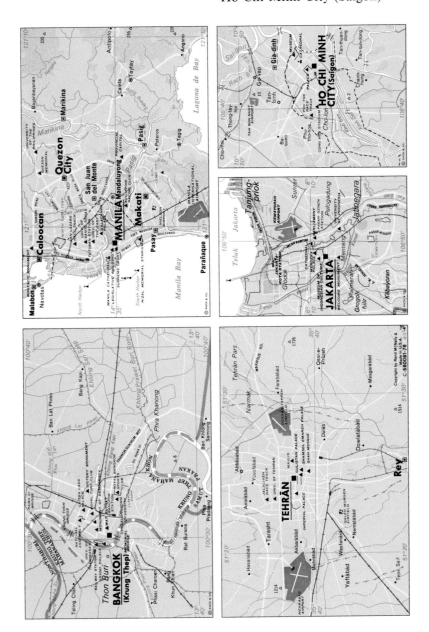

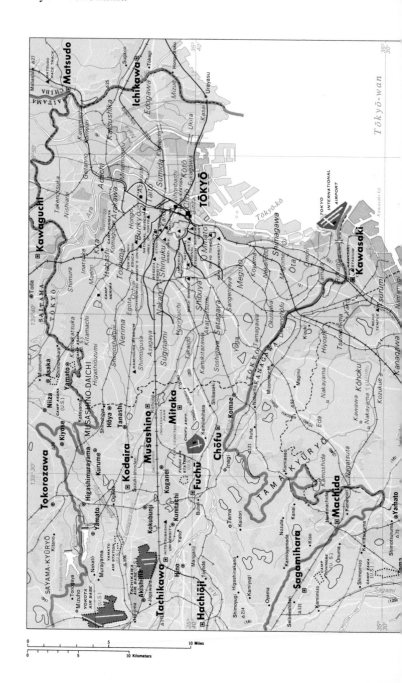

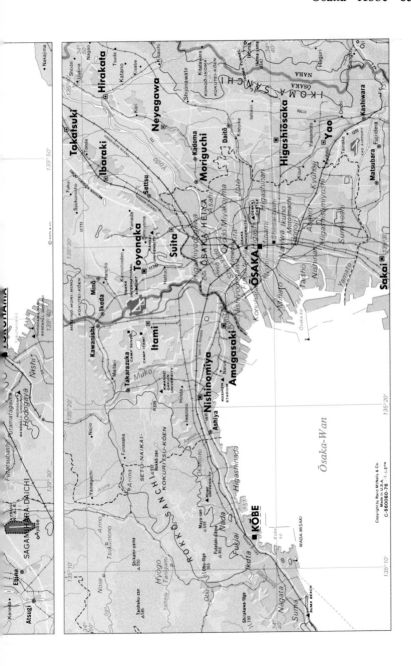

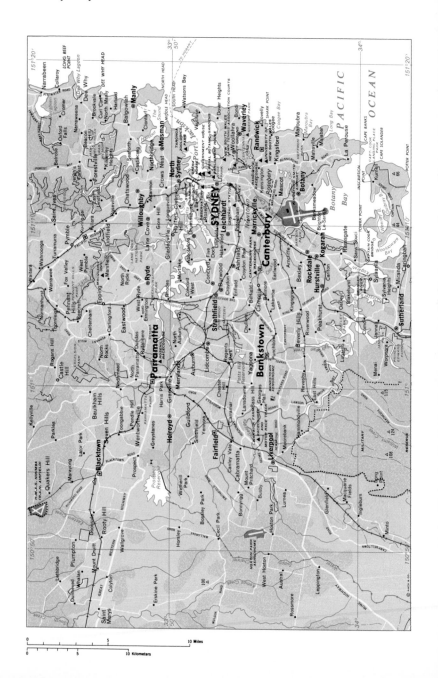

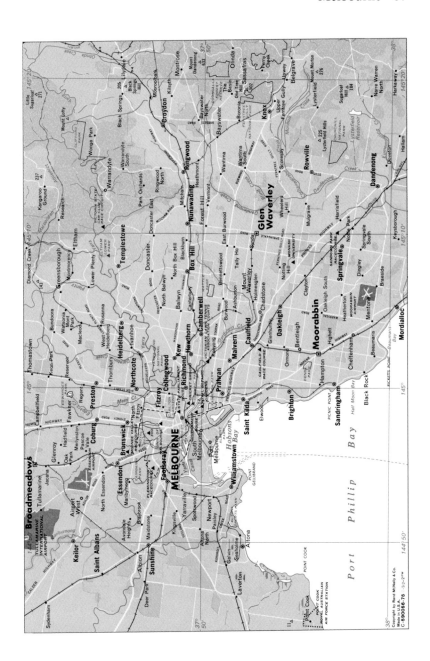

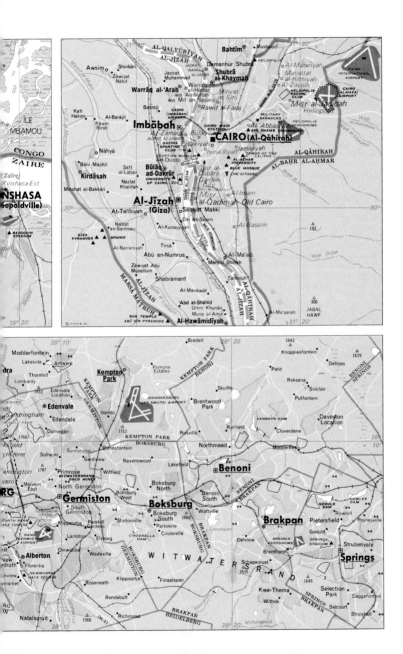

# Guide to Selected Cities

This alphabetical guide shows geographical and travel information for major international cities. The list includes metro area population figures, hotels, restaurants, additional information sources, and other details.

The population figures quoted represent the populations of entire metropolitan areas, which include one or more central cities, as well as socially and economically integrated surrounding areas.

## Amsterdam, Netherlands
**Population:** 1,860,000
**Altitude:** 5 ft. (1.5m.) below sea level
**Average Temp.:** Jan., 35°F. (2°C.); July, 64°F. (18°C.)
**Selected Hotels:**
Amsterdam Hilton, Apollolaan 138-140
De l'Europe, Nieuwe Doelenstraat 2-8
Grand Hotel Krasnapolsky, Dam 9
Marriott, Stadshouderskade 19-21
Okura Amsterdam, Ferd. Bolstraat 333
Sonesta, Kattengat 1
**Selected Restaurants:**
Bali, Christophe, De Boerderij, De Kersentuin, De Prinsenkelder, Dikker en Thijs, Excelsior, La Rive, Sama Sebo, 't Swarte Schaep
**Banking:** Hours are 9 A.M. to 4 P.M. Monday through Friday.
**Information Sources:**
Netherlands Board of Tourism
355 Lexington Avenue, 21st Floor
New York, New York 10017
212-370-7367

## Athens (Athínai), Greece
**Population:** 3,027,331
**Altitude:** 230 ft. (70m.)
**Average Temp.:** Jan., 52°F. (11°C.); July, 80°F. (27°C.)
**Selected Hotels:**
Amalia, 10 Amalias Ave.
Athenaeum Intercontinental, 89-93 Syngrou Ave.
Athens Hilton, 46 Vasilissis Sophias Ave.
Electra, 5 Hermou St.
Grande Bretagne, Constitution Sq.
Meridien, Constitution Sq.
Park, 10 Leoforos Alexandras Ave.
**Selected Restaurants:**
Cellar, Corfu, Dionyssos, Gerofinikas, Floca, L'Abreuvoir, Papakia, Stagecoach, Ta Nissia, Zonars
**Banking:** Hours are 8 A.M. to 2 P.M. Monday through Saturday.
**Information Sources:**
Greek National Tourist Organization
645 Fifth Avenue
New York, New York 10022
212-421-5777

## Atlanta, Georgia
**Population:** 2,833,511
**Altitude:** 1,050 feet
**Average Temp.:** Jan., 52°F. (11°C.); July, 85°F. (29°C.)

**Telephone Area Code:** 404
**Time Zone:** Eastern
**Selected Hotels:**
Atlanta Hilton & Towers, 255 Courtland St. NE, 659-2000
Atlanta Marriott Perimeter Center, 246 Perimeter Cente Pkwy. NE, 394-6500
Colony Square Hotel, 188 14th St. NE, 892-6000
Holiday Inn-Airport North, 1380 Virginia Ave., 762-8411
Hyatt Regency-Atlanta, 265 Peachtree St. NE, 577-1234
Omni Hotel at CNN Center, 100 CNN Center, 659-0000
Radisson Atlanta, 165 Courtland St., 659-6500
Westin Peachtree Plaza, 210 Peachtree St. NW, 659-1400
**Selected Restaurants:**
The Abbey, 163 Ponce de Leon Ave., 876-8831
Bugatti's, in the Omni Hotel at CNN Center, 659-0000
Cafe de la Paix, in the Atlanta Hilton & Towers, 659-2000
Coach and Six, 1776 Peachtree St. NW, 872-6666
La Grotta, 2637 Peachtree Rd. NE, 231-1368
Nikolai's Roof Restaurant, in the Atlanta Hilton & Towers, 659-2000
Pano's and Paul's, 1232 W. Paces Ferry Rd. NW, 261-3662
Terrace Garden Inn, 3405 Lenox Rd. NE, 261-9250
**Information Sources:**
Atlanta Convention & Visitors Bureau
233 Peachtree St. NE, Suite 2000
Atlanta, Georgia 30303 404-521-6600

## Beijing, China
**Population:** 7,320,000
**Altitude:** 165 ft. (50m.)
**Average Temp.:** Jan., 23°F. (-5°C.); July, 79°F. (26°C.)
**Selected Hotels:**
Although all travel arrangements are made by the China International Travel Service, here are the leading hotels and their telephone numbers:
Beijing-Toronto Hotel, 5002266
Great Wall Sheraton Hotel, 5005566
**Selected Restaurants:**
Beijing Orient Restaurant, Beijing Roast Duck Restaurant, Borom Piman, Champagne Room, Dynasty Grill Room, Yuen Tai
**Banking:** Hours vary from one branch to another of Bank of China - 9 A.M. to 5 P.M.

Information Sources:
China National Tourist Office
60 E. 42nd Street, Suite 3126
New York, New York 10165
212-867-0273

## Berlin, Germany

**Population:** 3,825,000
**Altitude:** 115 ft. (35m.)
**Average Temp.:** Jan., 31°F. (-1°C.); July, 66°F.
(19°C.)
**Selected Hotels:**
Ambassor, Bayreuther Str. 42-43
Berlin Hotel Intercontinental, Budapester Str. 2
Bristol Hotel Kempinski, Kurfürstendamm 27
Palace Hotel, Europa Center
Schweizerhof, Budapester Str. 21-31
**Selected Restaurants:**
Alt Luxembourg, Alt Nürnberg, Bamberger Reiter,
  Blockhaus Nikolskoe, Chalet Corniche, Forsthaus
  Paulsborn, Frühsammers Restaurant an der
  Rehwiese, Hemingway's, Ponte Vecchio,
  Rockendorf's Restaurant
**Banking:**
Hours are from 8:30 A.M. to 1 P.M. and 2:30 P.M.
  to 4 P.M. weekdays (Thursday to 5:30 P.M.).
  Closed Saturday and Sunday.
**Information Sources:**
German National Tourist Office
747 Third Ave., 33rd Floor
New York, New York 10017
212-308-3300

## Boston, Massachusetts

**Population:** 4,171,643
**Altitude:** Sea level to 330 feet
**Average Temp.:** Jan., 29°F. (-2°C.); July, 72°F.
(22°C.)
**Telephone Area Code:** 617
**Time Zone:** Eastern
**Selected Hotels:**
The Colonnade, 120 Huntington Ave., 424-7000
Copley Plaza Hotel, 138 St. James Ave., 267-5300
Hotel Meridien, 250 Franklin St., 451-1900
Logan Airport Hilton, 75 Service Rd., Logan
  International Airport, 569-9300
Omni Parker House, 60 School St., 227-8600
**Selected Restaurants:**
Anthony's Pier 4, 140 Northern Ave., 423-6363
The Cafe Budapest, 90 Exeter St., 266-1979
Copley's Restaurant, in the Copley Plaza Hotel,
  267-5300
The Dining Room, in The Ritz-Carlton, Boston,
  536-5700
Felicia's,145A Richmond St., up one flight,
  523-9885
Genji, 327 Newbury St., 267-5656
Julien, in the Hotel Meridien, 451-1900
Locke-Ober Cafe, 3 Winter Pl., 542-1340
Parker's, in the Omni Parker House Hotel,
  227-8600

Information Sources:
Greater Boston Convention & Visitors Bureau Inc.
  Prudential Plaza West, Box 490
  Boston, Massachusetts 02199
  617-536-4100

## Brussels (Bruxelles), Belgium

**Population:** 2,385,000
**Altitude:** 53 ft. (16m.)
**Average Temp.:** Jan., 38°F. (3°C.); July, 66°F.
(19°C.)
**Selected Hotels:**
Amigo, 1-3 Rue de l'Amigo
Atlanta, 7 Blvd. Adolphe Max
Brussels Europa, 107 Rue de la Loi
Brussels Hilton, 38 Blvd. de Waterloo
Metropole, 31 Place de Brouckère
Royal Windosr, 5-7 Rue Duquesnoy
Sheraton Brussels, 3 Place Rogier
**Selected Restaurants:**
Au Beurre Blanc, Bruneau, Comme Chez Soi,
  Dupont, En Plein Ciel, Francois, La Pomme
  Cannelle, La Truffe Noir, L'Ecailler Du Palais
  Royal, Villa Lorraine
**Banking:**
Hours are normally 9 A.M. to 1 P.M. and 2:30
  P.M. to 3:30 P.M. Tuesday through Thursday; 9
  A.M. to 1 P.M. and 2:30 to 4:30 P.M. Monday
  and Friday.
**Information Sources:**
Belgian Tourist Office
745 Fifth Avenue
New York, New York 10151
212-758-8130

## Buenos Aires, Argentina

**Population:** 10,750,000
**Altitude:** 65 ft. (20m.)
**Average Temp.:** Jan., 75°F. (24°C.); July, 51°F.
(11°C.)
**Selected Hotels:**
Bauen Hotel, Callao 360
Libertador Hotel, Cordoba 698
Plaza, Calle Florida
Presidente, Cerrito 850, Ave. 9 de Julio
**Selected Restaurants:**
A Los Amigos, Au Bec Fin, Clark's, El Repecho de
  San Telmo, La Cabaña, La Chacra, Los Años
  Locos, Plaza Hotel Grill
**Banking:** Hours are 10 A.M. to 4 P.M. Monday
  through Friday.
**Information Sources:**
Argentina National Tourist Office
12 West 56th Street
New York, New York 10019
212-603-0443

## Cairo (Al-Qahirah), Egypt

**Population:** 9,300,000
**Altitude:** 65 ft. (20m.)
**Average Temp.:** Jan., 57°F. (14°C.); July, 82°F.
(28°C.)
**Selected Hotels:**
El Salam, Abdel-Hamid Badawi St., Heliopolis
Holiday Inn Pyramids, Alexandria Desert Rd.

Mena House, in front of Pyramids of Giza
Nile Hilton, Tahrir Square
Cairo Marriott, Saray El Guezira, Zamalek
Cairo Meridien, Corniche El Nil, Garden City
Cairo-Sheraton, Gala Square, Giza
Sheraton Heliopolis, Oruba St.
Shepheards, Corniche El Nil, Garden City
**Selected Restaurants:**
Aladdin's, Al Rubayyat, Cairo Tower, El Haty, El
  Nile Rotisserie, Estoril, Falafel, Kebabgy el
  Gezirah, The Pharaohs, Semiramis Grill, Swiss
  Air Restaurant, Vue des Pyramides
**Banking:** Hours are 8:30 A.M. to 1 P.M. Saturday
  through Thursday; 10 A.M. to noon on Sunday.
  Closed Friday.
**Information Sources:**
Egyptian Tourist Authority
630 Fifth Avenue
New York, New York 10111
212-246-6960

## Calcutta, India
**Population:** 11,100,000
**Altitude:** 20 ft. (6m.)
**Average Temp.:** Jan., 68°F. (20°C.); July, 84°F.
(29°C.)
**Selected Hotels:**
Airport Ashok, Calcutta Airport
Great Eastern, Old Court House St.
Oberoi Grand, 15 J. Nehru Rd.
Park Hotel, 17 Park St.
**Selected Restaurants:**
Amber, Blue Fox, Kwality, Moulin Rouge, Sky
  Room, Trinca's, Waldorf
**Banking:** Hours are 10 A.M. to 2 P.M. Monday
  through Friday; 10 A.M. to noon on Saturday.
**Information Sources:**
Government of India Tourist Office
30 Rockefeller Plaza
New York, New York 10112
212-586-4901

## Chicago, Illinois
**Population:** 8,065,633
**Altitude:** 579 to 672 feet
**Average Temp.:** Jan., 27°F. (-3°C.); July 75°F.
(24°C.)
**Telephone Area Code:** 312
**Time Zone:** Central
**Selected Hotels:**
Ambassador West Hotel, 1300 N. State Pkwy.,
  787-7900
Barclay Chicago, 166 E. Superior, 787-6000
Chicago Marriott Hotel, 540 N. Michigan Ave.,
  836-0100
Days Inn, 644 N. Lake Shore Dr., 943-9200
Fairmont Hotel, 200 N. Columbus Dr. at Illinois
  Center, 565-9000
Holiday Inn, 350 N. Orleans St., 836-5000
Hotel Nikko, 320 N. Dearborn, 744-1900
Hyatt Regency O'Hare, 9300 W. Bryn Mawr Ave.,
  Rosemont, 708-696-1234
Palmer House & Towers, 17 E. Monroe St.,
  726-7500
Park Hyatt, 800 N. Michigan Ave., 280-2222
Tremont Hotel, 100 E. Chestnut St., 751-1900

The Whitehall, 105 E. Delaware Pl., 944-6300
**Selected Restaurants:**
Biggs Restaurant, 1150 N. Dearborn Pkwy.,
  787-0900
Cape Cod Room, in the Drake Hotel, 787-2200
Gordon Restaurant, 500 N. Clark, 467-9780
House of Hunan, 535 N. Michigan Ave., 329-9494
Lawry's The Prime Rib, 100 E. Ontario St.,
  787-5000
Nick's Fishmarket, 1 First National Plaza, Monroe
  at Dearborn, 621-0200
Ninety-Fifth, 172 E. Chestnut, in the John Hancock
  Center, 787-9596
Pizzeria Uno, 29 E. Ohio St., 321-1000
The Pump Room, Ambassador East Hotel, 1301
  State Pkwy., 266-0360
Su Casa, 49 E. Ontario St., 943-4041
**Information Sources:**
Chicago Convention & Visitors Bureau
McCormick Place-on-the-Lake
Chicago, Illinois 60616
312-567-8500

## Dallas-Fort Worth, Texas
**Population:** 3,885,415
**Altitude:** 450 to 750 feet
**Average Temp.:** Jan., 44°F. (7°C.); July, 86°F.
(30°C.)
**Telephone Area Code:** (Dallas) 214, (Fort Worth)
817
**Time Zone:** Central
**Selected Hotels: DALLAS**
Adolphus Hotel, 1321 Commerce St., 742-8200
Fairmont Hotel, 1717 N. Akard St., 720-2020
Hyatt Regency-Dallas-Fort Worth Airport,
  International Pkwy., 453-8400
Le Baron Hotel, 1055 Regal Row, 634-8550
Loew's Anatole Hotel, 2201 Stemmons Frwy.,
  748-1200
Plaza of the Americas Hotel, 650 N. Pearl St.,
  979-9000
Stouffer Dallas Hotel, 2222 N. Stemmons Frwy.,
  631-2222
The Westin Hotel, 13340 Dallas Pkwy., 934-9494
**Selected Restaurants: DALLAS**
Le Relais, Plaza of the Americas Hotel, 979-9000
Il Sorrento, 8616 Turtle Creek Blvd., 352-8759
Old Warsaw, 2610 Maple Ave., 528-0032
Plum Blossom, in the Loew's Anatole Hotel,
  748-1200
The Pyramid Room, Fairmont Hotel, 720-2020
**Information Sources: DALLAS**
Dallas Convention & Visitors Bureau
1201 Elm St., Suite 2000
Dallas, Texas 75270
214-746-6677
**Selected Hotels: FORT WORTH**
Green Oaks Inn, 6901 W. Freeway, 738-7311
Hyatt Regency Fort Worth, 815 Main St., 870-1234
La Quinta-Fort Worth West, 7888 I-30 W. at
  Cherry Ln., 246-5511
Park Central Inn, 1010 Houston St., 336-2011
Quality Inn South, I-35 W. South at Seminary Exit,
  923-8281
The Worthington, 200 Main St., 870-1000
**Selected Restaurants: FORT WORTH**
The Balcony, 6100 Camp Bowie Blvd., 731-3719

The Cattle Drive, 1900 Ben Ave., 534-4908
Crystal Cactus, in the Hyatt Regency Fort Worth,
  870-1234
Mac's House, 2400 Park Hill Dr., 921-4682
**Information Sources: FORT WORTH**
Fort Worth Convention & Visitors Bureau
100 E. 15th St., Suite 400
Fort Worth, Texas 76102
817-336-8791

## Denver, Colorado

**Population:** 1,848,319
**Altitude:** 5,130 to 5,470 feet
**Average Temp.:** Jan., 31°F. (-1°C.); July, 74°F.
(23°C.)
**Telephone Area Code:** 303
**Time Zone:** Mountain
**Selected Hotels:**
Brown Palace Hotel, 321 17th St., 297-3111
Burnsley Hotel, 1000 Grant St., 830-1000
Hotel Denver Downton, 1450 Glenarm Pl.,
  573-1450
Hyatt Regency Denver, 1750 Welton St., 295-1200
Radisson Hotel Denver, 1550 Court Pl., 893-3333
Stapleton Plaza Hotel and Fitness Center, 3333
  Quebec St., 321-3500
**Selected Restaurants:**
Churchill's, The Writers' Manor Hotel, 1730 S.
  Colorado Blvd., 756-8877
Ellyngton's, at the Brown Palace Hotel, 297-3111
Normandy French Restaurant, 1515 Madison St.,
  321-3311
Palace Arms, at the Brown Palace Hotel, 297-3111
Tante Louise, 4900 E. Colfax Ave., 355-4488
**Information Sources:**
Denver Metro Convention and Visitors Bureau
225 W. Colfax Avenue
Denver, Colorado 80202
303-892-1112

## Detroit, Michigan

**Population:** 4,665,236
**Altitude:** 573 to 672 feet
**Average Temp.:** Jan., 26°F. (-3°C.); July, 73°F.
(28°C.)
**Telephone Area Code:** 313
**Time Zone:** Eastern
**Selected Hotels:**
Holiday Inn Metro Airport, 31200 Industrial
  Expwy., 728-2800
Radisson Hotel Pontchartrain, 2 Washington Blvd.,
  965-0200
Hotel St. Regis, 3071 W. Grand Blvd., 873-3000
Hyatt Regency Dearborn, Fairlane Town Center
  Dr., Dearborn, 593-1234
Sheraton Southfield, 16400 J.L. Hudson Dr.,
  Southfield, 559-6500
Northfield Hilton, 5500 Crooks Rd., Troy,
  879-2100
The Westin Hotel, Renaissance Center, 568-8000
**Selected Restaurants:**
Captains, 260 Schweizer Place, 568-1862
Carl's Chop House, 3020 Grand River Ave.,
  833-0700
Caucus Club, 150 W. Congress St., 965-4970
Charley's Crab, 5498 Crooks Rd., Troy, 879-2060

Joe Muer's Sea Food, 2000 Gratiot Ave., 567-1088
London Chop House, 155 W. Congress St.,
  962-6735
Mario's Restaurant, 4222 2nd Ave., 833-9425
Pontchartrain Wine Cellars, 234 W. Larned St.,
  963-1785
Van Dyke Place, 649 Van Dyke Ave., 821-2620
**Information Sources:**
Metropolitan Detroit Convention & Visitors Bureau
100 Renaissance Center, Suite 1950
Detroit, Michigan 48243
313-259-4333

## Frankfurt am Main, Germany

**Population:** 1,855,000
**Altitude:** 325 ft. (99m.)
**Average Temp.:** Jan., 34°F. (1°C.); July, 67°F.
(19°C.)
**Selected Hotels:**
Steigenberger Frankfurter Hof, Kaiserplatz
Frankfurt Intercontinental, Wilhelm-Leuschner Str.
  43
Hessische Hof, Friedrich-Ebert Anlage 40
Parkhotel, Wiesenhüttenplatz 28-38
Schlosshotel Kronberg, in Kronberg at Hain Str. 25
Sheraton Rhein-Main, Airport
Steigenberger Airport Hotel
**Selected Restaurants:**
Bistrot 77, Börsenkeller, Da Franco, Erno's Bistro,
  Frankfurter Stubb, Humperdinck, Intercity,
  Restaurant Français, Weinhaus Brückenkeller
**Banking:** Hours 8:30 A.M. to 1 P.M. and 2:30 P.M.
  to 4 P.M., Monday through Friday; close at 5:30
  P.M. Thursday.
**Information Sources:**
German National Tourist Offices
747 Third Avenue, 33rd Floor
New York, New York 10017
212-308-3300

## Hong Kong (Victoria)

**Population:** 4,770,000
**Altitude:** 50 ft., (15m.)
**Average Temp.:** Jan., 59°F. (15°C.); July, 84°F.
(29°C.)
**Selected Hotels:**
Excelsior, Gloucester Rd., Causeway Bay
Furama Kempinski, 1 Connaught Rd. Central
Holiday Inn Harbour View, 70 Mody Rd., Kowloon
Hong Kong Hilton Hotel, 2 Queen's Rd. Central
Hyatt Regency Hong Kong, 67 Nathan Rd.,
  Kowloon
Lee Gardens, Hysan Ave., Causeway Bay
Mandarin Oriental, 5 Connaught Rd. Central
Omni Marco Polo, Harbour City, Kowloon
Miramar, 130 Nathan Rd., Kowloon
Peninsula, Salisbury Rd., Kowloon
Regal Meridien, 71 Mody Rd., Kowloon
Regent, Salisbury Rd., Kowloon
Royal Garden, 69 Mody Rd., Kowloon
Shangri-La, 64 Mody Rd., Kowloon
Sheraton Hong Kong, 20 Nathan Rd., Kowloon
**Selected Restaurants:**
Chesa, Gaddi's (Peninsula), Hilton's Eagle Nest,
  Hugo's (Hyatt), JK's, La Ronda, Mandarin Grill,
  Peacock, Peking Garden, Yung Kee

**Banking:** Hours are 9 A.M. to 3 P.M. Monday through Friday; 9 A.M. to noon on Saturday.
**Information Sources:**
Hong Kong Tourist Association
590 Fifth Avenue, 5th Floor
New York, New York 10036
212-869-5008

## Honolulu, Hawaii

**Population:** 836,231
**Altitude:** Sea level to 4,020 feet
**Average Temp.:** Jan., 72°F. (22°C.); July, 80°F. (27°C.)
**Telephone Area Code:** 808
**Time Zone:** Hawaiian (Two hours earlier than Pacific standard time)
**Selected Hotels:**
Halekulani, 2199 Kalia Rd., 923-2311
Hawaiian Regent, 2552 Kalakaua Ave., 922-6611
Hilton Hawaiian Village, 2005 Kalia Rd., 949-4321
Hyatt Regency Waikiki, 2424 Kalakaua Ave., 923-1234
The Ilikai, 1777 Ala Moana Blvd., 949-3811
Moana Surfrider, 2365 Kalakaua Ave., 922-3111
Outrigger Waikiki Hotel, 2335 Kalakaua Ave., 923-0711
Queen Kapiolani, 150 Kapahulu Ave., 922-1941
Royal Hawaiian, 2259 Kalakaua Ave., 923-7311
**Selected Restaurants:**
Furusato, 2500 Kalakaua Ave., 922-5502
Golden Dragon Room (Chinese), in the Hilton Hawaiian Village, 949-4321
Maile Room, in the Kahala Hilton, 734-2211
Michel's, in the Colony Surf Hotel, 2895 Kalakaua Ave., 923-6552
The Secret, in the Hawaiian Regent Hotel, 922-6611
The Willows, 901 Hausten St., 946-4808
**Information Sources:**
Hawaii Visitors Bureau Meetings & Convention Office
2270 Kalakaua Ave., Suite 801
Honolulu, Hawaii 96815
808-923-1811

## Istanbul, Turkey

**Population:** 7,550,000
**Altitude:** 30 ft. (9m.)
**Average Temp.:** Jan., 42°F. (6°C.); July, 74°F. (23°C.)
**Selected Hotels:**
Büyük Tarabya, Tarabya
Cinar Hotel, Yesilköy
Divan Hotel, Sisli
ETAP Hotel, Tepebasi
Istanbul Hilton, Harbiye
Macka Hotel, Tesvikiye
Marmara Hotel, Taksim Mey
Sheraton Hotel, Taksim
**Selected Restaurants:**
Abdullah Restaurant, Bebek Ambassadeurs, Divan Hotel Restaurant, Marmara Restaurant, Hotel Kalyon Restaurant, Konyali, Le Mangal (Sheraton Hotel), Liman (lunch), Orient Express, Restaurant 29, Ziya

**Banking:** Hours 9 A.M. to noon and 1:30 P.M. to 5:30 P.M. Monday through Friday.
**Information Sources:**
Turkish Government Tourist Office
821 United Nations Plaza
New York, New York 10017
212-687-2194

## Johannesburg, South Africa

**Population:** 3,650,000
**Altitude:** 5,750 ft. (1,753m.)
**Average Temp.:** Jan., 67°F., (19°C.); July, 51°F. (11°C.)
**Selected Hotels:**
Carlton, Main St.
Holiday Inn, Jan Smuts Airport
Milpark Holiday Inn, Empire Rd.
Rand International, 230 Bree St.
Rosebank, Tyrwhitt Ave.
Sandton Sun Hotel, Sandton
**Selected Restaurants:**
Bougainvillia, Chez Zimmerli, De Fistermann, El Gaucho, Jorissen at Devonshire, Le Francais, Leo, L'Escargot, Lien Wah Chinese, Linger Longer, Pot Luck, Rugantino, Scratch Caniels, Three Ships, Zoo Lake
**Banking:** Open at 9 A.M. and close at 3:30 P.M. except Wednesday, when closing hour is 1 P.M., and Saturday, when banks open at 8:30 A.M. and close at 11 A.M. On the last day of the month banks open at 8:30 A.M. and close at the normal hour for that day.
**Information Sources:**
South African Tourist Board
747 Third Avenue, 20th Floor
New York, New York 10017
212-838-8841

## Lisbon (Lisboa), Portugal

**Population:** 2,250,000
**Altitude:** 150 ft. (46m.)
**Average Temp.:** Jan., 51°F. (11°C.); July, 72°F. (22°C.)
**Selected Hotels:**
Alfa, Av. Columbano Bordalo Pinheiro
Altis, Rua Castilho 11
Avenida Palace, Rua 1.° de Dezembro 123
Diplomatico, Rua Castilho 74
Fénix, Praca Marquês de Pombal 8
Flórida, Rua Duque de Palmela 32
Lisbon-Sheraton, Rua Latino Coelho
Lisbon Penta, Av. Dos Combatentes
Mundial, Rua D. Duarte 4
Principe Real, Rua da Alegria 53
Ritz, Rua Rodrigo da Fonseca 88-A
Tivoli, Av. da Liberdade 185
**Selected Restaurants:**
Antonio Clara, Casa da Comida, Gambrinus, Michel's, Pabe, Ritz Hotel Grill, Solmar, Tagide, Tavares
**Banking:** Hours 8:30 A.M. to 11:45 A.M. and 1 P.M. to 2:45 P.M. Monday through Friday; closed Saturday.

**Information Sources:**
Portuguese National Tourist Office
590 Fifth Avenue, 4th Floor
New York, New York 10036
212-354-4403

## London, England

**Population:** 11,100,000
**Altitude:** 20 ft. (6m.)
**Average Temp.:** Jan., 40°F. (4°C.); July, 64°F.
(18°C.)
**Selected Hotels:**
Berkeley, Wilton Pl., Knightsbridge
Britannia Inter-Continental, Grosvenor Sq.
Capital, Basil St., Knightsbridge
Churchill, Portman Sq.
Connaught, Carlos Pl., Mayfair
Dorchester, Park Lane
Grosvenor House, Park Lane
Hilton, Park Lane
Ritz, Piccadilly
Savoy, The Strand
Tower Thistle, St. Katherine's Way
Waldorf, Aldwych
**Selected Restaurants:**
Café Royal, La Gavroche, La Tante Claire,
  Mirabelle, Rules, Simpson's-in-the-Strand,
  Walton's
**Banking:** Hours in England are 9:30 A.M. to 3:30
  P.M. Monday through Friday. Some banks are
  open Saturday.
**Information Sources:**
British Tourist Authority
40 West 57th Street, Suite 320
New York, New York 10019
212-581-4708

## Los Angeles, California

**Population:** 14,531,529
**Altitude:** Sea level to 5,074 feet
**Average Temp.:** Jan., 55°F. (13°C.); July, 73°F.
(23°C.)
**Telephone Area Code:** 213
**Time Zone:** Pacific
**Selected Hotels:**
Beverly Hills Hotel, 9641 Sunset Blvd., (310)
  276-2251
Biltmore Hotel, 506 S. Grand Ave., 624-1011
Century Plaza, 2025 Avenue of the Stars, (310)
  277-2000
Holiday Inn-Hollywood, 1755 N. Highland Ave.,
  462-7181
Hyatt Los Angeles Airport, 6225 W. Century Blvd.
  (310) 670-9000
L'Ermitage, 9291 Burton Way, 278-3344
Le Parc Hotel De Luxe, 733 N. West Knoll Dr.,
  (310) 855-8888
Los Angeles Airport Marriott, 5855 W. Century
  Blvd., (310) 641-5700
Los Angeles Hilton and Towers, 930 Wilshire Blvd.,
  629-4321
Sheraton Town Hotel, 2961 Wilshire Blvd.,
  382-7171
Sheraton-Universal, 333 Universal Terrace Pkwy.,
  Universal City, (818) 980-1212

University Hilton, 3540 S. Figueroa St., 748-4141
The Westin Bonaventure Hotel, 404 S. Figueroa St.,
  624-1000
**Selected Restaurants:**
Bernard's, in the Biltmore Hotel, 612-1580
Lawry's Prime Rib, 55 N. La Cienega Blvd.,
  652-2827
Madame Wu's Garden, 2201 Wilshire Blvd.,
  828-5656
Perino's, 4101 Wilshire Blvd., 487-0000
Scandia, 9040 Sunset Blvd., West Hollywood,
  278-3555
The Tower, 1150 S. Olive St., 746-1554
Yamato, in the Century Plaza Hotel, 277-1840
**Information Sources:**
Greater Los Angeles Visitors & Convention Bureau
515 S. Figueroa, 11th Floor
Los Angeles, California 90071
213-624-7300

## Madrid, Spain

**Population:** 4,650,000
**Altitude:** 2,100 ft. (640m.)
**Average Temp.:** Jan., 41°F. (5°C.); July, 76°F.
(24°C.)
**Selected Hotels:**
Alameda, Av. Logrono 100
Castellana, Paseo de la Castellana 49
Eurobuilding, Padre Damian 23
Melia Madrid, Princesa 27
Miguel Angel, Miguel Angel 31
Mindanao, S. Francisco De Sales 15
Monte Real, Arroyo Fresno 17
Plaza, Plaza de España 8
Palace, Plaza de las Cortes 7
Princesa Plaza, Serano Jover 3
Villa Magna, Castellana 22
Wellington, Velazquez 8
**Selected Restaurants:**
Club 31, Cafe Chinitas, El Cenador del Prado, Cafe
  de Oriente, Jockey Club, Zalacain
**Banking:** Hours are 9 A.M. to 2 P.M. Monday
  through Saturday.
**Information Sources:**
Spanish National Tourist Office
665 Fifth Avenue
New York, New York 10022
212-759-8822

## Manila, Phillipines

**Population:** 6,800,000
**Altitude:** 10 ft. (3m.)
**Average Temp.:** Jan. 78°F. (26°C.); July, 82°F.
(28°C.)
**Selected Hotels:**
Holiday Inn, 3001 Roxas Blvd., Pasay City
Hotel Intercontinental, Ayala Av., Makati
Hyatt Regency Manila, 2702 Roxas Blvd., Pasay
  City
Mandarin Oriental Manila, Makati Av., Makati
Manila Hotel, Rizal Park
Manila Peninsula, Ayala and Makati Av.
Philippine Plaza, Cultural Center Complex, Roxas
  Blvd.
Silahis International, 1990 Roxas Blvd.

**Selected Restaurants:**
Aristocrat, Au Bon Vivant, Barrio Fiesta,
Champagne Room in Manila Hotel,
Intercontinental Hotel Restaurant, Kamayan,
Maynila
**Banking:** Hours usually are 9 A.M. to 3 P.M.
Monday through Friday.
**Information Sources:**
Philippine Convention & Visitors Corp.
Philippine Center
556 Fifth Avenue
New York, New York 10036
212-575-7915

## Mexico City (Ciudad de México), Mexico
**Population:** 14,100,000
**Altitude:** 7,300 ft. (2,225m.)
**Average Temp.:** Jan., 54°F. (12°C.); July, 64°F.
(18°C.)
**Selected Hotels:**
Aristos, Paseo de la Reforma 276
Camino Real, Mariano Escobedo 700
Hotel El Presidenté Chapultepec, Campos Eliseos
218
Maria Isabel-Sheraton, Paseo de la Reforma 325
**Selected Restaurants:**
Anderson's, El Parador, Focolare, Fonda Santa
Anita, Hacienda de los Morales, La Cava,
Restaurant del Lago, Rivoli, San Angel Inn
**Banking:** Banks are open 9 A.M. to 1 P.M. Monday
through Friday; 9 A.M. to 12:30 P.M. on
Saturday.
**Information Sources:**
Mexican Government Tourism Office
405 Park Avenue, #1002
New York, New York 10022
212-755-7261

## Miami, Florida
**Population:** 3,192,582
**Altitude:** Sea level to 30 feet
**Average Temp.:** Jan., 69°F. (21°C.); July, 82°F.
(28°C.)
**Telephone Area Code:** 305
**Time Zone:** Eastern
**Selected Hotels:**
Doubletree, 2649 S. Bayshore Dr., 858-2500
Holiday Inn-Civic Center, 1170 NW. 11th St.,
324-0800
Best Western Marina Park Hotel, 340 Biscayne
Blvd., 371-4400
Marriott Airport Hotel, 1201 NW. LeJeune Rd.,
649-5000
Miami Lakes Inn, Athletic Club & Golf Resort,
Main St. & Bull Run Rd., Miami Lakes,
821-1150
Omni International Hotel, 1601 Biscayne Blvd.,
374-0000
Ramada Hotel-Miami International Airport, 3941
NW. 22nd St., 871-1700
**Selected Restaurants:**
Cafe Chauveron, 9561 E. Bay Harbor Dr.,
866-8779
Centro Vasco, 2235 SW. 8th St., 643-9606
Cye's Rivergate, 444 Brickell Ave., 358-9100

La Paloma, 10999 Biscayne Blvd., 891-0505
Raimondo, 4612 SW. LeJeune, 666-9355
**Information Sources:**
Greater Miami Convention and Visitors Bureau
701 Brickell Ave.
Miami, Florida 33131
305-539-3000

## Milan (Milano), Italy
**Population:** 3,750,000
**Altitude:** 400 ft. (122m.)
**Average Temp.:** Jan., 34°F. (1°C.); July, 73°F.
(23°C.)
**Selected Hotels:**
Dei Cavalieri, Piazza Missori 1
Excelsior Gallia, Piazza Duca d'Aosta 9
Grand Hotel Duomo, Via S. Raffaele 1
Grand Hotel et de Milan, Via Manzoni 29
Palace, Piazza della Repubblica 20
Principe Di Savoia, Piazza della Repubblica 17
Hilton, Via Galvani 12
**Selected Restaurants:**
Biffi Scala, Canoviano, Peck, St. Andrew's, Savini
**Banking:** Hours are 8:30 A.M. to 1 P.M. Monday
through Friday.
**Information Sources:**
Italian Government Travel Office
630 Fifth Avenue
New York, New York 10111
212-245-4822

## Montreal, Canada
**Population:** 2,921,357
**Altitude:** 50 ft. (15m.)
**Average Temp.:** Jan., 16°F. (-9°C.); July, 71°F.
(22°C.)
**Telephone Area Number:** 514
**Selected Hotels:**
Le Chateau Champlain, 1050 Ouest de
Lagauchetiere
Hotel Meridien-Montréal, 4 Complexe Desjardins
Montréal Aeroport Hilton International, 12505
Côte de Liesse Rd. in Dorval
Queen Elizabeth, 900 Blvd. Réné-Levesqne
Ritz-Carlton, 1228 Sherbrooke St. W
Ruby Foo's Hotel, 7655 Decaria Blvd.
**Selected Restaurants:**
Café de Paris, Chez la Mere Michel, Des Jardins,
Le Castillon in the Bonaventure Hilton
International, Le Neufchatel, Les Filles du Roy,
Les Halles
**Banking:**
Hours are generally from 10 A.M. to 3 P.M.
Monday through Thursday; 10 A.M. to 6 P.M. on
Friday. If Friday is a holiday, Friday hours are
observed on Thursday.
**Information Sources:**
Tourism Quebec
1001 Dorchester Square St.
Downtown Information Center
Montreal, Quebec
800-363-7777
514-873-2015

## Moscow (Moskva), Russia

**Population:** 13,100,000
**Altitude:** 395 ft. (120m.)
**Average Temp.:** Jan., 14°F. (-10°C.); July, 66°F. (19°C.)
**Selected Hotels:**
Intourist, 3/5 Gorky St.
Metropole, 1 Marx Ave.
National, 14-1 Marx Ave.
Rossiya Hotel, 6 Razin St.
Ukraina, 2/1 Kutuzovsky Ave.
**Selected Restaurants:**
Aragvi, Arbat, Baku, Budapest, Peking, Praga, Seventh Heaven, Sofia, Slavyansky Bazaar, Uzbekistan
**Banking:** Banks are open from 9 A.M. to 1 P.M. Monday through Friday; days before holidays they close at noon.
**Information Sources:**
Intourist Information Office
630 Fifth Ave., Suite 868
New York, New York 10111
212-757-3884

## New Orleans, Louisiana

**Population:** 1,238,816
**Altitude:** 5 to 25 feet
**Average Temp.:** Jan., 55°F. (13°C.); July, 82°F. (28°C.)
**Telephone Area Code:** 504
**Time Zone:** Central
**Selected Hotels:**
Fairmont Hotel, 123 Baronne St., 529-7111
Hyatt Regency New Orleans, 500 Poydras Plaza, 561-1234
The Monteleone, 214 Royal St., 523-3341
New Orleans Hilton Riverside and Towers, Poydras St. at the Mississippi River, 561-0500
New Orleans Marriott, 555 Canal St., 581-1000
The Omni Royal Orleans Hotel, 621 St. Louis St., 529-5333
The Pontchartrain Hotel, 2031 St. Charles Ave., 524-0581
Royal Sonesta Hotel, 300 Bourbon St., 586-0300
**Selected Restaurants:**
Broussard's, 819 Conti St., 581-3866
Caribbean Room, in The Pontchartrain Hotel, 524-0581
Commander's Palace Restaurant, 1403 Washington Ave., 899-8221
Galatoire's Restaurant, 209 Bourbon St., 525-2021
Louis XVI French Restaurant, 730 Bienville, 581-7000
Masson's Restaurant Français, 7200 Pontchartrain Blvd., 283-2525
Sazerac Restaurant, in the Fairmont Hotel, 529-7111
**Information Sources:**
Greater New Orleans Tourist & Convention Commission
1520 Sugar Bowl Dr.
New Orleans, Louisiana 70112
504-566-5011

## New York, New York

**Population:** 18,087,251
**Altitude:** Sea level to 410 feet
**Average Temp.:** Jan., 33°F. (-1°C.); July, 75°F. (24°C.)
**Telephone Area Code:** 212
**Time Zone:** Eastern
**Selected Hotels:**
Carlyle, Madison Ave. at E. 76th St., 744-1600
The Helmsley Palace, 455 Madison Ave., 888-7000
The Hotel Pierre, 2 E. 61st St. at 5th Ave., 838-8000
The Plaza, 768 5th Ave., 759-3000
Regency, 540 Park Ave., 759-4100
Sherry-Netherland, 781 5th Ave., 355-2800
United Nations Plaza Hotel, 1 U.N. Plaza, 355-3400
**Selected Restaurants:**
The Four Seasons, 99 E. 52nd St., 754-9494
La Cote Basque, 5 E. 55th St., 688-6525
Lutèce, 249 E. 50th St., 752-2225
Mitsukoshi, 461 Park Ave., 935-6444
"21" Club, 21 W. 52nd St., 582-7200
**Information Sources:**
New York Convention and Visitors Bureau, Inc.
Two Columbus Circle
New York City, New York 10019
212-397-8200

## Osaka, Japan

**Population:** 16,450,000
**Altitude:** 16 ft. (5m.)
**Average Temp.:** Jan., 40°F. (4°C.); July, 80°F. (27°C.)
**Selected Hotels:**
Hotel Osaka Grand, 2-3-18 Nakanoshima, Kita-ku
International Hotel, 2-33 Honmachibashi, Chou-ku
Osaka Miyako Hotel, 6-1-55 Uehonmachi, Tennoji-ku
Osaka Royal Hotel, 5-3-68 Nakanashima, Kita-ku
Plaza, 2-2-49 Oyodo-Minami, Kita-ku
Toyo Hotel, 3-16-19 Toyosaki, Kita-ku
**Selected Restaurants:**
Chambord, Hanagoyomi, Kobe Misono, Little Pirates, Osaka Boteju, Osaka Joe's, Suehiro Honten
**Banking:** Hours are 9 A.M. to 3 P.M. Monday through Friday; 9 A.M. to noon on Saturday.
**Information Sources:**
Japan National Tourist Organization
630 Fifth Avenue
New York, New York 10111
212-757-5640

## Paris, France

**Population:** 9,775,000
**Altitude:** 140 ft. (43m.)
**Average Temp.:** Jan., 44°F. (7°C.); July, 76°F. (24°C.)
**Selected Hotels:**
Le Bristol, 112 Rue du Faubourg St., Honoré
Crillon, 10 Place de la Concorde
George V, 31 Ave. George V
Intercontinental Paris, 3 Rue de Castiglione
Meridien Hotel, 81 Blvd. Gouvion-St. Cyr
Napoleon, 40 Ave. de Friedland

Paris Hilton, 18 Ave. de Suffren
Plaza Athenée, 25 Ave. Montaigne
Ritz, 15 Place Vendome, overlooking Place
Vendome
**Selected Restaurants:**
Drouant, Grand Vefour, La Maré, Lasserre,
Ledoyen, Le Vivarois, Lucas-Carton, Maxim's,
Pré Catelan, Taillevent, Tour d'Argent
**Banking:** From 9 A.M. to 4:30 P.M. Monday
through Friday; 9 A.M. to noon day before
holidays.
**Information Sources:**
French Government Tourist Office
610 Fifth Avenue
New York, New York 10020
212-757-1125

## Rio de Janeiro, Brazil

**Population:** 10,150,000
**Altitude:** 30 ft. (9m.)
**Average Temp.:** Jan., 79°F. (26°C.); July, 69°F.
(21°C.)
**Selected Hotels:**
Caesar Park, Ave. Vieira Souto 460
Copacabana Palace, Ave. Atlantica 1702
Everest Rio, Rua Prudente de Morais 1117
Leme Palace, Ave. Atlantica 656
Marina Palace, R. Delfim Moreira 630
Meridien Copacabana, Ave. Atlantica 1020
Miramar Palace, Ave. Atlantica 3668
Nacional Rio, Ave. Niemeyer 769
Rio Palace, Ave. Atlantica 4240
Sol Ipanema, Ave. Vieira Souto 320
Rio Sheraton, Ave. Niemeyer 121
**Selected Restaurants:**
Maxim's de Paris, La Streghe, Candido's,
Antiquarius, Chalé, La Tour, Mario's, L: Saint
Honoré, Petronio's, Club Gourmet, Nino, Rio's
**Banking:** Hours are 10 A.M. to 4:30 P.M. Monday
through Friday.
**Information Sources:**
Brazilian Tourism Office
551 Fifth Avenue
New York, New York 10176
212-286-9600

## Rome (Roma), Italy

**Population:** 3,175,000
**Altitude:** 80 ft. (24m.)
**Average Temp.:** Jan., 46°F. (8°C.); July, 75°F.
(24°C.)
**Selected Hotels:**
Ambasciatori Palace, Via Veneto 70
Bernini Bristol, Piazza Barberini 23
Cavalieri Hilton, Via Cadlolo 101
Eden, Via Ludovisi 49
Excelsior, Via Vittorio Veneto 125
Flora, Via Vittorio Veneto 191
Grand, Via V.E. Orlando 3
Hassler, Trinità dei Monti 6
Mediterraneo, Via Cavour 15
Parco dei Principi, Via G. Frescobaldi 5
Quirinale, Via Nazionale 7
Sheraton Roma, Viale del Pattinaggio

**Selected Restaurants:**
Albert Ciarla, Checchino dal 1887, La Rosetta, Le
Restaurant, Passetto, Patrizia e Roberto del
Pianeta Terra, Quinzi Gabrieli, Ranieri, Relais le
Jardin, San Souci
**Banking:** From 8:30 A.M. to 1:30 P.M. Monday
through Friday.
**Information Sources:**
Italian Government Travel Office
630 Fifth Avenue, #1565
New York, New York 10111
212-245-4822

## San Francisco, California

**Population:** 6,253,311
**Altitude:** Sea level to 934 feet
**Average Temp.:** Jan., 50°F. (10°C.); July, 59°F.
(15°C.)
**Telephone Area Code:** 415
**Time Zone:** Pacific
**Selected Hotels:**
The Fairmont Hotel, 950 Mason St., 772-5000
Four Seasons-Clift, 495 Geary St., 775-4700
Hilton Square, 333 O'Farrell St., 771-1400
The Holiday Inn Union Square, 480 Sutter St.,
398-8900
Huntington Hotel, 1075 California St., 474-5400
Hyatt on Union Square, 345 Stockton St., 398-1234
Hyatt Regency San Francisco, 5 Embarcadero
Center, 788-1234
Mark Hopkins Intercontinental, 999 California St.,
392-3434
Miyako Hotel, 1625 Post St., 922-3200
The Phoenix Inn, 601 Eddy St., 776-1380
Queen Anne, 1590 Sutter St., 441-2828
The Westin St. Francis, 335 Powell St., 397-7000
**Selected Restaurants:**
Amelio's 1630 Powell St., 397-4339
Blue Fox Restaurant, 659 Merchant St., 981-1177
Empress of China, 838 Grant Ave., 434-1345
Ernie's Restaurant, 847 Montgomery St., 397-5969
Fleur de Lys, 777 Sutter St., 673-7779
Fournou's Ovens, in The Stanford Court Hotel,
989-1910
**Information Sources:**
San Francisco Convention & Visitors Bureau
Convention Plaza 201 Third St., Suite 900
San Francisco, California 94103
415-974-6900

## Sao Paulo, Brazil

**Population:** 15,175,000
**Altitude:** 2,375 ft. (724m.)
**Average Temp.:** Jan., 71°F. (22°C.); July, 58°F.
(14°C.)
**Selected Hotels:**
Brasilton, Rua Martins Fontes 330
Caesar Park Hotel, Rua Augusta 1508
Eldorado, Ave. São Luis 234
Grande Hotel Ca D'Oro, Rua Augusta 129
Jaraguá, Viaduto Major Quedinho 40
Maksoud Plaza, Al. Campinas 150
Othon Palace, Rua Libero Badaró 190
Sao Paulo Center, Lgo. Sta. Ifigenia 40
Sao Paulo Hilton, Ave. Ipiranga 165

**Selected Restaurants:**
Abril em Portugal, Andrade, Baiúa, Bolinha, Chalet Suisse, La Casserole, Manhattan, Os Vikings, Presidente, Tarraço Italia, Via Veneto
**Banking:** Hours are 8 A.M. to 6:30 P.M. Monday through Friday.
**Information Sources:**
Brazilian Tourism Office
551 Fifth Avenue
New York, New York 10176
212-286-9600

## Singapore, Singapore

**Population:** 3,000,000
**Altitude:** 35 ft. (11m.)
**Average Temp.:** Jan., 79°F. (26°C.); July, 81°F. (27°C.)
**Selected Hotels:**
Dynasty Singapore, 320 Orchard Rd.
Goodwood Park, 22 Scotts Rd.
Hyatt Singapore, 10-12 Scotts Rd.
The Mandarin Singapore, 333 Orchard Rd.
The Marco Polo, Tanglin Circus
Shangri-La, 22 Orange Grove Rd.
Singapore Hilton, 581 Orchard Rd.
**Selected Restaurants:**
Aziza's, Casablanca, Compass Rose, Fourchettes, Harbour Grill, Moti Mahal, The Pinnacle
**Banking:** Hours are 10 A.M. to 3 P.M. Monday through Friday; 9:30 A.M. to 11:30 A.M. on Saturday.
**Information Sources:**
Singapore Tourist Promotion Board
590 Fifth Avenue, 12th Floor
New York, New York 10036
212-302-4861

## Stockholm, Sweden

**Population:** 1,449,972
**Altitude:** 55 ft. (17m.)
**Average Temp.:** Jan., 27°F. (-3°C.); July, 64°F. (18°C.)
**Selected Hotels:**
Birger Jarl, Tulegatan 8
Grand Hotel, Södra Blasieholmshamnen 8, opposite the Royal Palace
Strand, Nybrokajen 9
Diplomat, Strandvägen 7 C
Park, Karlavägen 43
Anglais, Humlegårdsgatan 23
Sheraton-Stockholm, Tegelbacken 6
**Selected Restaurants:**
Aurora, Den Glydene Freden, Fem Små Hus, Franska Matsalen, L'Escargot, Michel, Operakällaren, Riche, Solliden at Skansen, Stallmästaregarden
**Banking:** Hours from 9:30 A.M. to 3 P.M. on weekdays
**Information Sources:**
Swedish Tourist Board
655 Third Avenue
New York, New York 10017
212-949-2333

## Sydney, Australia

**Population:** 3,623,550
**Altitude:** 75 ft. (23m.)
**Average Temp.:** Jan., 71°F. (22°C.); July, 53°F. (12°C.)
**Selected Hotels:**
Boulevard Hotel, 90 William St.
Holiday Inn Menzies, 14-28 Carrington St.
Hyatt Kingsgate, Kings Cross Rd., Kings Cross
Regent of Sydney, 199 George St.
Sheraton Wentworth, 61-101 Phillip St.
Hilton International Sydney, 259 Pitt St.
**Selected Restaurants:**
Afrilanka, Beppi's, Chitose, Doyle's on the Beach, Harbor Restaurant, Jin Jiang, Kables, Le Trianon at King's Cross, San Francisco Grill
**Banking:**
Hours are 9:30 A.M. to 4 P.M. Monday through Thursday; 9:30 A.M. to 5 P.M. on Friday. Major branches are open for extended hours.
**Information Sources:**
Australian Tourist Commission
489 Fifth Avenue, 31st Floor
New York, New York 10017
212-687-6300

## Tel Aviv (Tel Aviv-Yafo), Israel

**Population:** 1,735,000
**Altitude:** 35 ft. (11m.)
**Average Temp.:** Jan., 57°F. (14°C.); July, 77°F. (25°C.)
**Selected Hotels:**
Carlton, 10 Hayarkon St.
Dan Tel Aviv, 99 Hayarkon St.
Diplomat, 145 Hayarkon St.
Hilton, Independence Park
Plaza, 155 Hayarkon St.
Ramada Continental, 121 Hayarkon St.
Sheraton, 115 Hayarkon St.
**Selected Restaurants:**
Alhambra, Casba, Taboon, Zion
**Banking:** Hours are 8:30 A.M. to 12:30 P.M. and 4 P.M. to 6 P.M. Sunday, Tuesday and Thursday; 8:30 A.M. to 12:30 P.M. Monday and Wednesday; and 8:30 A.M. to 12 noon Friday. Banks are closed on eves of holidays and on holidays.
**Information Sources:**
Israel Tourist Bureau
350 Fifth Avenue
New York, New York 10118
212-560-0650

## Tōkyō, Japan

**Population:** 27,700,000
**Altitude:** 20 ft. (6m.)
**Average Temp.:** Jan., 39°F. (4°C.); July, 77°F. (25°C.)
**Selected Hotels:**
Imperial Hotel, 1-1-1, Uchisaiwaicho, Chiyoda-ku
Hotel New Otani, 4-1, Kioicho, Chiyoda-ku
Hotel Okura, 2-10-4, Toranomon, Minato-ku
Keio Plaza Hotel, 2-2-1, Nishi-Shinjuku, Shinjuku-ku
Palace Hotel, 1-1-1, Marunouchi, Chiyoda-ku

The Tokyo Hilton, 6-6-2, Nishi-Shinjuku,
Shinjuku-ku
**Selected Restaurants:**
Attore, Bengawan Solo, Borsalino, Edo-Gin,
Fukudaya, Heichinrou, Inakaya, Ketel's, La Belle
Époque, L'Orangerie, Sabatini di Firenze,
Sasashu, Tokyo Joe's
**Banking:** Hours from 9 A.M. to 3 P.M. Monday
through Friday; 9 A.M. to noon on Saturday.
**Information Sources:**
Japan National Tourist Organization
650 Fifth Avenue
New York, New York 10111
212-757-5640

## Toronto, Canada
**Population:** 3,427,168
**Altitude:** 275 ft. (84m.)
**Average Temp.:** Jan., 23°F. (-5°C.); July, 69°F.
(21°C.)
**Telephone Area Number:** 416
**Selected Hotels:**
Four Seasons Motor Hotel, 21 Avenue Rd.
Holiday Inn-Downtown, 89 Chestnut St.
Park Plaza, 4 Avenue Rd.
Royal York, 100 Front St. W
Sheraton Centre, 123 Queen St.
Sutton Place, 955 Bay St.
**Selected Restaurants:**
Fisherman's Wharf, Imperial Room, Old Spaghetti
Factory, The Old Mill, Tanaka of Tokyo
**Banking:** Hours generally are from 10 A.M. to 3
P.M. Monday through Friday.
**Information Sources:**
Metropolitan Toronto Convention & Visitors Assn.
207 Quay West at Harbour Front
Toronto, Ontario M5J 1A7
416-368-9990

## Vienna (Wien), Austria
**Population:** 1,875,000
**Altitude:** 560 ft. (171m.)
**Average Temp.:** Jan., 30°F. (-1°C.); July, 68°F.
(20°C.)
**Selected Hotels:**
Ambassador, Neuer Markt 5
Bristol, Kärntner Ring 1, opposite Vienna Opera
Clima Villenhotel, Nussberggasse 2c
Imperial, Kärntner Ring 16
Parkhotel Schönbrunn, Hietzinger Haupstr. 12
Sacher, Philharmonikerstr. 4
Vienna Intercontinental, Johannesgasse 28
Hilton Wien, Am Stadtpark
**Selected Restaurants:**
Da Conte, Gottfried, Korso, Rotisserie Prinz Eugen
in the Hilton Hotel, Steirereck, Vier Jahreszeiten,
Zu den drei Husaren
**Banking:**
Hours are 8:00 A.M. to 12:30 P.M. and 1:30 P.M.
to 3:30 P.M. Monday, Tuesday, Wednesday, and
Friday; 1:30 P.M. to 5:30 P.M. on Thursday.

**Information Sources:**
Austrian National Tourist Office
500 Fifth Avenue
New York, New York 10110
212-944-6880

## Zurich, Switzerland
**Population:** 870,000
**Altitude:** 1,339 ft. (408m.)
**Average Temp.:** Jan., 31°F. (0°C.); July, 63°F.
(17°C.)
**Selected Hotels:**
Atlantis Sheraton, Doeltschiweg 234
Baur au Lac, Talstrasse 1
Bellerive au Lac, Utoquai 47
Carlton-Elite, Bahnhofstrasse 41
Dolder Grand, Kurhausstr. 65
Eden au Lac, Utoquai 45
Zum Storchen, Weinplatz 2
Zurich, Neumuhlequai 42
**Selected Restaurants:**
Agnes Amberg, Chez Max, Haus zum Ruden,
Kronenhalle, Rotisserie Lindenhofkeller, Veltliner
Keller, Zunfthaus zur Waage
**Banking:** Hours 8:30 A.M. to 4:30 P.M. Monday
through Friday; closed Saturday.
**Information Sources:**
Swiss National Tourist Office
608 Fifth Avenue
New York, New York 10020
212-757-5944

# World Travel Maps

## Inhabited Localities
The symbol represents the number of inhabitants within the locality

**At scales 1:6,000,000 to 1:12,000,000**
- •    0–10,000
- ○    10,000–25,000
- ◉    25,000–100,000
- ▣    100,000–250,000
- ▣    250,000–1,000,000
- ■    >1,000,000

**At 1:24,000,000 scale**
- •    0–50,000
- ◉    50,000–100,000
- ▣    100,000–250,000
- ▣    250,000–1,000,000
- ■    >1,000,000

**Urban Area** (area of continuous industrial, commercial, and residential development)

The size of type indicates the relative economic and political importance of the locality

| | | |
|---|---|---|
| Écommoy | Lisieux | **Rouen** |
| Trouville | **Orléans** | **PARIS** |

### Capitals of Political Units

**BUDAPEST**    Independent Nation

**Cayenne**    Dependency (Colony, protectorate, etc.)

Lasa    State, Province, etc.

### Alternate Names

**MOSKVA**
**MOSCOW**    English or second official language names are shown in reduced size lettering

**Volgograd**
(Stalingrad)    Historical or other alternates in the local language are shown in parentheses

## Political Boundaries

**International**
(First-order political unit)

— · — · — · —    Demarcated and Undemarcated

— — — — —    Indefinite or Undefined

— — — — — —    Demarcation Line (used in Korea)

**Internal**

**State, Province, etc.** (Second-order political unit)

*MURCIA*    **Historical Region** (No boundaries indicated)

## Transportation

—————————    Primary Road

—————————    Secondary Road

*Canal du Midi*    Navigable Canal

—]– – – – –[—    Tunnel

– – – – – – –    Ferry

## Hydrographic Features

Intermittent Stream

Rapids, Falls

Irrigation or Drainage Canal

Reef

*The Everglades*    Swamp

Glacier
VATNAJÖKULL

*L. Victoria*    Lake, Reservoir

*Tuz Gölü*    Salt Lake

Intermittent Lake, Reservoir

Dry Lake Bed

## Topographic Features

| | | |
|---|---|---|
| Matterhorn 4478 △ | Elevation Above Sea Level |
| 76 ▽ | Elevation Below Sea Level |
| Mount Cook 3764 ▲ | Highest Elevation in Country |
| Khyber Pass 1067 ✕ | Mountain Pass |
| 133 ▼ | Lowest Elevation in Country |

Elevations are given in meters, the Highest and Lowest Elevation in a continent are underlined

Sand Area

Lava

Salt Flat

ARCTIC OCEAN

GREENLAND
(Den.)

Beaufort Sea

75°

BAFFIN ISLAND

VICTORIA
ISLAND

Arctic Circle

RUSSIA

ICELAND

UNITED
STATES

Anchorage

Godthåb

60°

Yellowknife

Hudson
Bay

Bering Sea

Gulf of
Alaska

C A N A D A

UNITED
KINGDOM

IRELAND
LONDO

FRANC

ALEUTIAN ISLANDS

NEWFOUNDLAND

45°

Vancouver

Winnipeg

NORTH
AMERICA

Montréal

ATLANTIC   OCEAN

P A C I F I C

SAN
FRANCISCO

U N I T E D   S T A T E S

NEW YORK
Washington

PORTUGAL   SPA

LOS ANGELES

CHICAGO

AÇORES AZORES
(Port.)

30°

O C E A N

BERMUDA
(U.K.)

MOROCCO

Tropic of Cancer

Houston

Gulf of Mexico

Miami

H A W A I I A N   I S L A N D S
(U.S.)

MEXICO

CUBA

WESTERN S
SAHARA

AL

15°

CIUDAD
DE MÉXICO

HAITI

DOMINICAN
REPUBLIC
PUERTO RICO
(U.S.)

MAURI-
TANIA

MA

GUATEMALA

HONDURAS
NICARAGUA

SENEGAL

GUINEA

BURKIN
FAS

P

O

L

Y

N

E

Equator

TRINIDAD AND
TOBAGO

SIERRA
LEONE

IVORY
COAST

0°

PANAMA

VENEZUELA

GUYANA
FRENCH
SURINAME
GUIANA

ARCHIPIÉLAGO DE COLÓN
GALAPAGOS ISLANDS
(Ec.)

COLOMBIA

ECUADOR

Amazon

Belém

Equator

S

I

A

Recife

15°

FIJI

AM.
SAMOA

BRAZIL

SOUTH AMERICA

ATLANTIC OCEA

TONGA

COOK
ISLANDS
(N.Z.)

FRENCH
POLYNESIA

BOLIVIA

Brasilia

Tropic of Capricorn

PARAGUAY

RIO DE JANEIRO
SÃO PAULO

Asunción

International Date Line

CHILE

30°

P A C I F I C

Santiago

URUGUAY
BUENOS AIRES

ARGENTINA

O C E A N

45°

FALKLAND ISLANDS
(U.K.)

60°

CABO DE HORNOS
CAPE HORN

Antarctic Circle

Bellingshausen Sea

Weddell Sea

75°

A    N    T    A    R

Kilometres 0 1000 2000 3000 Km.

Miles 0 1000 2000 3000 Mi.

Robinson Projection

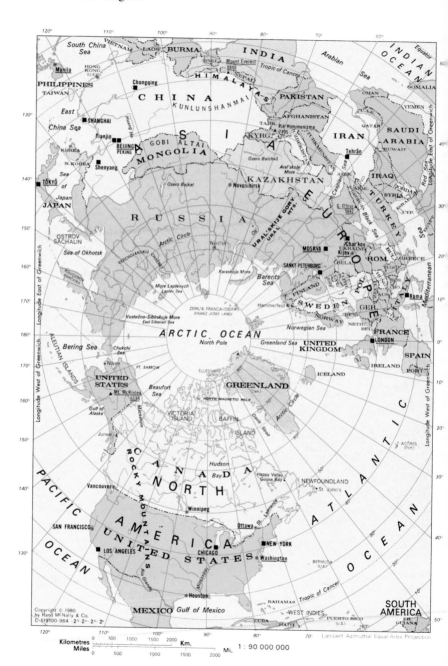

Kilometres 0 500 1000 1500 2000 Km.
Miles 0 500 1000 1500 2000 Mi.    1 : 90 000 000

Lambert Azimuthal Equal-Area Projection

Copyright © 1980
by Rand McNally & Co.
C-519100-964 -2ᵛ-2ᵛ-2ᵛ-2ᵛ

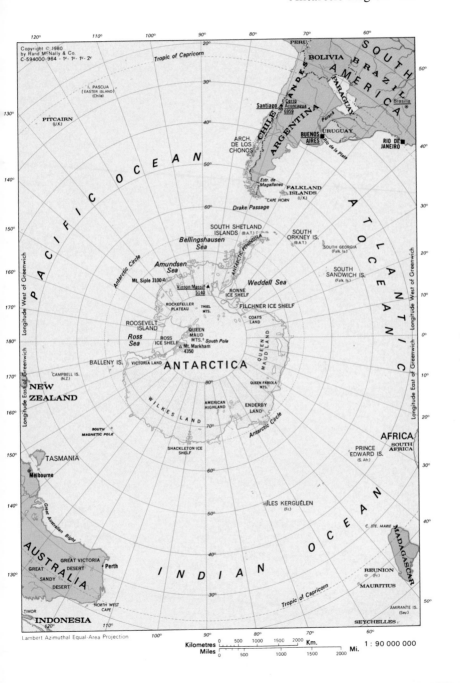

Tropic of Capricorn

PERU

SOUTH AMERICA

BOLIVIA

BRAZIL

PARAGUAY

Brasilia

URUGUAY

ARGENTINA

CHILE

ANDES

Santiago

Cerro Aconcagua 6959

BUENOS AIRES

Paraná

Río de la Plata

RIO DE JANEIRO

I. PASCUA
(EASTER ISLAND)
(Chile)

PITCAIRN
(U.K.)

ARCH. DE LOS CHONOS

Estr. de Magallanes

FALKLAND ISLANDS
(U.K.)

CAPE HORN

Drake Passage

PACIFIC OCEAN

SOUTH SHETLAND ISLANDS (B.A.T.)

Bellingshausen Sea

SOUTH ORKNEY IS.
(B.A.T.)

SOUTH GEORGIA
(Falk. Is.)

ATLANTIC OCEAN

Antarctic Circle

Amundsen Sea

Mt. Siple 3100

Vinson Massif 5140

ANTARCTIC PENINSULA

Weddell Sea

SOUTH SANDWICH IS.
(Falk. Is.)

ROCKEFELLER PLATEAU

THIEL MTS.

RONNE ICE SHELF

FILCHNER ICE SHELF

COATS LAND

ROOSEVELT ISLAND

Ross Sea

ROSS ICE SHELF

QUEEN MAUD MTS.

South Pole

Mt. Markham 4350

QUEEN MAUD LAND

Longitude West of Greenwich

Longitude East of Greenwich

BALLENY IS.

VICTORIA LAND

ANTARCTICA

QUEEN FABIOLA MTS.

NEW ZEALAND

WILKES LAND

AMERICAN HIGHLAND

ENDERBY LAND

CAMPBELL IS.
(N.Z.)

SOUTH MAGNETIC POLE

Antarctic Circle

AFRICA

SOUTH AFRICA

TASMANIA

SHACKLETON ICE SHELF

PRINCE EDWARD IS.
(S. Afr.)

Melbourne

Great Australian Bight

ÎLES KERGUÉLEN
(Fr.)

INDIAN OCEAN

C. STE. MARIE

MADAGASCAR

AUSTRALIA

GREAT VICTORIA DESERT

Perth

REUNION
(Fr.)

GREAT SANDY DESERT

MAURITIUS

NORTH WEST CAPE

TIMOR

INDONESIA

Tropic of Capricorn

AMIRANTE IS.
(Sey.)

SEYCHELLES

Lambert Azimuthal Equal-Area Projection

Kilometres
0   500   1000   1500   2000   Km.

Miles
0   500   1000   1500   2000   Mi.

1 : 90 000 000

Kilometres 0 200 400 600 Km.

Miles 0 200 400 600 Mi.    1 : 24 000 000

Copyright © 1980,1987
by Rand McNally & Co.

C-550000-964 — 7ᵛ — 7ᵛ — 7ᵛ — 13ᵛ

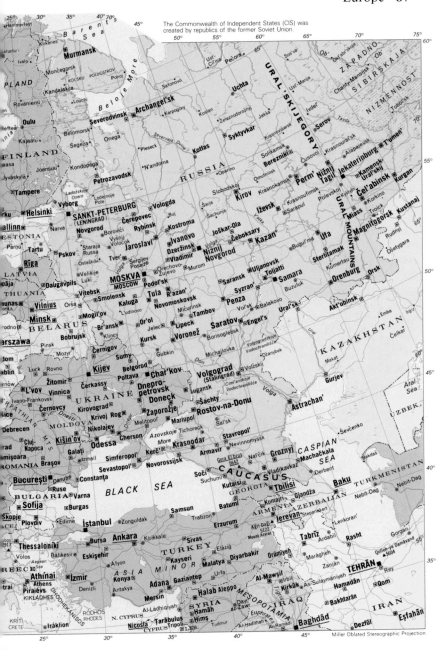

The Commonwealth of Independent States (CIS) was
created by republics of the former Soviet Union.

25° 30° 35° 40° 70° 45° 50° 55° 60° 65° 70° 75° 60°

Hammerfest
Kirkenes
ualuntuni
Ivalo
PLAND
Murmansk
Moncegorsk
KOLSKIJ POLUOSTROV
Ponoj
Ust-
Cil'ma
Pecora
Ob'
ZAPADNO
SIBIRSKAJA
Chanty-Mansijsk Ob
Tobol'sk
NIZMENNOST'
60°

Rovaniemi
Kandalaksa
Louchi
Safonovo
Uchta
Vdel'
Serov
Tavda
Alapaevsk
Tumen'

eftea
Oulu
Belomorsk
Severodvinsk
Archangel'sk
Karpogory
Koslan
Zeleznodoroznyj
Jaksa
Syktyvkar
Krasnojarsk
Krasnouralsk
Jekaterinburg
Kamensk-
Ural'skij
Cel'abinsk
Kurgan

Kajaani
Segeza
Onega
Plesetsk
Severnaja Dvina
Kottas
Solikamsk
Berezniki
Cusovoj
Perm'
Niznij
Tagil
Korkino
Miass
Magnitogorsk
kustanaj

FINLAND
aasa
Kondopoga
'N'andoma
Oparino
Omutninsk
Krasnokamsk
Perm'
Sarapul
Ufa
Bugul'ma
URAL
MOUNTAINS
Troick
Rudnyj
Dzetygara

Jyvaskyla
Joensuu
Petrozavodsk
RUSSIA
Slobodskoj
Kirov
Krasnoufimsk
Polevskoj

Tampere
Ladozskoje
Ozero
Lodejnoje
Pole
Vologda
Sarja
Sachunja
Izevsk
Sterlitamak
Kumertau
Orenburg
Orsk

Helsinki
Vyborg
Cerepovec
Buj
Joskar-Ola
Kazan'
Samara

allinn
SANKT-PETERBURG
(LENINGRAD)
Rybinsk
Kostroma
Ivanovo
Ceboksary
Buzuluk

ESTONIA
Narva
Novgorod
Borovici
Vysnij
Volocek
Jaroslavl'
Dzerzinsk
Niznij
Novgorod
Uljanovsk
Toljatti
Orenburg

Parnu
Tartu
Pskov
Staraja
Russa
Tver'
Volga
Vladimir
Murom
Saransk
Syzran'
Samara
AKT'ubinsk

Riga
Velikije
Luki
Ostaskov
Sergijev
Posad
Orechovo-
Zujevo
Penza
Vol'sk
Balakovo
Ural'sk
Emba
Irg

oaja
Daugavpils
Vitebsk
MOSKVA
MOSCOW
Podol'sk
R'azan'
Tambov
Engel's
KAZAKHSTAN
Celkar

THUANIA
Vilnius
Orsa
Smolensk
Kaluga
Tula
Novomoskovsk
Micurinsk
Penza
Saratov
Ul
Makat

unas
Minsk
Mogil'ov
'Ludinovo
Or'ol
Jelec
Lipeck
Voronez
Borisoglebsk
Volgogradskoje
Vodochranilisce
Olzanbek

rodno
BELARUS
Br'ansk
Kliney
Kursk
Michajlovka
Ižizel

arszawa
Bobrujsk
Mozyr'
Cernigov
Sumy
Gubkin
Don
Dneprodzerzinsk
Volgogradskoje
Vodochranilisce

Jom
Pinsk
Luck
Rovno
Kijev
Belgorod
Char'kov
Volgograd
(Stalingrad)
Volzskij

ablin
rnow
L'vov
Žitomir
Poltava
Dnepro-
petrovsk
Lugansk
Ciml'anskoje
Vodochranilisce

Ivano-Frankovsk
Vinnica
Cerkassy
Doneck
Sachty
Volga
Gurjev

ice
Cernovcy
Kirovograd
Krivoj Rog
Zaporozje
Rostov-na-Donu
Astrachan'
UZBEK

Debrecen
Dnestr
Melitopol'
Mariupol'
Sal'sk
Aral
Sea

rad
Cluj-
Napoca
KISIN'OV
Nikolajev
Cherson
Azovskoje
More
Tichoreck
Stavropol'
Sevcenko

misoara
Galati
Izmail
Simferopol'
Kerc
Krasnodar
Armavir
Nevinnomyssk
Bekdas

ROMANIA
Brasov
Odessa
Novorossijsk
Soci
Gora El'brus
5642
Nal'cik
Groznyj
Vladikavkaz
Macackala
CASPIAN
SEA
Derbent

Bucuresti
Danube
Constanta
Sevastopol'
Suchumi
CAUCASUS
Kutaisi
TURKMENISTAN
Nebit-Dag

BULGARIA
Ruse
Varna
BLACK SEA
GEORGIA
Tbilisi
Baku

Sofija
Burgas
Batumi
Gjandza
Gorgan
Nebit-Dag

Skopje
Plovdiv
Edirne
Istanbul
Zonguldak
Samsun
Trabzon
ARMENIA
AZERBAIJAN
Stepanakert
Lenkoran'

CE
Thessaloniki
Bursa
Ankara
Kirikkale
Sivas
Erzurum
Agri Dagi
Mount Ararat
5122
Jerevan
Tabriz
Ardabil
Rasht

917
Eskisehir
Kayseri
Elazig
Orumiyeh
Maragheh
Qollehye Damavand
5604

Athinai
Izmir
Afyon
Malatya
Diyarbakir
Zanjan
TEHRAN
Rey

trai
Piraievs
Denizli
Konya
ASIA
MINOR
TURKEY
Gaziantep
Urfa
Al-Mawsil
As-Sulaymaniyah
Hamadan
Qom

KIKLADHES
Antakya
Adana
Mersin
Halab Aleppo
MESOPOTAMIA
Kirkuk
IRAQ
Bakhtaran
IRAN

KRITI
CRETE
RODHOS
RHODES
Al-Ladhiqiyah
Tarabulus
SYRIA
Hamah
az-Zawr
Euphrates
Esfahan

Iraklion
Nicosia
N. CYPRUS
CYPRUS Tripoli
LEB.
Hims
Tudmur
Dezful

Blos
E
REECE
Vólos
Balikesir
Aegean
Sea
Denizli
Tarabulus
Al-Hadithah
An-Ramadi
Baghdad

25° 30° 35° 40° 45°
Miller Oblated Stereographic Projection

ATLANTIC
OCEAN

NORTH
SEA

Melby
House•
SHETLAND
ISLANDS
•Lerwick
•Virkie

ORKNEY
ISLANDS
MAINLAND
Stromness•  •Kirkwall
Durness•      •Burwick
Thurso•
•Wick
ISLE OF       Ben More
LEWIS         Assynt  •Helmsdale
Lochinver•  △998
SAINT KILDA   Ullapool•  •Bonarbridge
              Dingwall•  •Elgin  •Fraserburgh
Uig•  Kyle of      Inverness•  •Huntly
      Lochaish
ISLAND
OF SKYE
•Mallaig        Balmoral  •Aberdeen
        1343    Castle    •Stonehaven
      ▲Ben Nevis
•Tobermory
ISLAND        Perth  •Dundee
OF MULL       Ben More•  •Arbroath
      1174
Lochgilphead•        Kirkcaldy
        Greenock•  Firth of Forth
Port Ellen•ISLAND OF  GLASGOW  •Edinburgh
ARRAN          Motherwell•  Berwick-upon-Tweed
Campbeltown•  •Kilmarnock  Galashiels•
        •Ayr  Hawick•  Moffat•  NORTHUMBERLAND
Coleraine•              NATIONAL PARK
Londonderry•  Dumfries•  Blyth•
Lifford•  Larne•  Newton Stewart•  Newcastle upon Tyne
Donegal•  Omagh•  Bangor•  Stranraer•  Carlisle  Durham•  •Sunderland
Belmullet•  Enniskillen•  Newtownards•  Whitehaven•  Penrith•  Bishop  •Middlesbrough
Sligo•  Portadown•  Belfast  LAKE DISTRICT  Auckland•  NORTH YORK MOORS
Ballina•  ISLE OF      NATIONAL PARK      NATIONAL PARK  •Scarborough
ULSTER  MAN      Barrow-in-  YORKSHIRE DALES
Castlebar•  (U.K.)  Douglas•  Furness  NATIONAL PARK
CONNAUGHT  Cavan•  Castle-  Lancaster•  York  Kingston
Clifden•  Roscommon•  MEATH  town  Blackpool•  Black-  Leeds  upon Hull
ARAN  Athlone•  •Drogheda  IRISH  Preston•  burn  MANCHESTER•  •Grimsby
ISLANDS  Galway•  Tullamore•  SEA  Southport•  Liverpool•  Sheffield•  Lincoln•
Milltown  Ennis•  Naas•  Dublin  Chester•  PEAK DISTRICT  •Skegness
Malbay•  LEINSTER  Dún  Bangor•  Stoke-on-  Nottingham  Sheringham•
Limerick  Nenagh•  Laoghaire•  Holy-  Caernarvon•  Trent•  •Cromer
Tralee•  Tipperary•  Arklow•  head  Wrexham•  Derby•  Grantham•  Norwich
MUNSTER  Clonmel•  Wexford•  Barmouth•  Stafford•  King's Lynn  •Peterborough  Great
Dingle•  1041  Waterford•  Rosslare•  Aberystwyth•  Leicester•  Yarmouth
Carrauntoohil△  Aberystwyth  BIRMINGHAM  •Coventry  Cambridge
Cahirciveen•  WALES  Worcester•  Stratford-  Northampton  Ipswich•
Bantry•  Cork  Dungarvan•  Carmarthen•  CAMBRIAN  upon-  Banbury•  Luton  Chelmsford
      PEMBROKESHIRE  MTS.  Hereford•  Avon  •Gloucester  •Oxford  •Southend-
      COAST  BRECON BEACONS  Merthyr Tydfil•  LONDON  on-Sea
      NATIONAL PARK  NATIONAL PARK  •Newport  Reading  Thames
St. George's Channel  Milford Haven•  Swansea  Cardiff  Bristol  Windsor•  Canterbury•  Dover
      Bridgwater•  Bath•  Salisbury•  Basingstoke•  Guildford•  Folkestone•
ATLANTIC      EXMOOR NATIONAL  Yeovil•  Brighton•  Hastings
OCEAN      PARK  Exeter•  Southampton•  Portsmouth•  UNITED  Boulogne-
      DARTMOOR  Weymouth•  Bournemouth•  KINGDOM  sur-Mer
Newquay•  Plymouth  NATIONAL PARK  Torquay•
LAND'S END  Saint Austell  (Torbay)  English  Channel
•Falmouth      La  Manche  FRANCE  Le Tréport•
                  Cherbourg•  Fécamp•  Dieppe•
                  •Totes

Conic Projection, Two Standard Parallels

Kilometres 0  50  100  150 Km.
Miles 0    50    100   150 Mi.
1 : 7 500 000

Copyright © 1980
by Rand McNally & Co.
C-554300-964 - 5ᵛ- 5ᵛ- 5ᵛ- 9ᵛ

NORWEGIAN SEA

ATLANTIC

OCEAN

Arctic Circle

NORWAY

SWEDEN

FINLAND

LAPLAND

Gulf of Bothnia

Gulf of Finland

BALTIC SEA

DENMARK

GERMANY

POLAND

RUSSIA

ESTONIA

LATVIA

LITHUANIA

BELARUS

**STOCKHOLM**

**Helsinki** Helsingfors

**SANKT-PETERBURG**

**Tallinn**

**Riga**

**KØBENHAVN** COPENHAGEN

**HAMBURG**

Oslo

Trondheim

Göteborg Gothenburg

Malmö

Lambert Conformal Conic Projection

Kilometres 0 100 200 300 Km.
Miles 0 100 200 300 Mi.
1 : 13 000 000

Lambert Conformal Conic Projection

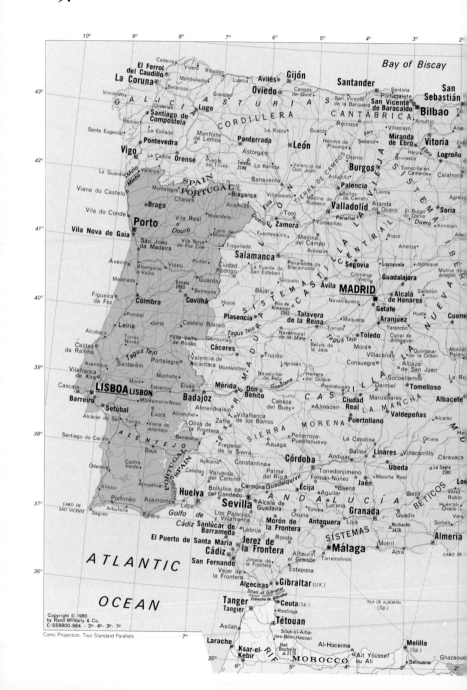

Bay of Biscay

10° 9° 8° 7° 6° 5° 4° 3° 2°

Cedeira
El Ferrol
del Caudillo
La Coruna
Vivero Ribadeo
Mondonedo
Betanzos
Avilés Gijón
Oviedo
Santander
San
Sebastián
Bilbao

43°
Vimianzo
GALICIA ASTURIAS
Lugo
Cangas
de Onis
Reinosa
CORDILLERA
CANTÁBRICA
San Vicente
de Baracaldo
Vitoria
Logroño

Santiago de
Compostela
La Robla
León
Miranda
de Ebro
Soria

42°
Pontevedra
Vigo
Orense
La Caniza
Ponferrada
Astorga
Burgos
Palencia
Valladolid

SPAIN
PORTUGAL
Braga
Porto
Vila Nova de Gaia

41°
Vila do Conde
Viana do Castelo
Chaves
Vila Real
Zamora
Salamanca
Segovia
Guadalajara
MADRID

40°
Coimbra
Covilhã
Plasencia
Ávila
Getafe
Aranjuez
Toledo

39°
Leiria
Castelo Branco
Cáceres
Mérida
Don
Benito
Ciudad
Real

LISBOA LISBON
Badajoz
Albacete

38°
Setúbal
Évora
Córdoba
Valdepeñas

37°
Huelva
Sevilla
Granada
Almería

ALENTEJO
Jerez de
la Frontera
Cádiz
Málaga

36°
ATLANTIC
Algeciras Gibraltar (U.K.)

OCEAN
Tanger
Tangier
Ceuta (Sp.)
Tétouan

Conic Projection, Two Standard Parallels

35°
Larache
Ksar-el-
Kebir
MOROCCO
Melilla
(Sp.)

Kilometres 0   50   100   150

Miles 0   50   100   150 Mi.    1: 6 000 000

Conic Projection, Two Standard Parallels

Copyright © 1980
by Rand McNally & Co.
C-559800-964-4-4-4½-4¾-8v

Conic Projection Two Standard Parallels

1 : 6 500 000

Kilometres 0    50    100    150  Km.
Miles 0    50    100    150  Mi.

**100**

SWEDEN
FINLAND

19° 20° 21° 22° 23° 24° 25° 26° 27° 28° 29° 30° 31° 3.

60° Storby Kastelholm **Turku** Salo Hyvinkää Mysrkylä Inkeroinen Soloviovka
Mariehamn Korpo Sauvo Vihti Borga Porvoo Kotka Sovetskij **Vyborg** Srednegorje *Ladožskoje Lake*
Degerby Korpo Kimito Karis Korso Lovisa Lovisa Primorsk Vaskelovo Lu
Hanko Hanko Esbo **Helsinki** FINLAND RUSSIA Sosnovyj Bor **Kronštadt** **Vsevoložsk**
**Helsingfors** **Kronštadt** **SANKT-PETERBUR**

Gulf of Finland Ust'-Luga Puškin (LENINGRAD)
59° Ristna **Tallinn** Loksa Kunda Begunici **ST. PETERSBURG**
Paldiski Vasalemma Rakvere Kohtla-Järve **Narva** Kikering **Gatčina** Kiriš
Kärdla Riguldi Kohila Tamsalu Kiviôli **Sillamäe** Ivangorod Družnaja Gorka
Emmaste Haapsalu Märjamaa Järva-Jaani Alajôe Slepino **Slancy** Čudovo
SAAREMAA Kirbla Türi Mustvee Čudskoje Krasnyje Gory Torkoviči Tosovskij
58° Saare Virtsu Tootsi **Pärnu** Põltsamaa Ozero Marjinsko **Luga** Bateckij
Kuresaare Vändra ESTONIA Mustla L'ady **Novgorod**
Kilingi-Nõmme Viljandi Elva **Tartu** Jamm Pl'usa Zapl'usje Proletarij
Ovisi LATVIA Otepää Veriora Pavy Nikolajevo Ozero Il'men'
**Ventspils** Kolka Mazsalaca Valga Võru Sol'cy **Staraja Russa**
57° Limbaži Valmiera **Pskov** Bol'šoje Zagorje Dno Morino
Pavilosta Kuldiga Saulkrasti Cesis Aluksne RUSSIA Palkino Dulovka Gorodno Bělebelka Zalucje
Valdemarpils Kandava Gauja Viļaka Ostrov Dedoviči Cichačovo
**Liepāja** Aizpute **Jūrmala** **Rīga** Ergli Gulbene Krutcy Krasnyj Luč **Cholm**
Priekule Saldus Dobele Madona Karsava Opočka Puškinskije Gory Kudever Lokn'a Bologovo
56° Mažeikiai Eleja **Jelgava** Plaviņas Preiļi Rēzekne Žilupe Makismo Novosokol'niki Nasva Toropec
Seda LATVIA Nereta LITHUANIA Dagda Sebež Lopatovo **Velikije Luki**
Palanga Kretinga Plunge **Šiauliai** Birži Dusetos Kraslava Osveja Rossony Never' Poreče Usmyn Sinkovo
**Klaipėda** Rietavas Užventis Radviliškis Zarasai Osveja RUSSIA BELARUS'
**(Memel)** Šilale **Panevėžys** Anykščiai Braslav Miory Dvina **Polock** Gorodok Veliž
55° Neringa LITHUANIA Tytuvenai Raseiniai Ramygala J. Vidzy Dvina Vetrino **Vitebsk** Demidov
Zelenogradsk Tauragė Ukmerge Ignalina Postavy Ulla Akatova
**Kaliningrad** **Sovetsk** Nemunas Švenčioneliai Glubokoje Bešenkoviči Liozno **Smolensk**
**Königsberg** **Tilsit** Kazlu Ruda Svir' M'adel' Lepel' Čašniki Bogušovsk ŠMOL.
Čern'achovsk Gumbinnen Vievis **Vilnius** Žodiški Krasnoluki Novolukoml' Kochanovo **Orša** **Gorki** Monastyrščina
54° RUSSIA Interburg Marijampole Alytus Osm'any Plešcenicy Mstiž Krupki Kopys' Dnepr
Bartosyce Suwałki Druskininkai Eišiškes **Molodečno** Borisov Novyje Gorodišče Gorki **Mogil'ov** Lobkoviči
Szczytno Kolno Jeziero Augustow LITHUANIA Lida **Minsk** Žodino Denisoviči Gorodišče Kričov Čausy
53° Ełk Spawskry BELARUS' Berozovka Voložin Dzeržinsk Smiloviči Berezina **Osipoviči** Slavgorod Kost'ukoviči
Łomža Grajewo **Grodno** Ščučin Novogrudok Uzda BELORUSSKAJA **Bobrujsk** Rogačov Krasnaja
Ostrołęka Szczecin Volkovysk Slonim **Baranoviči** Sin'avka Sluck Parici Zabolotje Žlobin Merkuloviči Gora
52° Biala **Białystok** Kossovo Ostrov Soligorsk L'uban' Svetlogorsk Čečorsk **Gomel'** **Novozybko**
Minsk Mazowiecki Podlaska ZAPOVEDNIK Gancevici Moroč Zabolotje Sosnovyj **Rečica** Dobruš
Wyszków BELOVEŽSKAJA Kobrin Telechany Lunínec Luban' L'achoviči POLESJE Bor Kalinkoviči
Ciechanowiec **Brest** Drogičin Divin **Pinsk** Petrikov Ple Kalinkoviči

22° 23° 24° 25° 26° 27° 28° 29° 30° 31° 32°

Copyright © 1980
by Rand McNally & Co.
C-579495-964 - 2⌄- 4⌄- 4⌄- 9⌄

Kilometres 0 50 100 150 Km.
Miles 0 50 100 150 Mi.
1: 6 000 000

BALTIC SEA
Gulf of Riga
HIIUMAA

Kilometres 0 200 400 600 Km.

Miles 0 200 400 600 Mi.

1 : 24 000 000

MORE LAPTEVYCH

LAPTEV SEA

NOVOSIBIRSKIJE OSTROVA

OSTROV NOVAJA SIBIR'

OSTROV KOTEL'NYJ

OSTROV BOL'ŠOJ L'ACHOVSKIJ

VOSTOČNO-SIBIRSKOJE MORE

EAST SIBERIAN SEA

OSTROV VRANGELJA

Chukchi Sea

Chuchi

EKIATAPSKIJ CHREBET

Arctic Circle

Providenija

Bering Strait

MTS SVATOJ NOS

80°

75°

180°

175°

170°

175°

170°

165°

Buolkalach

Sokol

Sklad

Udza

Sikt'ach

Dzardzan

Suchana

Lena

K'us'ur

Kazačje

Sedanich

SIBERIA

TIJE

Sologoncy

N'urba

Tuobuja

O'okminsk

Lensk

Kropotkin

Bodajbo

ANOVOJE NAGORJE

STANOVYJE MOUNTAINS

Bagdarin

Vitim

Bukačača

Mogoča

Stretensk

Nerčinskij Zavod

Borz'a

Čita

Chapceranga

Manzhouli

Cojbalsan

Hailar

NEI MONGGOL ZIZHIQU

INNER MONGOLIA

Butehaqi

Tailai

HEILONGJIANG

CHINA

Qiqihar

Harbin

Svalach

VERCHOJANSKIJ

CHREBET

Verchojansk

Suordach

Sartang

Batamaj

Lena

Chandyga

Amga

Ust'-Maja

Ulu

Aldan

Čagda

Gonam

STANOVOJ CHREBET

Tyndinskij

Never

Zeja

Zeja

Simanovsk

Svobodnyj

Blagoveščensk

Rajčichinsk

Birobidžan

Beian

Hegang

Shuangyashan

Jixi

Mudanjiang

JILINI

Ussurijsk

Vladivostok

Nachodka

CHREBET ČERSKOGO

Gora Pobeda 3147

Om'akon

Gora Mus-Chaja 2959

Omča

Ynykčanskij

Nel'kan

Ajan

ŠANTARSKIJE OSTROVA

Čumikan

Guga

Selimdža

Nikolajevsk-na-Amure

Ocha

OSTROV SACHALIN

SAKHALIN

Aleksandrovsk-Sachalinskij

Poronajsk

Sovetskaja Gavan'

Južno-Sachalinsk

Kuril'sk

SEA OF OKHOTSK

OCHOTSKOJE MORE

SEA OF JAPAN

POLUOSTROV KAMČATKA

Petropavlovsk Kamčatskij

KORJAKSKOJE NAGORJE

Bering Sea

Magadan

Ochotsk

Zaliv Šelichova

Palana

Tigil

 Key

Komsomol'sk-na-Amure

Chabarovsk

SICHOTE-ALIN'

Amur

KURIL'SKIJE OSTROVA

KURIL ISLANDS

PACIFIC OCEAN

Wakkanai

Nayoro

Asahikawa

Kushiro

Obihiro

Sapporo

Muroran

HOKKAIDO

Hakodate

Aomori

JAPAN

Hachinohe

Akita

HONSHU

Morioka

Le Perouse Strait

80°

60°

55°

50°

45°

40°

175°

180°

175°

170°

165°

160°

155°

150°

145°

120°

115°

Lambert Conformal Conic Projection

135°

140°

145°

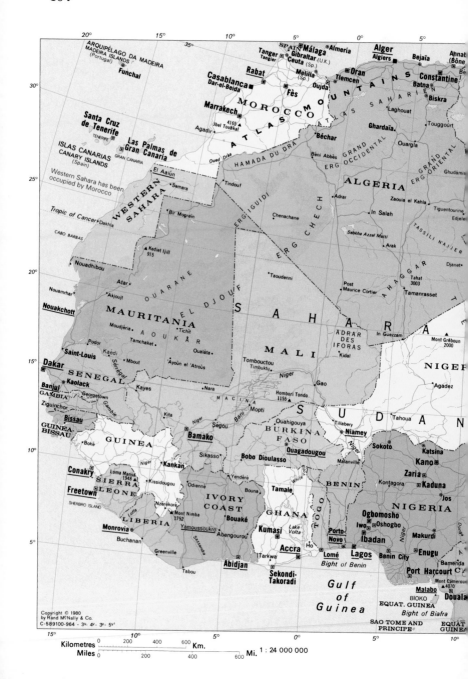

ARQUIPÉLAGO DA MADEIRA
MADEIRA ISLANDS
(Portugal)
Funchal

SPAIN ●Málaga ●Almeria
Tanger Gibraltar (U.K.) Alger
Tangier ●Ceuta (Sp.) Algiers Bejaïa Annat (Bône
Rabat ●Melilla (Sp.) ■Oran Constantine!
Casablanca Fès Oran Tlemcen Batna
Dar-el-Beïda Dujda Biskra
Marrakech MOROCCO Laghouat ATLAS SAHARIEN
Jbel Toubkal 4165 Ghardaïa● Touggourt
Agadir Béchar Ouargla
Santa Cruz de Tenerife
TENERIFE Béni Abbès ERG OCCIDENTAL Ghudamis
ISLAS CANARIAS Las Palmas de HAMADA DU DRÂ ALGERIA GRAND ERG ORIENTAL
CANARY ISLANDS Gran Canaria
(Spain) GRAN CANARIA Adrar Zaouia el Kahla Tiguentourine Edjelel
Western Sahara has been El Aaiún Tindouf In Salah
occupied by Morocco Semara Chenachane TASSILI N'AJJER
Bir Mogrein Arak Djanet
Tropic of Cancer Dakhla Sebkha Azzel Matti
CABO BARBAS Kediet Ijill 915 Taoudenni AHAGGAR Tahat 3003
Nouadhibou OUARANE EL DJOUF SAHARA Post Maurice Cortier Tamanrasset
Nouamrhar Atar Akjoujt
Nouakchott MAURITANIA Tichît In Guezzam Mont Gréboun 2000
Moudjéria AOUKÂR ADRAR DES IFORAS NIGER
Podor Tamchaket Oualâta MALI Kidal
Saint-Louis Kaédi Mbout Âyoûn el 'Atroûs Tombouctou Gao
Dakar SENEGAL Kayes Nara Timbuktu Niger Agadez
Banjul Kaolack Georgetown MACINA Hombori Tondo 1155
GAMBIA Ziguinchor Gambie Kita Mopti Niger Tahoua SUDAN
Bissau GUINEA- Ségou BURKINA Tillabery
BISSAU Boké GUINEA Sikasso Bamako Ouahigouya FASO Niamey Sokoto Katsina
Conakry Kankan Bobo Dioulasso Ouagadougou Malanville Kano
LOMA MANSA 1948 Kissidougou Odienne Yendéré White Volta Kontagora Zaria Kaduna
Freetown SIERRA LEONE Nzérékoré Bouna Tamale BENIN Jos
SHERBRO ISLAND Mont Nimba 1752 IVORY COAST TOGO NIGERIA
Monrovia LIBERIA Bouaké GHANA Ogbomosho Makurdi
Buchanan Yamoussoukro Abengourou Kumasi Lake Volta Iwo Oshogbo Enugu
Greenville Sassandra Ho Porto Ibadan
Tabou Tarkwa Accra Novo Benin City Port Harcourt C
Abidjan Lomé Lagos Bamenda
Sekondi- Bight of Benin Mont Cameroun 4070
Takoradi Malabo Douala
Gulf BIOKO
of EQUAT. GUINEA EQUAT
Guinea Bight of Biafra GUINEA
SAO TOME AND
PRINCIPE

Copyright © 1980
by Rand McNally & Co.
C-589100-964 - 3v. 4v. 3v. 5v'

Kilometres 0 200 400 600 Km.
Miles 0 200 400 600 Mi. 1 : 24 000 000

Miller Oblated Stereographic Projection

SAO TOME AND PRINCIPE
• São Tomé

EQUATORIAL GUINEA
Mitzic
Mekambo
• Ouesso
CAMEROON
Oubangui
Congo
Basankusu
Zaire
Basoko
Aruwimi
Bunia
Lake Albert
Margherita Pk. 5109
Kisangani (Stanleyville)
Kampala
UG
Entebbe

Libreville
Boque
GABON
Lambaréné
Fort-Rousset
Bikoro
Befale
Bokungu
Ikela
STANLEY FALLS
Ubundi
Lualaba
Kisangani (Stanleyville)
MONTS MITUMBA
RIFT
Kigali
RWANDA
BURUNDI
Bujumbura

Port-Gentil
▲ Mont Iboundji 1580
Franceville
Mossaka
Lac Mai-Ndombe
Kutu
Lomela
Kasese
Bukavu
Uvira
Lake Tanganyika

Iguéla
Mouila
Tchibanga
CONGO
Kibangou
Bandundu
Kasai
Lokolama
Bena-Dibele
Kindu
Kongolo
Kalémie (Albertville)
Mpanda

Dolisie
Brazzaville
Kinshasa (Léopoldville)
Kikwit
Ilebo
Tshofa
Kasongo
Manono
Lake Rukwa
Kasanga

Pointe-Noire
CABINDA (Angola)
Cabinda
Matadi
Boma
Popokabaka
Feshi
Tshikapa
Kananga (Luluabourg)
Mbuji-Mayi (Bakwanga)
Kaniama
Kawambwa
Kasenga
Kasama
Mbala

N'zeto
M'banza Congo
Cuango
Santa Pombo
Kahemba
Chitato
Camissombo
Kapanga
Kamina
Lake Mweru

Ambriz
Negage
Caungula
Kamina
Lubudi
Kolwezi
Likasi (Jadotville)
Lubumbashi (Elisabethville)
Mpika
MUCHINGA MTS.

Luanda
Caxito
Dondo
Malanje
Saurimo
Sandoa
Kasaji
Luau
Zambezi
Solwezi
Mufulira
Kitwe
Luanshya
Ndola

Porto Amboim
ANGOLA
Cela
Kuito
Luena
Balovale
Mankoya
Mumbwa
ZAMBIA
Kabwe (Broken Hill)

Lobito
Serra Mêco 2619 ▲
Huambo (Nova Lisboa)
Munhango
Luanguinga
Mussuma
Mongu
Lusaka
Zambezi
Zumbo

CABO DE SANTA MARIA
Caconda
Kuvango
Menongue
Senanga
Choma
Lake Kariba
Chinhoyi
Harare

ATLANTIC
Namibe
Lubango
Kassinga
Caiundo
N'Riquinha
Livingstone
Hwange
ZIMBABWE
Gweru
Kwekwe

OCEAN
Foz do Cunene
CAPE FRIA
Cunene
Xangongo
Ondangua
Cuangar
Okavango
Shakawe
CAPRIVI STRIP
Okavango Swamp
Bulawayo
Masvingo
Mwenezi

OVAMBOLAND
Sesfontein
Tsumeb
Toteng
Makgadikgadi Pans
Gwanda
Shashi
Messina
Pafuri

NAMIBIA
2606 ▲ Brandberg
Okahandja
Ghanzi
Francistown
BOTSWANA
Serowe
Palapye
Louis Trichardt
Potgietersrus
Limpopo

Walvisbaai Walvis Bay (S. Afr.)
Windhoek
KALAHARI
DESERT
Pietersburg
Thabazimbi
Maputo (Lourenço Marques)

Tropic of Capricorn
Mariental
Gibeon
Kakia
Kanye
Zeerust
Mochudi
Gaborone
Pretoria
Springs
Mbabane
SWAZI-LAND

Keetmanshoop
Koes
Askham
Kuruman
Vryburg
JOHANNESBURG
Klerksdorp
Vereeniging
Welkom
Kroonstad
Bethlehem
ZULULAND

Aus
Bogenfels
Karasburg
Upington
Virginia
Ladysmith
Injasuti 3408
Pietermaritzburg

Alexander Bay
Pofadder
Kenhardt
Kimberley
Bloemfontein
LESOTHO
Springfontein
DRAKENSBERG
Durban
Port Shepstone

Port Nolloth
Springbok
Garies
SOUTH AFRICA
De Aar
Middelburg
Queenstown
TRANSKEI
East London

Lambert's Bay
Vanrhynsdorp
Clanwilliam
Beaufort West
Graaff-Reinet
Murraysburg

Saldanha
Laingsburg
GREAT KARROO
30°

Paarl
Cape Town
Swellendam
Mosselbaai
Uitenhage
Port Elizabeth

CAPE OF GOOD HOPE
CAPE AGULHAS

Miller Oblated Stereographic Projection

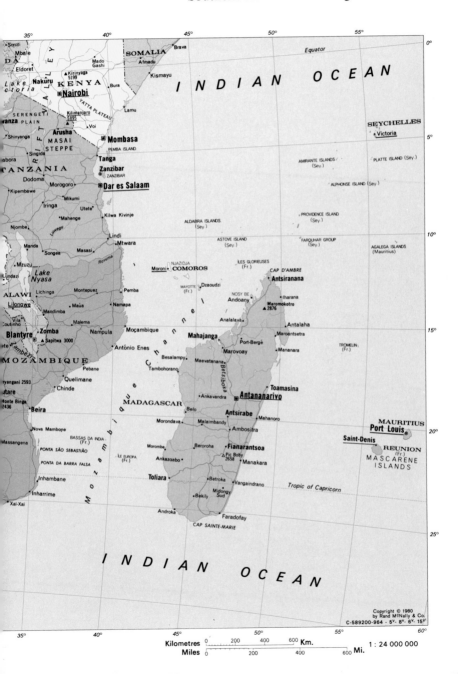

Kilometres  0  200  400  600 **Km.**

Miles  0  200  400  600 **Mi.**     1 : 24 000 000

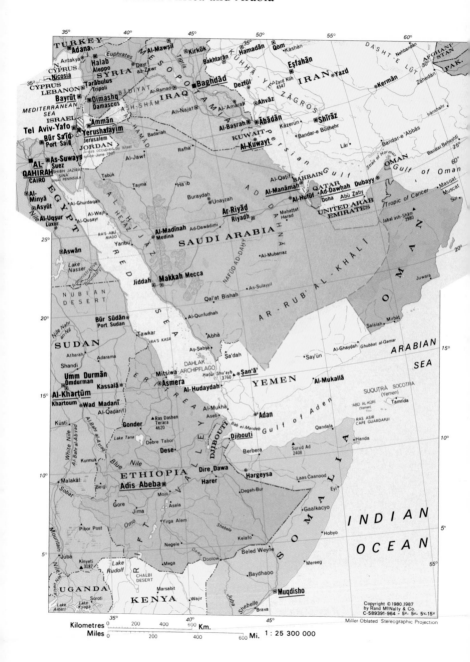

Kilometres 0   200   400   600 Km.
Miles 0   200   400   600 Mi.   1 : 25 300 000

Miller Oblated Stereographic Projection

Copyright ©1980,1987
by Rand McNally & Co.
C-589391-964 - 5¼- 5¼- 5¼-15½

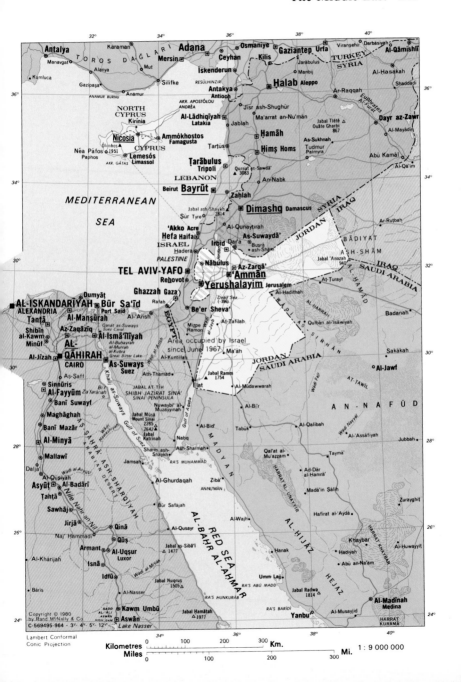

Lambert Conformal
Conic Projection

Kilometres | 0   100   200   300 Km.
Miles | 0   100   200   300 Mi.

1 : 9 000 000

The boundary between India and Pakistan through the disputed state of Jammu and Kashmir follows the "line of control" agreed upon by both countries in 1972.

Copyright © 1980, 1987
by Rand McNally & Co.
C-589400-964 - 7ᵛ- 7ᵛ- 5ᵛ- 15ᵛ

Lambert Conformal
Conic Projection
1 : 24 000 000

Kilometres 0  200  400  600 Km.
Miles 0  200  400  600 Mi.

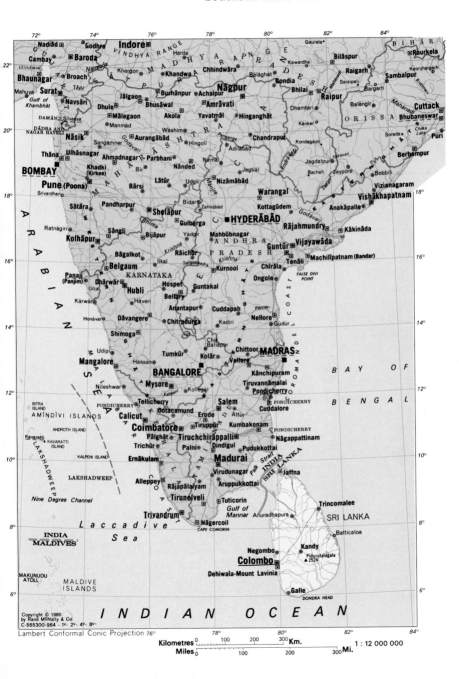

ARABIAN SEA

Copyright © 1980
by Rand McNally & Co.
C-565200-964 - 3v - 3v - 3v - 12v

The boundary between India and
Pakistan through the disputed
state of Jammu and Kashmir
follows the "line of control"
agreed to by both countries
in 1972.

Tropic of Cancer

Kilometres 0   100   200   300 Km.
Miles 0      100       200      300 Mi.

1 : 12 000 000

Lambert Conformal Conic Projection

Kilometres 0  200  400  600 Km.
Miles 0   200    400    600 Mi.   1: 24 000 000

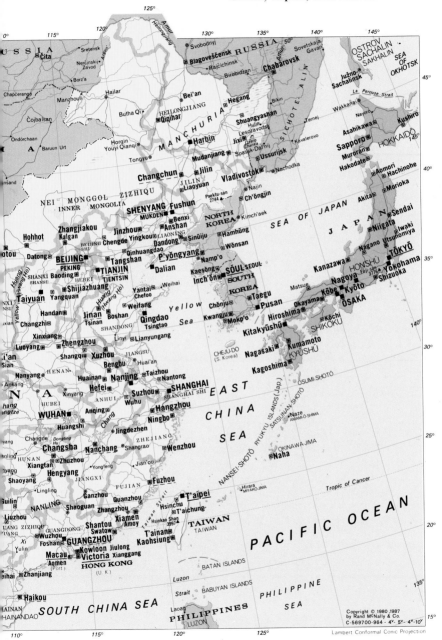

China, Japan, and Korea map

Copyright © 1980, 1987
by Rand McNally & Co.
C-569700-964 - 4V- 5V- 4V-10V

Lambert Conformal Conic Projection

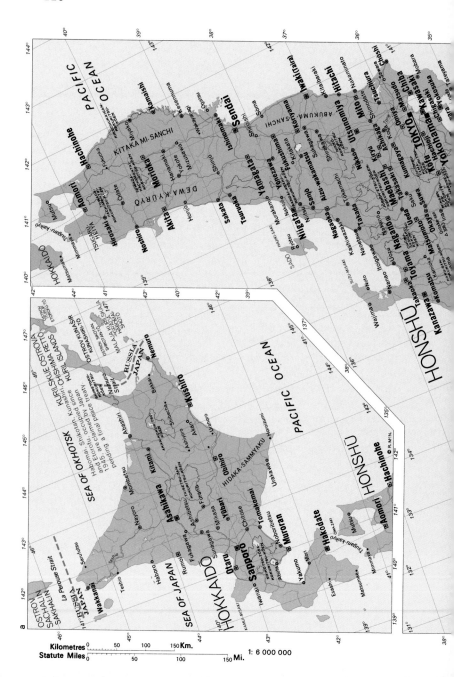

PACIFIC OCEAN

Hachinohe
Aomori
Morioka
Sendai
Akita
Yamagata
Niigata
Nagaoka
Toyama
Kanazawa
TOKYO
Yokohama
Kawasaki
Chiba

HONSHU

KITAKA MI-SANCHI
DEWA-KYŪRYO
ABUKUMA-SANCHI

Tsugaru-kaikyō
Mutsu
Mimmaya
Noshiro
TSUGARU HEIYA
Hirosaki
Ōdate
Fukuoka
Miyako
Ōfunato
Kamaishi
Kesennuma
Ōgatsu
Wakuya
Ishinomaki
Shiroishi
Sōma
Iwaki (Taira)
Hitachi
(Ibaraki)
Nakaminato
Mito
Shimodate
Utsunomiya
Nikkō
Kanuma
Ashikaga
Kiryū
Takasaki
Maebashi
Kumagaya
Hachiōji
Sabae
Chigasaki
Yokosuka
Odawara
Ōhū
Tsuchiura
Choshi
Matsudo
Ōami

Tsuruoka
Sakata
Shōnai-Heiya
Murakami
Shinjō
Nakada
Tsuchizawa
Yonezawa
Fukushima
Aizu-wakamatsu
Kitakata
Koriyama
Takamachi
Shirakawa
Sakai
Sendai
Suwa
Okaya
Matsumoto
Ueda
Nagano
Komatsu
Kiso
Inai
Kamiōka
Ōgaki

Takaoka
Takada
Naoetsu
Kashiwazaki
Itoigawa
SADO
HAIKU-SAKI
Nōetsu-shi
Noto
Nanao
Wajima
Suzu-misaki
Ishizaki

HOKKAIDŌ
Matsumae
Mimmaya

SEA OF OKHOTSK
OSTROVA KURILSKIJE RETTO
KURIL'SKIJE OSTROVA
CHISHIMA RETTO
KURIL ISLANDS
OSTROV KUNASIR
SIMONOSIRI-TO
KUNASHIR-TO
MALAJA KURIL'SKAJA
SHIKOTAN
SHIBOTSU-SHIMA
SHIOI
OSTROV ITURUP
ETOROFU-TO

RUSSIA
JAPAN

Nemuro
Nemuro Strait
Notsuke
Bakkai
Shibetsu
Shibecha
Akan
Akkeshi
Kushiro

Wakkanai
Teshio
Sarufutsu
Hoboro
Esashi
Monbetsu
Nayoro
Kitami
AKAN-KOKURITSU-KŌEN
Ashoro
Ōbihiro
Urakawa
Horoizumi
RUSSIA
JAPAN
La Perouse Strait
OSTROV SACHALIN
SAHALIN
SAKHALIN

Asahikawa
Ashibetsu
Furano
HIDAKA-SAMMYAKU
Mihasa
Yūbari
Funagawa
Sunagawa
Rumoi
Fukagawa
Chitose
Tomakomai
Mori
Abuta
Yakumo
Esashi
Noboribetsu
Muroran

HOKKAIDO
Sapporo
Otaru
Iwanai
KAMUI-MISAKI
Teshio

SEA OF JAPAN

Hakodate
Aomori
Hachinohe
HONSHU
Mutsu
Mimmaya
Tsugaru-kaikyō
SIRIYA-ZAKI
R. MtN.

PACIFIC OCEAN

a

1: 6 000 000
Kilometres  0  50  100  150 Km.
Statute Miles  0  50  100  150 Mi.

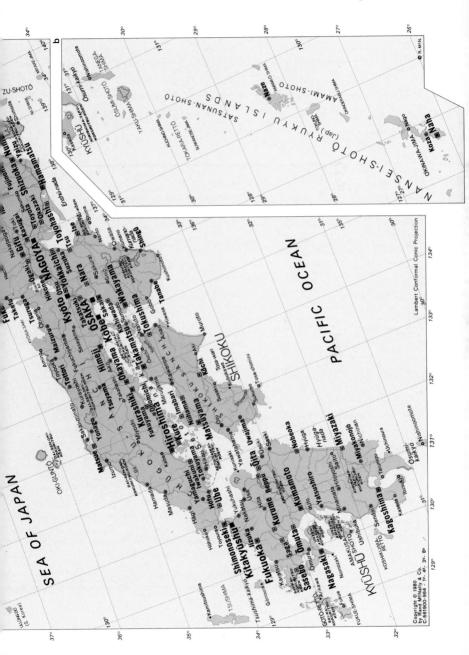

SEA OF JAPAN

PACIFIC OCEAN

RYUKYU ISLANDS

NANSEI-SHOTŌ

SATSUNAN-SHOTŌ

AMAMI-SHOTŌ

ŌSUMI-SHOTŌ

KYUSHU

SHIKOKU

Lambert Conformal Conic Projection

Copyright © 1980
by Rand McNally & Co.
C-561900-964 - 1v. 4v. 3v. 8v

INDIA  Shwebo
Chittagong
BANGLA-
DESH
Mandalay
CHINA  GUANGXI  Tsiang  GUANGDONG  GUANGZHOU  Shantou
Gejiu Koktu  ZHUANGZU  CANTON  Swatow
YUNNAN  Nanning  ZIZHIQU  Yulin  Foshan  New Kowloon
3143  Fan-si-pan  Beihai  Macau  VICTORIA
Phongsali  Aomen  HONG KONG
(Port.)  (U.K.)

Sittwe
(Akyab)
BURMA
MYANMAR
20°

Myingyan
Prome
(Pyè)
Keng Tung
Chiang Rai
Chiang
Mai
LAOS  Ha-noi
Louangphrabang  Hai-phong
Nam-dinh
Gulf of  Haikou
Tonkin  HAINAN  HAINANDAO

Henzada
BAY OF  RANGOON
BENGAL  YANGON  Bago
Mawlamyine
Viangchan
(Vientiane)
Udon
Thani
Vinh
Dong-hoi
15°
Dawei
Nakhon
Sawan
Khon Kaen
THAILAND
Nakhon
Ratchasima
Paksé
Hue
Da-nang
VIETNAM
ANDAMAN
SEA
Mergui
MERGUI
ARCHIPELAGO
KRUNG THEP
BANGKOK
CAMBODIA
Stœng Trêng
Qui-nhon
SOUTH CHINA
Port Blair
Gulf of
Thailand
Phnum Pénh
Kâmpóng Saôm
Rach-gia
Gia-dinh
Nha-trang
Phan-thiet
THANH-PHO HO CHI MINH
(SAI-GON)
Can-tho
SEA
10°
ISTHMUS
OF
KRA
Chumphon
Puerto Princesa
PALAWAN
Phuket
Nakhon Si
Thammarat
Songkhla
Alor Setar
Kota Baharu
Kudat
Kota Kinabalu
Gunung
Kinabalu
4094
Sandakan
Banda Aceh
George Town
(Pinang)
MALAYSIA
MALAYA
KEPULAUAN
BUNGURAN
UTARA
Bandar Seri Begawan
BRUNEI
Bukit
Pagon
1850
Tarakę
5°
Medan
Pematangsiantar
Kuala Lumpur
Melaka
MALAYSIA
Sibu
Kayan
2053
Kong Kemul
Sibolga
PULAU
NIAS
SINGAPORE  SINGAPORE
Kuching
BORNEO
KALIMANTAN
Talc
Equator
Pakanbaru
SUMATERA
KEPULAUAN LINGGA
Pontianak
Samarinda
Balikpapan
0°
Padang
KEPULAUAN
MENTAWAI
SUMATRA
Jambi
Gunung
Kerinci
3800
Pangkalpinang
BELITUNG
Sampit
Banjarmasin
Palembang
GREATER  SU
Bengkulu  Lahat
INDONESIA  ISLAND
5°
Telukbetung
LAUT JAWA  JAVA SEA
JAKARTA
Bogor
BANDUNG
Tasikmalaya
Cirebon  Semarang  MADURA
Surakarta
Yogyakarta  Madiun
SURABAYA
Malang
Lau
Denpasar
BALI
LOMBOK
SUMBAWA
LESSER
INDIAN  OCEAN
JAWA
JAVA
10°

Copyright © 1980
by Rand McNally & Co.
C-569800-964 - 4v. 7v. 6v. 9v²

CHRISTMAS ISLAND
(Austr.)

Kilometres  0  200  400  600 Km.
Miles  0  200  400  600 Mi.
1 : 24 000 000

0°

TAIWAN
T'AIWAN
T'ainan
KAOHSIUNG

*Tropic of Cancer*

OKINO-TORI-SHIMA
(Japan)

MAUG ISLANDS

20°

uzon BATAN ISLANDS

trait BABUYAN ISLANDS

Laoag

LUZON

Baguio

Lingayen

Angeles

Quezon
City

MANILA  Naga

PHILIPPINES

CATANDUANES
ISLAND

DORO

Catarman

CALAMIAN
GROUP  PANAY

Iloilo  Bacolod
Cebu

NEGROS

ULU

SEA

Zamboanga

ISLAND

TAWITAWI
ISLAND

SULU ARCHIPELAGO

PANAY

SAMAR

LEYTE
Leyte Gulf

Surigao

Butuan

MINDANAO

Moro
Gulf  2954▲Davao
Mount Apo

CAPE SAN
AGUSTIN

PHILIPPINE

SEA

PACIFIC

P H I L I P P I N E

MARIANA ISLANDS
(U.S.)

PAGAN

SAIPAN

TINIAN

15°

GUAM
Agana  (U.S.)

S E A

O C E A N

YAP

FAIS

GAFERUT

10°

SOROL

OLIMARAO

PALAU ISLANDS  BABELTHUAP
(Trust Ter. of Pac. Is.)

WOLEAI

C A R O L I N E
I S L A N D S

5°

PULAU
KARAKELONG  KEPULAUAN
TALAUD

C E L E B E S

SEA

PULAU
SANGIHE

Manado

HELEN ISLAND

HALMAHERA

Bukit Malino
2443  Gorontalo

Sabang

Teluk
Tomini

LAUT
MALUKU

M
A
L

PULAU
WAIGEO

Labuha

PULAU
BATANTA

Equator

0°

LAWESI
ELEBES

KEPULAUAN
BANGGAI  KEPULAUAN
SULA

KEPULAUAN  PULAU
OBI  MISOOL

LAUT SERAM

SERAM

PULAU
BATANTA

Manokwari

JAZIRAH DOBERAI

Steenkool

BIAK

Sarmi

Teluk
Cenderawasih

Jayapura
(Sukarnapura)

PAPUA
NEW
GUINEA

Parepare

ung Pandang

Namlea
BURU

Kendari

Ambon

PULAU
BUTUNG

Fakfak

Kaimana

Puncak Jaya

5030▲

PEGUNUNGAN
MAOKE

Angoram

N E W

Angoram

5°

Bulukumba

Baubau

LAUT

BANDA

M
O
L
U
C
C
A
S

Tual

KEPULAUAN
KAI

KEPULAUAN
ARU

Mapi

G U I N E A  Mount
Wilhelm
4509

res

Reo

FLORES

NDA ISLANDS

MBA

Dili

KEPULAUAN BABAR
LETI

Kupang

TIMOR
SEA

PULAU
YAMDENA  KEPULAUAN
TANIMBAR

A R A F U R A  S E A

TIMOR

PULAU
YOS
SUDARSA

Merauke

Daru

Torres Strait

A U S T R A L I A

FLY

Gulf
of
Papua

CAPE YORK

CAPE YORK
PENINSULA

10°

120°  125°  130°  135°

Lambert Conformal Conic Projection

Lambert Conformal
Conic Projection

ANDAMAN
ISLANDS

Karen

SOUTH ANDAMAN

Port Blair

NICOBAR ISLANDS

Ten Degree Channel

Duncan Passage

GREAT NICOBAR

Sombrero Channel

CAR NICOBAR ISLAND

Kohoa

CAMORTA ISLAND

Baranga

Banda Aceh

Sabang

Sigli

Rigaih

Tangse

Keudepasi

Isak

Susoh

Tapaktuan

Sibigo

Singkil

Gunungsitoli

PULAU SIMEULUE

PULAU NIAS

Teludalem

KEPULAUAN BANYAK

ANDAMAN AND

NICOBAR ISLANDS

ANDAMAN SEA

MERGUI

Mergui Myeik

TAVOY

Ye

KAWKAREIK

ZADETKYI KYUN

LAUNGLON

Bokpyin

ARCHIPELAGO

ISTHMUS OF KRA

KRA

Prachuap Khiri Khan

Hua Hin

Ban Na San

KO SAMUI

Si Chon

Surat Thani
(Ban Don)

Chumphon

Lang Suan

Krabi

Phangnga

Phuket

Hual Yot

Trang

Phatthalung

Ban Khlong Kua

Satun

Kangar

Alor Setar

George Town
(Pinang)

Butterworth

Taiping

Ipoh

Teluk Anson

BURMA
THAILAND

BURMA

THAILAND

GULF

OF

THAILAND

Rayong

Chanthaburi

Ban Pak Phraek

Nakhon
Si Thammarat

Songkhla

Hat Yai

Pattani

Narathiwat

Yala

Kuala
Kerai

Gua
Musang

Kuala Terengganu

Kuala Dungun

Kuantan

MALAYSIA

MALAYA

Kuala Lumpur

Seremban

Melaka

Johor Baharu

SINGAPORE

Pekan

Mersing

Keluang

Kota Baharu

Kuala Lipah

Muar.
(Bandar
Maharani)

Batupahat

Kuala Pilah

Jemerioh

Matan

Teluk Intan

Kampar

Kuala Kubu

Lahat

Simpang-ampat

S U M A T E R A

Medan

Binjai

Langsa

Lhokseumawe

Peureulak

Idi

Pematangsiantar

Tebingtinggi

Tanjungbalai

Rantauprapat

Tarutung

Sibolga

SUMATERA

Padangsidimpuan

Natal

Pakanbaru

Bangkinang

Rantau

Bagansiapi-api

Tanahputih

Sikasinderapura

Dumai

INDIA

INDONESIA

INDONESIA

I N D I A N

O C E A N

Selat Malaka

Strait

Malacca

SINGAPORE

Tanjungpinang

KEPULAUAN RIAU

Sawang

Selat Berhala

Lingga

KEPULAUAN TAMBELAN

KEPULAUAN BUNGURAN
SELATAN

KEPULAUAN BUNGURAN
UTARA

BUNGURAN BESAR

NATUNA BESAR

PULAU SUBI

PULAU SERASAN

Selat Karimata

KEPULAUAN
ANAMBAS

PULAU
JEMAJA

Midai

Serasan

MALAYSIA

INDONESIA

Kuching

MALAYSIA
INDONESIA

BORNEO
KALIMANTAN

Bengkayang

Singkawang

Mempawah

Sambas

Sanggau

Pemangkat

Sematan

S O U T H

C H I N A

S E A

Nha-trang

Cam-ranh

Phan-rang

Phan-thiet

Da-lat

Lac-giao

Dong-hai

Sen-monorom

Buon-mthuot

Buon-thach-hon

Xuan-loc

Bien-hoa

THANH-PHO
HO-CHI MINH
(SAI-GON)

Gia-dinh

Long-xuyen

Chau-phu

Rach-gia

Vinh-long

Phu-vinh

Bac-lieu
(Vinh-loi)

Khanh-hung

Quan-long
(Ca-mau)

MUI CA-MAU

DAO PHU-QUOC

Duong-dong

Kien-an

Prey
Veng

Kracheh

Kampong Cham

Kampot

Kampong
Thum

Kampong
Chhnang

Phnum Penh

Poudhisato

Pailin

Kratie

Phumi Krek

Tay-ninh

Kampong
Trach

Kampong
Trabaek

Sre Ambel

DAO PHU-QUOC

Sre Khlong

An-loc

Kampong
Saôm

Batdambang

Sisophon

Siem Réab

Ile Sap

Tonle Sab

Phnum Tbêng Méanchey

Krong
Koh Kong

Khlong Yai

Kilometres
Miles

0    100    200    300 Km.

0              100              200 Mi.

1 : 12 000 000

Copyright © 1980
by Rand McNally &
C.-581100-964-2'-6°-6°-10'6'

110° 115° 120° 125° 130°

Surakarta Malang BALI SUMBAWA SUNDA ISLANDS
Yogyakarta Blitar Jember LOMBOK LESSER SUMBA Laut Sawu TIMOR Arat
JAWA JAVA SUMBA Kupang Timor MELVILLE
INDONESIA PULAU ROTI ISLAND
PULAU Van Diemen
SAWU BATHURST Gulf
10° ISLAND Darwin
CARTIER ISLAND CAPE Rum Jungle ARNH
LONDONDERRY Joseph LANI
I N D I A N Bonaparte Katheri
Gulf
BONAPARTE Victoria
ARCHIPELAGO Wyndham Birdu
CAPE LEVEQUE KIMBERLEY PLATEAU
15° ROWLEY △Mount Ord Newca
O C E A N SHOALS 936 NORTHE Wate
Broome Fitzroy Halls
Creek
EIGHTY MILE BEACH GREAT SANDY DESERT TERRITOR
DAMPIER Port
ARCHIPELAGO Hedland Barrow C
Roebourne Lake Mackay
20° Onslow Fortescue Nullagine (Dry Salt Lake) Mount Zeil
NORTH WEST CAPE HAMERSLEY RANGE Lake 1511
Disappointment Mount Leisler MACDONN Spe
1235 (Dry Salt Lake) 901
Mount Bruce
WESTERN GIBSON DESERT A U S T R
Lake Macleod △Mount Augustus Mount
Tropic of Capricorn 1105 Essendon Lake Carnegie Mount Aloysius
BERNIER ISLAND Carnarvon 906 (Dry) 1085 Mount Wood
105° Wooramel 1439
DIRK HARTOG Wiluna
ISLAND Meekatharra GREAT VICTORIA DESE
25°
Mount A U S T R A L I A SOUT
Magnet Lake Carey
Geraldton Lake Leonora (Dry Salt Lake) Forrest Ooldea
Barlee
Dongara CAPE ADIEU
Dalwallinu Kalgoorlie Eucla
DARLING RANGE
Perth Southern Norseman Great Australian Big
30° Northam Cross
Bunbury Esperance
CAPE NATURALISTE Ravensthorpe CAPE
Augusta ARID
CAPE LEEUWIN Albany
CAPE VANCOUVER

35°

I N D I A N O C E

40° Copyright © 1980
by Rand McNally & Co.
C-590200-964 - 4° - 5° - 5° - 9°

105° 110° 115° 120° 125° 130°
Kilometres 0 200 400 600 Km.
Statute Miles 0 200 400 600 Mi. 1 : 24 000 000

Sea

135°

a  Sea

WESSEL ISLANDS

CAPE ARNHEM

GROOTE
EYLANDT

Limmen Bight

140°

Daru

Torres  Strait

CAPE
YORK

Gulf
of
Carpentaria

MORNINGTON
ISLAND

145°

Gulf of
Papua

**Port
Moresby**

OWEN STANLEY RANGE

**PAPUA
NEW GUINEA**
NEW GUINEA

D'ENTRECASTEAUX ISLANDS

LOUISIADE ARCHIPELAGO

TAGULA
ISLAND

ROSSEL
ISLAND

150°

TROBRIAND
ISLANDS

WOODLARK
ISLAND

155°

VELLA
LAVELLA  Gizo  NEW
GEORGIA

SANTA
ISABEL

**SOLOMON
ISLANDS**

Honiara 160°
Mt. Popomanaseu ▲
2331

Solomon Sea

10°

RENNELL

CAPE
YORK

PENINSULA

GREAT BARRIER REEF

Cooktown

CAPE GRAFTON
**Cairns**

HINCHINBROOK
ISLAND

GREAT BARRIER REEF

C o r a l    S e a

WILLIS GROUP
(Austl.)

TREGOSSE ISLETS
(Austl.)

15°

ÎLES
CHESTERFIELD
(N. Cal.)

ÎLE DE SABLE
(N. Cal.)

BARKLY  TABLELAND

ennant
reek

Mount
Isa

Cloncurry

Normanton

Mitchell

Ravenshoe

Flinders

Hughenden

GREAT  DIVIDING  RANGE

●**Townsville**

CUMBERLAND
ISLAND

Mackay

20°

ÎLE DE SABLE
(N. Cal.)

SAUMAREZ
REEF

CAYE DE
L'OBSERVATOIRE
(N. Cal.)

Winton

Georgina

QUEENSLAND

GREAT  ARTESIAN

Emerald

SWAIN
REEFS

**Rockhampton**

RANGES

Hay

SIMPSON

A    L    I    A

DESERT

BASIN

Blackall

Theodore

CURTIS I.

CATO
ISLAND

Tropic of Capricorn

Quilpie

GREY  RANGE

Charleville

Bundaberg

FRASER ISLAND

Maryborough

25°

Lake Eyre
North
(Dry Salt Lake)

Eyre

Lake Eyre
South

STURT
DESERT

Milparinka

Paroo

Saint George

Mount Kiangarow
1135
△

**Toowoomba**●

**Ipswich**●

**Brisbane**

PACIFIC

AUSTRALIA

Lake
Torrens

Woomera

GAWLER RANGES

Lake
Gairdner

FLINDERS  RANGE

△Saint Mary
Peak
1165

**Broken
Hill**

Darling

Tenterfield●

Lismore●

Walgett

Bourke

Nyngan

Warrego

Round Mountain
1608
△

Grafton

Tamworth

Port
Macquarie

MIDDLETON REEF

OCEAN

30°

Port
Augusta

Peterborough

NEW  SOUTH  WALES

Dubbo

Macquarie

GREAT

DIVIDING

RANGE

LORD HOWE ISLAND
(N.S.W.)

165°

EYRE PENINSULA

Port Pirie

Spencer
Gulf

Murray

Mildura

Orange●

●**Newcastle**

Port
Lincoln

Gulf
Saint
Vincent

**Adelaide**

Hay

Wagga
Wagga

**SYDNEY**●

●**Wollongong**

CAPE
CATASTROPHE

NGAROO
SLAND

Encounter
Bay

Murray

**Albury**

**Canberra**●
A.C.T.

T  a  s  m  a  n

Bordertown

VICTORIA

**Bendigo**

GREAT  DIVIDING

Mount
Kosciusko
2228
△

S  e  a

35°

Mount Gambier●

**Geelong**  **MELBOURNE**

CAPE HOWE

Portland

Warrnambool

CAPE OTWAY

SOUTH POINT

NINETY MILE BEACH

N

135°

Bass Strait

KING ISLAND

FLINDERS ISLAND

Barks Strait

Smithton

Burnie

Launceston

Mount Ossa △
1617

TASMANIA

**Hobart**

SOUTH
WEST
CAPE

SOUTH
EAST
CAPE

140°

145°

150°

155°

160°  Lambert Conformal Conic Projection

40°

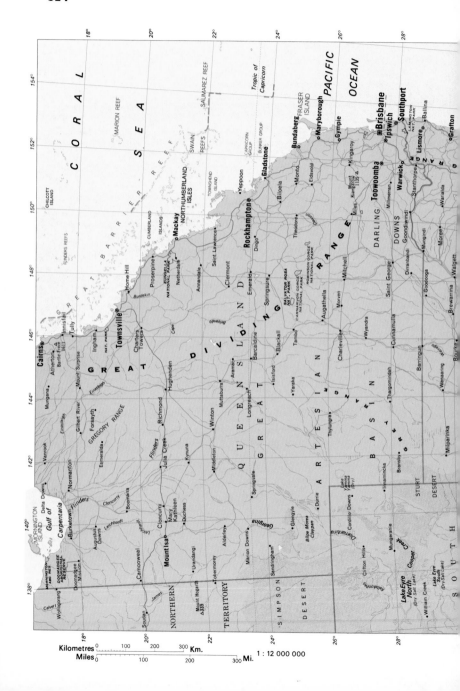

Kilometres 0 100 200 300 Km.

Miles 0 100 200 300 Mi.

1 : 12 000 000

Lambert Conformal Conic Projection

168°   170°   172°   174°   176°   178°

*PACIFIC*

*OCEAN*

NORTH CAPE

Doubtless Bay

TAUROA POINT

Okaihau

**Whangarei**

Dargaville

36°

GREAT
BARRIER
ISLAND

Wellsford

Kaipara
Harbour

**Takapuna**

Devonport

COROMANDEL
PENINSULA

**Auckland**

Thames

Waihi

Morrinsville

Bay of
Plenty

**Hamilton**

EAST
CAPE

*NORTH*

**Tauranga**

38°

*ISLAND*

Te Kuiti

Taupo

**Rotorua**

Opotiki

Murupara

*TASMAN*

Taumarunui

Lake
Taupo

**New Plymouth**

Ruapehu
△ 2797

Wairoa

**Gisborne**

MAHIA
PENINSULA

Opunake

Raetihi

**Napier**

Hawke
Bay

*SEA*

Hawera

Taihape

**Wanganui**

Waipukurau

**Hastings**

40°

CAPE FAREWELL

**Palmerston North**

D'URVILLE
ISLAND

Levin

Woodville

Takaka

*Tasman
Bay*

**Masterton**

Karamea
Bight

**Nelson**

*Cook*

**Lower Hutt**

**Wellington**

**Westport**

**Blenheim**

Tapuaenuku
2885

*Strait*

CAPE PALLISER

42°

Reefton

Kaikoura

Greymouth

Waiau

Hokitika

Waipara

*SOUTH*

Whataroa

Sheffield

*Pegasus Bay*

*ISLAND*

Mount Cook
3764

**Christchurch**

**Ashburton**

Southbridge

BANKS
PENINSULA

CASCADE
POINT

Haast

*Canterbury
Bight*

44°

Mount
Aspiring
3039

Fairlie

Omarama

**Timaru**

Wanaka

*Waitaki*

Queenstown

**Oamaru**

Lake
Anau

Kingston

Alexandra

Palmerston

*PACIFIC*

Te Anau

Mossburn

Beaumont

**Dunedin**

*OCEAN*

CAPE
PROVIDENCE

Winton

**Invercargill**

Gore

Kaitangata

*Foveaux*

Bluff

*Strait*

STEWART
ISLAND

SOUTHERN ALPS

Copyright © 1980
by Rand McNally & Co.
C-591600-964 - 2ᴵ- 2ᴵᴵ- 4ᴵᴵᴵ- 7ᵛ

Conic Projection

170°   172°   174°   176°

Kilometres   0   100   200   300   Km.

Miles   0   100   200   300   Mi.

1 : 9 000 000

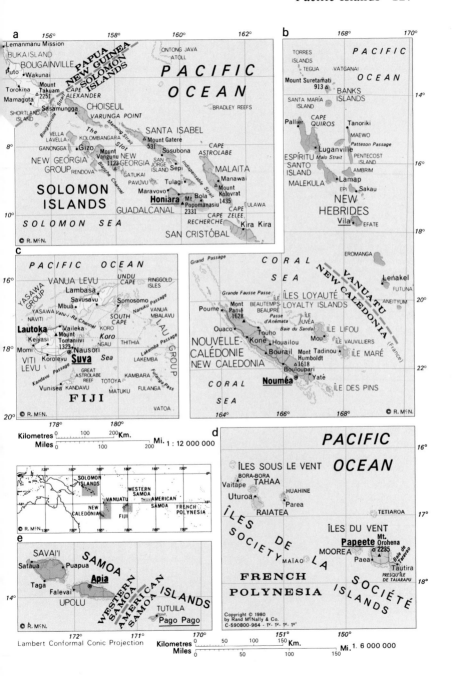

**a**

Lemanmanu Mission
BUKA ISLAND
BOUGAINVILLE
Puto • Wakunai
PAPUA NEW GUINEA
SOLOMON ISLANDS
Torokina
Takuam Mount 2251
Mamagota
CAPE ALEXANDER
SHORTLAND ISLAND
Sasamungga
CHOISEUL
VARUNGA POINT
VELLA LAVELLA
KOLOMBANGARA
GANONGGA • Gizo
NEW GEORGIA GROUP
Mount Vangunu 1123
NEW GEORGIA
SAN JORGE ISLAND
RENDOVA
GATUKAI
PAVUVU
Tulagi •
Maravovo •
GUADALCANAL
Mt Bola • Popomanasiu 2331
SANTA ISABEL
Mount Gatere
531
Susubona
Sepi
Manawai
Mount Kolovrat 1435
MALAITA
Honiara
CAPE ASTROLABE
Indispensable Strait
ULAWA
CAPE ZELEE
RECHERCHE
Kira Kira
SAN CRISTÓBAL
SOLOMON ISLANDS
SOLOMON SEA
ONTONG JAVA ATOLL
PACIFIC OCEAN
BRADLEY REEFS
The Slot
Manning Strait
Blanche Channel
© R. McN.

156° 158° 160° 162° 8° 10°

**b**

TORRES ISLANDS
TEGUA VATGANAI
Mount Suretamati 913
SANTA MARÍA ISLAND
Pallier
CAPE QUIROS
ESPÍRITU SANTO ISLAND
MALEKULA
BANKS ISLANDS
Tanoriki
MAEWO
Patteson Passage
Luganville
Malo Strait
PENTECOST ISLAND
AMBRIM
Lamap
EPI • Sakau
NEW HEBRIDES
Vila •
EFATE
PACIFIC OCEAN

168° 170° 14° 16° 18°

**c**

PACIFIC OCEAN
YASAWA GROUP
VANUA LEVU
UNDU CAPE
RINGGOLD ISLES
Lambasa
Savusavu
YASAWA
Mbua •
Somosomo
VANUA MBALAVU
NAVITI
Vatu-i-Ra Channel
KORO
Lautoka
Vaileka
Mount Tomanivi 1323
Koro
THITHIA
Keiyasi
NGAU
Momi
Korolevu
Nausori
Suva
Koro Sea
LAU GROUP
LAKEMBA
GREAT ASTROLABE REEF
KAMBARA
Vunisea KANDAVU
TOTOYA
MATUKU
FULANGA
VATOA
FIJI
VITI LEVU
Kandavu Passage
Nanuku Passage
Lakemba Passage
Fulanga Pass
© R. McN.

Grand Passage
CORAL SEA
Grande Fausse Passe
Poume
Mont Panié 1628
Passe d'Anemata
Ouaco
NOUVELLE-CALÉDONIE NEW CALEDONIA
Kone
Bourail
Bouloupari
CORAL SEA
BEAUTEMPS-BEAUPRÉ
ÎLE UVÉA
Touho
Houailou
Mont Tadinou Humboldt 1618
Yaté
Nouméa
ÎLES LOYAUTÉ LOYALTY ISLANDS
ÎLE LIFOU
Mou
ÎLE VAUVILLIERS
ÎLE MARÉ
ÎLE DES PINS
NEW CALEDONIA
VANUATU
(France)
EROMANGA
Lenakel
FUTUNA
ANEITYUM

178° 180° 16° 18° 20°
164° 166° 168° 20° 22°
© R. McN.

Kilometres 0 100 200 Km.
Miles 0 100 200 Mi. 1 : 12 000 000

SOLOMON ISLANDS
WESTERN SAMOA
VANUATU
AMERICAN SAMOA
NEW CALEDONIA
FIJI
FRENCH POLYNESIA
© R. McN.

**d**

PACIFIC OCEAN
ÎLES SOUS LE VENT
BORA-BORA
TAHAA
Vaitape
Uturoa •
HUAHINE
Parea
RAIATEA
TETIAROA
ÎLES DU VENT
Papeete Mt. Orohena 2235
MOOREA
Paea •
Tautira
MAĪAO
PRESQU'ÎLE DE TAIARAPU
FRENCH POLYNESIA
SOCIETY ISLANDS
SOCIÉTÉ
Baie de Taarapu
Copyright © 1980 by Rand McNally & Co.
C-590800-964 - 1ʸ - 1ʸ- 1ʸ- 1ᵛ- 1ᵛ

16° 17° 18°
151° 150°

**e**

SAVAI'I
Sataua
Puapua
SAMOA
Taga
Falevai
UPOLU
Apia
WESTERN SAMOA
AMERICAN SAMOA ISLANDS
TUTUILA
Pago Pago
© R. McN.

172° 171° 170° 14°

Lambert Conformal Conic Projection
Kilometres 0 50 100 150 Km.
Miles 0 50 100 150 Mi. 1: 6 000 000

Copyright © 1980
by Rand McNally & Co.
C-531600-964 · 3ᵛ· 3ᵛ· 4ᵛ· 8ᵛᴵ

Kilometres  0   100   200   300   Km.
Miles       0        100        200        300   Mi.

1 : 13 300 000

Lambert Conformal Conic Projection

**GULF OF MEXICO**

Fort Myers○ **UNITED STATES** ●**West Palm Beach**
FLORIDA GRAND BAHAMA
The Everglades □**Fort Lauderdale** GREAT ABAC
EVERGLADES NATIONAL PARK ●**Miami Beach** ELEUTH
**MIAMI**

Key West○ FLORIDA KEYS Straits of Florida **Nassa**
ANDROS ISLAND **NEW PROVIDENCE**

**LA HABANA** Straits of Florida
HAVANA Nicholas Channel
Marianao○ **Cárdenas**
Artemisa○ ●**Güines** **Sagua**
**Pinar del Río**○ Golfo de Batabanó ●**Matanzas** **la Grande** Old Bahama Channel **W E**
**Güines**○ **Santa Clara**◉○ ●**Placetas**
○Santa Fe **Cienfuegos** **Sancti Spíritus** **Ciego de Avila** **GREAT BAHAMA BA**
ISLA DE LA JUVENTUD (ISLA DE PINOS) **C U B A** **Florida**○ ○**Nuevita**
**Camagüey**◉

Progreso○ CABO CATOCHE **Ba**
**Mérida**◉ ○Tizimin **Holguin**
Celestún○ **Bay**
CABO SAN ANTONIO CABO CORRIENTES Manzanillo○ 1994 Pico Turquino **Sant**
Halachó○ ○Ticul Chichen Itzá ○Cozumel **de C**
Tenabo○ ○Peto ISLA DE COZUMEL
**20°** 92° YUCATÁN ○Tulum **CAYMAN ISLANDS** **GREATE**
○**Campeche**◉ ○Hopelchén Georgetown (U.K.)
Champotón○ PENINSULA ○Felipe Carrillo Puerto
**Ciudad del Carmen**○ **Montego Bay**○
**MEXICO** Ciudad ○Chetumal **Kingston**
Frontera○ Escárcega de○ **JAMAICA** Spanish Town
Matamoros Chetumal Bay
Usumacinta Orange Walk○ **BELIZE**
Palenque○ ○Tiradero ○**Belize**
○Ocozingo Piedras Negras○ **Belmopan**
Comitán○ ○San Benito 1122 Gulf of
Sayaxché○ Victoria Honduras ISLAS DE LA BAHÍA
○San Luis Peak
**GUATEMALA** Puerto○ Brus
Volcán Tajumulco Barrios **La** ○Limón Laguna
○Huehuetenango El Estor○ Puerto○ ○**Ceiba**
**Tapachula**○ SIERRA DE LAS MINAS Cortés **San Pedro Sula** CABO GRACIAS **CAR**
○El Progreso ○Yoro A DIOS
Cerro Las Coco○ Waspán
**14°** Tiquisate○ Minas 2865 CORDILLERA DE AGALTA
Escuintla○ Juticalpa○ Patuca
Santa Ana○ **HONDURAS** San○ Puerto○
Nueva◉○**San** Ramón ○Cabezas
**San Salvador** **Salvador** ○**Tegucigalpa** ○Cerro Mogotón 2107
San○ ○**San Miguel** Cerro Pìu
**EL SALVADOR** Vicente La○ ○Estelí 1800
Union ○La Cruz ○Prinzapolca
Chinandega○ El Sauce○ ○Matagalpa ○Río Grande ISLA DE SAN ANDRES (COL.)
**León**◉ **NICARAGUA** ○San Andrés
**Managua**◉ ○**Granada** ○Rama CORN ISLANDS (NIC.)
Diriambo○ Lago de Nicaragua ○Punta Gorda
Rivas○ ○San Carlos
ISLA DE OMETEPE Volcán ○San Juan del Norte
**PACIFIC** Liberia○ △Miravalles
2028
**OCEAN** **COSTA RICA**
PENÍNSULA DE NICOYA ○**Limón**
Puntarenas○ ○Cartago
CABO BLANCO **San** Cerro Chirripó
**José** 3819 ○Bocas del Toro **Colón** ISTMO DE PANAMÁ
Puerto○ ○Portobelo **Lo**
Cortés Golfo de los ○Chepo ○Mulatupo **Ce**
PEN. DE OSA Volcán Barú Mosquitos ISLA **Monte**
3475 **La Chorrera**○ DEL REY ○Acandi
Puerto○ **PANAMA** **Panamá** ○La Palma
Armuelles ○David Río Hato○ ○Yaviza ○Turbe
PUNTA BURICA ○Aguadulce Gulf ○Acandi
Golfo de of
Chiriquí PENÍNSULA Panama
DE Jaqué○
ISLA DE AZUERO
COIBA

Kilometres 0 100 200 300 Km.
Miles 0 100 200 300 Mi. 1 : 12 000 000

74° 72° 70° 68° 66° 64° 62° 60°

26°

**BAHAMAS**

CAT ISLAND

24°

LONG
ISLAND

*Tropic of Cancer*

Sound
Crooked
Passage

CROOKED
ISLAND

22°

MAYAGUANA

**TURKS AND
CAICOS ISLANDS**
(U.K.)

**A T L A N T I C**

LITTLE
INAGUA

CAICOS
ISLANDS

TURKS
ISLANDS
Grand
Turk

**O C E A N**

20°

Matthew
Town

GREAT
INAGUA

Sagua de
Tánamo

**HAITI** **I N D I E S**

**Guantánamo** Cap-
Haitien

Montecristi

VIRGIN
ISLANDS

POINTE DU
CHEVAL BLANC
Golfe de
la Gonâve

Gonaïves
**Santiago**

San Francisco
de Macoris

(U.S.)(U.K.)

**ANGUILLA**
(U.K.)

18°

Jérémie

ÎLE DE LA
GONÂVE

PicoDuarte3175

Concepcion de la Vega **PUERTO RICO**
(U.S.) **San Juan**

Charlotte
Amalie

Arecibo
Higüey

SAINT CHRISTOPHER
(SAINT KITTS)

BARBUDA

LEEWARD ISLANDS

**Port-au-
Prince**

**HISPANIOLA**

Azuar **Santo**

San Pedro
de Macoris Mayagüez

**Caguas**

**Ponce**

SAINT
CROIX

**ANTIGUA**

Les
Cayes

Chaîne de
la Selle
2674

**Domingo**

Basseterre

ST. KITTS AND NEVIS

GRANDE-
TERRE

16°

**A N T I L L E S**

**DOMINICAN
REPUBLIC**

**Pointe-à-Pitre**
(U.K.)
BASSE-TERRE (Fr.)

MONTSERRAT

**GUADELOUPE**

**DOMINICA**

Roseau

Montagne
Pelée 1397

60°

**B E A N     S E A**

Fort-de-France
**MARTINIQUE**

Castries

14°

**SAINT LUCIA**
**SAINT
VINCENT**

Kingstown **Bridgetown**
**BARBADOS**

WINDWARD ISLANDS

ARUBA **NETHERLANDS**
(Neth.)
Oranjestad **ANTILLES**
BONAIRE

**GRENADA**

Saint George's

12°

CABO DE LA VELA

PENÍNSULA DE
LA GUAJIRA

CURAÇAO **Willemstad**

LA BLANQUILLA
(Ven.)

TOBAGO

**Barran-
quilla**

Santa
Marta

Riohacha

COLOMBIA

PENÍNSULA
DE PARAGUANÁ

**Punto
Fijo**

ISLAS LOS ROQUES
(Ven.)

ISLA DE
MARGARITA

**Port of Spain**

Ciénaga

VENEZUELA

Golfe de
Venezuela Coro

Puerto Cumarebo

ISLA LA TORTUGA
(Ven.)

Porlamar

Carúpano

**TRINIDAD
AND**

**Cartagena**

Pico Cristóbal
5775

San Luis

Los Cayes

San Juan de
los Morros

PARQ.
NAC.
HENRY
PITTIER

Güiria TRINIDAD

San
Fernando

TOBAGO

Arjona
Colón

**Maracaibo** San Felipe

Puerto
Cabello

**Maiquetía** Cumaná
**CARACAS**

Puerto la Cruz

San
Jacinto

Villa del
Rosario

**Cabimas**

PARQ. NAC.
GUATOPO

**Barcelona**

**Maturin**

SanOnofre

Augustin

**Ciudad** Barqui-
simeto **Valencia Maracay**

San Mateo

DELTA

60°

Sincelejo

Codazzi

Lago de

Ojeda

Maracaibo

Trujillo **Acarigua**

de los Morros

Altagracia
de Orituco

Tucupita

ORINOCO

**Magangué**

SIERRA

Rio Ariguaisa

**Valera**

CORDDE MÉRIDA

Villa
Bruzual

Calabozo

Valle de
la Pascua

Zaraza Cantaura

**El
Tigre**

San José
de Guanipa

Barrancas

Orinoco

**Ciudad
Guayana**

8°

Planeta Rica

El Banco

Gamarra

San Carlos
del Zulia

**Barinas**

Arismendi

**Mérida**

Pico Bolívar
5002

Libertad

Puerto
de Nutrias

Ciudad Bolívar

Caroní

Upata

El Palmar

Nechí
Ocaña

Apure

**San Fernando
de Apure**

Mapire

Cerro Bolívar

802

El Manteco

Cáceres

**Cúcuta** **San Cristóbal**

Achaguas

Orinoco

Maripa

74° 72° 70° 68° 66° 64°

Lambert Conformal Conic Projection

**CARIBBEAN SEA**

**PACIFIC OCEAN**

NICARAGUA

COSTA RICA

PANAMÁ

COLOMBIA

VENEZUELA

ECUADOR

PERU

BOLIVIA

CHILE

ARGENTINA

NETH. ANTILLES

LESSER ANTILLES

SAINT VINCENT

TRINIDAD

Kilometres 0 200 400 600 Km.
Miles 0 200 400 600
Mi. 1 : 24 000 000

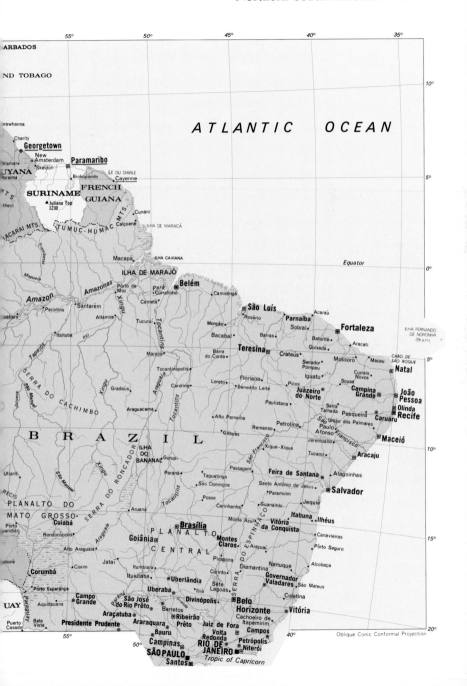

ARBADOS

ND TOBAGO

*ATLANTIC   OCEAN*

rawhanna
.Charity
**Georgetown**
.New
.Amsterdam   **Paramaribo**
Vismar
.Skeldon
.Foraima
.Brokópondo
ÎLE DU DIABLE
**UYANA**
.Cayenne
**SURINAME**   **FRENCH**
▲Juliana Top   **GUIANA**
.them   1230
.Cunani
ACARAI MTS.
.Calçoene
TUMUC-HÚMAC   MTS.
ILHA DE MARACÁ
.Macapá
ILHA CAVIANA
*Equator*   0°
ILHA DE MARAJÓ

.Mapuera
.Pôrto de   .Para
.Moz   .Curralinho   **Belém**
**Amazon**   **Amazonas**   .Camirangá
.Cametá
.Parintins   .Santarém   **São Luís**
oatiara   .Altamira   .Rosário   **Parnaíba**   .Acaraú
.Itaituba   .Tucuruí   .Monção   .Sobral   **Fortaleza**
**Tapajós**   .Bacabal   .Barras   .Baturité   .Aracati   ILHA FERNANDO
DE NORONHA
(Brazil)
.Marabá   **Teresina**   .Crateús   .Quixadá   .Macau   CABO DE
SÃO ROQUE   5°
SERRA   .Barra   .Senador   .Mossoró   **Natal**
DO CACHIMBO   do Corda   Pompeu
.Tocantinópolis   .Floriano   .Iguatú   Currais
.Gradaús   .Loreto   .Picos   .Sousa   .Novos
.Carolina   .Benedito Leite   .Paulistana   **Juàzeiro**   **Campina**   **João**
**do Norte**   **Grande**   **Pessoa**
.Araguacema   .Alto Parnaíba   Serra   .Pesqueira   **Olinda**
.Talhada   **Caruaru**   **Recife**
**B   R   A   Z   I   L**   .Remanso   .União dos Palmares
.Gilbués   São   .Paulo   **Maceió**
.Afonso   .Jeremoabo
ILHA   .Gurupí   Xique-Xique   .Tucano   **Aracaju**
DO
BANANAL   .Paraná   .Passagem   **Feira de Santana**   .Alagoinhas
Utiariti   .Taguatinga
.São Domingos   Santo Antônio de Jesus   **Salvador**
PLANALTO   DO   .Posse   .Carinhanha
MATO   GROSSO   .Guanambi   .Jequié
.Pôrto   **Cuiabá**   Monte Azul   **Vitória**   **Itabuna**   .Ilhéus
peridiga   .Rondonópolis   **Brasília**   Montes   **da Conquista**
**Goiânia**   **Claros**   .Araçuaí   .Canavieiras
obore   .Alto Araguaia   C   E   N   T   R   A   L   .Pirapora   .Pôrto Seguro
**Corumbá**   .Jataí   .Itumbiara   .Corinto   .Diamantina   .Nanuque   .Alcobaça
.Pôrto Esperança   .Ituiutaba   .Sete   **Governador**
**Uberlândia**   Lagoas   **Valadares**   .São Mateus
**UAY**   .Aquidauana   **Uberaba**   .Ibiá   .Colatina
.Coxim   **Divinópolis**   **Belo**   .Vitória
Puerto   Bela   **Campo**   .São José   .Barretos   **Horizonte**
Casado   Vista   **Grande**   do Rio Prêto   Cachoeiro de
**Araçatuba**   **Ribeirão**   Juiz de Fora   Itapemirim
**Presidente Prudente**   **Araraquara**   **Prêto**   Volta   .Campos
.Bauru   Redonda   **Petrópolis**
**Campinas**   **RIO DE**   .Niterói   20°
**SÃO PAULO**   **JANEIRO**
.Santos   *Tropic of Capricorn*

Oblique Conic Conformal Projection

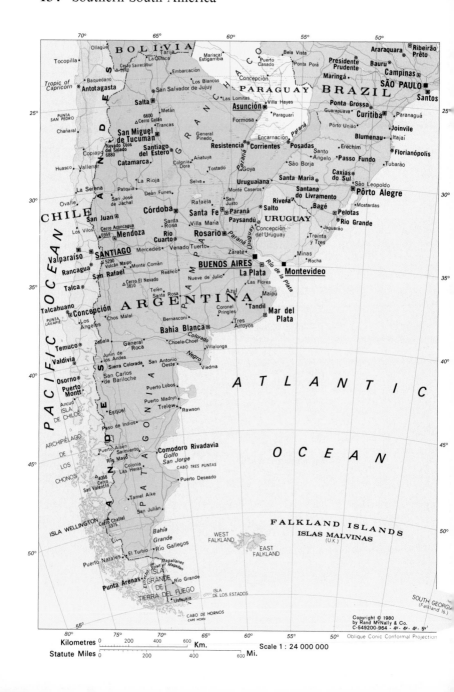

Oblique Conic Conformal Projection

Kilometres 0  200  400  600 Km.

Statute Miles 0     200     400     600 Mi.

Scale 1 : 24 000 000

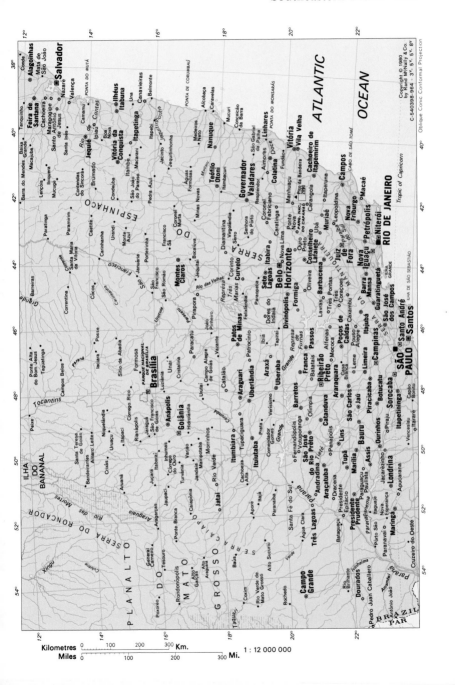

ATLANTIC

OCEAN

Kilometres 0  100  200  300 Km.

Miles 0  100  200  300 Mi.

1 : 12 000 000

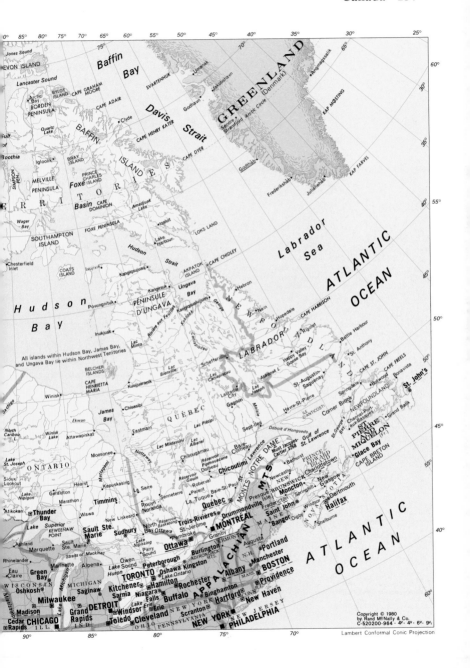

Lambert Conformal Conic Projection

PACIFIC OCEAN

CANADA

UNITED STATES

MEXICO

BRITISH COLUMBIA

ALBERTA

SASKATCHEWAN

MANITOBA

WASHINGTON

OREGON

IDAHO

MONTANA

NORTH DAKOTA

SOUTH DAKOTA

WYOMING

NEBRASKA

NEVADA

UTAH

COLORADO

KANSAS

CALIFORNIA

ARIZONA

NEW MEXICO

OKLAHOMA

TEXAS

ROCKY MOUNTAINS

GREAT BASIN

SIERRA MADRE OCCIDENTAL

SIERRA MADRE ORIENTAL

Golfo de California

BAJA CALIFORNIA

Vancouver Island

Edmonton
Calgary
Vancouver
Victoria
Seattle
Tacoma
Spokane
Portland
Salem
Eugene
Boise
Great Falls
Helena
Billings
Regina
Winnipeg
Fargo
Bismarck
Rapid City
Sioux Falls
Salt Lake City
Ogden
Provo
Denver
Colorado Springs
Pueblo
San Francisco
Oakland
Sacramento
San Jose
Fresno
Bakersfield
Las Vegas
Los Angeles
Long Beach
San Diego
San Bernardino
Phoenix
Tucson
Albuquerque
Santa Fe
El Paso
Wichita
Oklahoma City
Dallas
Fort Worth
Austin
San Antonio
Houston
Tijuana
Mexicali
Hermosillo
Chihuahua
Ciudad Juarez
Monterrey
Guadalajara
Mazatlan
Durango
Torreon
Tampico

Copyright © 1980
by Rand McNally & Co.
C-520500-964 - 6ᵛ- 6ᵛ- 7ᵛ- 10ᵛ

Kilometres
Miles
1 : 24 000 000

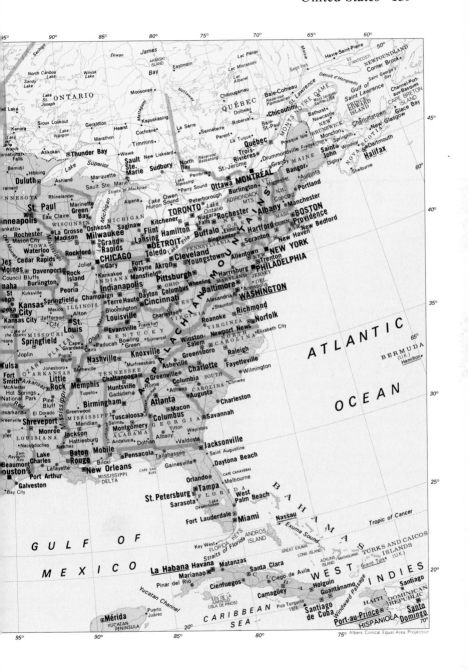

Albers Conical Equal-Area Projection

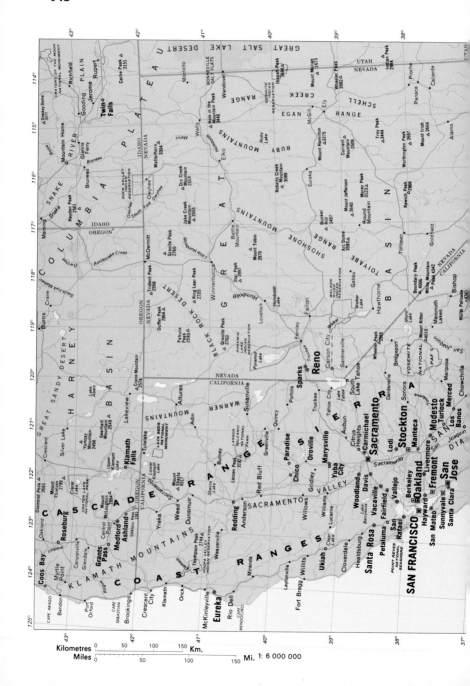

Kilometres | 0  50  100  150 | Km.
Miles | 0  50  100  150 | Mi.  1: 6 000 000

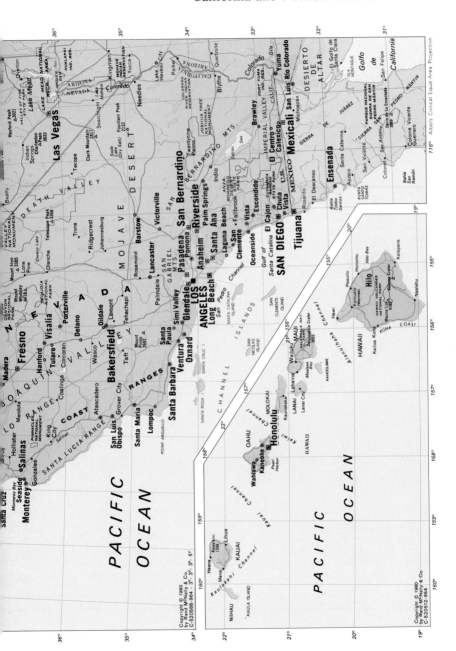

PACIFIC OCEAN

NEVADA

ARIZONA

CALIFORNIA

Las Vegas

Fresno

Bakersfield

LOS ANGELES
Long Beach

San Bernardino

Riverside

SAN DIEGO

Tijuana

Mexicali

Ensenada

DESIERTO DE ALTAR

Golfo de California

Honolulu

OAHU

MAUI

HAWAII

Hilo

KAUAI

NIIHAU

Albers Conical Equal Area Projection

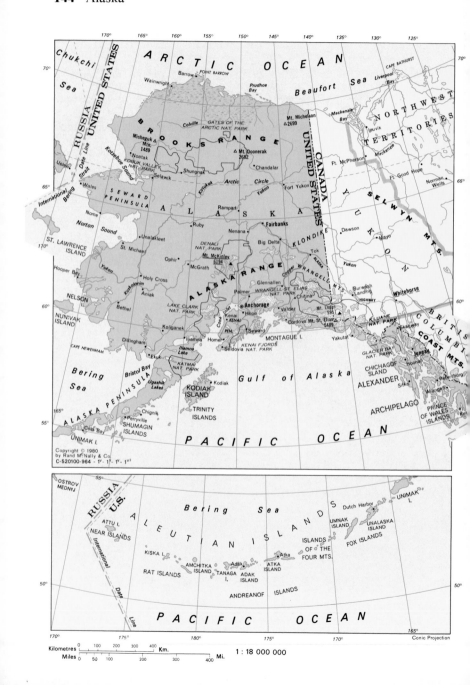

Kilometres 0 100 200 300 400 Km.

Miles 0 50 100 200 300 400 Mi.

1 : 18 000 000

Conic Projection

## THE CONTINENTS

| Continent | Area | Estimated Population | Population Density | Mean Elevation | Highest Elevation | Lowest Elevation |
|---|---|---|---|---|---|---|
| Africa | 11,700,000 sq. mi. (30,300,000 sq. km.) | 694,000,000 | 59/sq. mi. (23/sq. km.) | 1,900 ft. (600 m.) | Kilimanjaro, Tanzania, 19,340 ft. (5,895 m.) | Lac Assal, Djibouti, -502 ft. (-153 m.) |
| Antarctica | 5,400,000 sq. mi. (14,000,000 sq. km.) | ... | ... | 6,000 ft. (1,800 m.) | Vinson Massif, 16,864 ft. (5,140 m.) | Sea level |
| Asia | 17,300,000 sq. mi. (44,900,000 sq. km.) | 3,331,500,000 | 193/sq. mi. (74/sq. km.) | 3,000 ft. (900 m.) | Mt. Everest, China (Tibet)-Nepal, 29,028 ft. (8,848 m.) | Dead Sea, Israel-Jordan, -1,299 ft. (-396 m.) |
| Australia | 2,966,155 sq. mi. (7,682,300 sq. km.) | 17,420,000 | 5.8/sq. mi. (2.2/sq. km.) | 1,000 ft. (300 m.) | Mt. Kosciusko, New South Wales, 7,310 ft. (2,228 m.) | Lake Eyre, South Australia, -52 ft. (-16 m.) |
| Europe | 3,800,000 sq. mi. (9,900,000 sq. km.) | 695,200,000 | 183/sq. mi. (70/sq. km.) | 1,000 ft. (300 m.) | Gora El'brus, Russia, 18,510 ft. (5,642 m.) | Caspian Sea, -92 ft. (-28 m.) |
| North America | 9,500,000 sq. mi. (24,700,000 sq. km.) | 436,300,000 | 46/sq. mi. (18/sq. km.) | 2,000 ft. (600 m.) | Mt. McKinley, U.S. (Alaska), 20,320 ft. (6,194 m.) | Death Valley, U.S. (Calif.), -282 ft. (-86 m.) |
| Oceania, incl. Australia | 3,300,000 sq. mi. (8,500,000 sq. km.) | 27,300,000 | 8.3/sq. mi. (3.2/sq. km.) | ... | Mt. Wilhelm, Papua New Guinea, 14,793 ft. (4,509 m.) | Lake Eyre, South Australia, -52 ft. (-16 m.) |
| South America | 6,900,000 sq. mi. (17,800,000 sq. km.) | 306,700,000 | 44/sq. mi. (17/sq. km.) | 1,800 ft. (550 m.) | Cerro Aconcagua, Argentina, 22,831 ft. (6,959 m.) | Salinas Chicas, Argentina, -138 ft. (-42 m.) |
| WORLD | 57,900,000 sq. mi. (150,100,000 sq. km.) | 5,491,000,000 | 93/sq. mi. (36/sq. km.) | ... | Mt. Everest, China (Tibet)-Nepal, 29,028 ft. (8,848 m.) | Dead Sea, Israel-Jordan, -1,299 ft. (-396m.) |

## Principal Mountains

| Mountains | Location | Feet | Meters |
|---|---|---|---|
| Aconcagua, Cerro | Argentina | 22,831 | 6,959 |
| Adams, Mt. | U.S. | 12,276 | 3,742 |
| Annapurna | Nepal | 26,503 | 8,078 |
| Apo, Mt. | Philippines | 9,692 | 2,954 |
| Barú, Volcán | Panama | 11,401 | 3,475 |
| Blanc, Mont | France-Italy | 15,771 | 4,807 |
| Bolívar, Pico | Venezuela | 16,411 | 5,002 |
| Boundary Pk. | U.S. | 13,143 | 4,006 |
| Büyük Ağrı Daği (Mt. Ararat) | Turkey | 17,011 | 5,185 |
| Cameroun, Mont | Cameroon | 13,353 | 4,070 |
| Chimborazo | Ecuador | 20,702 | 6,310 |
| Chirripó, Cerro | Costa Rica | 12,530 | 3,819 |
| Citlaltépetl, Volcán | Mexico | 18,701 | 5,700 |
| Columbia, Mt. | Canada | 12,293 | 3,747 |
| Cook, Mt. | New Zealand | 12,349 | 3,764 |
| Cristóbal Colón, Pico | Colombia | 18,947 | 5,775 |
| Dhaulāgiri | Nepal | 26,811 | 8,172 |
| Dimlang | Nigeria | 6,699 | 2,042 |
| Duarte, Pico | Dominican Republic | 10,417 | 3,175 |
| Dufour Spitze | Italy-Switzerland | 15,203 | 4,634 |
| Elbert, Mt. | U.S. | 14,433 | 4,399 |
| El'brus, Gora | Russia | 18,510 | 5,642 |
| Etna, Monte | Italy | 10,902 | 3,323 |
| Everest, Mt. | China-Nepal | 29,028 | 8,848 |
| Fuji-san | Japan | 12,388 | 3,776 |
| Gannett Pk. | U.S. | 13,804 | 4,207 |
| Glittertinden | Norway | 8,110 | 2,472 |
| Grand Teton | U.S. | 13,770 | 4,197 |
| Grossglockner | Austria | 12,457 | 3,797 |
| Guadalupe Pk. | U.S. | 8,749 | 2,667 |
| Hood, Mt. | U.S. | 11,234 | 3,424 |
| Huascarán, Nevado | Peru | 22,205 | 6,768 |
| Humphreys Pk. | U.S. | 12,633 | 3,851 |
| Hvannadalshnúkur | Iceland | 6,952 | 2,119 |
| Illimani, Nevado | Bolivia | 21,004 | 6,402 |
| Inthanon, Doi | Thailand | 8,513 | 2,595 |
| Inyangani | Zimbabwe | 8,507 | 2,593 |
| Jaya, Puncak | Indonesia | 16,503 | 5,030 |
| Jungfrau | Switzerland | 13,642 | 4,158 |
| K2 (Qogir Feng) | China-Pakistan | 28,251 | 8,611 |
| Kānchenjunga | Nepal-India | 28,209 | 8,598 |
| Kāmet | China-India | 25,446 | 7,756 |
| Katrīnah, Jabal | Egypt | 8,668 | 2,642 |
| Kebnekaise | Sweden | 6,926 | 2,111 |
| Kerinci, Gunung | Indonesia | 12,467 | 3,800 |
| Kilimanjaro | Tanzania | 19,341 | 5,895 |
| Kinabalu, Gunong | Malaysia | 13,432 | 4,094 |
| Kirinyaga (Mt. Kenya) | Kenya | 17,057 | 5,199 |
| Kommunizma, Pik | Tajikistan | 24,590 | 7,495 |
| Kosciusko, Mt. | Australia | 7,310 | 2,228 |
| Koussi, Emi | Chad | 11,204 | 3,415 |
| Kula Kangri | Bhutan | 24,783 | 7,554 |
| Las Minas, Cerro | Honduras | 9,400 | 2,865 |
| Lassen Pk. | U.S. | 10,457 | 3,187 |
| Logan, Mt. | Canada | 19,524 | 5,951 |
| Makālu | China-Nepal | 27,825 | 8,481 |
| Marcy, Mt. | U.S. | 5,344 | 1,629 |
| Margherita Pk. | Uganda-Zaire | 16,762 | 5,109 |
| Maromokotro | Madagascar | 9,436 | 2,876 |
| Matterhorn | Italy-Switzerland | 14,692 | 4,478 |
| Mauna Loa | U.S. | 13,679 | 4,169 |
| McKinley, Mt. | U.S. (Alaska) | 20,320 | 6,194 |
| Mitchell, Mt. | U.S. | 6,684 | 2,037 |
| Mogotón, Cerro | Nicaragua | 6,913 | 2,107 |
| Mulhacén | Spain | 11,411 | 3,478 |
| Nanda Devi | India | 25,646 | 7,817 |
| Nānga Parbat | Pakistan | 26,660 | 8,126 |
| Narodnaja, Gora | Russia | 6,214 | 1,894 |
| Nevis, Ben | U.K. | 4,406 | 1,343 |
| Ojos del Salado, Nevado | Argentina-Chile | 22,572 | 6,880 |
| Ólimbos (Mt. Olympus) | Greece | 9,570 | 2,917 |
| Olympus, Mt. | U.S. | 7,965 | 2,428 |
| Orohena, Mt. | French Polynesia | 7,333 | 2,235 |
| Ossa, Mt. | Australia | 5,305 | 1,617 |
| Pelée, Montagne | Martinique | 4,583 | 1,397 |
| Pidurutalagala | Sri Lanka | 8,281 | 2,524 |
| Pikes Pk. | U.S. | 14,110 | 4,301 |
| Pobedy, pik | China-Russia | 24,406 | 7,439 |
| Popocatépetl, Volcán | Mexico | 17,887 | 5,452 |
| Rainier, Mt. | U.S. | 14,410 | 4,392 |
| Ras Dashen | Ethiopia | 15,157 | 4,620 |
| Sajama, Nevado | Bolivia | 21,463 | 6,540 |
| Selle, Chaîne de la | Haiti | 8,773 | 2,674 |
| Shasta, Mt. | U.S. | 14,162 | 4,317 |
| Tahat | Algeria | 9,852 | 3,003 |
| Tajumulco, Volcán | Guatemala | 13,845 | 4,220 |
| Toubkal, Jbel | Morocco | 13,665 | 4,165 |
| Triglav | Yugoslavia | 9,393 | 2,863 |
| Uncompahgre Pk. | U.S. | 14,309 | 4,361 |
| Vesuvio | Italy | 4,190 | 1,277 |

## Oceans, Seas, and Gulfs

| Name | Location | Sq. Mi. | Sq. Km. | Name | Location | Sq. Mi. | Sq. Km. |
|---|---|---|---|---|---|---|---|
| Arabian Sea | Asia-Africa | 1,492,000 | 3,864,000 | Mexico, Gulf | | | |
| Arctic Ocean | | 5,400,000 | 14,000,000 | of | N.A. | 596,000 | 1,544,000 |
| Atlantic | | | | North Sea | Eur. | 222,000 | 575,000 |
| Ocean | | 31,800,000 | 82,400,000 | Norwegian | | | |
| Baltic Sea | Eur. | 163,000 | 422,000 | Sea | Eur.-N.A. | 597,000 | 1,546,000 |
| Bengal, Bay of | Asia | 839,000 | 2,173,000 | Pacific Ocean | | 63,800,000 | 165,200,000 |
| Bering Sea | Asia-N.A. | 876,000 | 2,269,000 | Red Sea | Africa-Asia | 169,000 | 438,000 |
| Black Sea | Eur.-Asia | 178,000 | 461,000 | South China | | | |
| Caribbean Sea | N.A.-S.A. | 1,063,000 | 2,753,000 | Sea | Asia | 1,331,000 | 3,447,000 |
| Greenland Sea | Eur.-N.A. | 465,000 | 1,204,000 | Yellow Sea | China- | | |
| Hudson Bay | Canada | 475,000 | 1,230,000 | | Korea | 480,000 | 1,200,000 |
| Indian Ocean | | 28,900,000 | 74,900,000 | | | | |
| Mediterranean | | | | | | | |
| Sea | | 967,000 | 2,505,000 | | | | |

## Principal Islands

| Name | Location | Sq. Mi. | Sq. Km. | Name | Location | Sq. Mi. | Sq. Km. |
|---|---|---|---|---|---|---|---|
| Baffin I. | Canada | 195,928 | 507,451 | Negros | Philippines | 4,907 | 12,710 |
| Banks I. | Canada | 27,038 | 70,028 | New Britain | Papua New | | |
| Borneo | Asia | 287,300 | 744,100 | | Guinea | 14,093 | 36,500 |
| Bougainville | Papua New | | | New Caledonia | Oceania | 6,252 | 16,192 |
| | Guinea | 3,600 | 9,300 | Newfoundland | Canada | 42,031 | 108,860 |
| Cape Breton I. | Canada | 3,981 | 10,311 | New Guinea | Oceania | 309,000 | 800,000 |
| Corse (Corsica) | France | 3,352 | 8,681 | North I. | New Zealand | 44,274 | 114,669 |
| Cuba | N.A. | 42,800 | 110,800 | Novaja Zeml'a | Russia | 31,900 | 82,600 |
| Devon I. | Canada | 21,331 | 55,247 | Palawan | Philippines | 4,550 | 11,785 |
| Ellesmere I. | Canada | 75,767 | 196,236 | Prince of | | | |
| Great Britain | United | | | Wales I. | Canada | 12,872 | 33,339 |
| | Kingdom | 88,795 | 229,978 | Puerto Rico | N.A. | 3,500 | 9,100 |
| Greenland | N.A. | 840,000 | 2,175,600 | Sachalin, | | | |
| Hainan Dao | China | 13,100 | 34,000 | Ostrov | Russia | 29,500 | 76,400 |
| Hawaii | U.S. | 4,034 | 10,448 | Samar | Philippines | 5,100 | 13,080 |
| Hispaniola | N.A. | 29,300 | 76,000 | Sardegna | | | |
| Hokkaidō | Japan | 32,245 | 83,515 | (Sardinia) | Italy | 9,301 | 24,090 |
| Honshū | Japan | 89,176 | 230,966 | Seram (Ceram) | Indonesia | 7,191 | 18,625 |
| Ireland | Europe | 32,600 | 84,400 | Shikoku | Japan | 7,258 | 18,799 |
| Ísland | Europe | 39,800 | 103,000 | Sicilia (Sicily) | Italy | 9,926 | 25,708 |
| Jamaica | N.A. | 4,200 | 11,000 | Somerset I. | Canada | 9,570 | 24,786 |
| Jawa (Java) | Indonesia | 51,038 | 132,187 | Southampton | | | |
| Kípros / Kıbrıs | Asia | 3,572 | 9,251 | I. | Canada | 15,913 | 41,214 |
| Kodiak I. | U.S. | 3,670 | 9,505 | South I. | New Zealand | 57,870 | 149,883 |
| Kríti (Crete) | Greece | 3,189 | 8,259 | Spitsbergen | Norway | 15,260 | 39,523 |
| Kyūshū | Japan | 17,129 | 44,363 | Sri Lanka | Asia | 24,900 | 64,600 |
| Long I. | U.S. | 1,377 | 3,566 | Sulawesi | | | |
| Luzon | Philippines | 40,420 | 104,688 | (Celebes) | Indonesia | 73,057 | 189,216 |
| Madagascar | Africa | 227,000 | 587,000 | Sumatera | | | |
| Melville I. | Canada | 16,274 | 42,149 | (Sumatra) | Indonesia | 182,860 | 473,606 |
| Mindanao | Philippines | 36,537 | 94,630 | T'aiwan | Asia | 13,900 | 36,000 |
| Mindoro | Philippines | 3,759 | 9,735 | Tasmania | Austl. | 26,200 | 67,800 |

## Principal Lakes

| Name | Location | Sq. Mi. | Sq. Km. |
|------|----------|---------|---------|
| Albert, L. | Uganda-Zaire | 2,160 | 5,594 |
| Aral Sea | Kazakhstan-Uzbekistan | 24,700 | 64,100 |
| Athabasca, L. | Canada | 3,064 | 7,935 |
| Bajkal, Ozero (L. Baikal) | Russia | 12,200 | 31,500 |
| Balchaš, Ozero (L. Balkhash) | Kazakhstan | 7,100 | 18,300 |
| Caspian Sea | Asia-Europe | 143,240 | 370,990 |
| Chad, L. | Cameroon-Chad-Nigeria | 6,300 | 16,300 |
| Erie, L. | Canada-U.S. | 9,910 | 25,667 |
| Eyre, L. | Australia | 3,700 | 9,500 |
| Great Bear L. | Canada | 12,095 | 31,326 |
| Great Salt L. | U.S. | 1,680 | 4,351 |
| Great Slave L. | Canada | 11,030 | 28,568 |
| Huron, L. | Canada-U.S. | 23,000 | 60,000 |
| Mai-Ndombe, Lac | Zaire | 3,100 | 8,000 |
| Michigan, L. | U.S. | 22,300 | 57,800 |
| Nicaragua, Lago de | Nicaragua | 3,150 | 8,158 |
| Nyasa, L. | Malawi-Mozambique-Tanzania | 11,150 | 28,878 |
| Ontario, L. | Canada-U.S. | 7,540 | 19,529 |
| Rudolf, L. | Ethiopia-Kenya | 2,473 | 6,405 |
| Superior, L. | Canada-U.S. | 31,700 | 82,100 |
| Tanganyika. L. | Africa | 12,350 | 31,986 |
| Titicaca, Lago | Bolivia-Peru | 3,200 | 8,300 |
| Tônlé Sab | Cambodia | 2,500 | 6,500 |
| Vänern | Sweden | 2,156 | 5,584 |
| Victoria, L. | Kenya-Tanzania-Uganda | 26,820 | 69,463 |
| Winnipeg, L. | Canada | 9,416 | 24,387 |
| Woods, Lake of the | Canada-U.S. | 1,727 | 4,472 |

## Principal Rivers

| Name | Location | Mi. | Km. |
|------|----------|-----|-----|
| Amazon-Ucayali | S.A. | 4,000 | 6,400 |
| Amur (Heilong) | Asia | 2,744 | 4,416 |
| Angara | Asia | 1,105 | 1,779 |
| Arkansas | N.A. | 1,459 | 2,348 |
| Ayeyarwady (Irrawaddy) | Asia | 1,300 | 2,100 |
| Brahmaputra | Asia | 1,770 | 2,849 |
| Changjiang (Yangtze) | Asia | 3,900 | 6,300 |
| Churchill | N.A. | 1,000 | 1,600 |
| Colorado | N.A. | 1,450 | 2,334 |
| Columbia | N.A. | 1,200 | 2,000 |
| Congo (Zaïre) | Africa | 2,900 | 4,700 |
| Danube | Europe | 1,776 | 2,858 |
| Darling | Australia | 864 | 1,390 |
| Dnepr | Europe | 1,400 | 2,200 |
| Dnestr | Europe | 840 | 1,352 |
| Don | Europe | 1,162 | 1,870 |
| Euphrates (Al-Furāt) | Asia | 1,510 | 2,430 |
| Ganges | Asia | 1,560 | 2,511 |
| Grande, Rio | N.A. | 1,885 | 3,034 |
| Huanghe (Yellow) | Asia | 3,395 | 5,464 |
| Indus | Asia | 1,800 | 2,900 |
| Jenisej (Yenisey) | Asia | 2,543 | 4,092 |
| Kasai | Africa | 1,338 | 2,153 |
| Lena | Asia | 2,700 | 4,400 |
| Limpopo | Africa | 1,100 | 1,800 |
| Mackenzie | N.A. | 2,635 | 4,241 |
| Madeira | S.A. | 2,013 | 3,240 |
| Mekong | Asia | 2,600 | 4,200 |
| Mississippi | N.A. | 2,348 | 3,779 |
| Mississippi-Missouri | N.A. | 3,740 | 6,019 |
| Murray | Australia | 1,566 | 2,520 |
| Negro | S.A. | 1,300 | 2,100 |
| Niger | Africa | 2,600 | 4,200 |
| Nile | Africa | 4,145 | 6,671 |
| Ob'-Irtyš | Asia | 3,362 | 5,410 |
| Ohio | N.A. | 981 | 1,579 |
| Orange | Africa | 1,300 | 2,100 |
| Orinoco | S.A. | 1,600 | 2,600 |
| Paraguay | S.A. | 1,610 | 2,591 |
| Peace | N.A. | 1,195 | 1,923 |
| Pečora | Europe | 1,124 | 1,809 |
| Purus | S.A. | 1,860 | 2,993 |
| Red | N.A. | 1,270 | 2,044 |
| Rhine (Rhein) | Europe | 820 | 1,320 |
| Rio de la Plata--Paraná | S.A. | 3,030 | 4,876 |
| St. Lawrence | N.A. | 800 | 1,300 |
| Salween (Nu) | Asia | 1,750 | 2,816 |
| São Francisco | S.A. | 1,988 | 3,199 |
| Saskatchewan--Bow | N.A. | 1,205 | 1,939 |
| Snake | N.A. | 1,038 | 1,670 |
| Tennessee | N.A. | 652 | 1,049 |
| Tigris | Asia | 1,180 | 1,899 |
| Ural | Asia | 1,509 | 2,428 |
| Uruguay | S.A. | 1,025 | 1,650 |
| Volga | Europe | 2,194 | 3,531 |
| Yukon | N.A. | 1,770 | 2,849 |
| Zambezi | Africa | 1,700 | 2,700 |

## Largest Countries: Area

| | Country | Sq. Mi. | Sq. Km. |
|---|---|---|---|
| 1 | Russia | 6,592,849 | 17,075,400 |
| 2 | Canada | 3,849,674 | 9,970,610 |
| 3 | United States | 3,787,425 | 9,809,431 |
| 4 | China | 3,689,631 | 9,556,100 |
| 5 | Brazil | 3,286,488 | 8,511,965 |
| 6 | Australia | 2,966,155 | 7,682,300 |
| 7 | India | 1,237,062 | 3,203,975 |
| 8 | Argentina | 1,073,400 | 2,780,092 |
| 9 | Kazakhstan | 1,049,156 | 2,717,300 |
| 10 | Sudan | 967,500 | 2,505,813 |
| 11 | Algeria | 919,595 | 2,381,741 |
| 12 | Zaire | 905,446 | 2,345,095 |
| 13 | Greenland | 840,004 | 2,175,600 |
| 14 | Saudi Arabia | 830,000 | 2,149,690 |
| 15 | Mexico | 756,066 | 1,958,201 |
| 16 | Indonesia | 752,410 | 1,948,732 |
| 17 | Libya | 679,362 | 1,759,540 |
| 18 | Iran | 632,457 | 1,638,057 |
| 19 | Mongolia | 604,829 | 1,566,500 |
| 20 | Peru | 496,225 | 1,285,216 |
| 21 | Chad | 495,755 | 1,284,000 |
| 22 | Niger | 489,191 | 1,267,000 |
| 23 | Ethiopia | 483,123 | 1,251,282 |
| 24 | Angola | 481,354 | 1,246,700 |
| 25 | Mali | 478,767 | 1,240,000 |
| 26 | Colombia | 440,831 | 1,141,748 |
| 27 | South Africa | 433,680 | 1,123,226 |
| 28 | Bolivia | 424,165 | 1,098,581 |
| 29 | Mauritania | 395,956 | 1,025,520 |
| 30 | Egypt | 386,662 | 1,001,449 |
| 31 | Tanzania | 364,900 | 945,087 |
| 32 | Nigeria | 356,669 | 923,768 |
| 33 | Venezuela | 352,145 | 912,050 |
| 34 | Pakistan | 339,732 | 879,902 |
| 35 | Namibia | 317,818 | 823,144 |
| 36 | Mozambique | 308,642 | 799,380 |
| 37 | Turkey | 300,948 | 779,452 |
| 38 | Chile | 292,135 | 756,626 |
| 39 | Zambia | 290,586 | 752,614 |
| 40 | Burma | 261,228 | 676,577 |
| 41 | Afghanistan | 251,826 | 652,225 |
| 42 | Somalia | 246,201 | 637,657 |
| 43 | Central African Republic | 240,535 | 622,984 |
| 44 | Ukraine | 233,090 | 603,700 |
| 45 | Madagascar | 226,658 | 587,041 |
| 46 | Kenya | 224,961 | 582,646 |
| 47 | Botswana | 224,711 | 582,000 |
| 48 | France | 211,208 | 547,026 |
| 49 | Yemen | 205,356 | 531,869 |
| 50 | Thailand | 198,115 | 513,115 |
| 51 | Spain | 194,885 | 504,750 |
| 52 | Turkmenistan | 188,456 | 488,100 |
| 53 | Cameroon | 183,569 | 475,442 |
| 54 | Papua New Guinea | 178,704 | 462,840 |
| 55 | Sweden | 173,732 | 449,964 |

## Smallest Countries: Area

| | Country | Sq. Mi. | Sq. Km. |
|---|---|---|---|
| 1 | Vatican City | 0.2 | 0.4 |
| 2 | Monaco | 0.7 | 1.9 |
| 3 | Nauru | 8.1 | 21 |
| 4 | Tuvalu | 10 | 26 |
| 5 | San Marino | 24 | 61 |
| 6 | Anguilla | 35 | 91 |
| 7 | Liechtenstein | 62 | 160 |
| 8 | Marshall Islands | 70 | 181 |
| 9 | Aruba | 75 | 193 |
| 10 | Cook Islands | 91 | 236 |
| 11 | Niue | 100 | 258 |
| 12 | St. Kitts and Nevis | 104 | 269 |
| 13 | Maldives | 115 | 298 |
| 14 | Malta | 122 | 316 |
| 15 | Grenada | 133 | 344 |
| 16 | St. Vincent and the Grenadines | 150 | 388 |
| 17 | Barbados | 166 | 430 |
| 18 | Antigua and Barbuda | 171 | 443 |
| 19 | Andorra | 175 | 453 |
| | Seychelles | 175 | 453 |
| 20 | Northern Mariana Islands | 184 | 477 |
| 21 | Palau | 196 | 508 |
| 22 | Isle of Man | 221 | 572 |
| 23 | St. Lucia | 238 | 616 |
| 24 | Singapore | 246 | 636 |
| 25 | Bahrain | 267 | 691 |
| 26 | Micronesia, Federated States of | 271 | 702 |
| 27 | Tonga | 290 | 750 |
| 28 | Dominica | 305 | 790 |
| 29 | Netherlands Antilles | 309 | 800 |
| 30 | Kiribati | 313 | 811 |
| 31 | Sao Tome and Principe | 372 | 964 |
| 32 | Faeroe Islands | 540 | 1,399 |
| 33 | Mauritius | 788 | 2,040 |
| 34 | Comoros | 863 | 2,235 |
| 35 | Luxembourg | 998 | 2,586 |
| 36 | Western Samoa | 1,093 | 2,831 |
| 37 | Cyprus, North | 1,295 | 3,355 |
| 38 | Cape Verde | 1,557 | 4,033 |
| 39 | Trinidad and Tobago | 1,980 | 5,128 |
| 40 | Brunei | 2,226 | 5,765 |
| 41 | Cyprus | 2,276 | 5,896 |
| 42 | Venda | 2,393 | 6,198 |
| 43 | Ciskei | 2,996 | 7,760 |
| 44 | Puerto Rico | 3,515 | 9,104 |
| 45 | Lebanon | 4,015 | 10,400 |
| 46 | Gambia | 4,127 | 10,689 |
| 47 | Jamaica | 4,244 | 10,991 |
| 48 | Qatar | 4,416 | 11,437 |
| 49 | Vanuatu | 4,707 | 12,190 |
| 50 | Bahamas | 5,382 | 13,939 |
| 51 | Swaziland | 6,704 | 17,364 |
| 52 | Kuwait | 6,880 | 17,818 |
| 53 | Fiji | 7,078 | 18,333 |

## Largest Countries: Population

| | Country | Population |
|---|---|---|
| 1 | China | 1,181,580,000 |
| 2 | India | 874,150,000 |
| 3 | United States | 253,510,000 |
| 4 | Indonesia | 195,300,000 |
| 5 | Brazil | 156,750,000 |
| 6 | Russia | 150,505,000 |
| 7 | Nigeria | 124,300,000 |
| 8 | Japan | 124,270,000 |
| 9 | Pakistan | 119,000,000 |
| 10 | Bangladesh | 118,000,000 |
| 11 | Mexico | 91,000,000 |
| 12 | Germany | 79,710,000 |
| 13 | Vietnam | 68,310,000 |
| 14 | Philippines | 62,380,000 |
| 15 | Iran | 60,000,000 |
| 16 | Turkey | 58,850,000 |
| 17 | Italy | 57,830,000 |
| 18 | United Kingdom | 57,630,000 |
| 19 | Thailand | 57,200,000 |
| 20 | France | 57,010,000 |
| 21 | Egypt | 55,105,000 |
| 22 | Ethiopia | 54,040,000 |
| 23 | Ukraine | 52,800,000 |
| 24 | Korea, South | 43,305,000 |
| 25 | Burma | 42,615,000 |
| 26 | Spain | 39,465,000 |
| 27 | Zaire | 38,475,000 |
| 28 | Poland | 37,840,000 |
| 29 | South Africa | 36,765,000 |
| 30 | Colombia | 33,170,000 |
| 31 | Argentina | 32,860,000 |
| 32 | Sudan | 27,630,000 |
| 33 | Tanzania | 27,325,000 |
| 34 | Canada | 26,985,000 |
| 35 | Morocco | 26,470,000 |
| 36 | Algeria | 26,360,000 |
| 37 | Kenya | 25,695,000 |
| 38 | Romania | 23,465,000 |
| 39 | Peru | 22,585,000 |
| 40 | Korea, North | 22,250,000 |
| 41 | Taiwan | 20,785,000 |
| 42 | Venezuela | 20,430,000 |
| 43 | Uzbekistan | 20,325,000 |
| 44 | Iraq | 19,915,000 |
| 45 | Nepal | 19,845,000 |
| 46 | Uganda | 18,485,000 |
| 47 | Malaysia | 18,200,000 |
| 48 | Sri Lanka | 17,530,000 |
| 49 | Australia | 17,420,000 |
| 50 | Kazakhstan | 16,880,000 |
| | Afghanistan | 16,880,000 |
| 51 | Saudi Arabia | 16,690,000 |
| 52 | Ghana | 15,865,000 |
| 53 | Czechoslovakia | 15,755,000 |
| 54 | Mozambique | 15,460,000 |

## Smallest Countries: Population

| | Country | Population |
|---|---|---|
| 1 | Vatican City | 800 |
| 2 | Niue | 1,800 |
| 3 | Anguilla | 7,000 |
| 4 | Tuvalu | 9,000 |
| | Nauru | 9,000 |
| 5 | Palau | 15,000 |
| 6 | Cook Islands | 18,000 |
| 7 | San Marino | 23,000 |
| 8 | Liechtenstein | 28,000 |
| 9 | Monaco | 30,000 |
| 10 | St. Kitts and Nevis | 42,000 |
| 11 | Northern Mariana Islands | 46,000 |
| 12 | Faeroe Islands | 48,000 |
| 13 | Marshall Islands | 49,000 |
| 14 | Andorra | 54,000 |
| 15 | Greenland | 57,000 |
| 16 | Isle of Man | 64,000 |
| | Aruba | 64,000 |
| | Antigua and Barbuda | 64,000 |
| 18 | Seychelles | 69,000 |
| 19 | Kiribati | 72,000 |
| 20 | Dominica | 87,000 |
| 21 | Grenada | 98,000 |
| 22 | Tonga | 103,000 |
| 23 | Micronesia, Fed. States of | 109,000 |
| 24 | St. Vincent and the Grenadines | 115,000 |
| 25 | Sao Tome and Principe | 130,000 |
| 26 | Vanuatu | 153,000 |
| 27 | St. Lucia | 155,000 |
| 28 | Netherlands Antilles | 190,000 |
| 29 | Cyprus, North | 192,000 |
| | Western Samoa | 192,000 |
| 30 | Maldives | 230,000 |
| 31 | Belize | 232,000 |
| 32 | Barbados | 257,000 |
| 33 | Bahamas | 260,000 |
| 34 | Iceland | 261,000 |
| 35 | Djibouti | 351,000 |
| 36 | Solomon Islands | 353,000 |
| 37 | Malta | 357,000 |
| 38 | Equatorial Guinea | 384,000 |
| 39 | Luxembourg | 390,000 |
| 40 | Cape Verde | 393,000 |
| 41 | Suriname | 405,000 |
| 42 | Brunei | 411,000 |
| 43 | Comoros | 484,000 |
| 44 | Qatar | 532,000 |
| 45 | Bahrain | 546,000 |
| 46 | Cyprus | 713,000 |
| 47 | Fiji | 747,000 |
| 48 | Guyana | 748,000 |
| 49 | Swaziland | 875,000 |
| 50 | Gambia | 889,000 |
| 51 | Venda | 925,000 |

## Highest Urban Population

| Country | Percent Urban |
|---|---|
| 1 Monaco | 100% |
| Singapore | 100% |
| Vatican City | 100% |
| 2 Belgium | 97% |
| 3 Kuwait | 96% |
| 4 United Kingdom | 93% |
| 5 Israel | 92% |
| 6 Iceland | 91% |
| Venezuela | 91% |
| 7 Qatar | 90% |
| 8 Netherlands | 89% |
| 9 Malta | 87% |
| 10 Argentina | 86% |
| Australia | 86% |
| Chile | 86% |
| Denmark | 86% |
| Uruguay | 86% |
| 11 Germany | 84% |
| Lebanon | 84% |
| Luxembourg | 84% |
| New Zealand | 84% |
| Sweden | 84% |

## Lowest Urban Population

| Country | Percent Urban |
|---|---|
| 1 Bhutan | 5% |
| 2 Burundi | 7% |
| 3 Rwanda | 8% |
| 4 Burkina Faso | 9% |
| 5 Nepal | 10% |
| Uganda | 10% |
| 6 Oman | 11% |
| Solomon Islands | 11% |
| 7 Cambodia | 12% |
| 8 Ethiopia | 13% |
| 9 Bangladesh | 14% |
| 10 Grenada | 15% |
| Malawi | 15% |
| 11 Northern Mariana Islands | 16% |
| Papua New Guinea | 16% |
| 12 Laos | 19% |
| Mali | 19% |
| Micronesia, Fed. States of | 19% |
| 13 Lesotho | 20% |
| Niger | 20% |
| 14 China | 21% |
| Sri Lanka | 21% |

## Highest Life Expectancy

| Country | Years M | F |
|---|---|---|
| 1 Japan | 76 | 82 |
| 2 Iceland | 75 | 81 |
| Sweden | 75 | 81 |
| Switzerland | 75 | 81 |
| 3 Andorra | 74 | 81 |
| Canada | 74 | 81 |
| Netherlands | 74 | 81 |
| Norway | 74 | 81 |
| 4 France | 73 | 81 |
| 5 Australia | 74 | 80 |
| Spain | 74 | 80 |
| 6 Cyprus | 74 | 79 |
| Greece | 74 | 79 |
| 7 Faeroe Islands | 73 | 80 |
| Italy | 73 | 80 |
| United States | 73 | 80 |
| 9 Denmark | 73 | 79 |
| New Zealand | 73 | 79 |
| Puerto Rico | 73 | 79 |
| United Kingdom | 73 | 79 |
| 10 Finland | 72 | 80 |
| Monaco | 72 | 80 |

## Lowest Life Expectancy

| Country | Years M | F |
|---|---|---|
| 1 Gambia | 34 | 47 |
| Sierra Leone | 41 | 45 |
| 2 Ethiopia | 41 | 45 |
| Sierra Leone | 41 | 45 |
| 3 Afghanistan | 43 | 44 |
| 4 Guinea | 43 | 46 |
| 5 Mali | 44 | 48 |
| 6 Angola | 45 | 48 |
| Niger | 45 | 48 |
| 7 Guinea-Bissau | 45 | 49 |
| Somalia | 45 | 49 |
| 8 Central African Republic | 46 | 49 |
| Chad | 46 | 49 |
| 9 Mauritania | 46 | 50 |
| Senegal | 46 | 50 |
| 10 Benin | 47 | 50 |
| Equatorial Guinea | 47 | 50 |
| Mozambique | 47 | 50 |
| 11 Djibouti | 47 | 51 |
| 12 Malawi | 48 | 50 |
| 13 Burkina Faso | 48 | 51 |
| 14 Bhutan | 49 | 47 |

## Highest Literacy

| Country | Percent Literate |
|---------|------------------|
| 1 Australia | 100% |
| Finland | 100% |
| Iceland | 100% |
| Liechtenstein | 100% |
| Luxembourg | 100% |
| Tonga | 100% |
| Vatican City | 100% |
| 2 Armenia | 99% |
| Austria | 99% |
| Barbados | 99% |
| Belarus | 99% |
| Belgium | 99% |
| Canada | 99% |
| Czechoslovakia | 99% |
| Denmark | 99% |
| France | 99% |
| Georgia | 99% |
| Germany | 99% |
| Hungary | 99% |
| Japan | 99% |
| Netherlands | 99% |
| New Zealand | 99% |
| Norway | 99% |
| Poland | 99% |
| Russia | 99% |
| Slovenia | 99% |
| Sweden | 99% |
| Switzerland | 99% |
| United Kingdom | 99% |

## Lowest Literacy

| Country | Percent Literate |
|---------|------------------|
| 1 Burkina Faso | 18% |
| 2 Sierra Leone | 21% |
| 3 Malawi | 22% |
| 4 Benin | 23% |
| Botswana | 23% |
| 5 Guinea | 24% |
| Somalia | 24% |
| 6 Nepal | 26% |
| 7 Central African Republic | 27% |
| Gambia | 27% |
| Sudan | 27% |
| 8 Niger | 28% |
| 9 Afghanistan | 29% |
| 10 Chad | 30% |
| 11 Mali | 32% |
| 12 Mozambique | 33% |
| 13 Mauritania | 34% |
| 14 Bangladesh | 35% |
| Cambodia | 35% |
| Pakistan | 35% |
| 16 Guinea-Bissau | 36% |
| 17 Namibia | 38% |
| Senegal | 38% |
| Yemen | 38% |
| 18 Liberia | 40% |
| 19 Angola | 42% |
| 20 Tanzania | 46% |
| 21 Egypt | 48% |
| India | 48% |

## Highest GDP U.S. $ / Capita

| Country | GDP/ Capita |
|---------|-------------|
| 1 Liechtenstein | $22,500 |
| 2 United States | *21,847* |
| 3 Qatar | 20,625 |
| 4 Canada | 19,561 |
| 5 Switzerland | 19,025 |
| 6 Luxembourg | 18,110 |
| 7 Norway | 17,658 |
| 8 Japan | *17,148* |
| 9 Iceland | 16,535 |
| 10 San Marino | 16,375 |
| 11 Sweden | 16,206 |
| 12 France | 15,540 |
| 13 Finland | 15,507 |
| 14 Denmark | 15,190 |
| 15 Australia | 15,009 |
| 16 United Kingdom | 14,970 |
| 17 Germany | 14,798 |
| 18 Netherlands | 14,705 |
| 19 Belgium | 14,660 |
| 20 Italy | 14,659 |

## Lowest GDP U.S. $ / Capita

| Country | GDP/ Capita |
|---------|-------------|
| 1 Mozambique | $ 91 |
| 2 Cambodia | 132 |
| 3 Ethiopia | 136 |
| 4 Laos | 151 |
| 5 Nepal | 158 |
| 6 Guinea-Bissau | 160 |
| 7 Bhutan | 183 |
| 8 Zaire | 188 |
| 9 Bangladesh | 190 |
| 10 Malawi | 192 |
| 11 Burkina Faso | 204 |
| Burundi | 204 |
| 12 Afghanistan | 205 |
| 13 Madagascar | 207 |
| 14 Chad | 209 |
| 15 Somalia | 216 |
| 16 Mali | 221 |
| 17 Vietnam | *232* |
| 18 Lesotho | 237 |
| 19 Gambia | 242 |

**Figures in italics are GNP.**

# Index

## Introduction to the Index

This universal index includes in a single alphabetical list more than 7,000 names of features that appear on the world travel maps on pages 81 through 144. Each name is followed by latitude and longitude coordinates and a page reference.

**Names:** Local official names are used on the maps and in the index. The names are shown in full, including diacritical marks. Features that extend beyond the boundaries of one country and have no single official name are usually named in English. Many conventional English names and former names are cross-referenced to the official names. Names that appear in shortened versions on the maps due to space limitiations are spelled out in full in the index. The portions of these names omitted from the maps are enclosed in brackets—for example, Acapulco [de Juárez].

**Transliteration:** For names in languages not written in the Roman alphabet, the locally official transliteration system has been used where one exists. Thus, names in Russia and Bulgaria have been transliterated according to the systems adopted by the academies of science of these countries. Similarly, the transliteration for mainland Chinese names follows the Pinyin system, which has been officially adopted in mainland China. For languages with no one locally accepted system, notably Arabic, transliteration closely follows a system adopted by the United States Board on Geographic Names.

**Abbreviation and Capitalization:** Abbreviations of names on the maps have been standardized as much as possible. Names that are abbreviated on the maps are generally spelled out in full in the index. Periods are used after all abbreviations regardless of local practice. The abbreviation "St." is used only for "Saint". "Sankt" and other forms of this term are spelled out.

Most initial letters of names are capitalized, except for a few Dutch names, such as "'s-Gravenhage". Capitalization of noninitial words in a name generally follows local practice.

**Alphabetization:** Names are alphabetized in the order of the letters of the English alphabet. Spanish *ll* and *ch,* for example, are not treated as distinct letters. Furthermore, diacritical marks are disregarded in alphabetization—German or Scandinavian *ä* or *ö* are treated as *a* or *o.*

The names of physical features may appear inverted, since they are always alphabetized under the proper, not the generic, part of the name, thus: "Gibraltar, Strait of ꭒ". Otherwise every entry, whether consisting of one word or more, is alphabetized as a single continuous entity. "La Habana," for example, appears after "Lagunillas" and before "Lahaina." Names beginning with articles (Le Havre, Den Helder, Al-Qāhirah, As-Suways) are not inverted. Names beginning "St.", "Ste." and "Sainte" are alphabetized as though spelled "Saint."

In the case of identical names, towns are listed first, then political divisions, then physical features. Entries that are completely identical (including symbols, discussed below) are distinguished by abbreviations of their country names. The country abbreviations used for places in the United States, Canada and United Kingdom indicate the state, province or political division in which the feature is located. (See List of Abbreviations on page 154).

**Symbols:** City names are not followed by symbols. The names of all other features are followed by symbols that graphically represent broad categories of features, for example, ᴧ for mountain (Everest, Mount ᴧ). Superior numbers indicate finer distinctions, for example, ᴧ¹ for volcano (Fuji-san ᴧ¹). A complete list of symbols, including those with superior numbers, follows the List of Abbreviations.

All cross-references are indicated by the symbol →.

**Page References and Geographical Coordinates:** The page references and geographical coordinates are found in the last three columns of each entry.

The page number generally refers to the map that shows the feature at the best scale. Countries, mountain ranges and other extensive features are usually indexed to maps that both show the features completely and also show them in their relationship to broad areas. Page references to two-page maps always refer to the left-hand page. If a page contains several maps or insets, a lowercase letter may identify the specific map or inset.

Latitude and longitude coordinates for point features, such as cities and mountain peaks, indicate the locations of the symbols. For extensive areal features, such as countries or mountain ranges, locations are given for the approximate center of the feature. Those for linear features, such as canals and rivers, are given to the mouth or terminal point.

## List of Abbreviations

| | English | Local Name | | English | Local Name |
|---|---|---|---|---|---|
| **Ab., Can.** | Alberta, Can. | Alberta | **Burkina** | Burkina Faso | Burkina Faso |
| **Afg.** | Afghanistan | Afghānestān | **Burma** | Burma | Myanmar |
| **Afr.** | Africa | — | **Ca., U.S.** | California, U.S. | California |
| **Ak., U.S.** | Alaska, U.S. | Alaska | | | |
| **Al., U.S.** | Alabama, U.S. | Alabama | **Camb.** | Cambodia | Kâmpŭchéa |
| **Alb.** | Albania | Shqipëri | **Cam.** | Cameroon | Cameroun |
| **Alg.** | Algeria | Algérie | | | (French) / |
| | | (French) / | | | Cameroon |
| | | Djazaïr | | | (English) |
| | | (Arabic) | **Can.** | Canada | Canada |
| **Am. Sam.** | American | American | **C.A.R.** | Central | République |
| | Samoa | Samoa | | African | centrafricaine |
| | | (English) / | | Republic | |
| | | Amerika | **Cay. Is.** | Cayman | Cayman |
| | | Samoa | | Islands | Islands |
| | | (Samoan) | **Chad** | Chad | Tchad |
| **And.** | Andorra | Andorra | **Chile** | Chile | Chile |
| **Ang.** | Angola | Angola | **China** | China | Zhongguo |
| **Anguilla** | Anguilla | Anguilla | **Christ. I.** | Christmas | Christmas |
| **Ant.** | Antarctica | — | | Island | Island |
| **Antig.** | Antigua and | Antigua and | **Ciskei** | Ciskei | Ciskei |
| | Barbuda | Barbuda | **Co., U.S.** | Colorado, U.S. | Colorado |
| **Ar., U.S.** | Arkansas, U.S. | Arkansas | **Cocos Is.** | Cocos | Cocos |
| **Arg.** | Argentina | Argentina | | (Keeling) | (Keeling) |
| **Arm.** | Armenia | Hayastan | | Islands | Islands |
| **Aruba** | Aruba | Aruba | **Col.** | Colombia | Colombia |
| **Asia** | Asia | — | **Com.** | Comoros | Comores |
| **Aus.** | Austria | Österreich | | | (French) / |
| **Austl.** | Australia | Australia | | | Al-Qumur |
| **Az., U.S.** | Arizona, U.S. | Arizona | | | (Arabic) |
| **Azer.** | Azerbaijan | Azerbaijan | **Congo** | Congo | Congo |
| **Bah.** | Bahamas | Bahamas | **Cook Is.** | Cook Islands | Cook Islands |
| **Bahr.** | Bahrain | Al-Baḥrayn | **C.R.** | Costa Rica | Costa Rica |
| **Barb.** | Barbados | Barbados | **Cro.** | Croatia | Hrvatska |
| **B.C., Can.** | British | British | **Ct., U.S.** | Connecticut, | Connecticut |
| | Columbia, | Columbia | | U.S. | |
| | Can. | (English) / | **Cuba** | Cuba | Cuba |
| | | Colombie- | **C.V.** | Cape Verde | Cabo Verde |
| | | Britannique | **Cyp.** | Cyprus | Kípros (Greek) |
| | | (French) | | | / Kıbrıs |
| **Bdi.** | Burundi | Burundi | | | (Turkish) |
| **Bel.** | Belgium | Belgique | **Czech.** | Czechoslovakia | Československo |
| | | (French) / | **D.C., U.S.** | District of | District of |
| | | België | | Columbia, | Columbia |
| | | (Flemish) | | U.S. | |
| **Bela.** | Belarus | Belarus | **De., U.S.** | Delaware, U.S. | Delaware |
| **Belize** | Belize | Belize | **Den.** | Denmark | Danmark |
| **Benin** | Benin | Bénin | **Dji.** | Djibouti | Djibouti |
| **Ber.** | Bermuda | Bermuda | **Dom.** | Dominica | Dominica |
| **Bhu.** | Bhutan | Druk-Yul | **Dom. Rep.** | Dominican | República |
| **B.I.O.T.** | British Indian | British Indian | | Republic | Dominicana |
| | Ocean | Ocean | **Ger.** | Germany | Deutschland |
| | Territory | Territory | **Ec.** | Ecuador | Ecuador |
| **Bngl.** | Bangladesh | Bangladesh | **Egypt** | Egypt | Miṣr |
| **Bol.** | Bolivia | Bolivia | **El Sal.** | El Salvador | El Salvador |
| **Boph.** | Bophuthatswana | Bophuthatswana | **Eng., U.K.** | England, U.K. | England |
| **Bos.** | Bosnia and | Bosna i | **Eq. Gui.** | Equatorial | Guinea |
| | Hercegovina | Hercegovina | | Guinea | Ecuatorial |
| **Bots.** | Botswana | Botswana | **Est.** | Estonia | Eesti |
| **Braz.** | Brazil | Brasil | **Eth.** | Ethiopia | Ityopiya |
| **Br. Vir. Is.** | British Virgin | British Virgin | **Eur.** | Europe | — |
| | Islands | Islands | **Faer. Is.** | Faeroe Islands | Føroyar |
| **Bru.** | Brunei | Brunei | **Falk. Is.** | Falkland | Falkland |
| **Bul.** | Bulgaria | Bålgarija | | Islands | Islands |

| | English | Local Name | | English | Local Name |
|---|---|---|---|---|---|
| Fiji | Fiji | Fiji | Kir. | Kiribati | Kiribati |
| Fin. | Finland | Suomi (Finnish) / Finland (Swedish) | Kor., N. | North Korea | Chosŏn-minjujuŭi-inmīn-konghwaguk |
| Fl., U.S. | Florida, U.S. | Florida | Kor., S. | South Korea | Taehan-min'guk |
| Fr. | France | France | | | |
| Fr. Gu. | French Guiana | Guyane française | Ks., U.S. | Kansas, U.S. | Kansas |
| | | | Kuw. | Kuwait | Al-Kuwayt |
| Fr. Poly. | French Polynesia | Polynésie française | Ky., U.S. | Kentucky, U.S. | Kentucky |
| | | | Kyrg. | Kyrgyzstan | Kyrgyzstan |
| Ga., U.S. | Georgia, U.S. | Georgia | La., U.S. | Louisiana, U.S. | Louisiana |
| Gabon | Gabon | Gabon | | | |
| Gam. | Gambia | Gambia | Laos | Laos | Lao |
| Geor. | Georgia | Sakartvelo | Lat. | Latvia | Latvija |
| Ghana | Ghana | Ghana | Leb. | Lebanon | Lubnān |
| Gib. | Gibraltar | Gibraltar | Leso. | Lesotho | Lesotho |
| Grc. | Greece | Ellás | Lib. | Liberia | Liberia |
| Gren. | Grenada | Grenada | Libya | Libya | Lībiyā |
| Grnld. | Greenland | Kalaallit Nunaat (Eskimo) / Grønland (Danish) | Liech. | Liechtenstein | Liechtenstein |
| | | | Lith. | Lithuania | Lietuva |
| | | | Lux. | Luxembourg | Luxembourg |
| | | | Ma., U.S. | Massachusetts, U.S. | Massachusetts |
| Guad. | Guadeloupe | Guadeloupe | Macao | Macao | Macau |
| Guam | Guam | Guam | Mac. | Macedonia | Makedonija |
| Guat. | Guatemala | Guatemala | Madag. | Madagascar | Madagasikara (Malagasy) / Madagascar (French) |
| Guernsey | Guernsey | Guernsey | | | |
| Gui. | Guinea | Guinée | | | |
| Gui.-B. | Guinea-Bissau | Guiné-Bissau | | | |
| Guy. | Guyana | Guyana | Malay. | Malaysia | Malaysia |
| Haiti | Haiti | Haïti | Mald. | Maldives | Maldives |
| Hi., U.S. | Hawaii, U.S. | Hawaii | Mali | Mali | Mali |
| H.K. | Hong Kong | Hong Kong | Malta | Malta | Malta |
| Hond. | Honduras | Honduras | Marsh. Is. | Marshall Islands | Marshall Islands |
| Hung. | Hungary | Magyarország | | | |
| Ia., U.S. | Iowa, U.S. | Iowa | Mart. | Martinique | Martinique |
| I.C. | Ivory Coast | Côte d'Ivoire | Maur. | Mauritania | Mauritanie (French) / Mūrītāniyā (Arabic) |
| Ice. | Iceland | Ísland | | | |
| Id., U.S. | Idaho, U.S. | Idaho | | | |
| Il., U.S. | Illinois, U.S. | Illinois | | | |
| In., U.S. | Indiana, U.S. | Indiana | | | |
| India | India | India (English) / Bharat (Hindi) | May. | Mayotte | Mayotte |
| | | | Mb., Can. | Manitoba, Can. | Manitoba |
| Indon. | Indonesia | Indonesia | Md., U.S. | Maryland, U.S. | Maryland |
| I. of Man | Isle of Man | Isle of Man | | | |
| Iran | Iran | Īrān | Me., U.S. | Maine, U.S. | Maine |
| Iraq | Iraq | Al-'Irāq | Mex. | Mexico | México |
| Ire. | Ireland | Ireland (English) / Éire (Gaelic) | Mi., U.S. | Michigan, U.S. | Michigan |
| | | | Micron. | Federated States of Micronesia | Federated States of Micronesia |
| Isr. | Israel | Yisra'el (Hebrew) / Isrā'īl (Arabic) | Mid. Is. | Midway Islands | Midway Islands |
| | | | Mn., U.S. | Minnesota, U.S. | Minnesota |
| Isr. Occ. | Israeli Occupied Areas | — | Mo., U.S. | Missouri, U.S. | Missouri |
| | | | Mol. | Moldova | Moldova |
| Italy | Italy | Italia | Mon. | Monaco | Monaco |
| Jam. | Jamaica | Jamaica | Mong. | Mongolia | Mongol Ard Uls |
| Japan | Japan | Nihon | | | |
| Jersey | Jersey | Jersey | Monts. | Montserrat | Montserrat |
| Jord. | Jordan | Al-Urdun | Mor. | Morocco | Al-Magreb |
| Kaz. | Kazakhstan | Kazachstan | Moz. | Mozambique | Moçambique |
| Kenya | Kenya | Kenya | Mrts. | Mauritius | Mauritius |

# 158 Index

## Key to Symbols

| | | | | | | | | |
|---|---|---|---|---|---|---|---|---|
| ∧ | Mountain | ‖ | Islands | ᴄ¹ | Estuary | □³ | State, Canton, |
| ∧¹ | Volcano | | | ᴄ² | Fjord | | Republic |
| ∧² | Hill | ≛ | Other Topographic | ᴄ³ | Bight | □⁴ | Province, Region, |
| ⋆ | Mountains | | Features | | | | Oblast |
| ⋆¹ | Plateau | ≛¹ | Continent | ⊜ | Lake, Lakes | □⁵ | Department, District, |
| ⋆² | Hills | ≛² | Coast, Beach | ⊜¹ | Reservoir | | Prefecture |
| )( | Pass | ≛³ | Isthmus | | | □⁸ | Miscellaneous |
| | | ≛⁴ | Cliff | ≕ | Swamp | □⁹ | Historical |
| ∨ | Valley, Canyon | ≛⁶ | Crater | ⋈ | Ice Features, Glacier | | |
| ≍ | Plain | ≛⁸ | Dunes | | | ♦ | Recreational Site |
| ≍¹ | Basin | ≛⁹ | Lava Flow | ⟙ | Other Hydrographic | | |
| ≍² | Delta | ≏ | River | | Features | ♦ | Miscellaneous |
| | | | | ⟙¹ | Ocean | ♦¹ | Region |
| ≻ | Cape | ⊠ | Canal | ⟙² | Sea | ♦² | Desert |
| ≻¹ | Peninsula | | | ⟙⁴ | Oasis, Well, Spring | ♦³ | Forest, Moor |
| | | ∟ | Waterfall, Rapids | | | ♦⁴ | Reserve, Reservation |
| ı | Island | | | □ | Political Unit | ♦⁶ | Dam |
| ı¹ | Atoll | ⨆ | Strait | □¹ | Independent Nation | ♦⁸ | Neighborhood |
| | | ᴄ | Bay, Gulf | □² | Dependency | | |

## Index to the Maps

| Name | Page No. | Lat. | Long. |
|---|---|---|---|
| Alaska □³ | 144 | 65.00N | 153.00W |
| Alaska, Gulf of ⊂ | 144 | 58.00N | 146.00W |
| Alaska Peninsula ➤¹ | 144 | 57.00N | 158.00W |
| Alaska Range ⋏ | 144 | 62.30N | 150.00W |
| Albacete | 94 | 38.59N | 1.51W |
| Albanel, Lac ⊜ | 136 | 50.55N | 73.12W |
| Albania □¹ | 86 | 41.00N | 20.00E |
| Albany, Austl. | 122 | 35.02S | 117.53E |
| Albany, Ga., U.S. | 138 | 31.34N | 84.09W |
| Albany, N.Y., U.S. | 140 | 42.39N | 73.45W |
| Al-Baṣrah | 108 | 30.30N | 47.47E |
| Albert, Lake ⊜ | 106 | 1.40N | 31.00E |
| Alberta □⁴ | 136 | 54.00N | 113.00W |
| Albert Nile ≏ | 108 | 3.36N | 32.02E |
| Ålborg | 89 | 57.03N | 9.56E |
| Albuquerque | 138 | 35.05N | 106.39W |
| Albury | 122 | 36.05S | 146.55E |
| Alcalá de Guadaira | 94 | 37.20N | 5.50W |
| Alcalá de Henares | 94 | 40.29N | 3.22W |
| Alcira | 94 | 39.09N | 0.26W |
| Alcoy | 94 | 38.42N | 0.28W |
| Aldabra Islands I¹ | 106 | 9.25S | 46.22E |
| Aldama | 128 | 28.51N | 105.54W |
| Aldan | 102 | 58.37N | 125.24E |
| Aleksandrovsk-Sachalinskij | 102 | 50.54N | 142.10E |
| Alentejo □⁹ | 94 | 38.00N | 8.00W |
| Alenuihaha Channel ʯ | 143 | 20.26N | 156.00W |
| Alessandria | 96 | 44.54N | 8.37E |
| Aleutian Islands II | 144 | 52.00N | 176.00W |
| Alexander, Cape ➤ | 127a | 6.35S | 156.30E |
| Alexander Archipelago II | 144 | 56.30N | 134.00W |
| Alexander Bay | 106 | 28.40S | 16.30E |
| Alexandra | 126 | 45.15S | 169.24E |
| Alexandria, Rom. | 98 | 43.58N | 25.20E |
| Alexandria, La., U.S. | 128 | 31.18N | 92.26W |
| Alexandria, Va., U.S. | 140 | 38.48N | 77.02W |
| Alexandria → Al-Iskandarīyah | 104 | 31.12N | 29.54E |
| Alexandria Bay | 140 | 44.20N | 75.55W |
| Alexandroúpolis | 98 | 40.50N | 25.52E |
| Al-Fāshir | 104 | 13.38N | 25.21E |
| Al-Fayyūm | 104 | 29.19N | 30.50E |
| Alfenas | 135 | 21.25S | 45.57W |
| Alfred | 140 | 45.34N | 74.53W |
| Algeciras | 94 | 36.08N | 5.30W |
| Alger (Algiers) | 104 | 36.47N | 3.03E |
| Algeria □¹ | 104 | 28.00N | 3.00E |
| Alghero | 96 | 40.34N | 8.19E |
| Algiers → El Djazaïr | 104 | 36.47N | 3.03E |
| Al-Ḥarrah ⌁⁹ | 109 | 31.00N | 38.30E |
| Al-Ḥijāz ◆¹ | 109 | 24.30N | 38.30E |
| Al-Ḥudaydah | 108 | 14.48N | 42.57E |
| Al-Ḥufūf | 108 | 25.22N | 49.34E |
| Alicante | 94 | 38.21N | 0.29W |
| Alice | 128 | 27.45N | 98.04W |
| Alice Springs | 122 | 23.42S | 133.53E |
| Alīgarh | 112 | 27.54N | 78.05E |
| Al-Iskandarīyah (Alexandria) | 104 | 31.12N | 29.54E |
| Al-Ismāʿīlīyah | 109 | 30.35N | 32.16E |
| Al-Jawf | 108 | 29.50N | 39.52E |
| Al-Jīzah | 104 | 30.01N | 31.13E |
| Al-Khandaq | 104 | 18.36N | 30.34E |
| Al-Kharṭūm (Khartoum) | 104 | 15.36N | 32.32E |
| Alkmaar | 90 | 52.37N | 4.44E |
| Al-Kuwayt | 108 | 29.20N | 47.59E |
| Al-Lādhiqīyah (Latakia) | 109 | 35.31N | 35.47E |
| Allāhābād | 112 | 25.27N | 81.51E |
| Allegheny Mountains ⋏ | 140 | 38.30N | 80.00W |
| Allentown | 140 | 40.36N | 75.28W |
| Alma-Ata | 102 | 43.15N | 76.57E |
| Al-Madīnah (Medina) | 108 | 24.28N | 39.36E |
| Al-Manāmah | 108 | 26.13N | 50.35E |
| Al-Manṣūrah | 109 | 31.03N | 31.23E |
| Al-Mawṣil | 108 | 36.20N | 43.08E |
| Almendralejo | 94 | 38.41N | 6.24W |
| Almería | 94 | 36.50N | 2.27W |
| Al-Minyā | 104 | 28.06N | 30.45E |
| Al-Mukallā | 108 | 14.32N | 49.08E |
| Al-Mukhā | 108 | 13.19N | 43.15E |
| Alor Setar | 120 | 6.07N | 100.22E |
| Alpena | 140 | 45.03N | 83.25W |
| Alpine | 128 | 30.21N | 103.39W |
| Alps ⋏ | 92 | 46.25N | 10.00E |
| Al-Qaḍārif | 104 | 14.02N | 35.24E |
| Al-Qāhirah (Cairo) | 104 | 30.03N | 31.15E |
| Al-Qāmishlī | 109 | 37.02N | 41.14E |
| Al-Qaṭrūn | 104 | 24.56N | 14.38E |
| Alsace □⁹ | 92 | 48.30N | 7.30E |
| Alta | 89 | 69.55N | 23.12E |
| Altagracia de Orituco | 130 | 9.52N | 66.23W |
| Altamura | 96 | 40.50N | 16.33E |
| Altiplano ⋏¹ | 132 | 18.00S | 68.00W |
| Alton | 138 | 38.53N | 90.11W |
| Altoona | 140 | 40.31N | 78.23W |
| Al-Ubayyiḍ | 104 | 13.11N | 30.13E |
| Al-Uqṣur (Luxor) | 104 | 25.41N | 32.39E |
| Alva | 138 | 36.48N | 98.39W |
| Alvarado | 128 | 18.46N | 95.46W |
| Amami-shotō II | 117b | 28.16N | 129.21E |
| Amarillo | 138 | 35.13N | 101.49W |
| Amazon (Solimões) (Amazonas) ≏ | 132 | 0.05S | 50.00W |
| Amberg | 90 | 49.27N | 11.52E |
| Ambon | 118 | 3.43S | 128.12E |
| Ambositra | 106 | 20.31S | 47.15E |
| Ambre, Cap d'➤ | 106 | 11.57S | 49.17E |
| Amecameca [de Juárez] | 128 | 19.07N | 98.46W |
| American Highland ⋏¹ | 85 | 72.30S | 78.00E |
| American Samoa □² | 127e | 14.20S | 170.00W |
| Amherstburg | 140 | 42.06N | 83.06W |
| Amiens | 92 | 49.54N | 2.18E |
| Amīndīvi Islands II | 111 | 11.23N | 72.23E |
| Amirante Islands II | 106 | 6.00S | 53.10E |
| ʿAmmān | 109 | 31.57N | 35.56E |
| Ammókhostos (Famagusta) | 109 | 35.07N | 33.57E |
| Åmot | 89 | 59.35N | 8.00E |
| Amoy → Xiamen | 114 | 24.28N | 118.07E |
| Amrāvati | 112 | 20.56N | 77.45E |
| Amritsar | 112 | 31.35N | 74.53E |
| Amsterdam, Neth. | 90 | 52.22N | 4.54E |
| Amsterdam, N.Y., U.S. | 140 | 42.56N | 74.11W |
| Amu Darya (Amudarja) ≏ | 110 | 42.30N | 59.15E |
| Amundsen Gulf ⊂ | 136 | 71.00N | 124.00W |
| Amundsen Sea ⊤² | 85 | 72.30S | 112.00W |
| Amur (Heilongjiang) ≏ | 102 | 52.56N | 141.10E |
| Anaheim | 142 | 33.50N | 117.54W |
| Anakāpalle | 111 | 17.41N | 83.01E |
| Anápolis | 135 | 16.20S | 48.58W |
| Añatuya | 134 | 28.28S | 62.50W |
| Anchorage | 144 | 61.13N | 149.54W |
| Ancona | 96 | 43.38N | 13.30E |
| Ancud | 134 | 41.52S | 73.50W |
| Andalucía □⁹ | 94 | 37.36N | 4.30W |
| Andaman Islands II | 120 | 12.00N | 92.45E |
| Andaman Sea ⊤² | 120 | 10.00N | 95.00E |
| Andes ⋏ | 82 | 20.00S | 68.00W |
| Andfjorden ʯ | 89 | 69.10N | 16.20E |
| Andhra Pradesh □³ | 111 | 16.00N | 79.00E |
| Andkhvoy | 112 | 36.56N | 65.08E |
| Andoany | 106 | 13.25S | 48.16E |
| Andorra | 94 | 42.30N | 1.31E |
| Andorra □¹ | 86 | 42.30N | 1.30E |
| Andradina | 135 | 20.54S | 51.23W |
| Andreanof Islands II | 144 | 52.00N | 176.00W |

| Name | Page No. | Lat. | Long. |
|---|---|---|---|
| Andrews | 128 | 32.19N | 102.32W |
| Ándros I | 98 | 37.45N | 24.42 E |
| Andros Island I | 130 | 24.26N | 77.57W |
| Andújar | 94 | 38.03N | 4.04W |
| Anegada Passage ⋓ | 130 | 18.30N | 63.40W |
| Aneto, Pico de ⋀ | 94 | 42.38N | 0.40 E |
| Angarsk | 102 | 52.34N | 103.54 E |
| Ángel, Salto (Angel Falls) ⌣ | 132 | 5.57N | 62.30W |
| Ángel de la Guarda, Isla I | 128 | 29.20N | 113.25W |
| Angeles | 118 | 15.09N | 120.35 E |
| Angel Falls → Ángel, Salto ⌣ | 132 | 5.57N | 62.30W |
| Ångermanälven ≃ | 89 | 62.48N | 17.56 E |
| Angermünde | 90 | 53.01N | 14.00 E |
| Angers | 92 | 47.28N | 0.33W |
| Angmagssalik | 136 | 65.36N | 37.41W |
| Angola | 140 | 42.38N | 79.01W |
| Angola □[1] | 106 | 12.30S | 18.30 E |
| Angoram | 118 | 4.04S | 144.04 E |
| Angoulême | 92 | 45.39N | 0.09 E |
| Anguilla □[2] | 130 | 18.15N | 63.05W |
| Aniak | 144 | 61.35N | 159.33W |
| Anina | 98 | 45.05N | 21.51 E |
| Ankara | 86 | 39.56N | 32.52 E |
| Annaba (Bône) | 104 | 36.54N | 7.46 E |
| An-Nafūd ◆[2] | 109 | 28.30N | 41.00 E |
| An-Najaf | 108 | 31.59N | 44.20 E |
| Annapolis | 140 | 38.58N | 76.29W |
| Annapurna ⋀ | 112 | 28.34N | 83.50 E |
| Ann Arbor | 140 | 42.16N | 83.43W |
| Annecy | 92 | 45.54N | 6.07 E |
| An-Nuhūd | 104 | 12.42N | 28.26 E |
| Anqing | 114 | 30.31N | 117.02 E |
| Ansbach | 90 | 49.17N | 10.34 E |
| Anshan | 114 | 41.08N | 122.59 E |
| Antalaha | 106 | 14.53S | 50.16 E |
| Antalya | 86 | 36.53N | 30.42 E |
| Antananarivo | 106 | 18.55S | 47.31 E |
| Antarctica ⋤[1] | 85 | 90.00S | 0.00 |
| Antarctic Peninsula ⋗[1] | 85 | 69.30S | 65.00W |
| Antequera | 94 | 37.01N | 4.33W |
| Anticosti, Île d' I | 138 | 49.30N | 63.00W |
| Antigua and Barbuda □[1] | 130 | 17.03N | 61.48W |
| Antofagasta | 134 | 23.39S | 70.24W |
| António Enes | 106 | 16.14S | 39.54 E |
| Antsirabe | 106 | 19.51S | 47.02 E |
| Antsiranana | 106 | 12.16S | 49.17 E |
| Antwerp → Antwerpen | 90 | 51.13N | 4.25 E |
| Antwerpen (Anvers) | 90 | 51.13N | 4.25 E |
| Anvers → Antwerpen | 90 | 51.13N | 4.25 E |
| Aomori | 116 | 40.49N | 140.45 E |
| Aôral, Phnum ⋀ | 120 | 12.02N | 104.10 E |
| Aosta | 96 | 45.44N | 7.20 E |
| Aoukâr ◆[1] | 104 | 18.00N | 9.30W |
| Apatzingán [de la Constitución] | 128 | 19.05N | 102.21W |
| Apeldoorn | 90 | 52.13N | 5.58 E |
| Apia | 127e | 13.50S | 171.44W |
| Apo, Mount ⋀ | 118 | 6.59N | 125.16 E |
| Apostólou Andréa, Akrotírion ⋗ | 109 | 35.42N | 34.35 E |
| Appalachian Mountains ⋌ | 138 | 41.00N | 77.00W |
| Appennino (Apennines) ⋌ | 96 | 43.00N | 13.00 E |
| Appennino Abruzzese ⋌ | 96 | 42.00N | 14.00 E |
| Appennino Calabrese ⋌ | 96 | 39.00N | 16.30 E |
| Appennino Ligure ⋌ | 96 | 44.30N | 9.00 E |
| Appennino Tosco-Emiliano ⋌ | 96 | 44.00N | 11.30 E |
| Appennino Umbro-Marchigiano ⋌ | 96 | 43.00N | 13.00 E |
| Apure ≃ | 130 | 7.37N | 66.25W |
| Aqaba, Gulf of ⊂ | 109 | 29.00N | 34.40 E |
| 'Arab, Bahr al- ≃ | 104 | 9.02N | 29.28 E |
| Arabian Sea ⊤[2] | 82 | 15.00N | 65.00 E |
| Aracaju | 132 | 10.55S | 37.04W |
| Araçatuba | 132 | 21.12S | 50.25W |
| Arad | 98 | 46.11N | 21.20 E |
| Arafura Sea ⊤[2] | 118 | 11.00S | 135.00 E |
| Arago, Cape ⋗ | 142 | 43.18N | 124.25W |
| Aragón □[9] | 94 | 41.00N | 1.00W |
| Aragón ≃ | 94 | 42.13N | 1.44W |
| Araguaia ≃ | 132 | 5.21S | 48.41W |
| Araguari | 135 | 18.38S | 48.11W |
| Árakhthos ≃ | 98 | 39.01N | 21.03 E |
| Aral Sea ⊤[2] | 86 | 45.00N | 59.00 E |
| Aran Islands II | 88 | 53.07N | 9.43W |
| Aranjuez | 94 | 40.02N | 3.36W |
| Aranyaprathet | 120 | 13.41N | 102.30 E |
| Araraquara | 132 | 21.47S | 48.10W |
| Araxá | 135 | 19.35S | 46.55W |
| Arbroath | 88 | 56.34N | 2.35W |
| Arc Dome ⋀ | 142 | 38.51N | 117.22W |
| Archangel'sk (Archangel) | 86 | 64.34N | 40.32 E |
| Arctic Bay | 136 | 73.02N | 85.11W |
| Arctic Ocean ⊤[1] | 84 | 85.00N | 170.00 E |
| Ardennes ◆[1] | 92 | 50.10N | 5.45 E |
| Arecibo | 130 | 18.28N | 66.43W |
| Arendal | 89 | 58.27N | 8.48 E |
| Arequipa | 132 | 16.24S | 71.33W |
| Arezzo | 96 | 43.25N | 11.53 E |
| Argentina □[1] | 134 | 34.00S | 64.00W |
| Argonne ◆[1] | 92 | 49.30N | 5.00 E |
| Argos | 98 | 37.39N | 22.44 E |
| Arguello, Point ⋗ | 142 | 34.35N | 120.39W |
| Argun' (Eergu'nahe) ≃ | 114 | 53.20N | 121.28 E |
| Århus | 89 | 56.09N | 10.13 E |
| Arica, Chile | 132 | 18.29S | 70.20W |
| Arica, Col. | 132 | 2.08S | 71.47W |
| 'Arīsh, Wādī al- ∨ | 109 | 31.09N | 33.49 E |
| Arismendi | 130 | 8.29N | 68.22W |
| Arizona □[3] | 138 | 34.00N | 112.00W |
| Arjona | 130 | 10.15N | 75.21W |
| Arkansas □[3] | 138 | 34.50N | 93.40W |
| Arkansas ≃ | 138 | 33.48N | 91.04W |
| Armant | 109 | 25.37N | 32.32 E |
| Armavir | 86 | 45.00N | 41.08 E |
| Armenia □[1] | 86 | 40.00N | 45.00 E |
| Armentières | 92 | 50.41N | 2.53 E |
| Arnhem | 90 | 51.59N | 5.55 E |
| Arnhem Land ◆[1] | 122 | 13.10S | 134.30 E |
| Arran, Island of I | 88 | 55.35N | 5.15W |
| Arras | 92 | 50.17N | 2.47 E |
| Ar-Riyāḍ (Riyadh) | 108 | 24.38N | 46.43 E |
| Ar-Rub' al-Khālī ◆[2] | 108 | 20.00N | 51.00 E |
| Artemisa | 130 | 22.49N | 82.46W |
| Artesia | 128 | 32.50N | 104.24W |
| Aru, Kepulauan II | 118 | 6.00S | 134.30 E |
| Aruba □[2] | 130 | 12.30N | 69.58W |
| Arunachal Pradesh □[8] | 112 | 28.30N | 95.00 E |
| Arusha | 106 | 3.22S | 36.41 E |
| Aruwimi ≃ | 106 | 1.13N | 23.36 E |
| Asahikawa | 116a | 43.46N | 142.22 E |
| Asansol | 112 | 23.41N | 86.59 E |
| Asbestos | 140 | 45.46N | 71.57W |
| Ascensión | 128 | 31.06N | 107.59W |
| Aseb | 108 | 13.00N | 42.45 E |
| Asenovgrad | 98 | 42.01N | 24.52 E |
| Ashburton | 126 | 43.55S | 171.45 E |
| Asheville | 138 | 35.36N | 82.33W |
| Ashikaga | 116 | 36.20N | 139.27 E |
| Ashland, Ky., U.S. | 140 | 38.28N | 82.38W |
| Ashland, N.H., U.S. | 140 | 43.41N | 71.37W |
| Ashland, Or., U.S. | 142 | 42.11N | 122.42W |
| Ashland, Wi., U.S. | 138 | 46.35N | 90.53W |

| Name | Page No. | Lat. | Long. |
|---|---|---|---|
| Ashtabula | 140 | 41.51N | 80.47W |
| Ashville | 140 | 39.42N | 82.57W |
| Asia ♠[1] | 82 | 50.00N | 100.00E |
| Asia Minor ✦[1] | 86 | 39.00N | 32.00E |
| Askham | 106 | 26.59S | 20.47E |
| Asmera | 108 | 15.20N | 38.53E |
| Aspiring, Mount ʌ | 126 | 44.23S | 168.44E |
| Assam □[3] | 112 | 26.00N | 92.00E |
| Assen | 90 | 52.59N | 6.34E |
| Assiniboine, Mount ʌ | 136 | 50.52N | 115.39W |
| As-Sulaymānīyah | 86 | 35.33N | 45.26E |
| As-Suwaydā' | 109 | 32.42N | 36.34E |
| As-Suways (Suez) | 104 | 29.58N | 32.33E |
| Asti | 96 | 44.54N | 8.12E |
| Astrachan' | 86 | 46.21N | 48.03E |
| Astrolabe, Cape ➤ | 127a | 8.20S | 160.34E |
| Asunción | 134 | 25.16S | 57.40W |
| Aswān | 104 | 24.05N | 32.53E |
| Aswān High Dam ✦[6] | 108 | 24.05N | 32.53E |
| Asyūṭ | 104 | 27.11N | 31.11E |
| Atacama, Desierto de ✦[2] | 132 | 20.00S | 69.15W |
| Atar | 104 | 20.31N | 13.03W |
| Atbarah | 104 | 17.42N | 33.59E |
| Atbasar | 102 | 51.48N | 68.20E |
| Athabasca | 136 | 54.43N | 113.17W |
| Athabasca, Lake ◎ | 136 | 59.07N | 110.00W |
| Athens, Ga., U.S. | 138 | 33.57N | 83.22W |
| Athens, Oh., U.S. | 140 | 39.19N | 82.06W |
| Athens, Pa., U.S. | 140 | 41.57N | 76.31W |
| Athens → Athínai | 98 | 37.58N | 23.43E |
| Athínai (Athens) | 98 | 37.58N | 23.43E |
| Athlone | 88 | 53.25N | 7.56W |
| Atikokan | 136 | 48.45N | 91.37W |
| Atikonak Lake ◎ | 136 | 52.40N | 64.30W |
| Atka Island I | 144 | 52.15N | 174.30W |
| Atlanta | 138 | 33.44N | 84.23W |
| Atlantic City | 140 | 39.21N | 74.25W |
| Atlantic Ocean ▼[1] | 82 | 0.00 | 25.00W |
| Atlas Mountains ⟋ | 104 | 33.00N | 2.00W |
| Atlas Saharien ⟋ | 104 | 33.25N | 1.20E |
| Atotonilco el Alto | 128 | 20.33N | 102.31W |
| Atrato ≃ | 130 | 8.17N | 76.58W |
| Attawapiskat | 136 | 52.55N | 82.26W |
| Attu Island I | 144 | 52.55N | 173.00E |
| Auburn | 140 | 42.55N | 76.33W |
| Auckland | 126 | 36.52S | 174.46E |
| Augsburg | 90 | 48.23N | 10.53E |
| Augusta, Austl. | 122 | 34.19S | 115.10E |
| Augusta, Italy | 96 | 37.13N | 15.13E |
| Augusta, Ga., U.S. | 138 | 33.28N | 82.01W |
| Augusta, Ky., U.S. | 140 | 38.46N | 84.00W |
| Augusta, Me., U.S. | 140 | 44.18N | 69.46W |
| Augustus, Mount ʌ | 122 | 24.20S | 116.50E |
| Aurillac | 92 | 44.56N | 2.26E |
| Aurora | 140 | 44.00N | 79.28W |
| Aus | 106 | 26.40S | 16.15E |
| Austin | 138 | 30.16N | 97.44W |
| Australia □[1] | 122 | 25.00S | 135.00E |
| Australian Capital Territory □[8] | 124 | 35.30S | 149.00E |
| Austria □[1] | 86 | 47.20N | 13.20E |
| Autlán de Navarro | 128 | 19.46N | 104.22W |
| Auvergne □[9] | 92 | 45.25N | 2.30E |
| Auxerre | 92 | 47.48N | 3.34E |
| Aveiro | 94 | 40.38N | 8.39W |
| Avellino | 96 | 40.54N | 14.47E |
| Avesta | 89 | 60.09N | 16.12E |
| Avezzano | 96 | 42.02N | 13.25E |
| Avignon | 92 | 43.57N | 4.49E |
| Ávila | 94 | 40.39N | 4.42W |
| Avilés | 94 | 43.33N | 5.55W |
| Avon | 140 | 42.54N | 77.44W |
| Axiós (Vardar) ≃ | 98 | 40.31N | 22.43E |
| Aydın | 98 | 37.51N | 27.51E |
| Ayeyarwady ≃ | 120 | 15.50N | 95.06E |
| Aylmer West | 140 | 42.46N | 80.59W |
| Ayr | 88 | 55.28N | 4.38W |
| Azerbaijan □[1] | 86 | 40.30N | 47.30E |
| Azogues | 132 | 2.44S | 78.50W |
| Azores → Açores II | 82 | 38.30N | 28.00W |
| Azovskoje More ▼[2] | 86 | 46.00N | 36.00E |
| Azraq, Al-Bahr al- (Blue Nile) ≃ | 104 | 15.38N | 32.31E |
| Azua | 130 | 18.27N | 70.44W |
| Azuaga | 94 | 38.16N | 5.41W |
| Azuero, Península de ➤[1] | 130 | 7.40N | 80.35W |
| Azul | 134 | 36.47S | 59.51W |
| Az-Zaqāzīq | 104 | 30.35N | 31.31E |
| Az-Zarqā' | 109 | 32.05N | 36.06E |

**B**

| Name | Page No. | Lat. | Long. |
|---|---|---|---|
| Babaeski | 98 | 41.26N | 27.06E |
| Babelthuap I | 118 | 7.30N | 134.36E |
| Babuyan Islands II | 118 | 19.10N | 121.40E |
| Bacău | 98 | 46.34N | 26.55E |
| Bac-lieu (Vinh-loi) | 120 | 9.17N | 105.44E |
| Bacolod | 118 | 10.40N | 122.57E |
| Badajoz | 94 | 38.53N | 6.58W |
| Badalona | 94 | 41.27N | 2.15E |
| Baden, Aus. | 90 | 48.00N | 16.14E |
| Baden, Switz. | 92 | 47.29N | 8.18E |
| Baden-Baden | 90 | 48.46N | 8.14E |
| Bad Ischl | 90 | 47.43N | 13.37E |
| Bad Kreuznach | 90 | 49.52N | 7.51E |
| Baffin Bay c | 136 | 73.00N | 66.00W |
| Baffin Island I | 136 | 68.00N | 70.00W |
| Bāgalkot | 111 | 16.11N | 75.42E |
| Bagdad → Baghdād | 108 | 33.21N | 44.25E |
| Bagé | 134 | 31.20S | 54.06W |
| Baghdād | 108 | 33.21N | 44.25E |
| Bagheria | 96 | 38.05N | 13.30E |
| Baghlān | 112 | 36.13N | 68.46E |
| Bago | 120 | 17.20N | 96.29E |
| Baguio | 118 | 16.25N | 120.36E |
| Bahamas □[1] | 130 | 24.15N | 76.00W |
| Bahāwalnagar | 112 | 29.59N | 73.16E |
| Bahāwalpur | 110 | 29.24N | 71.41E |
| Bahía, Islas de la II | 130 | 16.20N | 86.30W |
| Bahía Blanca | 134 | 38.43S | 62.17W |
| Bahrain □[1] | 108 | 26.00N | 50.30E |
| Baia-Mare | 98 | 47.40N | 23.35E |
| Baie-Comeau | 136 | 49.13N | 68.10W |
| Baie-Saint-Paul | 136 | 47.27N | 70.30W |
| Băilești | 98 | 44.02N | 23.21E |
| Baja | 90 | 46.11N | 18.57E |
| Baja California ➤[1] | 128 | 28.00N | 113.30W |
| Bajkal, Ozero (Lake Baikal) ◎ | 102 | 53.00N | 107.40E |
| Baker, Mt., U.S. | 138 | 46.22N | 104.17W |
| Baker, Or., U.S. | 138 | 44.46N | 117.49W |
| Baker Lake | 136 | 64.15N | 96.00W |
| Bakersfield | 142 | 35.22N | 119.01W |
| Bakhtaran | 108 | 34.19N | 47.04E |
| Baku | 86 | 40.23N | 49.51E |
| Balakovo | 86 | 52.02N | 47.47E |
| Balaton ◎ | 90 | 46.50N | 17.45E |
| Balchaš | 102 | 46.49N | 74.59E |
| Balchaš, Ozero ◎ | 102 | 46.00N | 74.00E |
| Baleares, Islas (Balearic Islands) II | 94 | 39.30N | 3.00E |
| Bâle → Basel | 92 | 47.33N | 7.35E |
| Bali I | 118 | 8.20S | 115.00E |
| Balikesir | 98 | 39.39N | 27.53E |
| Balikpapan | 118 | 1.17S | 116.50E |
| Balkan Mountains → Stara Planina ⟋ | 98 | 43.15N | 25.00E |

| Name | Page No. | Lat. | Long. | Name | Page No. | Lat. | Long. |
|---|---|---|---|---|---|---|---|
| Ballina | 88 | 54.07N | 9.09W | Barrie | 140 | 44.24N | 79.40W |
| Ballinger | 128 | 31.44N | 99.56W | Barrow, Point ≻ | 144 | 71.23N | 156.30W |
| Balmoral Castle | 88 | 57.02N | 3.15W | Barrow Creek | 122 | 21.33S | 133.53 E |
| Balsas ≏ | 128 | 17.55N | 102.10W | Barrow-in-Furness | 88 | 54.07N | 3.14W |
| Baltic Sea ᵀ² | 89 | 57.00N | 19.00 E | Barstow | 142 | 34.53N | 117.01W |
| Baltimore | 140 | 39.17N | 76.36W | Barú, Volcán ▲¹ | 130 | 8.48N | 82.33W |
| Baluchistan □⁹ | 110 | 28.00N | 63.00 E | Basatongwula Shan ▲ | 114 | 33.05N | 91.30 E |
| Bamako | 104 | 12.39N | 8.00W | Basel (Bâle) | 92 | 47.33N | 7.35 E |
| Bambari | 104 | 5.45N | 20.40 E | Baskatong, Réservoir ⊜¹ | 136 | 46.48N | 75.50W |
| Bamenda | 104 | 5.56N | 10.10 E | Basseterre | 130 | 17.18N | 62.43W |
| Banbury | 88 | 52.04N | 1.20W | Basse-Terre I | 130 | 16.10N | 61.40W |
| Banda, Laut (Banda Sea) ᵀ² | 118 | 5.00S | 128.00 E | Bass Harbor | 140 | 44.14N | 68.20W |
| Banda Aceh | 118 | 5.34N | 95.20 E | Bass Strait ⋃ | 124 | 39.20S | 145.30 E |
| Bandar-e 'Abbās | 108 | 27.11N | 56.17 E | Bastia | 92 | 42.42N | 9.27 E |
| Bandar Seri Begawan | 118 | 4.56N | 114.55 E | Bastogne | 90 | 50.00N | 5.43 E |
| Bandırma | 98 | 40.20N | 27.58 E | Bastrop | 128 | 32.46N | 91.54W |
| Bandon | 142 | 43.07N | 124.24W | Batabanó, Golfo de c | 130 | 22.15N | 82.30W |
| Bandundu | 106 | 3.18S | 17.20 E | Batamaj | 102 | 63.31N | 129.27 E |
| Bandung | 118 | 6.54S | 107.36 E | Batan Islands II | 118 | 20.30N | 121.50 E |
| Banes | 130 | 20.58N | 75.43W | Batatais | 135 | 20.53S | 47.37W |
| Bangalore | 111 | 12.59N | 77.35 E | Batavia | 140 | 42.59N | 78.11W |
| Bangassou | 104 | 4.50N | 23.07 E | Bātdâmbâng | 120 | 13.06N | 103.12 E |
| Banggai, Kepulauan II | 118 | 1.30S | 123.15 E | Bath, Eng., U.K. | 88 | 51.23N | 2.22W |
| Banghāzī | 104 | 32.07N | 20.04 E | Bath, Me., U.S. | 140 | 43.54N | 69.49W |
| Bangkok<br>→ Krung Thep | 120 | 13.45N | 100.31 E | Bath, N.Y., U.S. | 140 | 42.20N | 77.19W |
| Bangladesh □¹ | 110 | 24.00N | 90.00 E | Bathurst | 136 | 47.36N | 65.39W |
| Bangor, N. Ire., U.K. | 88 | 54.40N | 5.40W | Bathurst Island I, Austl. | 122 | 11.37S | 130.27 E |
| Bangor, Wales, U.K. | 88 | 53.13N | 4.08W | Bathurst Island I, N.T., Can. | 136 | 76.00N | 100.30W |
| Bangor, Me., U.S. | 140 | 44.48N | 68.46W | Batna | 104 | 35.34N | 6.11 E |
| Bangui | 104 | 4.22N | 18.35 E | Baton Rouge | 138 | 30.27N | 91.09W |
| Bani ≏ | 104 | 14.30N | 4.12W | Batouri | 104 | 4.26N | 14.22 E |
| Banī Mazār | 104 | 28.30N | 30.48 E | Battle Creek | 140 | 42.19N | 85.10W |
| Banī Suwayf | 104 | 29.05N | 31.05 E | Battle Harbour | 136 | 52.16N | 55.35W |
| Banja Luka | 96 | 44.46N | 17.11 E | Battle Mountain | 142 | 40.38N | 116.56W |
| Banjarmasin | 118 | 3.20S | 114.35 E | Batumi | 86 | 41.38N | 41.38 E |
| Banjul | 104 | 13.28N | 16.39W | Bauru | 132 | 22.19S | 49.04W |
| Banks Island I | 136 | 73.15N | 121.30W | Bautzen | 90 | 51.11N | 14.26 E |
| Banks Islands II | 127b | 13.50S | 167.30 E | Bayamo | 130 | 20.23N | 76.39W |
| Banks Peninsula ≻¹ | 126 | 43.45S | 173.00 E | Bay City, Mi., U.S. | 140 | 43.35N | 83.53W |
| Bannu | 112 | 32.59N | 70.36 E | Bay City, Tx., U.S. | 138 | 28.58N | 95.58W |
| Ban Pak Phraek | 120 | 8.13N | 100.12 E | Baydhaoo | 108 | 3.04N | 43.48 E |
| Banská Bystrica | 90 | 48.44N | 19.07 E | Bayerische Alpen ⋏ | 90 | 47.30N | 11.00 E |
| Baoding | 114 | 38.52N | 115.29 E | Bayonne | 92 | 43.29N | 1.29W |
| Baoji | 114 | 34.22N | 107.14 E | Bayreuth | 90 | 49.57N | 11.35 E |
| Baotou | 114 | 40.40N | 109.59 E | Bayrūt (Beirut) | 109 | 33.53N | 35.30 E |
| Baquedano | 134 | 23.20S | 69.51W | Bay Shore | 140 | 40.43N | 73.14W |
| Baraawe | 108 | 1.05N | 44.02 E | Be, Nosy I | 106 | 13.20S | 48.15 E |
| Barbacena | 135 | 21.14S | 43.46W | Beatrice | 138 | 40.16N | 96.44W |
| Barbados □¹ | 130 | 13.10N | 59.32W | Beatty | 142 | 36.54N | 116.45W |
| Barbaros | 98 | 40.54N | 27.27 E | Beaufort Sea ᵀ² | 84 | 73.00N | 140.00W |
| Barbas, Cabo ≻ | 104 | 22.18N | 16.41W | Beaufort West | 106 | 32.18S | 22.36 E |
| Barbuda I | 130 | 17.38N | 61.48W | Beaumont, N.Z. | 126 | 45.49S | 169.32 E |
| Barcelona, Mex. | 128 | 26.12N | 103.25W | Beaumont, Tx., U.S. | 138 | 30.05N | 94.06W |
| Barcelona, Spain | 94 | 41.23N | 2.11 E | Beautemps-Beaupré, Île I | 127b | 20.24S | 166.09 E |
| Barcelona, Ven. | 130 | 10.08N | 64.42W | Beaver Falls | 140 | 40.45N | 80.19W |
| Bardufoss | 89 | 69.04N | 18.30 E | Bečej | 98 | 45.37N | 20.03 E |
| Bareilly | 112 | 28.21N | 79.25 E | Béchar | 104 | 31.37N | 2.13W |
| Barents Sea ᵀ² | 84 | 74.00N | 36.00 E | Beckley | 140 | 37.46N | 81.11W |
| Bar Harbor | 140 | 44.23N | 68.12W | Be'er Sheva' | 109 | 31.14N | 34.47 E |
| Bari | 96 | 41.07N | 16.52 E | Beeville | 128 | 28.24N | 97.44W |
| Barinas | 130 | 8.38N | 70.12W | Beian | 114 | 48.15N | 126.30 E |
| Barīsāl | 112 | 22.42N | 90.22 E | Beihai | 114 | 21.29N | 109.05 E |
| Barlee, Lake ⊜ | 122 | 29.10S | 119.30 E | Beijing (Peking) | 114 | 39.55N | 116.25 E |
| Barletta | 96 | 41.19N | 16.17 E | Beira | 106 | 19.49S | 34.52 E |
| Barmouth | 88 | 52.43N | 4.03W | Beirut<br>→ Bayrūt | 109 | 33.53N | 35.30 E |
| Barnaul | 102 | 53.22N | 83.45 E | Beja, Port. | 94 | 38.01N | 7.52W |
| Barnegat | 140 | 39.45N | 74.13W | Béja, Tun. | 104 | 36.44N | 9.11 E |
| Baroda | 112 | 22.18N | 73.12 E | Bejaïa | 104 | 36.45N | 5.05 E |
| Barqah (Cyrenaica) ◆¹ | 104 | 31.00N | 22.30 E | Békéscsaba | 90 | 46.41N | 21.06 E |
| Barquisimeto | 132 | 10.04N | 69.19W | Belarus □¹ | 86 | 53.00N | 28.00 E |
| Barra Falsa, Ponta da ≻ | 106 | 22.55S | 35.37 E | Belcher Islands II | 136 | 56.20N | 79.30W |
| Barranquilla | 132 | 10.59N | 74.48W | Beled Weyne | 108 | 4.47N | 45.12 E |
| Barre | 140 | 44.11N | 72.30W | | | | |
| Barreiro | 94 | 38.40N | 9.04W | | | | |
| Barretos | 132 | 20.33S | 48.33W | | | | |

| Name | Page No. | Lat. | Long. |
|---|---|---|---|
| Bluffton | 140 | 40.44N | 85.10W |
| Blumenau | 134 | 26.56S | 49.03W |
| Blyth | 88 | 55.07N | 1.30W |
| Blythe | 142 | 33.36N | 114.35W |
| Blytheville | 138 | 35.55N | 89.55W |
| Boa Vista | 132 | 2.49N | 60.40W |
| Bobcaygeon | 140 | 44.33N | 78.33W |
| Bobo Dioulasso | 104 | 11.12N | 4.18W |
| Bobrujsk | 100 | 53.09N | 29.14 E |
| Boby, Pic ▲ | 106 | 22.12S | 46.55 E |
| Bocas del Toro | 130 | 9.20N | 82.15W |
| Bocholt | 90 | 51.50N | 6.36 E |
| Bochum | 90 | 51.28N | 7.13 E |
| Bodele ◆¹ | 104 | 16.30N | 16.30 E |
| Boden | 89 | 65.50N | 21.42 E |
| Bodensee ᴓ | 90 | 47.35N | 9.25 E |
| Bodø | 89 | 67.17N | 14.23 E |
| Bogalusa | 128 | 30.47N | 89.50W |
| Bogenfels | 106 | 27.23S | 15.22 E |
| Bogor | 118 | 6.35S | 106.47 E |
| Bogotá → Santa Fe de Bogotá | 132 | 4.36N | 74.05W |
| Bohai ᴄ | 114 | 38.30N | 120.00 E |
| Bohemian Forest ⚔ | 90 | 49.15N | 12.45 E |
| Boise | 138 | 43.36N | 116.12W |
| Boise, South Fork ≃ | 142 | 43.36N | 115.51W |
| Bola | 127a | 9.37S | 160.39 E |
| Bolesławiec | 90 | 51.16N | 15.34 E |
| Bolívar, Cerro ▲ | 130 | 7.28N | 63.25W |
| Bolívar, Pico ▲ | 132 | 8.30N | 71.02W |
| Bolivia □¹ | 132 | 17.00S | 65.00W |
| Bollnäs | 89 | 61.21N | 16.25 E |
| Bologna | 96 | 44.29N | 11.20 E |
| Bol'ševik, Ostrov I | 102 | 78.40N | 102.30 E |
| Bol'šoj L'achovskij, Ostrov I | 102 | 73.35N | 142.00 E |
| Bolzano (Bozen) | 96 | 46.31N | 11.22 E |
| Boma | 106 | 5.51S | 13.03 E |
| Bombay | 111 | 18.58N | 72.50 E |
| Bomu (Mbomou) ≃ | 104 | 4.08N | 22.26 E |
| Bonaire I | 130 | 12.10N | 68.15W |
| Bonarbridge | 88 | 57.53N | 4.21W |
| Bonavista | 136 | 48.39N | 53.07W |
| Bône → Annaba | 104 | 36.54N | 7.46 E |
| Bonn | 90 | 50.44N | 7.05 E |
| Boonville | 140 | 43.29N | 75.20W |
| Boothia, Gulf of ᴄ | 136 | 71.00N | 91.00W |
| Bora-Bora I | 127d | 16.30S | 151.45W |
| Boraha, Nosy I | 106 | 16.50S | 49.55 E |
| Borås | 89 | 57.43N | 12.55 E |
| Bordeaux | 92 | 44.50N | 0.34W |
| Bordertown | 122 | 36.19S | 140.47 E |
| Bordj Bou Arreridj | 94 | 36.04N | 4.46 E |
| Bordj Omar Idriss | 104 | 28.09N | 6.43 E |
| Borisoglebsk | 86 | 51.23N | 42.06 E |
| Borlänge | 89 | 60.29N | 15.25 E |
| Borneo (Kalimantan) I | 118 | 0.30N | 114.00 E |
| Bornholm I | 89 | 55.10N | 15.00 E |
| Boronga Islands II | 120 | 19.58N | 93.06 E |
| Borovici | 100 | 58.24N | 33.55 E |
| Borz'a | 102 | 50.38N | 115.38 E |
| Boshan | 114 | 36.29N | 117.50 E |
| Bosnia and Hercegovina □¹ | 96 | 44.15N | 17.50 E |
| Bosporus → İstanbul Boğazı ᴜ | 98 | 41.06N | 29.04 E |
| Boston | 140 | 42.21N | 71.03W |
| Botev ▲ | 98 | 42.43N | 24.55 E |
| Bothnia, Gulf of ᴄ | 89 | 63.00N | 20.00 E |
| Botoşani | 98 | 47.45N | 26.40 E |
| Botswana □¹ | 106 | 22.00S | 24.00 E |
| Bottenhavet (Selkämeri) ᴄ | 89 | 62.00N | 20.00 E |
| Botwood | 136 | 49.09N | 55.21W |
| Bouaké | 104 | 7.41N | 5.02W |
| Bouar | 104 | 5.57N | 15.36 E |
| Bougainville I | 127a | 6.00S | 155.00 E |
| Bougainville Strait ᴜ | 127a | 6.40S | 156.10 E |
| Bouillon | 90 | 49.48N | 5.04 E |
| Boulder | 138 | 40.00N | 105.16W |
| Boulogne-sur-Mer | 92 | 50.43N | 1.37 E |
| Bouloupari | 127b | 21.52S | 166.04 E |
| Boundary Peak ▲ | 142 | 37.51N | 118.21W |
| Bourail | 127b | 21.34S | 165.30 E |
| Bourges | 92 | 47.05N | 2.24 E |
| Bourgogne □⁹ | 92 | 47.00N | 4.30 E |
| Bourke | 122 | 30.05S | 145.56 E |
| Bournemouth | 88 | 50.43N | 1.54W |
| Bøvågen | 89 | 60.40N | 4.58 E |
| Bøverdal | 89 | 61.43N | 8.21 E |
| Bowie | 140 | 39.00N | 76.46W |
| Bowling Green, Ky., U.S. | 138 | 36.59N | 86.26W |
| Bowling Green, Oh., U.S. | 140 | 41.22N | 83.39W |
| Bowling Green, Va., U.S. | 140 | 38.02N | 77.20W |
| Boyoma Falls (Stanley Falls) ᴸ | 106 | 0.15N | 25.30 E |
| Brač, Otok I | 96 | 43.20N | 16.40 E |
| Brad | 98 | 46.08N | 22.47 E |
| Bradford, On., Can. | 140 | 44.07N | 79.34W |
| Bradford, Pa., U.S. | 140 | 41.57N | 78.38W |
| Braga | 94 | 41.33N | 8.26W |
| Bragança | 94 | 41.49N | 6.45W |
| Brāhmanbāria | 112 | 23.59N | 91.07 E |
| Brahmaputra (Yaluzangbujiang) ≃ | 112 | 24.02N | 90.59 E |
| Brăila | 98 | 45.16N | 27.58 E |
| Brainerd | 138 | 46.21N | 94.12W |
| Branco ≃ | 132 | 1.24S | 61.51W |
| Brandberg ▲ | 106 | 21.10S | 14.33 E |
| Brandenburg | 90 | 52.24N | 12.32 E |
| Brandenburg □⁹ | 90 | 52.00N | 13.30 E |
| Br'ansk | 100 | 53.15N | 34.22 E |
| Brantford | 140 | 43.08N | 80.16W |
| Brasília | 132 | 15.47S | 47.55W |
| Braşov | 98 | 45.39N | 25.37 E |
| Brateş, Lacul ᴓ | 98 | 45.30N | 28.05 E |
| Bratislava | 90 | 48.09N | 17.07 E |
| Bratsk | 102 | 56.05N | 101.48 E |
| Brattleboro | 140 | 42.51N | 72.33W |
| Braunschweig | 90 | 52.16N | 10.31 E |
| Bravo del Norte (Rio Grande) ≃ | 138 | 25.55N | 97.09W |
| Brawley | 142 | 32.58N | 115.31W |
| Brazil □¹ | 132 | 10.00S | 55.00W |
| Brazzaville | 106 | 4.16S | 5.17 E |
| Breda | 90 | 51.35N | 4.46 E |
| Bremen | 90 | 53.04N | 8.49 E |
| Bremerhaven | 90 | 53.33N | 8.34 E |
| Brenner Pass )( | 92 | 47.00N | 11.30 E |
| Brescia | 96 | 45.33N | 13.15 E |
| Brest, Bela. | 100 | 52.06N | 23.42 E |
| Brest, Fr. | 92 | 48.24N | 4.29W |
| Bretagne □⁹ | 92 | 48.00N | 3.00W |
| Bridgeport | 140 | 41.10N | 73.12W |
| Bridgeton | 140 | 39.25N | 75.14W |
| Bridgetown | 130 | 13.06N | 59.37W |
| Bridgeville | 140 | 38.44N | 75.36W |
| Brighton | 88 | 50.50N | 0.08W |
| Brindisi | 96 | 40.38N | 17.56 E |
| Brisbane | 122 | 27.28S | 153.02 E |
| Bristol, Eng., U.K. | 88 | 51.27N | 2.35W |
| Bristol, Ct., U.S. | 140 | 41.41N | 72.57W |
| Bristol Bay ᴄ | 144 | 58.00N | 159.00W |
| British Columbia □⁴ | 136 | 54.00N | 125.00W |
| Brno | 90 | 49.12N | 16.37 E |
| Brochet | 136 | 57.53N | 101.40W |
| Brockton | 140 | 42.05N | 71.01W |
| Brockville | 140 | 44.35N | 75.41W |
| Broken Hill | 122 | 31.57S | 141.27 E |

| Name | Page No. | Lat. | Long. |
|------|----------|------|-------|
| Chang (Yangtze) ≃ | 114 | 31.48N | 121.10 E |
| Changchun | 114 | 43.53N | 125.19 E |
| Changsha | 114 | 28.11N | 113.01 E |
| Changzhi | 114 | 36.11N | 113.08 E |
| Chanka, Ozero (Xingkathu) ⊜ | 114 | 45.00N | 132.24 E |
| Channel Islands II, Eur. | 92 | 49.20N | 2.20W |
| Channel Islands II, Ca., U.S. | 142 | 34.00N | 120.00W |
| Channel-Port-aux-Basques | 136 | 47.34N | 59.09W |
| Chanthaburi | 120 | 12.36N | 102.09 E |
| Chao Phraya ≃ | 120 | 13.32N | 100.36 E |
| Chapala, Lago de ⊜ | 128 | 20.15N | 103.00W |
| Chapmanville | 140 | 37.58N | 82.01W |
| Charcas | 128 | 23.08N | 101.07W |
| Charente ≃ | 92 | 45.57N | 1.05W |
| Chari ≃ | 104 | 12.58N | 14.31 E |
| Charity | 132 | 7.24N | 58.36W |
| Char'kov | 86 | 50.00N | 36.15 E |
| Charleroi | 90 | 50.25N | 4.26 E |
| Charleston, S.C., U.S. | 138 | 32.46N | 79.55W |
| Charleston, W.V., U.S. | 140 | 38.20N | 81.37W |
| Charleston Peak ʌ | 142 | 36.16N | 115.42W |
| Charleville | 122 | 26.24S | 146.15 E |
| Charlotte | 138 | 35.13N | 80.50W |
| Charlotte Amalie | 130 | 18.21N | 64.56W |
| Charlottesville | 140 | 38.01N | 78.28W |
| Charlottetown | 136 | 46.14N | 63.08W |
| Chārsadda | 112 | 34.09N | 71.44 E |
| Chartres | 92 | 48.27N | 1.30 E |
| Chatanga | 102 | 71.58N | 102.30 E |
| Châtellerault | 92 | 46.49N | 0.33 E |
| Chatham | 140 | 42.24N | 82.11W |
| Chattahoochee ≃ | 138 | 30.52N | 84.57W |
| Chattanooga | 138 | 35.02N | 85.18W |
| Chauk | 120 | 20.54N | 94.50 E |
| Chau-phu | 120 | 10.42N | 105.07 E |
| Chaves | 94 | 41.44N | 7.28W |
| Cheb | 90 | 50.01N | 12.25 E |
| Cheboygan | 140 | 45.38N | 84.28W |
| Chech, Erg ◆² | 104 | 25.00N | 2.15W |
| Cheju-do I | 114 | 33.20N | 126.30 E |
| Chełm | 90 | 51.10N | 23.28 E |
| Chelmsford | 88 | 51.44N | 0.28 E |
| Chelyabinsk → Čel'abinsk | 86 | 55.10N | 61.24 E |
| Chemnitz | 90 | 50.50N | 12.55 E |
| Chénéville | 140 | 45.53N | 75.03W |
| Chengde | 114 | 40.58N | 117.53 E |
| Chengdu | 114 | 30.39N | 104.04 E |
| Chepo | 130 | 9.10N | 79.06W |
| Cher ≃ | 92 | 47.21N | 0.29 E |
| Cherbourg | 92 | 49.39N | 1.39W |
| Cherson | 86 | 46.38N | 32.35 E |
| Chesapeake Bay c | 140 | 38.40N | 76.25W |
| Chesapeake Beach | 140 | 38.41N | 76.32W |
| Chester | 140 | 39.50N | 75.21W |
| Chesterfield, Îles II | 122 | 19.30S | 158.00 E |
| Chesterfield Inlet | 136 | 63.21N | 90.42W |
| Chesuncook Lake ⊜ | 140 | 46.00N | 69.20W |
| Cheyenne | 138 | 41.08N | 104.49W |
| Chiang Mai | 120 | 18.47N | 98.59 E |
| Chiang Rai | 120 | 19.54N | 99.50 E |
| Chiautla de Tapia | 128 | 18.17N | 98.36W |
| Chiba | 116 | 35.36N | 140.07 E |
| Chibougamau | 136 | 49.55N | 74.22W |
| Chicago | 138 | 41.51N | 87.39W |
| Chichagof Island I | 144 | 57.30N | 135.30W |
| Chichén Itzá | 128 | 20.40N | 88.34W |
| Chiclayo | 132 | 6.46S | 79.51W |
| Chico | 142 | 39.43N | 121.50W |
| Chicoutimi | 136 | 48.26N | 71.04W |
| Chidley, Cape ⊁ | 136 | 60.23N | 64.26W |
| Chieti | 96 | 42.21N | 14.10 E |
| Chigasaki | 116 | 35.19N | 139.24 E |
| Chihuahua | 128 | 28.38N | 106.05W |
| Chile □¹ | 134 | 30.00S | 71.00W |
| Chillicothe | 140 | 39.19N | 82.58W |
| Chiloé, Isla de I | 134 | 42.30S | 73.55W |
| Chilpancingo [de los Bravos] | 128 | 17.33N | 99.30W |
| Chimborazo ʌ¹ | 132 | 1.28S | 78.48W |
| Chimbote | 132 | 9.05S | 78.36W |
| China □¹ | 114 | 35.00N | 105.00 E |
| Chinandega | 130 | 12.37N | 87.09W |
| Chindwinn ≃ | 120 | 21.26N | 95.15 E |
| Chinhoyi | 106 | 17.22S | 30.12 E |
| Chinko ≃ | 104 | 4.50N | 23.53 E |
| Chioggia | 96 | 45.13N | 12.17 E |
| Chirāla | 111 | 15.49N | 80.21 E |
| Chiricahua National Monument ♦ | 128 | 32.02N | 109.19W |
| Chiriquí, Golfo c | 130 | 8.00N | 82.20W |
| Chirripó, Cerro ʌ | 130 | 9.29N | 83.30W |
| Chisasibi | 136 | 53.50N | 79.00W |
| Chittagong | 112 | 22.20N | 91.50 E |
| Choapan | 128 | 17.20N | 95.57W |
| Choele-Choel | 134 | 39.16S | 65.41W |
| Choiseul I | 127a | 7.05S | 157.00 E |
| Chomutov | 90 | 50.28N | 13.26 E |
| Chon Buri | 120 | 13.22N | 100.59 E |
| Ch'ŏngjin | 114 | 41.47N | 129.50 E |
| Chongqing | 114 | 29.39N | 106.34 E |
| Chŏnju | 114 | 35.49N | 127.08 E |
| Chonos, Archipiélago de los II | 134 | 45.00S | 74.00W |
| Chōshi | 116 | 35.44N | 140.50 E |
| Chos Malal | 134 | 37.23S | 70.16W |
| Chovd | 114 | 48.01N | 91.38 E |
| Christchurch | 126 | 43.32S | 172.38 E |
| Christmas Island □² | 118 | 10.30S | 105.40 E |
| Chukchi Sea ⊤² | 84 | 69.00N | 171.00W |
| Chula Vista | 142 | 32.38N | 117.05W |
| Chum Saeng | 120 | 15.54N | 100.19 E |
| Chungking → Chongqing | 114 | 29.39N | 106.34 E |
| Chur | 92 | 46.51N | 9.32 E |
| Churchill | 136 | 58.46N | 94.10W |
| Churchill ≃ | 136 | 58.47N | 94.12W |
| Churchill Lake ⊜ | 136 | 55.55N | 108.20W |
| Ciego de Avila | 130 | 21.51N | 78.46W |
| Ciénaga | 130 | 11.01N | 74.15W |
| Cienfuegos | 130 | 22.09N | 80.27W |
| Cieza | 94 | 38.14N | 1.25W |
| Čimkent | 110 | 42.18N | 69.36 E |
| Cincinnati | 140 | 39.09N | 84.27W |
| Çirebon | 118 | 6.44S | 108.34 E |
| Čita | 102 | 52.03N | 113.30 E |
| Citrus Heights | 142 | 38.42N | 121.16W |
| Ciudad Acuña | 128 | 29.18N | 100.55W |
| Ciudad Anáhuac | 128 | 27.14N | 100.09W |
| Ciudad Bolívar | 132 | 8.08N | 63.33W |
| Ciudad Camargo | 128 | 26.19N | 98.50W |
| Ciudad Chetumal | 128 | 18.30N | 88.18W |
| Ciudad del Carmen | 128 | 18.38N | 91.50W |
| Ciudad de México (Mexico City) | 128 | 19.24N | 99.09W |
| Ciudad de Valles | 128 | 21.59N | 99.01W |
| Ciudad de Villaldama | 128 | 26.30N | 100.26W |
| Ciudad Guayana | 132 | 8.22N | 62.40W |
| Ciudad Guerrero | 128 | 28.33N | 107.30W |
| Ciudad Ixtepec | 128 | 16.34N | 95.06W |
| Ciudad Jiménez | 128 | 27.08N | 104.55W |
| Ciudad Juárez | 128 | 31.44N | 106.29W |
| Ciudad Madero | 128 | 22.16N | 97.50W |
| Ciudad Mante | 128 | 22.44N | 98.57W |
| Ciudad Melchor Múzquiz | 128 | 27.53N | 101.31W |
| Ciudad Obregón | 128 | 27.29N | 109.56W |
| Ciudad Ojeda | 130 | 10.12N | 71.19W |
| Ciudad Real | 94 | 38.59N | 3.56W |
| Ciudad Victoria | 128 | 23.44N | 99.08W |
| Clanwilliam | 106 | 32.11S | 18.54 E |

| Name | Page No. | Lat. | Long. |
|---|---|---|---|
| Denver | 138 | 39.44N | 104.59W |
| Dera Ghāzi Khān | 110 | 30.03N | 70.38 E |
| Dera Ismāīl Khān | 112 | 31.50N | 70.54 E |
| Derby | 88 | 52.55N | 1.29W |
| Derby Line | 140 | 45.00N | 72.05W |
| Dese | 108 | 11.05N | 39.41 E |
| Des Moines | 138 | 41.36N | 93.36W |
| Des Moines ≃ | 138 | 40.22N | 91.26W |
| Dessau | 90 | 51.50N | 12.14 E |
| Detmold | 90 | 51.56N | 8.52 E |
| Detroit | 140 | 42.20N | 83.03W |
| Deutsche Bucht c | 90 | 54.30N | 7.30 E |
| Deva | 98 | 45.53N | 22.55 E |
| Deventer | 90 | 52.15N | 6.10 E |
| Devon Island I | 136 | 75.00N | 87.00W |
| Devonport | 126 | 36.49S | 174.48 E |
| Dexter | 140 | 45.01N | 69.17W |
| Dezfūl | 108 | 32.23N | 48.24 E |
| Dhaka | 112 | 23.43N | 90.25 E |
| Dhodhekánisos (Dodecanese) II | 98 | 36.30N | 27.00 E |
| Dhorāji | 112 | 21.44N | 70.27 E |
| Diable, Île du I | 132 | 5.17N | 52.35W |
| Diablo Range ⋋ | 142 | 37.00N | 121.20W |
| Diamantina | 132 | 18.15S | 43.36W |
| Diamond Peak ⋀ | 142 | 43.33N | 122.09W |
| Dieppe | 92 | 49.56N | 1.05 E |
| Digby | 136 | 44.37N | 65.46W |
| Dijon | 92 | 47.19N | 5.01 E |
| Dili | 118 | 8.33S | 125.35 E |
| Dillingham | 144 | 59.02N | 158.29W |
| Dillon | 138 | 45.12N | 112.38W |
| Dimashq (Damascus) | 109 | 33.30N | 36.18 E |
| Dimitrovgrad | 98 | 42.03N | 25.36 E |
| Dimlang ⋀ | 104 | 8.24N | 11.47 E |
| Dinant | 90 | 50.16N | 4.55 E |
| Dinara (Dinaric Alps) ⋋ | 96 | 43.50N | 16.35 E |
| Dingle | 88 | 52.08N | 10.15W |
| Dingwall | 88 | 57.35N | 4.29W |
| Dire Dawa | 108 | 9.37N | 41.52 E |
| Diriamba | 130 | 11.51N | 86.14W |
| Disappointment, Cape ⋋ | 138 | 46.18N | 124.03W |
| Disappointment, Lake ⊜ | 122 | 23.30S | 122.50 E |
| Diu | 112 | 20.42N | 70.59 E |
| Diu □ ³ | 112 | 20.42N | 70.59 E |
| Divinópolis | 132 | 20.09S | 44.54W |
| Diyarbakir | 86 | 37.55N | 40.14 E |
| Dja ≃ | 104 | 2.02N | 15.12 E |
| Djerba, Île de I | 104 | 33.48N | 10.54 E |
| Djibouti | 108 | 11.36N | 43.09 E |
| Djibouti □ ¹ | 108 | 11.30N | 43.00 E |
| Dnepr ≃ | 86 | 46.30N | 32.18 E |
| Dnepropetrovsk | 86 | 48.27N | 34.59 E |
| Dnestr ≃ | 86 | 46.18N | 30.17 E |
| Doberai, Jazirah ⊁ ¹ | 118 | 1.30S | 132.30 E |
| Dobrič | 98 | 43.34N | 27.50 E |
| Dodecanese → Dhodhekánisos II | 98 | 36.30N | 27.00 E |
| Dodge City | 138 | 37.45N | 100.01W |
| Dodoma | 106 | 6.11S | 35.45 E |
| Doha → Ad-Dawḥah | 108 | 25.17N | 51.32 E |
| Dolbeau | 136 | 48.53N | 72.14W |
| Dolisie | 106 | 4.12S | 12.41 E |
| Dolomiti ⋋ | 96 | 46.25N | 11.50 E |
| Dominica □ ¹ | 130 | 15.30N | 61.20W |
| Dominican Republic □ ¹ | 130 | 19.00N | 70.40W |
| Don ≃ | 86 | 47.04N | 39.18 E |
| Donau → Danube ≃ | 90 | 45.20N | 29.40 E |
| Don Benito | 94 | 38.57N | 5.52W |
| Dondra Head ⊁ | 111 | 5.55N | 80.35 E |
| Doneck | 86 | 48.00N | 37.48 E |
| Donegal | 88 | 54.39N | 8.07W |
| Donga ≃ | 104 | 8.19N | 9.58 E |
| Dongara | 122 | 29.15S | 114.56 E |
| Dongting Hu ⊜ | 114 | 29.20N | 112.54 E |
| Dordogne ≃ | 92 | 45.02N | 0.35W |
| Dordrecht | 90 | 51.49N | 4.40 E |
| Dores do Indaiá | 135 | 19.27S | 45.36W |
| Dortmund | 90 | 51.31N | 7.28 E |
| Dothan | 138 | 31.13N | 85.23W |
| Douala | 104 | 4.03N | 9.42 E |
| Doubtless Bay c | 126 | 34.55S | 173.25 E |
| Douglas | 88 | 54.09N | 4.28W |
| Dourados | 135 | 22.13S | 54.48W |
| Douro (Duero) ≃ | 94 | 41.08N | 8.40W |
| Dover, Eng., U.K. | 88 | 51.08N | 1.19 E |
| Dover, De., U.S. | 140 | 39.09N | 75.31W |
| Dover, N.H., U.S. | 140 | 43.11N | 70.52W |
| Dover, Strait of (Pas de Calais) ⊍ | 92 | 51.00N | 1.30 E |
| Dra'a, Hamada du ⊶ ² | 104 | 29.00N | 6.45W |
| Drâa, Oued ⋁ | 104 | 28.43N | 11.09W |
| Drachten | 90 | 53.06N | 6.05 E |
| Drakensberg ⋋ | 106 | 27.00S | 30.00 E |
| Drake Passage ⊍ | 85 | 58.00S | 70.00W |
| Dráma | 98 | 41.09N | 24.08 E |
| Drammen | 89 | 59.44N | 10.15 E |
| Dranov, Ostrovul I | 98 | 44.52N | 29.15 E |
| Drava (Dráva) (Drau) ≃ | 90 | 45.33N | 18.55 E |
| Dresden | 90 | 51.03N | 13.44 E |
| Drina ≃ | 98 | 44.53N | 19.21 E |
| Drobeta-Turnu-Severin | 98 | 44.38N | 22.39 E |
| Drogheda | 88 | 53.43N | 6.21W |
| Drummondville | 140 | 45.53N | 72.29W |
| Duarte, Pico ⋀ | 130 | 19.02N | 70.59W |
| Dubayy | 108 | 25.18N | 55.18 E |
| Dubbo | 122 | 32.15S | 148.36 E |
| Dublin (Baile Átha Cliath) | 88 | 53.20N | 6.15W |
| Du Bois | 140 | 41.07N | 78.45W |
| Dubrovnik | 98 | 42.38N | 18.07 E |
| Duero (Douro) ≃ | 94 | 41.08N | 8.40W |
| Dufourspitze ⋀ | 92 | 45.55N | 7.52 E |
| Dugi Otok I | 96 | 44.00N | 15.04 E |
| Duisburg | 90 | 51.25N | 6.46 E |
| Duluth | 138 | 46.45N | 92.07W |
| Dumfries | 88 | 55.04N | 3.37W |
| Dumyāṭ | 109 | 31.25N | 31.48 E |
| Duna → Danube ≃ | 90 | 45.20N | 29.40 E |
| Dunaj → Danube ≃ | 90 | 45.20N | 29.40 E |
| Dunaújváros | 90 | 46.58N | 18.57 E |
| Dundalk | 88 | 54.01N | 6.25W |
| Dundee | 88 | 56.28N | 3.00W |
| Dunedin | 126 | 45.52S | 170.30 E |
| Dungarvan | 88 | 52.05N | 7.37W |
| Dunkirk, In., U.S. | 140 | 40.22N | 85.12W |
| Dunkirk, N.Y., U.S. | 140 | 42.28N | 79.20W |
| Dunkirk, Oh., U.S. | 140 | 40.47N | 83.38W |
| Dun Laoghaire | 88 | 53.17N | 6.08W |
| Dunnville | 140 | 42.54N | 79.36W |
| Durance ≃ | 94 | 43.55N | 4.44 E |
| Durango | 128 | 24.02N | 104.40W |
| Durban | 106 | 29.55S | 30.56 E |
| Durham | 140 | 44.10N | 80.49W |
| Durmitor ⋀ | 98 | 43.08N | 19.01 E |
| Durness | 88 | 58.33N | 4.45W |
| Durrësi | 98 | 41.19N | 19.26 E |
| D'Urville Island I | 126 | 40.50S | 173.52 E |
| Dušanbe | 110 | 38.35N | 68.48 E |
| Düsseldorf | 90 | 51.12N | 6.47 E |
| Dzaoudzi | 106 | 12.47S | 45.17 E |
| Dzierżoniów (Reichenbach) | 90 | 50.44N | 16.39 E |

| Name | Page No. | Lat. | Long. |
|---|---|---|---|
| **E** | | | |
| Eagle Pass | 138 | 28.42N | 100.29W |
| East Aurora | 140 | 42.46N | 78.36W |
| East Cape ‣ | 126 | 37.41S | 178.33 E |
| East China Sea ₮² | 114 | 30.00N | 126.00 E |
| Eastern Ghāts ⚹ | 111 | 14.00N | 78.50 E |
| East Falkland ∎ | 134 | 51.55S | 59.00W |
| East Lansing | 140 | 42.44N | 84.29W |
| East Liverpool | 140 | 40.37N | 80.34W |
| East London | | | |
| (Oos-Londen) | 106 | 33.00S | 27.55 E |
| Eastmain | 136 | 52.15N | 78.30W |
| Easton | 140 | 40.41N | 75.13W |
| East Stroudsburg | 140 | 40.59N | 75.10W |
| East Tawas | 140 | 44.16N | 83.29W |
| Eau Claire | 138 | 44.48N | 91.29W |
| Eberswalde | 90 | 52.50N | 13.49 E |
| Ebro ≏ | 94 | 40.43N | 0.54 E |
| Ebro, Delta del ⌣² | 94 | 40.43N | 0.54 E |
| Écija | 94 | 37.32N | 5.05W |
| Ecuador □¹ | 132 | 2.00S | 77.30W |
| Edinburg, Tx., U.S. | 128 | 26.18N | 98.09W |
| Edinburg, Va., U.S. | 140 | 38.49N | 78.33W |
| Edinburgh | 88 | 55.57N | 3.13W |
| Edirne | 98 | 41.40N | 26.34 E |
| Edmonton | 136 | 53.33N | 113.28W |
| Edremit | 98 | 39.35N | 27.01 E |
| Edson | 136 | 53.35N | 116.26W |
| Eel ≏ | 142 | 40.40N | 124.20W |
| Efate ∎ | 127b | 17.40S | 168.25 E |
| Eganville | 140 | 45.32N | 77.06W |
| Eger | 90 | 47.54N | 20.23 E |
| Egypt □¹ | 104 | 27.00N | 30.00 E |
| Eindhoven | 90 | 51.26N | 5.28 E |
| Eisenach | 90 | 50.59N | 10.19 E |
| Eisenhüttenstadt | 90 | 52.10N | 14.39 E |
| Eisenstadt | 90 | 47.51N | 16.32 E |
| Eisleben | 90 | 51.31N | 11.32 E |
| Ekibastuz | 102 | 51.42N | 75.22 E |
| Ekwan ≏ | 136 | 53.14N | 82.13W |
| El Aaiún | 104 | 27.09N | 13.12W |
| El Asnam | | | |
| (Orléansville) | 94 | 36.10N | 1.20 E |
| Elat | 109 | 29.33N | 34.57 E |
| Elba, Isola d' ∎ | 96 | 42.46N | 10.17 E |
| El Banco | 130 | 9.00N | 73.58W |
| Elbasani | 98 | 41.06N | 20.05 E |
| Elbe (Labe) ≏ | 90 | 53.50N | 9.00 E |
| Elbląg (Elbing) | 90 | 54.10N | 19.25 E |
| El'brus, Gora ⋀ | 86 | 43.21N | 42.26 E |
| El Cajon | 142 | 32.47N | 116.57W |
| El Campo | 128 | 29.11N | 96.16W |
| El Capitan ⋀ | 138 | 46.01N | 114.23W |
| Elche | 94 | 38.15N | 0.42W |
| Elda | 94 | 38.29N | 0.47W |
| El Djouf ⬥² | 104 | 20.30N | 8.00W |
| El Dorado | 138 | 33.12N | 92.39W |
| Eldoret | 106 | 0.31N | 35.17 E |
| El Encanto | 132 | 1.37S | 73.14W |
| Elephant Mountain ⋀ | 140 | 44.46N | 70.46W |
| El Estor | 130 | 15.32N | 89.21W |
| Eleuthera ∎ | 130 | 25.10N | 76.14W |
| Elgin | 88 | 57.39N | 3.20W |
| Elizabeth City | 138 | 36.18N | 76.13W |
| Elk | 90 | 53.50N | 22.22 E |
| El Kairouan | 96 | 35.41N | 10.07 E |
| El Kef | 96 | 36.11N | 8.43 E |
| Elkins | 140 | 38.55N | 79.50W |
| Elko | 142 | 40.49N | 115.45W |
| Elk Rapids | 140 | 44.53N | 85.24W |
| Elkton | 140 | 39.36N | 75.50W |
| Ellesmere Island ∎ | 84 | 81.00N | 80.00W |
| Ellsworth | 140 | 44.32N | 68.25W |
| Elmer | 140 | 39.35N | 75.10W |
| Elmira | 140 | 42.05N | 76.48W |
| Elmore | 124 | 36.30S | 144.37 E |
| Elmshorn | 90 | 53.45N | 9.39 E |
| El Nevado, Cerro ⋀ | 134 | 35.35S | 68.30W |
| El Palmar | 130 | 7.58N | 61.53W |
| El Paso | 138 | 31.45N | 106.29W |
| El Progreso | 130 | 15.21N | 87.49W |
| El Salvador □¹ | 130 | 13.50N | 88.55W |
| El Sauce | 130 | 12.53N | 86.32W |
| El Tigre | 132 | 8.55N | 64.15W |
| El Turbio | 134 | 51.41S | 72.05W |
| Elvas | 94 | 38.53N | 7.10W |
| Ely | 142 | 39.14N | 114.53W |
| Embarcación | 134 | 23.13S | 64.06W |
| Emden | 90 | 53.22N | 7.12 E |
| Emerald | 122 | 23.32S | 148.10 E |
| Empoli | 96 | 43.43N | 10.57 E |
| Emporia | 138 | 38.24N | 96.10W |
| Emporium | 140 | 41.30N | 78.14W |
| Encarnación | 134 | 27.20S | 55.54W |
| Encontrados | 130 | 9.03N | 72.14W |
| Enderby Land ⬥¹ | 85 | 67.30S | 53.00 E |
| Endicott | 140 | 42.05N | 76.02W |
| Engel's | 86 | 51.30N | 46.07 E |
| England □⁸ | 88 | 52.30N | 1.30W |
| English Channel (La | | | |
| Manche) ⋃ | 92 | 50.20N | 1.00W |
| Enns ≏ | 96 | 48.14N | 14.32 E |
| Enschede | 90 | 52.12N | 6.53 E |
| Ensenada | 128 | 31.52N | 116.37W |
| Entebbe | 106 | 0.04N | 32.28 E |
| Enugu | 104 | 6.27N | 7.27 E |
| Eolie, Isole ∎∎ | 96 | 38.30N | 15.00 E |
| Épinal | 92 | 48.11N | 6.27 E |
| Equatorial Guinea □¹ | 104 | 2.00N | 9.00 E |
| Erechim | 134 | 27.38S | 52.17W |
| Erfurt | 90 | 50.58N | 11.01 E |
| Erie | 140 | 42.07N | 80.05W |
| Erie, Lake ⊜ | 138 | 42.15N | 81.00W |
| Eritrea □⁹ | 108 | 15.20N | 39.00 E |
| Erlangen | 90 | 49.36N | 11.01 E |
| Eromanga ∎ | 127b | 18.45S | 169.05 E |
| Erzurum | 86 | 39.55N | 41.17 E |
| Esbjerg | 89 | 55.28N | 8.27 E |
| Esch-sur-Alzette | 90 | 49.30N | 5.59 E |
| Escondido | 142 | 33.07N | 117.05W |
| Escuintla | 130 | 14.18N | 90.47W |
| Esfahān | 108 | 32.40N | 51.38 E |
| Eskilstuna | 89 | 59.22N | 16.30 E |
| Eskimo Point | 136 | 61.07N | 94.03W |
| Eskişehir | 86 | 39.46N | 30.32 E |
| Esmeraldas | 132 | 0.59N | 79.42W |
| Esperance | 122 | 33.51S | 121.53 E |
| Espinhaço, Serra do ⚹ | 132 | 17.30S | 43.30W |
| Espíritu Santo ∎ | 127b | 15.50S | 166.50 E |
| Espoo (Esbo) | 89 | 60.13N | 24.40 E |
| Esquel | 134 | 42.54S | 71.19W |
| Essen | 90 | 51.28N | 7.01 E |
| Estados, Isla de los ∎ | 134 | 54.47S | 64.15W |
| Estelí | 130 | 13.05N | 86.23W |
| Estonia □¹ | 86 | 59.00N | 26.00 E |
| Estrela ⋀ | 94 | 40.19N | 7.37W |
| Ethiopia □¹ | 108 | 9.00N | 39.00 E |
| Etna, Monte ⋀¹ | 96 | 37.46N | 15.00 E |
| Ettelbruck | 90 | 49.52N | 6.05 E |
| Eucla | 122 | 31.43S | 128.52 E |
| Eugene | 138 | 44.03N | 123.05W |
| Eugenia, Punta ‣ | 138 | 27.50N | 115.05W |
| Euphrates (Al-Furāt) ≏ | 108 | 31.00N | 47.25 E |
| Eureka, Ca., U.S. | 142 | 40.48N | 124.09W |
| Eureka, Nv., U.S. | 142 | 39.30N | 115.57W |
| Europa, Île ∎ | 106 | 22.20S | 40.22 E |
| Europe ⬩¹ | 82 | 50.00N | 20.00 E |
| Evansville | 138 | 37.58N | 87.33W |
| Everest, Mount ⋀ | 112 | 27.59N | 86.56 E |
| Everglades National | | | |
| Park ⬥ | 130 | 25.27N | 80.53W |
| Évora | 94 | 38.34N | 7.54W |
| Évreux | 92 | 49.01N | 1.09 E |

| Name | Page No. | Lat. | Long. |
|---|---|---|---|
| Ilhéus | 132 | 14.49S | 39.02W |
| Iliamna Lake ⊜ | 144 | 59.30N | 155.00W |
| Ilion | 140 | 43.00N | 75.02W |
| Illimani, Nevado ∧ | 132 | 16.39S | 67.48W |
| Illinois □[3] | 138 | 40.00N | 89.00W |
| Ilo | 132 | 17.38S | 71.20W |
| Iloilo | 118 | 10.42N | 122.34 E |
| Imabari | 116 | 34.03N | 133.00 E |
| Imperia | 96 | 43.53N | 8.03 E |
| Imperial Valley V | 142 | 32.50N | 115.30W |
| Inari | 89 | 68.54N | 27.01 E |
| Inari ⊜ | 89 | 69.00N | 28.00 E |
| Inch'ŏn | 114 | 37.28N | 126.38 E |
| India □[1] | 110 | 20.00N | 77.00 E |
| Indiana | 140 | 40.37N | 79.09W |
| Indiana □[3] | 138 | 40.00N | 86.15W |
| Indianapolis | 138 | 39.46N | 86.09W |
| Indian Ocean ⊤[1] | 82 | 10.00S | 70.00 E |
| Indian Peak ∧ | 142 | 38.16N | 113.53W |
| Indian Springs | 142 | 36.34N | 115.40W |
| Indigirka ≃ | 102 | 70.48N | 148.54 E |
| Indio | 142 | 33.43N | 116.12W |
| Indispensable Strait ʊ | 127a | 9.00S | 160.30 E |
| Indonesia □[1] | 118 | 5.00S | 120.00 E |
| Indore | 112 | 22.43N | 75.50 E |
| Indus ≃ | 112 | 24.20N | 67.47 E |
| İnegöl | 98 | 40.05N | 29.31 E |
| Inez | 140 | 37.51N | 82.32W |
| Infiernillo, Presa del ⊜[1] | 128 | 18.35N | 101.45W |
| In Guezzam | 104 | 19.32N | 5.42 E |
| Inhambane | 106 | 23.51S | 35.29 E |
| Inharrime | 106 | 24.29S | 35.01 E |
| Injasuti ∧ | 106 | 29.09S | 29.23 E |
| Inn (En) ≃ | 92 | 48.35N | 13.28 E |
| Inner Mongolia → Nei Monggol Zizhiqu □[4] | 114 | 43.00N | 115.00 E |
| Innsbruck | 90 | 47.16N | 11.24 E |
| Inowrocław | 90 | 52.48N | 18.15 E |
| In Salah | 104 | 27.12N | 2.28 E |
| Interlaken | 92 | 46.41N | 7.51 E |
| International Falls | 138 | 48.36N | 93.24W |
| Inthanon, Doi ∧ | 120 | 18.35N | 98.29 E |
| Inukjuak | 136 | 58.27N | 78.06W |
| Inuvik | 136 | 68.25N | 133.30W |
| Invercargill | 126 | 46.24S | 168.21 E |
| Inverness | 88 | 57.27N | 4.15W |
| Inyangani ∧ | 106 | 18.20S | 32.50 E |
| Ioánnina | 98 | 39.40N | 20.50 E |
| Ionia | 140 | 42.59N | 85.04W |
| Ionian Islands → Iónioi Nísoi ∥ | 98 | 38.30N | 20.30 E |
| Ionian Sea ⊤[2] | 86 | 39.00N | 19.00 E |
| Iónioi Nísoi ∥ | 98 | 38.30N | 20.30 E |
| Iowa □[3] | 138 | 42.15N | 93.15W |
| Ípeiros ◆[1] | 98 | 39.40N | 20.50 E |
| Ipiaú | 135 | 14.08S | 39.44W |
| Ipoh | 120 | 4.35N | 101.05 E |
| Ipswich, Austl. | 122 | 27.36S | 152.46 E |
| Ipswich, Eng., U.K. | 88 | 52.04N | 1.10 E |
| Iqaluit | 136 | 63.44N | 68.28W |
| Iquique | 132 | 20.13S | 70.10W |
| Iquitos | 132 | 3.46S | 73.15W |
| Iráklion | 98 | 35.20N | 25.09 E |
| Iran □[1] | 82 | 32.00N | 53.00 E |
| Irapuato | 128 | 20.41N | 101.21W |
| Iraq □[1] | 108 | 33.00N | 44.00 E |
| Irbīl | 86 | 36.11N | 44.01 E |
| Ireland □[1] | 86 | 53.00N | 8.00W |
| Iringa | 106 | 7.46S | 35.42 E |
| Irish Sea ⊤[2] | 88 | 53.30N | 5.20W |
| Irkutsk | 102 | 52.16N | 104.20 E |
| Iron Gate Reservoir ⊜[1] | 98 | 44.30N | 22.00 E |
| Iroquois | 140 | 44.51N | 75.19W |
| Irtyš ≃ | 102 | 61.04N | 68.52 E |
| Irún | 94 | 43.21N | 1.47W |

| Name | Page No. | Lat. | Long. |
|---|---|---|---|
| Isabelia, Cordillera ⋏ | 130 | 13.45N | 85.15W |
| Isar ≃ | 92 | 48.49N | 12.58 E |
| Ise | 116 | 34.29N | 136.42 E |
| Išim | 102 | 56.09N | 69.27 E |
| İskenderun | 109 | 36.37N | 36.07 E |
| Islāmābād | 110 | 33.42N | 73.10 E |
| Island Pond | 140 | 44.48N | 71.52W |
| Islas Malvinas → Falkland Islands □[2] | 134 | 51.45S | 59.00W |
| Isle of Man □[2] | 86 | 54.15N | 4.30W |
| Israel □[1] | 109 | 31.30N | 35.00 E |
| İstanbul | 98 | 41.01N | 28.58 E |
| İstanbul Boğazı (Bosporus) ʊ | 98 | 41.06N | 29.04 E |
| Itabira | 135 | 19.37S | 43.13W |
| Itabuna | 132 | 14.48S | 39.16W |
| Itajaí | 134 | 26.53S | 48.39W |
| Itajubá | 135 | 22.26S | 45.27W |
| Italy □[1] | 86 | 42.50N | 12.50 E |
| Itapetinga | 135 | 15.15S | 40.15W |
| Itapetininga | 135 | 23.36S | 48.03W |
| Itararé | 135 | 24.07S | 49.20W |
| Ithaca | 140 | 42.26N | 76.29W |
| Ituiutaba | 132 | 18.58S | 49.28W |
| Itumbiara | 135 | 18.25S | 49.13W |
| Itzehoe | 90 | 53.55N | 9.31 E |
| Ivano-Frankovsk | 86 | 48.55N | 24.43 E |
| Ivanovo | 100 | 57.00N | 40.59 E |
| Ivory Coast □[1] | 104 | 8.00N | 5.00W |
| Iwaki (Taira) | 116 | 37.03N | 140.55 E |
| Iwakuni | 116 | 34.09N | 132.11 E |
| Iwo | 104 | 7.38N | 4.11 E |
| Iževsk | 86 | 56.51N | 53.14 E |
| Izmail | 86 | 45.21N | 28.50 E |
| İzmir | 98 | 38.25N | 27.09 E |
| Izu-shotō ∥ | 116 | 34.30N | 139.30 E |

## J

| Name | Page No. | Lat. | Long. |
|---|---|---|---|
| Jabalpur | 112 | 23.10N | 79.57 E |
| Jablonec nad Nisou | 90 | 50.44N | 15.10 E |
| Jacarèzinho | 135 | 23.09S | 49.59W |
| Jackson, Mi., U.S. | 140 | 42.14N | 84.24W |
| Jackson, Ms., U.S. | 138 | 32.17N | 90.11W |
| Jacksonville, Fl., U.S. | 138 | 30.19N | 81.39W |
| Jacksonville, Tx., U.S. | 128 | 31.57N | 95.16W |
| Jacobābād | 112 | 28.17N | 68.26 E |
| Jacques-Cartier, Mont ∧ | 136 | 48.59N | 65.57W |
| Jaén, Peru | 132 | 5.42S | 78.47W |
| Jaén, Spain | 94 | 37.46N | 3.47W |
| Jaffna | 111 | 9.40N | 80.00 E |
| Jaipur | 112 | 26.55N | 75.49 E |
| Jakarta | 118 | 6.10S | 106.48 E |
| Jakobstad (Pietarsaari) | 89 | 63.40N | 22.42 E |
| Jakutsk | 102 | 62.13N | 129.49 E |
| Jalālābād | 112 | 34.26N | 70.28 E |
| Jalapa Enríquez | 128 | 19.32N | 96.55W |
| Jamaica □[1] | 130 | 18.15N | 77.30W |
| Jamal, Poluostrov ≻[1] | 102 | 70.00N | 70.00 E |
| Jambi | 118 | 1.36S | 103.37 E |
| Jambol | 98 | 42.29N | 26.30 E |
| James Bay C | 136 | 53.30N | 80.30W |
| Jamestown | 140 | 42.05N | 79.14W |
| Jammu | 112 | 32.42N | 74.52 E |
| Jammu and Kashmir □[2] | 112 | 34.00N | 76.00 E |
| Jāmnagar | 112 | 22.28N | 70.04 E |
| Jamshedpur | 112 | 22.48N | 86.11 E |
| Jamsk | 102 | 59.35N | 154.10 E |
| Jamuna ≃ | 112 | 23.51N | 89.45 E |
| Japan □[1] | 114 | 36.00N | 138.00 E |
| Japan, Sea of ⊤[2] | 114 | 40.00N | 135.00 E |
| Japurá (Caquetá) ≃ | 132 | 3.08S | 64.46W |
| Jaqué | 130 | 7.31N | 78.10W |

| Name | Page No. | Lat. | Long. |
|---|---|---|---|
| Jaroslavl' | 100 | 57.37N | 39.52 E |
| Jarosław | 90 | 50.02N | 22.42 E |
| Jataí | 135 | 17.53S | 51.43W |
| Játiva | 94 | 38.59N | 0.31W |
| Jawa (Java) **I** | 118 | 7.30S | 110.00 E |
| Jawa, Laut (Java Sea) | | | |
| ▼ ² | 118 | 5.00S | 110.00 E |
| Jaya, Puncak ᴧ | 118 | 4.05S | 137.11 E |
| Jayapura | | | |
| (Sukarnapura) | 118 | 2.32S | 140.42 E |
| Jefferson City | 138 | 38.34N | 92.10W |
| Jekaterinburg | 102 | 56.51N | 60.36 E |
| Jelec | 100 | 52.37N | 38.30 E |
| Jelenia Góra | | | |
| (Hirschberg) | 90 | 50.55N | 15.46 E |
| Jena | 90 | 50.56N | 11.35 E |
| Jenisej ≃ | 102 | 71.50N | 82.40 E |
| Jenisejsk | 102 | 58.27N | 92.10 E |
| Jennings | 128 | 30.13N | 92.39W |
| Jequié | 132 | 13.51S | 40.05W |
| Jérémie | 130 | 18.39N | 74.07W |
| Jerevan | 86 | 40.11N | 44.30 E |
| Jerez de la Frontera | 94 | 36.41N | 6.08W |
| Jerome | 142 | 42.43N | 114.31W |
| Jersey □ ² | 92 | 49.15N | 2.10W |
| Jersey City | 140 | 40.43N | 74.04W |
| Jerusalem | | | |
| → Yerushalayim | 109 | 31.46N | 35.14 E |
| Jessore | 112 | 23.10N | 89.13 E |
| Jezerce ᴧ | 98 | 42.26N | 19.49 E |
| Jhang Maghiāna | 110 | 31.16N | 72.19 E |
| Jhānsi | 112 | 25.26N | 78.35 E |
| Jhelum | 112 | 32.56N | 73.44 E |
| Jiddah | 108 | 21.30N | 39.12 E |
| Jilin | 114 | 43.51N | 126.33 E |
| Jima | 108 | 7.36N | 36.50 E |
| Jinan (Tsinan) | 114 | 36.40N | 116.57 E |
| Jingdezhen | 114 | 29.16N | 117.11 E |
| Jinshajiang (Yangtze) | | | |
| ≃ | 120 | 26.40N | 102.55 E |
| Jinzhou | 114 | 41.07N | 121.08 E |
| Jirjā | 104 | 26.20N | 31.53 E |
| Jixi | 114 | 45.17N | 130.59 E |
| João Pessoa | 132 | 7.05S | 34.52W |
| Jodhpur | 112 | 26.17N | 73.02 E |
| Joensuu | 89 | 62.36N | 29.46 E |
| Johannesburg | 106 | 26.15S | 28.00 E |
| Johnstown | 140 | 40.19N | 78.55W |
| Johor Baharu | 120 | 1.28N | 103.45 E |
| Joinvile | 134 | 26.18S | 48.50W |
| Joliet | 138 | 41.31N | 88.04W |
| Joliette | 140 | 46.01N | 73.27W |
| Jonesboro | 138 | 35.50N | 90.42W |
| Jönköping | 89 | 57.47N | 14.11 E |
| Joplin | 138 | 37.05N | 94.30W |
| Jordan □ ¹ | 109 | 31.00N | 36.00 E |
| Jordan ≃ | 109 | 31.46N | 35.33 E |
| Jos | 104 | 9.55N | 8.53 E |
| Joseph, Lac ⊜ | 136 | 52.45N | 65.15W |
| Joseph Bonaparte Gulf | | | |
| ⊂ | 122 | 14.15S | 128.30 E |
| Joškar-Ola | 86 | 56.38N | 47.52 E |
| Juàzeiro do Norte | 132 | 7.12S | 39.20W |
| Jūbā | 104 | 4.51N | 31.37 E |
| Jubba ≃ | 108 | 0.12N | 42.40 E |
| Juiz de Fora | 132 | 21.45S | 43.20W |
| Juliaca | 132 | 15.30S | 70.08W |
| Juliana Top ᴧ | 132 | 3.41N | 56.32W |
| Julianeháb | 136 | 60.43N | 46.01W |
| Junction | 128 | 30.29N | 99.46W |
| Juneau | 144 | 58.20N | 134.27W |
| Jungfrau ᴧ | 92 | 46.32N | 7.58 E |
| Junín de los Andes | 134 | 39.56S | 71.05W |
| Jura ⼂ | 92 | 46.45N | 6.30 E |
| Juticalpa | 130 | 14.42N | 86.15W |
| Juventud, Isla de la | | | |
| (Isla de Pinos) **I** | 130 | 21.40N | 82.50W |

| Name | Page No. | Lat. | Long. |
|---|---|---|---|
| Južno-Sachalinsk | 102 | 46.58N | 142.42 E |
| Jylland ⋗ ¹ | 89 | 56.00N | 9.15 E |
| Jyväskylä | 89 | 62.14N | 25.44 E |

**K**

| | | | |
|---|---|---|---|
| K2 (Qogir Feng) ᴧ | 112 | 35.53N | 76.30 E |
| Kābol | 112 | 34.31N | 69.12 E |
| Kabwe (Broken Hill) | 106 | 14.27S | 28.27 E |
| Kaduna | 104 | 10.33N | 7.27 E |
| Kaédi | 104 | 16.09N | 13.30W |
| Kaesŏng | 114 | 37.59N | 126.33 E |
| Kagoshima | 116 | 31.36N | 130.33 E |
| Kahoolawe **I** | 143 | 20.33N | 156.37W |
| Kaikoura | 126 | 42.25S | 173.41 E |
| Kailua Kona | 143 | 19.22N | 155.59W |
| Kaipara Harbour ⊂ | 126 | 36.25S | 174.13 E |
| Kaitangata | 126 | 46.18S | 169.51 E |
| Kaiwi Channel ⋃ | 143 | 21.15N | 157.30W |
| Kajaani | 89 | 64.14N | 27.41 E |
| Kalahari Desert ◆ ² | 106 | 24.00S | 21.30 E |
| Kalámai | 98 | 37.04N | 22.07 E |
| Kalasin | 120 | 16.29N | 103.30 E |
| Kalašnikovo | 100 | 57.17N | 35.13 E |
| Kalemie (Albertville) | 106 | 5.56S | 29.12 E |
| Kalgoorlie | 122 | 30.45S | 121.28 E |
| Kalimantan | | | |
| → Borneo **I** | 118 | 0.30N | 114.00 E |
| Kaliningrad | | | |
| (Königsberg) | 100 | 54.43N | 20.30 E |
| Kalispell | 138 | 48.11N | 114.18W |
| Kalixälven ≃ | 89 | 65.50N | 23.11 E |
| Kalmar | 89 | 56.40N | 16.22 E |
| Kaluga | 100 | 54.31N | 36.16 E |
| Kamālia | 112 | 30.44N | 72.39 E |
| Kamčatka, Poluostrov | | | |
| ⋗ ¹ | 102 | 56.00N | 160.00 E |
| Kamen'-na-Obi | 102 | 53.47N | 81.20 E |
| Kamensk-Ural'skij | 102 | 56.28N | 61.54 E |
| Kamina | 106 | 8.44S | 25.00 E |
| Kamloops | 136 | 50.40N | 120.20W |
| Kampala | 106 | 0.19N | 32.25 E |
| Kampen | 90 | 52.33N | 5.54 E |
| Kâmpóng Cham | 120 | 12.00N | 105.27 E |
| Kâmpóng Chhnăng | 120 | 12.15N | 104.40 E |
| Kâmpóng Thum | 120 | 12.42N | 104.54 E |
| Kâmpôt | 120 | 10.37N | 104.11 E |
| Kananga (Luluabourg) | 106 | 5.54S | 22.25 E |
| Kanazawa | 116 | 36.34N | 136.39 E |
| Kanchanaburi | 120 | 14.01N | 99.32 E |
| Kandavu **I** | 127c | 19.03S | 178.13 E |
| Kandavu Passage ⋃ | 127c | 18.45S | 178.00 E |
| Kandy | 111 | 7.18N | 80.38 E |
| Kane | 140 | 41.39N | 78.48W |
| Kangaroo Island **I** | 124 | 35.50S | 137.06 E |
| Kangiqsualujjuaq | 136 | 58.32N | 65.54W |
| Kangiqsujuaq | 136 | 61.36N | 71.58W |
| Kangirsuk | 136 | 60.01N | 70.01W |
| Kankakee | 138 | 41.07N | 87.51W |
| Kankan | 104 | 10.23N | 9.18W |
| Kano | 104 | 12.00N | 8.30 E |
| Kānpur | 112 | 26.28N | 80.21 E |
| Kansas □ ³ | 138 | 38.45N | 98.15W |
| Kansas City, Ks., U.S. | 138 | 39.06N | 94.37W |
| Kansas City, Mo., U.S. | 138 | 39.05N | 94.34W |
| Kansk | 102 | 56.13N | 95.41 E |
| Kanye | 106 | 24.59S | 25.19 E |
| Kaohsiung | 114 | 22.38N | 120.17 E |
| Kaolack | 104 | 14.09N | 16.04W |
| Kapfenberg | 90 | 47.26N | 15.18 E |
| Kaposvár | 90 | 46.22N | 17.47 E |
| Kapuas ≃ | 118 | 0.25S | 109.40 E |
| Kapuskasing | 136 | 49.25N | 82.26W |
| Karaköy | 98 | 41.24N | 28.22 E |
| Karāchi | 110 | 24.52N | 67.03 E |
| Karaganda | 102 | 49.50N | 73.10 E |

# 180   Kiro—Kurg

| Name | Page No. | Lat. | Long. |
|------|----------|------|-------|
| Kirovograd | 86 | 48.30N | 32.18 E |
| Kīrthar Range ⚑ | 112 | 27.00N | 67.10 E |
| Kiruna | 89 | 67.51N | 20.16 E |
| Kiryū | 116 | 36.24N | 139.20 E |
| Kisangani (Stanleyville) | 106 | 0.30N | 25.12 E |
| Kishiwada | 116 | 34.28N | 135.22 E |
| Kišin'ov | 86 | 47.00N | 28.50 E |
| Kiskörei-víztároló ◙ ¹ | 90 | 47.35N | 20.40 E |
| Kiskunfélegyháza | 90 | 46.43N | 19.52 E |
| Kiskunhalas | 90 | 46.26N | 19.30 E |
| Kismaayo | 106 | 0.23S | 42.30 E |
| Kissidougou | 104 | 9.11N | 10.06W |
| Kita | 104 | 13.03N | 9.29W |
| Kitakyūshū | 116 | 33.53N | 130.50 E |
| Kitami | 116a | 43.48N | 143.54 E |
| Kitchener | 136 | 43.27N | 80.29W |
| Kíthira ▮ | 98 | 36.20N | 22.58 E |
| Kitwe | 106 | 12.49S | 28.13 E |
| Kjustendil | 98 | 42.17N | 22.41 E |
| Kladno | 90 | 50.08N | 14.05 E |
| Klagenfurt | 90 | 46.38N | 14.18 E |
| Klamath ≏ | 142 | 41.33N | 124.04W |
| Klamath Falls | 138 | 42.13N | 121.46W |
| Klamath Mountains ⚑ | 142 | 41.40N | 123.20W |
| Klarälven ≏ | 89 | 59.23N | 13.32 E |
| Klerksdorp | 106 | 26.58S | 26.39 E |
| Klincy | 100 | 52.47N | 32.14 E |
| Kłodzko | 90 | 50.27N | 16.39 E |
| Klondike □ ⁹ | 144 | 63.30N | 139.00W |
| Kl'učevskaja Sopka, Vulkan ᴧ ¹ | 102 | 56.04N | 160.38 E |
| Kneža | 98 | 43.30N | 24.05 E |
| Knoxville | 138 | 35.57N | 83.55W |
| Kōbe | 116 | 34.41N | 135.10 E |
| København (Copenhagen) | 89 | 55.40N | 12.35 E |
| Koblenz | 90 | 50.21N | 7.35 E |
| Kōchi | 116 | 33.33N | 133.33 E |
| Kodiak | 144 | 57.48N | 152.23W |
| Kodiak Island ▮ | 144 | 57.30N | 153.30W |
| Koes | 106 | 25.59S | 19.08 E |
| Kōfu | 116 | 35.39N | 138.35 E |
| Kokkola (Gamlakarleby) | 89 | 63.50N | 23.07 E |
| Koksoak ≏ | 136 | 58.32N | 68.10W |
| Kola Peninsula → Kol'skij Poluostrov ⋗ ¹ | 102 | 67.30N | 37.00 E |
| Kolhāpur | 111 | 16.42N | 74.13 E |
| Koliganek | 144 | 59.48N | 157.25W |
| Köln (Cologne) | 90 | 50.56N | 6.59 E |
| Kolovrat, Mount ᴧ | 127a | 9.10S | 161.05 E |
| Kolpaševo | 102 | 58.20N | 82.50 E |
| Kol'skij Poluostrov (Kola Peninsula) ⋗ ¹ | 102 | 67.30N | 37.00 E |
| Kolwezi | 106 | 10.43S | 25.28 E |
| Kolyma ≏ | 102 | 69.30N | 161.00 E |
| Komárno | 90 | 47.45N | 18.09 E |
| Komatsu | 116 | 36.24N | 136.27 E |
| Komló | 90 | 46.12N | 18.16 E |
| Kommunizma, Pik (Communism Peak) ᴧ | 110 | 38.57N | 72.01 E |
| Komotiní | 98 | 41.08N | 25.25 E |
| Komsomolec, Ostrov ▮ | 102 | 80.30N | 95.00 E |
| Komsomol'sk-na-Amure | 102 | 50.35N | 137.02 E |
| Kona Coast ≗ ² | 143 | 19.25N | 155.55W |
| Koné | 127b | 21.04S | 164.52 E |
| Kŏng, Kaôh ▮ | 120 | 11.20N | 103.00 E |
| Königsberg → Kaliningrad | 100 | 54.43N | 20.30 E |
| Konin | 90 | 52.13N | 18.16 E |
| Könkämäälven ≏ | 89 | 68.29N | 22.17 E |
| Konstanz | 90 | 47.40N | 9.10 E |
| Kontagora | 104 | 10.24N | 5.28 E |

| Name | Page No. | Lat. | Long. |
|------|----------|------|-------|
| Konya | 86 | 37.52N | 32.31 E |
| Kor'akskoje Nagorje ⚑ | 102 | 62.30N | 172.00 E |
| Korça | 98 | 40.37N | 20.46 E |
| Korea, North □ ¹ | 114 | 40.00N | 127.00 E |
| Korea, South □ ¹ | 114 | 36.30N | 128.00 E |
| Korinthiakós Kólpos ⊂ | 98 | 38.19N | 22.04 E |
| Kórinthos (Corinth) | 98 | 37.56N | 22.56 E |
| Korolevu | 127c | 18.13S | 177.44 E |
| Koro Sea ≂ ² | 127c | 18.00S | 179.50 E |
| Korsør | 89 | 55.20N | 11.09 E |
| Kortrijk (Courtrai) | 90 | 50.50N | 3.16 E |
| Kos ▮ | 98 | 36.50N | 27.10 E |
| Kosciusko, Mount ᴧ | 124 | 36.27S | 148.16 E |
| Košice | 90 | 48.43N | 21.15 E |
| Kosovska Mitrovica | 98 | 42.53N | 20.52 E |
| Kostroma | 100 | 57.46N | 40.55 E |
| Koszalin (Köslin) | 90 | 54.12N | 16.09 E |
| Kota Baharu | 120 | 6.08N | 102.15 E |
| Kota Kinabalu | 118 | 5.59N | 116.04 E |
| Kotel'nyj, Ostrov ▮ | 102 | 75.45N | 138.44 E |
| Kotka | 89 | 60.28N | 26.55 E |
| Kotuj ≏ | 102 | 71.55N | 102.05 E |
| Kotzebue Sound ⨆ | 144 | 66.20N | 163.00W |
| Koussi, Emi ᴧ | 104 | 19.50N | 18.30 E |
| Kouvola | 89 | 60.52N | 26.42 E |
| Kowloon | 114 | 22.18N | 114.10 E |
| Koyukuk ≏ | 144 | 64.56N | 157.30W |
| Koza | 117b | 26.20N | 127.50 E |
| Kra, Isthmus of ≗ ³ | 120 | 10.20N | 99.00 E |
| Krâchéh | 120 | 12.29N | 106.01 E |
| Kragerø | 89 | 58.52N | 9.25 E |
| Kragujevac | 98 | 44.01N | 20.55 E |
| Kraków | 90 | 50.03N | 19.58 E |
| Kraljevo | 98 | 43.43N | 20.41 E |
| Kranj | 96 | 46.15N | 14.21 E |
| Krasnodar | 86 | 45.02N | 39.00 E |
| Krasnojarsk | 102 | 56.01N | 92.50 E |
| Krasnokamsk | 86 | 58.04N | 55.48 E |
| Krasnoural'sk | 102 | 58.21N | 60.03 E |
| Krems an der Donau | 90 | 48.25N | 15.36 E |
| Kričov | 100 | 53.42N | 31.43 E |
| Kristiansand | 89 | 58.10N | 8.00 E |
| Kristianstad | 89 | 56.02N | 14.08 E |
| Kristiansund | 89 | 63.07N | 7.45 E |
| Kríti ▮ | 98 | 35.29N | 24.42 E |
| Kritikón Pélagos ≂ ² | 98 | 35.46N | 23.54 E |
| Krivoj Rog | 86 | 47.55N | 33.21 E |
| Krnov | 90 | 50.05N | 17.41 E |
| Kroonstad | 106 | 27.46S | 27.12 E |
| Kropotkin | 102 | 58.30N | 115.17 E |
| Krung Thep (Bangkok) | 120 | 13.45N | 100.31 E |
| Kruševac | 98 | 43.35N | 21.20 E |
| Ksar-el-Kebir | 94 | 35.01N | 5.54W |
| Kuala Lumpur | 120 | 3.10N | 101.42 E |
| Kuala Terengganu | 120 | 5.20N | 103.08 E |
| Kuantan | 120 | 3.48N | 103.20 E |
| Kuching | 120 | 1.33N | 110.20 E |
| Kuhmo | 89 | 64.08N | 29.31 E |
| Kujbyšev | 102 | 55.27N | 78.19 E |
| Kujbyšev → Samara | 86 | 53.12N | 50.09 E |
| Kula Kangri ᴧ | 112 | 28.03N | 90.27 E |
| Kumagaya | 116 | 36.08N | 139.23 E |
| Kumajri | 86 | 40.48N | 43.50 E |
| Kumamoto | 116 | 32.48N | 130.43 E |
| Kumanovo | 98 | 42.08N | 21.43 E |
| Kumasi | 104 | 6.41N | 1.35W |
| Kumo | 104 | 10.03N | 11.13 E |
| Kumon Range ⚑ | 120 | 26.30N | 97.15 E |
| Kunlun Shan ⚑ | 112 | 36.30N | 88.00 E |
| Kunming | 114 | 25.05N | 102.40 E |
| Kuopio | 89 | 62.54N | 27.41 E |
| Kupang | 118 | 10.10S | 123.35 E |
| Kupino | 102 | 54.22N | 77.18 E |
| Kurashiki | 116 | 34.35N | 133.46 E |
| Kure | 116 | 34.14N | 132.34 E |
| Kurgan | 102 | 55.26N | 65.18 E |

| Name | Page No. | Lat. | Long. |
|---|---|---|---|
| Kuril'skije Ostrova | | | |
| (Kuril Islands) ‖ | 102 | 46.10N | 152.00 E |
| Kurmuk | 104 | 10.33N | 34.17 E |
| Kursk | 86 | 51.42N | 36.12 E |
| Kuruman | 106 | 27.28S | 23.28 E |
| Kurume | 116 | 33.19N | 130.31 E |
| Kuskokwim ≈ | 144 | 60.17N | 162.27W |
| Kustanaj | 86 | 53.10N | 63.35 E |
| Küsti | 104 | 13.10N | 32.40 E |
| Kutch, Gulf of c | 112 | 22.36N | 69.30 E |
| Kutno | 90 | 52.15N | 19.23 E |
| Kuwait □¹ | 108 | 29.30N | 47.45 E |
| Kwangju | 114 | 35.09N | 126.54 E |
| Kwekwe | 106 | 18.55S | 29.49 E |
| Kyle of Lochalsh | 88 | 57.17N | 5.43W |
| Kyoga, Lake ⊛ | 106 | 1.30N | 33.00 E |
| Kyōto | 116 | 35.00N | 135.45 E |
| Kyrgyzstan □¹ | 82 | 41.00N | 75.00 E |
| Kyūshū ‖ | 116 | 33.00N | 131.00 E |
| Kyzyl | 102 | 51.42N | 94.27 E |

**L**

| Name | Page No. | Lat. | Long. |
|---|---|---|---|
| Labe (Elbe) ≈ | 90 | 53.50N | 9.00 E |
| La Blanquilla ‖ | 130 | 11.51N | 64.37W |
| Labrador ⬦¹ | 136 | 54.00N | 62.00W |
| Labrador City | 136 | 52.57N | 66.55W |
| Labrador Sea ≈² | 136 | 57.00N | 53.00W |
| Labutta | 120 | 16.09N | 94.46 E |
| Laccadive Sea ≈² | 111 | 8.00N | 75.00 E |
| La Ceiba | 130 | 15.47N | 86.50W |
| Lac-giao | 120 | 12.40N | 108.03 E |
| Lachlan ≈ | 124 | 34.21S | 143.57 E |
| La Chorrera | 130 | 8.53N | 79.47W |
| Lac la Biche | 136 | 54.46N | 111.58W |
| Lac-Mégantic | 140 | 45.36N | 70.53W |
| Laconia | 140 | 43.31N | 71.28W |
| La Coruña | 94 | 43.22N | 8.23W |
| La Crosse | 138 | 43.48N | 91.14W |
| Ladožskoje Ozero | | | |
| (Lake Ladoga) ⊛ | 89 | 61.00N | 31.30 E |
| Ladysmith | 106 | 28.34S | 29.45 E |
| Lafayette | 138 | 30.13N | 92.01W |
| Laghouat | 104 | 33.50N | 2.59 E |
| Lagos | 104 | 6.27N | 3.24 E |
| Lagrange | 140 | 41.39N | 85.25W |
| La Gran Sabana ≍ | 132 | 5.30N | 61.30W |
| La Guajira, Península | | | |
| de ⋗¹ | 132 | 12.00N | 71.40W |
| Laguna Beach | 142 | 33.32N | 117.46W |
| Lagunillas | 132 | 19.38S | 63.43W |
| La Habana (Havana) | 130 | 23.08N | 82.22W |
| Lahaina | 143 | 20.52N | 156.40W |
| Lahore | 110 | 31.35N | 74.18 E |
| Lahti | 89 | 60.58N | 25.40 E |
| Laingsburg | 106 | 33.11S | 20.51 E |
| Lake Charles | 138 | 30.13N | 93.13W |
| Lake Harbour | 136 | 62.51N | 69.53W |
| Lake Havasu City | 142 | 34.29N | 114.19W |
| Lake Placid | 140 | 44.16N | 73.58W |
| Lake Pleasant | 140 | 43.28N | 74.25W |
| Lakeview | 142 | 42.11N | 120.20W |
| Lakonikós Kólpos c | 98 | 36.25N | 22.37 E |
| Lakshadweep □³ | 111 | 10.00N | 73.00 E |
| Lakshadweep ‖ | 111 | 10.00N | 73.00 E |
| La Loche | 136 | 56.29N | 109.27W |
| La Mancha ⬦¹ | 94 | 39.05N | 3.00W |
| La Manche (English | | | |
| Channel) ⊔ | 92 | 50.20N | 1.00W |
| Lamap | 127b | 16.26S | 167.43 E |
| Lambaréné | 106 | 0.42S | 10.13 E |
| Lambasa | 127c | 16.26S | 179.24 E |
| Lambert's Bay | 106 | 32.05S | 18.17 E |
| Lamesa | 128 | 32.44N | 101.57W |
| Lamía | 98 | 38.54N | 22.26 E |
| Lamont | 142 | 35.15N | 118.54W |

| Name | Page No. | Lat. | Long. |
|---|---|---|---|
| Lampang | 120 | 18.18N | 99.31 E |
| Lamphun | 120 | 18.35N | 99.01 E |
| Lamu | 106 | 2.16S | 40.54 E |
| Lanai ‖ | 143 | 20.50N | 156.55W |
| Lanai City | 143 | 20.49N | 156.55W |
| Lancaster, On., Can. | 140 | 45.15N | 74.30W |
| Lancaster, Eng., U.K. | 88 | 54.03N | 2.48W |
| Lancaster, Ca., U.S. | 142 | 34.41N | 118.08W |
| Lancaster, Oh., U.S. | 140 | 39.43N | 82.36W |
| Lancaster, Pa., U.S. | 140 | 40.02N | 76.18W |
| Lancaster Sound ⊔ | 136 | 74.13N | 84.00W |
| Lanchow | | | |
| → Lanzhou | 114 | 36.03N | 103.41 E |
| Land's End ⋗ | 88 | 50.03N | 5.44W |
| Landshut | 90 | 48.33N | 12.09 E |
| Langenhagen | 90 | 52.27N | 9.44 E |
| Langsa | 120 | 4.28N | 97.58 E |
| L'Annonciation | 140 | 46.25N | 74.52W |
| Lansing | 140 | 42.43N | 84.33W |
| Lanzhou | 114 | 36.03N | 103.41 E |
| Laos □¹ | 118 | 18.00N | 105.00 E |
| La Palma | 130 | 8.25N | 78.09W |
| La Paragua | 132 | 6.50N | 63.20W |
| La Paz, Bol. | 132 | 16.30S | 68.09W |
| La Paz, Mex. | 128 | 24.10N | 110.18W |
| La Perouse Strait | | | |
| (Sōya-kaikyō) ⊔ | 116a | 45.45N | 142.00 E |
| La Piedad [Cavadas] | 128 | 20.21N | 102.00W |
| Lapland ⬦¹ | 89 | 68.00N | 25.00 E |
| La Plata, Arg. | 134 | 34.55S | 57.57W |
| La Plata, Md., U.S. | 140 | 38.31N | 76.58W |
| Lappeenranta | 89 | 61.04N | 28.11 E |
| Laptevych, More | | | |
| (Laptev Sea) ≈² | 102 | 76.00N | 126.00 E |
| La Quiaca | 134 | 22.06S | 65.37W |
| L'Aquila | 96 | 42.22N | 13.22 E |
| Larache | 94 | 35.12N | 6.10W |
| Laramie | 138 | 41.18N | 105.35W |
| Laredo | 138 | 27.30N | 99.30W |
| La Rioja | 134 | 29.26S | 66.51W |
| Lárisa | 98 | 39.38N | 22.25 E |
| Lärkäna | 112 | 27.33N | 68.13 E |
| La Rochelle | 92 | 46.10N | 1.10W |
| La Roche-sur-Yon | 92 | 46.40N | 1.26W |
| La Ronge | 136 | 55.06N | 105.17W |
| La Sarre | 136 | 48.48N | 79.12W |
| Las Cruces | 128 | 32.18N | 106.46W |
| La Serena | 134 | 29.54S | 71.16W |
| Las Flores | 134 | 36.03S | 59.07W |
| Las Lomitas | 134 | 24.42S | 60.36W |
| Las Minas, Cerro ⋀ | 130 | 14.33N | 88.39W |
| Las Palmas de Gran | | | |
| Canaria | 104 | 28.06N | 15.24W |
| La Spezia | 96 | 44.07N | 9.50 E |
| Lassen Peak ⋀¹ | 142 | 40.29N | 121.31W |
| Las Vegas | 142 | 36.10N | 115.08W |
| La Tortuga, Isla ‖ | 130 | 10.56N | 65.20W |
| La Tuque | 136 | 47.26N | 72.47W |
| Lātūr | 111 | 18.24N | 76.35 E |
| Latvia □¹ | 86 | 57.00N | 25.00 E |
| Lauchhammer | 90 | 51.30N | 13.47 E |
| Lau Group ‖ | 127c | 18.20S | 178.30W |
| Launceston | 122 | 41.26S | 147.08 E |
| La Union | 130 | 13.20N | 87.57W |
| Laurel | 128 | 31.41N | 89.07W |
| Lausanne | 92 | 46.31N | 6.38 E |
| Lautoka | 127c | 17.37S | 177.27 E |
| Laval, P.Q., Can. | 140 | 45.33N | 73.44W |
| Laval, Fr. | 92 | 48.04N | 0.46W |
| Lavapié, Punta ⋗ | 134 | 37.09S | 73.35W |
| La Vela, Cabo de ⋗ | 130 | 12.13N | 72.11W |
| Lavras | 135 | 21.14S | 45.00W |
| Lawrenceburg | 140 | 39.05N | 84.51W |
| Lawton | 138 | 34.36N | 98.23W |
| Lead | 138 | 44.21N | 103.45W |
| Leamington | 140 | 42.03N | 82.36W |
| Lebanon, N.H., U.S. | 140 | 43.38N | 72.15W |

| Name | Page No. | Lat. | Long. |
|---|---|---|---|
| Lebanon, Pa., U.S. | 140 | 40.20N | 76.24W |
| Lebanon □¹ | 109 | 33.50N | 35.50 E |
| Lecce | 96 | 40.23N | 18.11 E |
| Lecco | 96 | 45.51N | 9.23 E |
| Leeds | 88 | 53.50N | 1.35W |
| Leeuwarden | 90 | 53.12N | 5.46 E |
| Leeward Islands II | 130 | 17.00N | 63.00W |
| Legnica (Liegnitz) | 90 | 51.13N | 16.09 E |
| Le Havre | 92 | 49.30N | 0.08 E |
| Lehighton | 140 | 40.50N | 75.42W |
| Leicester | 88 | 52.38N | 1.05W |
| Leinster □⁹ | 88 | 53.05N | 7.00W |
| Leipzig | 90 | 51.19N | 12.20 E |
| Leland | 140 | 45.01N | 85.45W |
| Lemanmanu Mission | 127a | 5.02S | 154.35 E |
| Le Mans | 92 | 48.00N | 0.12 E |
| Leme | 135 | 22.12S | 47.24W |
| Lemesós (Limassol) | 109 | 34.40N | 33.02 E |
| Lemmon | 138 | 45.56N | 102.09W |
| Lena ≏ | 102 | 72.25N | 126.40 E |
| Lenakel | 127b | 19.32S | 169.16 E |
| Leningrad | | | |
| → Sankt-Peterburg | 100 | 59.55N | 30.15 E |
| Leninsk-Kuzneckij | 102 | 54.38N | 86.10 E |
| Lens | 92 | 50.26N | 2.50 E |
| Leoben | 90 | 47.23N | 15.06 E |
| León, Nic. | 130 | 12.26N | 86.53W |
| León, Spain | 94 | 42.36N | 5.34W |
| León [de los Aldamas] | 128 | 21.07N | 101.40W |
| Leonora | 122 | 28.53S | 121.20 E |
| Leopoldina | 135 | 21.32S | 42.38W |
| Lérida | 94 | 41.37N | 0.37 E |
| Lerwick | 88 | 60.09N | 1.09W |
| Lesbos | | | |
| → Lésvos I | 98 | 39.10N | 26.20 E |
| Les Cayes | 130 | 18.12N | 73.45W |
| Leskovac | 98 | 42.59N | 21.57 E |
| Lesotho □¹ | 106 | 29.30S | 28.30 E |
| Lesozavodsk | 102 | 45.28N | 133.27 E |
| Lesser Antilles II | 130 | 15.00N | 61.00W |
| Lesser Sunda Islands II | 118 | 9.00S | 120.00 E |
| Lésvos I | 98 | 39.10N | 26.20 E |
| Leszno | 90 | 51.51N | 16.35 E |
| Letea, Ostrovul I | 98 | 45.20N | 29.20 E |
| Lethbridge | 136 | 49.42N | 112.50W |
| Lethem | 132 | 3.23N | 59.48W |
| Leticia | 132 | 4.09S | 69.57W |
| Levanger | 89 | 63.45N | 11.18 E |
| Leverkusen | 90 | 51.03N | 6.59 E |
| Levin | 126 | 40.37S | 175.17 E |
| Levkás I | 98 | 38.39N | 20.27 E |
| Lewis, Isle of I | 88 | 58.10N | 6.40W |
| Lewiston, Id., U.S. | 138 | 46.25N | 117.01W |
| Lewiston, Me., U.S. | 140 | 44.06N | 70.12W |
| Lewistown | 140 | 40.35N | 77.34W |
| Lexington, Ky., U.S. | 140 | 38.02N | 84.30W |
| Lexington, Ma., U.S. | 140 | 42.26N | 71.13W |
| Lexington Park | 140 | 38.16N | 76.27W |
| Leyte I | 118 | 10.50N | 124.50 E |
| Leyte Gulf c | 118 | 10.50N | 125.25 E |
| Lhasa | 114 | 29.40N | 91.09 E |
| Lianyungang | 114 | 34.39N | 119.16 E |
| Liaoyuan | 114 | 42.54N | 125.07 E |
| Liberal | 138 | 37.02N | 100.55W |
| Liberec | 90 | 50.46N | 15.03 E |
| Liberia | 130 | 10.38N | 85.27W |
| Liberia □¹ | 104 | 6.00N | 10.00W |
| Libertad | 130 | 8.20N | 69.37W |
| Libīyah, Aṣ-Ṣaḥrā' al- (Libyan Desert) ◆² | 104 | 24.00N | 25.00 E |
| Libreville | 106 | 0.23N | 9.27 E |
| Libya □¹ | 104 | 27.00N | 17.00 E |
| Licata | 96 | 37.05N | 13.56 E |
| Lichinga | 106 | 13.18S | 35.14 E |
| Liechtenstein □¹ | 86 | 47.09N | 9.35 E |
| Liège | 90 | 50.38N | 5.34 E |
| Lier | 90 | 51.08N | 4.34 E |

| Name | Page No. | Lat. | Long. |
|---|---|---|---|
| Liezen | 90 | 47.35N | 14.15 E |
| Lifou, Île I | 127b | 20.53S | 167.13 E |
| Ligurian Sea ▼² | 92 | 43.00N | 8.00 E |
| Lihue | 143 | 21.58N | 159.22W |
| Likasi (Jadotville) | 106 | 10.59S | 26.44 E |
| Lille | 92 | 50.38N | 3.04 E |
| Lilongwe | 106 | 13.59S | 33.44 E |
| Lima, Peru | 132 | 12.03S | 77.03W |
| Lima, Oh., U.S. | 140 | 40.44N | 84.06W |
| Limeira | 135 | 22.34S | 47.24W |
| Limerick | 88 | 52.40N | 8.38W |
| Límnos I | 98 | 39.54N | 25.21 E |
| Limoges | 92 | 45.50N | 1.16 E |
| Limón, C.R. | 130 | 10.00N | 83.02W |
| Limón, Hond. | 130 | 15.52N | 85.33W |
| Limpopo ≏ | 106 | 25.15S | 33.30 E |
| Linares | 94 | 38.05N | 3.38W |
| Lincoln, Eng., U.K. | 88 | 53.14N | 0.33W |
| Lincoln, Ne., U.S. | 138 | 40.48N | 96.40W |
| Lindi | 106 | 10.00S | 39.43 E |
| Lingga, Kepulauan II | 118 | 0.05S | 104.35 E |
| Linköping | 89 | 58.25N | 15.37 E |
| Lins | 135 | 21.40S | 49.45W |
| Linton | 138 | 46.16N | 100.13W |
| Linz | 90 | 48.18N | 14.18 E |
| Lion, Golfe du c | 92 | 43.00N | 4.00 E |
| Lipeck | 100 | 52.37N | 39.35 E |
| Lippstadt | 90 | 51.40N | 8.19 E |
| Lisboa (Lisbon) | 94 | 38.43N | 9.08W |
| Lismore | 122 | 28.48S | 153.17 E |
| Lithuania □¹ | 86 | 56.00N | 24.00 E |
| Little Current | 140 | 45.58N | 81.56W |
| Little Inagua I | 130 | 21.30N | 73.00W |
| Little Minch ʉ | 88 | 57.35N | 6.45W |
| Little Rock | 138 | 34.44N | 92.17W |
| Liuzhou | 114 | 24.22N | 109.32 E |
| Livermore Falls | 140 | 44.28N | 70.11W |
| Liverpool | 88 | 53.25N | 2.55W |
| Livingston | 138 | 45.39N | 110.33W |
| Livingstone | 106 | 17.50S | 25.53 E |
| Livny | 100 | 52.25N | 37.37 E |
| Livonia | 140 | 42.22N | 83.21W |
| Livorno (Leghorn) | 96 | 43.33N | 10.19 E |
| Ljubljana | 96 | 46.03N | 14.31 E |
| Ljusnan ≏ | 89 | 61.12N | 17.08 E |
| Llanos ≃ | 132 | 5.00N | 70.00W |
| Lloydminster | 136 | 53.17N | 110.00W |
| Lobito | 106 | 12.20S | 13.34 E |
| Lochgilphead | 88 | 56.03N | 5.26W |
| Lochinver | 88 | 58.09N | 5.15W |
| Lock Haven | 140 | 41.08N | 77.26W |
| Lockport | 140 | 43.10N | 78.41W |
| Lodi | 142 | 38.07N | 121.16W |
| Łódź | 90 | 51.46N | 19.30 E |
| Lofoten II | 89 | 68.30N | 15.00 E |
| Logan, Mount ʌ | 136 | 60.34N | 140.24W |
| Logroño | 94 | 42.28N | 2.27W |
| Loire ≏ | 92 | 47.16N | 2.11W |
| Loja | 132 | 4.00S | 79.13W |
| Lom | 98 | 43.49N | 23.14 E |
| Loma Mansa ʌ | 104 | 9.13N | 11.07W |
| Lombok I | 118 | 8.45S | 116.30 E |
| Lomé | 104 | 6.08N | 1.13 E |
| Lompoc | 142 | 34.38N | 120.27W |
| Łomża | 90 | 53.11N | 22.05 E |
| London, On., Can. | 140 | 42.59N | 81.14W |
| London, Eng., U.K. | 88 | 51.30N | 0.10W |
| Londonderry | 88 | 55.00N | 7.19W |
| Londrina | 135 | 23.18S | 51.09W |
| Long Beach | 142 | 33.46N | 118.11W |
| Long Branch | 140 | 40.18N | 73.59W |
| Long Island I, Bah. | 130 | 23.15N | 75.07W |
| Long Island I, N.Y., U.S. | 140 | 40.50N | 73.00W |
| Long Point ꜱ¹ | 140 | 42.34N | 80.15W |
| Longview | 128 | 32.30N | 94.44W |
| Longwy | 92 | 49.31N | 5.46 E |

| Name | Page No. | Lat. | Long. |
|---|---|---|---|
| Mahajanga | 106 | 15.43S | 46.19 E |
| Mahārāshtra □ ³ | 111 | 19.00N | 76.00 E |
| Mahia Peninsula ❯ ¹ | 126 | 39.10S | 177.53 E |
| Mahón | 94 | 39.53N | 4.15 E |
| Maiduguri | 104 | 11.51N | 13.10 E |
| Mai-Ndombe, Lac ⊜ | 106 | 2.00S | 18.20 E |
| Maine □ ³ | 138 | 45.15N | 69.15 W |
| Mainland I | 88 | 59.00N | 3.10 W |
| Mainz | 90 | 50.01N | 8.16 E |
| Maipo, Volcán ▲ ¹ | 134 | 34.10S | 69.50 W |
| Maipú | 134 | 36.52S | 57.52 W |
| Maiquetía | 130 | 10.36N | 66.57 W |
| Majorca |  |  |  |
| → Mallorca I | 94 | 39.30N | 3.00 E |
| Makasar, Selat |  |  |  |
| (Makassar Strait) ⊔ | 118 | 2.00S | 117.30 E |
| Makat | 86 | 47.39N | 53.19 E |
| Makgadikgadi Pans ≊ | 106 | 20.45S | 25.30 E |
| Makinsk | 102 | 52.37N | 70.26 E |
| Makkah (Mecca) | 108 | 21.27N | 39.49 E |
| Makó | 90 | 46.13N | 20.29 E |
| Makunudu Atoll I ¹ | 111 | 6.20N | 72.36 E |
| Makurdi | 104 | 7.45N | 8.32 E |
| Malabar Coast ▴ ² | 111 | 10.00N | 76.15 E |
| Malabo | 104 | 3.45N | 8.47 E |
| Malacca, Strait of ⊔ | 120 | 2.30N | 101.20 E |
| Málaga | 94 | 36.43N | 4.25 W |
| Malaita I | 127a | 9.00S | 161.00 E |
| Malakāl | 104 | 9.31N | 31.39 E |
| Malang | 118 | 7.59S | 112.37 E |
| Malange | 106 | 9.32S | 16.20 E |
| Malatya | 86 | 38.21N | 38.19 E |
| Malawi □ ¹ | 106 | 13.30S | 34.00 E |
| Malay Peninsula ❯ ¹ | 120 | 4.00N | 102.00 E |
| Malaysia □ ¹ | 118 | 2.30N | 112.30 E |
| Malbork | 90 | 54.02N | 19.01 E |
| Maldive Islands II | 111 | 5.00N | 73.00 E |
| Maldives □ ¹ | 111 | 3.15N | 73.00 E |
| Malekula I | 127b | 16.15S | 167.30 E |
| Malheur, South Fork ≃ | 142 | 43.33N | 118.10 W |
| Mali □ ¹ | 104 | 17.00N | 4.00 W |
| Malik, Wādī al- V | 104 | 18.02N | 30.58 E |
| Malino, Bukit ▲ | 118 | 0.45N | 120.47 E |
| Malkara | 98 | 40.53N | 26.54 E |
| Mallaig | 88 | 57.00N | 5.50 W |
| Mallawī | 104 | 27.44N | 30.50 E |
| Mallorca I | 94 | 39.30N | 3.00 E |
| Malmö | 89 | 55.36N | 13.00 E |
| Małopolska ◂■ ¹ | 90 | 50.10N | 21.30 E |
| Malpelo, Isla de I | 132 | 3.59N | 81.35 W |
| Malta □ ¹ | 86 | 35.50N | 14.35 E |
| Malta I | 96 | 35.53N | 14.27 E |
| Maluku (Moluccas) II | 118 | 2.00S | 128.00 E |
| Maluku, Laut (Molucca |  |  |  |
| Sea) ▼ ² | 118 | 0.00 | 125.00 E |
| Mamagota | 127a | 6.46S | 155.24 E |
| Manado | 118 | 1.29N | 124.51 E |
| Managua | 130 | 12.09N | 86.17 W |
| Manakara | 106 | 22.08S | 48.01 E |
| Manaus | 132 | 3.08S | 60.01 W |
| Manawai | 127a | 9.05S | 161.11 E |
| Manchester, Eng., U.K. | 88 | 53.30N | 2.15 W |
| Manchester, N.H., U.S. | 140 | 42.59N | 71.27 W |
| Manchester, Vt., U.S. | 140 | 43.09N | 73.04 W |
| Manchuria □ ⁹ | 114 | 47.00N | 125.00 E |
| Mandal | 89 | 58.02N | 7.27 E |
| Mandalay | 120 | 22.00N | 96.05 E |
| Mandeb, Bāb el- ⊔ | 108 | 12.40N | 43.20 E |
| Manfredonia | 96 | 41.38N | 15.55 E |
| Manfredonia, Golfo di |  |  |  |
| c | 96 | 41.35N | 16.05 E |
| Mangalore | 111 | 12.52N | 74.53 E |
| Manhattan | 138 | 39.11N | 96.34 W |
| Manhuaçu | 135 | 20.15S | 42.02 W |
| Manila | 118 | 14.35N | 121.00 E |
| Manipur □ ⁸ | 112 | 25.00N | 94.00 E |
| Manitoba □ ⁴ | 136 | 54.00N | 97.00 W |
| Manitoba, Lake ⊜ | 136 | 51.00N | 98.45 W |
| Manitoulin Island I | 140 | 45.45N | 82.30 W |
| Manizales | 132 | 5.05N | 75.32 W |
| Mankato | 138 | 44.09N | 93.59 W |
| Mannar, Gulf of c | 111 | 8.30N | 79.00 E |
| Mannheim | 90 | 49.29N | 8.29 E |
| Mannington | 140 | 39.31N | 80.20 W |
| Manono | 106 | 7.18S | 27.25 E |
| Manresa | 94 | 41.44N | 1.50 E |
| Mansfield | 140 | 40.45N | 82.30 W |
| Mansfield, Mount ▲ | 140 | 44.33N | 72.49 W |
| Manta | 132 | 0.57S | 80.44 W |
| Mantes-la-Jolie | 92 | 48.59N | 1.43 E |
| Manton | 140 | 44.24N | 85.23 W |
| Mantova | 96 | 45.09N | 10.48 E |
| Manzanares | 94 | 39.00N | 3.22 W |
| Manzanillo, Cuba | 130 | 20.21N | 77.07 W |
| Manzanillo, Mex. | 128 | 19.03N | 104.20 W |
| Maoke, Pegunungan ⋏ | 118 | 4.00S | 138.00 E |
| Mapire | 130 | 7.45N | 64.42 W |
| Maputo (Lourenço |  |  |  |
| Marques) | 106 | 25.58S | 32.35 E |
| Maracaibo | 132 | 10.40N | 71.37 W |
| Maracaibo, Lago de ⊜ | 130 | 9.50N | 71.30 W |
| Maracay | 132 | 10.15N | 67.36 W |
| Maragogipe | 135 | 12.46S | 38.55 W |
| Maramureşului, Munţii |  |  |  |
| ⋏ | 98 | 47.50N | 24.45 E |
| Marañón ≃ | 132 | 4.30S | 73.27 W |
| Marathon | 136 | 48.40N | 86.25 W |
| Maravovo | 127a | 9.17S | 159.38 E |
| Marcy, Mount ▲ | 140 | 44.07N | 73.56 W |
| Mardān | 112 | 34.12N | 72.02 E |
| Mar del Plata | 134 | 38.00S | 57.33 W |
| Maré, Île I | 127b | 21.30S | 168.00 E |
| Margarita, Isla de I | 130 | 11.00N | 64.00 W |
| Margherita Peak ▲ | 106 | 0.22N | 29.51 E |
| Mariana Islands II | 118 | 16.00N | 145.30 E |
| Marianao | 130 | 23.05N | 82.26 W |
| Marías, Islas II | 128 | 21.25N | 106.28 W |
| Maribor | 96 | 46.33N | 15.39 E |
| Mariental | 106 | 24.36S | 17.59 E |
| Marietta | 140 | 39.24N | 81.27 W |
| Marília | 135 | 22.13S | 49.56 W |
| Marinette | 138 | 45.06N | 87.37 W |
| Maringá | 134 | 23.25S | 51.55 W |
| Marion, Mi., U.S. | 140 | 44.06N | 85.08 W |
| Marion, Oh., U.S. | 140 | 40.35N | 83.07 W |
| Maripa | 130 | 7.26N | 65.09 W |
| Mariscal Estigarribia | 134 | 22.02S | 60.38 W |
| Maritime Alps ⋏ | 92 | 44.15N | 7.10 E |
| Mariupol | 86 | 47.06N | 37.33 E |
| Markham, Mount ▲ | 85 | 82.51S | 161.21 E |
| Marlborough | 140 | 42.20N | 71.33 W |
| Marmara Denizi (Sea |  |  |  |
| of Marmara) ▼ ² | 98 | 40.40N | 28.15 E |
| Marmara Gölü ⊜ | 98 | 38.37N | 28.02 E |
| Marmet | 140 | 38.14N | 81.34 W |
| Marne ≃ | 92 | 48.49N | 2.24 E |
| Maroa | 132 | 2.43N | 67.33 W |
| Maromokotro ▲ | 106 | 14.01S | 48.59 E |
| Maroua | 104 | 10.36N | 14.20 E |
| Marovoay | 106 | 16.06S | 46.39 E |
| Marquette | 138 | 46.32N | 87.23 W |
| Marrah, Jabal ▲ | 104 | 14.04N | 24.21 E |
| Marrakech | 104 | 31.38N | 8.00 W |
| Marsabit | 108 | 2.20N | 37.59 E |
| Marsala | 96 | 37.48N | 12.26 E |
| Marseille | 92 | 43.18N | 5.24 E |
| Marshall | 138 | 32.32N | 94.22 W |
| Marsh Island I | 128 | 29.35N | 91.53 W |
| Marsing | 142 | 43.32N | 116.48 W |
| Martaban, Gulf of c | 120 | 16.30N | 97.00 E |
| Martha's Vineyard I | 140 | 41.25N | 70.40 W |
| Martigny | 92 | 46.06N | 7.04 E |
| Martigues | 92 | 43.24N | 5.03 E |

| Name | Page No. | Lat. | Long. |
|------|----------|------|-------|
| Martin | 90 | 49.05N | 18.55 E |
| Martinique □ ² | 130 | 14.40N | 61.00W |
| Martinsburg | 140 | 39.27N | 77.57W |
| Maryborough | 122 | 25.32S | 152.42 E |
| Maryland □ ³ | 138 | 39.00N | 76.45W |
| Marysville | 142 | 39.08N | 121.35W |
| Masai Steppe ⩗ ¹ | 106 | 4.45S | 37.00 E |
| Mascarene Islands **‖** | 106 | 21.00S | 57.00 E |
| Masherbrum ∧ | 112 | 35.38N | 76.18 E |
| Mason City | 138 | 43.09N | 93.12W |
| Masqaṭ (Muscat) | 108 | 23.37N | 58.35 E |
| Massa | 96 | 44.01N | 10.09 E |
| Massachusetts □ ³ | 138 | 42.15N | 71.50W |
| Massachusetts Bay ⊂ | 140 | 42.20N | 70.50W |
| Massena | 140 | 44.55N | 74.53W |
| Massillon | 140 | 40.48N | 81.32W |
| Masterton | 126 | 40.57S | 175.40 E |
| Matadi | 106 | 5.49S | 13.27 E |
| Matagalpa | 130 | 12.55N | 85.55W |
| Matagorda Island **I** | 128 | 28.15N | 96.30W |
| Matamoros | 128 | 25.53N | 97.30W |
| Matanzas | 130 | 23.03N | 81.35W |
| Matías Romero | 128 | 16.53N | 95.02W |
| Mato Grosso, Planalto do ⩗ ¹ | 132 | 15.30S | 56.00W |
| Matsue | 116 | 35.28N | 133.04 E |
| Matsumoto | 116 | 36.14N | 137.58 E |
| Matsuyama | 116 | 33.50N | 132.45 E |
| Mattagami ⩳ | 136 | 50.43N | 81.29W |
| Mattawamkeag | 140 | 45.30N | 68.21W |
| Matterhorn ∧ | 92 | 45.59N | 7.43 E |
| Matthew Town | 130 | 20.57N | 73.40W |
| Maturín | 132 | 9.45N | 63.11W |
| Maubeuge | 92 | 50.17N | 3.58 E |
| Maug Islands **‖** | 118 | 20.01N | 145.13 E |
| Maui **I** | 143 | 20.45N | 156.15W |
| Maumee | 140 | 41.33N | 83.39W |
| Mauna Loa ∧ ¹ | 143 | 19.29N | 155.36W |
| Maunath Bhanjan | 112 | 25.57N | 83.33 E |
| Mauritania □ ¹ | 104 | 20.00N | 12.00W |
| Mauritius □ ¹ | 106 | 20.17S | 57.33 E |
| Mawlamyine | 120 | 16.30N | 97.38 E |
| Mayaguana **I** | 130 | 22.23N | 72.57W |
| Mayagüez | 130 | 18.12N | 67.09W |
| Maymyo | 120 | 22.02N | 96.28 E |
| Mayotte □ ² | 106 | 12.50S | 45.10 E |
| Mayotte **I** | 106 | 12.50S | 45.10 E |
| Maysville | 140 | 38.38N | 83.44W |
| Mazara del Vallo | 96 | 37.39N | 12.36 E |
| Mazār-e-Sharīf | 112 | 36.42N | 67.06 E |
| Mazatlán | 128 | 23.13N | 106.25W |
| Mazury ⬥ ¹ | 90 | 53.45N | 21.00 E |
| Mbabane | 106 | 26.18S | 31.06 E |
| Mbala | 106 | 8.50S | 31.22 E |
| Mbale | 106 | 1.05N | 34.10 E |
| Mbandaka (Coquilhatville) | 106 | 0.04N | 18.16 E |
| Mbomou (Bomu) ⩳ | 104 | 4.08N | 22.26 E |
| Mbuji-Mayi (Bakwanga) | 106 | 6.09S | 23.38 E |
| McAdam | 140 | 45.36N | 67.20W |
| McAlester | 138 | 34.56N | 95.46W |
| McAllen | 128 | 26.12N | 98.13W |
| McComb | 128 | 31.14N | 90.27W |
| McConnellsburg | 140 | 39.55N | 77.59W |
| McCook | 138 | 40.12N | 100.37W |
| McGill | 142 | 39.24N | 114.46W |
| Mcgrath | 144 | 62.58N | 155.38W |
| McKinley, Mount ∧ | 144 | 63.30N | 151.00W |
| M'Clintock Channel ⸮ | 136 | 71.00N | 101.00W |
| McLoughlin, Mount ∧ | 142 | 42.27N | 122.19W |
| Mead, Lake ⊜ ¹ | 142 | 36.05N | 114.25W |
| Meadville | 140 | 41.38N | 80.09W |
| Meander River | 136 | 59.02N | 117.42W |
| Meath □ ⁹ | 88 | 53.36N | 6.54W |
| Mecca → Makkah | 108 | 21.27N | 39.49 E |

| Name | Page No. | Lat. | Long. |
|------|----------|------|-------|
| Mechelen | 90 | 51.02N | 4.28 E |
| Mecklenburg □ ⁹ | 90 | 53.30N | 13.00 E |
| Medan | 118 | 3.35N | 98.40 E |
| Médéa | 94 | 36.12N | 2.50 E |
| Medellín | 132 | 6.15N | 75.35W |
| Médenine | 104 | 32.21N | 10.30 E |
| Medford | 142 | 42.19N | 122.52W |
| Medgidia | 98 | 44.15N | 28.16 E |
| Medicine Hat | 136 | 50.03N | 110.40W |
| Mediterranean Sea ⴹ ² | 82 | 35.00N | 20.00 E |
| Medjerda, Monts de la ⩗ | 96 | 36.35N | 8.15 E |
| Meekatharra | 122 | 26.36S | 118.29 E |
| Meerut | 112 | 28.59N | 77.42 E |
| Meiktila | 120 | 20.52N | 95.52 E |
| Meiningen | 90 | 50.34N | 10.25 E |
| Meissen | 90 | 51.10N | 13.28 E |
| Mekambo | 106 | 1.01N | 13.56 E |
| Mekong ⩳ | 120 | 10.33N | 105.24 E |
| Melaka | 120 | 2.12N | 102.15 E |
| Melanesia **‖** | 82 | 13.00S | 164.00 E |
| Melbourne, Austl. | 122 | 37.49S | 144.58 E |
| Melbourne, Fl., U.S. | 138 | 28.04N | 80.36W |
| Melby House | 88 | 60.18N | 1.39W |
| Melilla | 104 | 35.19N | 2.58W |
| Melita | 136 | 49.16N | 101.00W |
| Melitopol' | 86 | 46.50N | 35.22 E |
| Melville Island **I**, Austl. | 122 | 11.40S | 131.00 E |
| Melville Island **I**, N.T., Can. | 136 | 75.15N | 110.00W |
| Melville Peninsula ⴲ ¹ | 136 | 68.00N | 84.00W |
| Memmingen | 90 | 47.59N | 10.11 E |
| Memphis | 138 | 35.08N | 90.02W |
| Mendocino, Cape ⴲ | 142 | 40.25N | 124.25W |
| Mendoza | 134 | 32.53S | 68.49W |
| Menorca **I** | 94 | 40.00N | 4.00 E |
| Mentawai, Kepulauan **‖** | 118 | 2.00S | 99.30 E |
| Menzel Bourguiba | 96 | 37.10N | 9.48 E |
| Merano (Meran) | 96 | 46.40N | 11.09 E |
| Merced | 142 | 37.18N | 120.28W |
| Mercedes | 134 | 33.40S | 65.28W |
| Mergui (Myeik) | 120 | 12.26N | 98.36 E |
| Mergui Archipelago **‖** | 120 | 12.00N | 98.00 E |
| Mérida, Mex. | 128 | 20.58N | 89.37W |
| Mérida, Spain | 94 | 38.55N | 6.20W |
| Mérida, Ven. | 130 | 8.30N | 71.10W |
| Meriden | 140 | 41.32N | 72.48W |
| Meridian | 138 | 32.21N | 88.42W |
| Merseburg | 90 | 51.21N | 11.59 E |
| Mersin | 109 | 36.48N | 34.38 E |
| Merthyr Tydfil | 88 | 51.46N | 3.23W |
| Mesa | 138 | 33.25N | 111.49W |
| Mesopotamia ⬥ ¹ | 108 | 34.00N | 44.00 E |
| Mesquite | 142 | 36.48N | 114.03W |
| Messina, Italy | 96 | 38.11N | 15.33 E |
| Messina, S. Afr. | 106 | 22.23S | 30.00 E |
| Metán | 134 | 25.29S | 64.57W |
| Metz | 92 | 49.08N | 6.10 E |
| Meuse (Maas) ⩳ | 90 | 51.49N | 5.01 E |
| Mexicali | 128 | 32.40N | 115.29W |
| Mexico | 138 | 39.10N | 91.52W |
| Mexico □ ¹ | 128 | 23.00N | 102.00W |
| Mexico, Gulf of ⊂ | 128 | 24.00N | 93.00W |
| Mexico City → Ciudad de México | 128 | 19.24N | 99.09W |
| Meymaneh | 112 | 35.55N | 64.47 E |
| Miami | 138 | 25.46N | 80.11W |
| Miānwāli | 112 | 32.35N | 71.33 E |
| Miass | 86 | 54.59N | 60.06 E |
| Michigan □ ³ | 138 | 44.00N | 85.00W |
| Michigan, Lake ⊜ | 138 | 44.00N | 87.00W |
| Micronesia **‖** | 82 | 11.00N | 159.00 E |
| Micronesia, Federated States of □ ¹ | 118 | 5.00N | 152.00 E |
| Mičurinsk | 100 | 52.54N | 40.30 E |
| Middelburg | 106 | 31.30S | 25.00 E |

| Name | Page No. | Lat. | Long. | Name | Page No. | Lat. | Long. |
|---|---|---|---|---|---|---|---|
| Moscos Islands ॥ | 120 | 14.00N | 97.45 E | Muscat | | | |
| Moscow | | | | → Masqaṭ | 108 | 23.37N | 58.35 E |
| → Moskva | 100 | 55.45N | 37.35 E | Mustafakemalpaşa | 98 | 40.02N | 28.24 E |
| Mosel (Moselle) ≊ | 92 | 50.22N | 7.36 E | Mutá, Ponta do ➤ | 135 | 13.52S | 38.56W |
| Moselle (Mosel) ≊ | 92 | 50.22N | 7.36 E | Mutare | 106 | 18.58S | 32.40 E |
| Moskva (Moscow) | 100 | 55.45N | 37.35 E | Mwanza | 106 | 2.31S | 32.54 E |
| Moskva ≊ | 100 | 55.05N | 38.50 E | Myanaung | 120 | 18.17N | 95.19 E |
| Mosquitos, Golfo de | | | | Myanmar | | | |
| los ⊂ | 130 | 9.00N | 81.15W | → Burma □[1] | 118 | 22.00N | 98.00 E |
| Mossburn | 126 | 45.40S | 168.15 E | Myingyan | 120 | 21.28N | 95.23 E |
| Mosselbaai | 106 | 34.11S | 22.08 E | Myitkyinā | 120 | 25.23N | 97.24 E |
| Mossoró | 132 | 5.11S | 37.20W | Mymensingh | 112 | 24.45N | 90.24 E |
| Most | 90 | 50.32N | 13.39 E | Myrtle Point | 142 | 43.03N | 124.08W |
| Mostaganem | 94 | 35.51N | 0.07 E | Mysore | 111 | 12.18N | 76.39 E |
| Mostar | 96 | 43.20N | 17.49 E | | | | |
| Motala | 89 | 58.33N | 15.03 E | | | | |
| Motherwell | 88 | 55.48N | 4.00W | **N** | | | |
| Moulins | 92 | 46.34N | 3.20 E | | | | |
| Moundou | 104 | 8.34N | 16.05 E | Naalehu | 143 | 19.03N | 155.35W |
| Moundsville | 140 | 39.55N | 80.44W | Naas | 88 | 53.13N | 6.39W |
| Mountain Home | 142 | 43.07N | 115.41W | Nabeul | 96 | 36.27N | 10.44 E |
| Mountain Nile (Baḥr | | | | Nābulus | 109 | 32.13N | 35.16 E |
| al-Jabal) ≊ | 108 | 9.30N | 30.30 E | Nacogdoches | 138 | 31.36N | 94.39W |
| Mount Forest | 140 | 43.59N | 80.44W | Næstved | 89 | 55.14N | 11.46 E |
| Mount Gambier | 122 | 37.50S | 140.46 E | Naga | 118 | 13.37N | 123.11 E |
| Mount Isa | 122 | 20.44S | 139.30 E | Nāgāland □[3] | 112 | 26.00N | 95.00 E |
| Mount Magnet | 122 | 28.04S | 117.49 E | Nagano | 116 | 36.39N | 138.11 E |
| Mount Morris | 140 | 42.43N | 77.52W | Nagaoka | 116 | 37.27N | 138.51 E |
| Mount Olivet | 140 | 38.31N | 84.02W | Nagasaki | 116 | 32.48N | 129.55 E |
| Mount Pleasant | 140 | 43.35N | 84.46W | Nagoya | 116 | 35.10N | 136.55 E |
| Mount Union | 140 | 40.23N | 77.52W | Nāgpur | 112 | 21.09N | 79.06 E |
| Mozambique □[1] | 106 | 18.15S | 35.00 E | Nagykanizsa | 90 | 46.27N | 17.00 E |
| Mozambique Channel | | | | Naha | 117b | 26.13N | 127.40 E |
| ⋓ | 106 | 19.00S | 41.00 E | Nain | 136 | 56.32N | 61.41W |
| Mozyr' | 86 | 52.03N | 29.14 E | Nairobi | 106 | 1.17S | 36.49 E |
| Mrhila, Djebel ⋀ | 96 | 35.25N | 9.14 E | Najin | 114 | 42.15N | 130.18 E |
| Mtwara | 106 | 10.16S | 40.11 E | Nakhon Pathom | 120 | 13.49N | 100.03 E |
| Muang Không | 120 | 14.07N | 105.51 E | Nakhon Ratchasima | 120 | 14.58N | 102.07 E |
| Muang Khôngxédôn | 120 | 15.34N | 105.49 E | Nakhon Sawan | 120 | 15.41N | 100.07 E |
| Muang Xaignabouri | 120 | 19.15N | 101.45 E | Nakhon Si Thammarat | 120 | 8.26N | 99.58 E |
| Muar (Bandar | | | | Nakuru | 106 | 0.17S | 36.04 E |
| Maharani) | 120 | 2.02N | 102.34 E | Nal'čik | 86 | 43.29N | 43.37 E |
| Muchinga Mountains ⋌ | 106 | 12.00S | 31.45 E | Namangan | 110 | 41.00N | 71.40 E |
| Mudanjiang | 114 | 44.35N | 129.36 E | Nam-dinh | 120 | 20.25N | 106.10 E |
| Mufulira | 106 | 12.33S | 28.14 E | Namib Desert ➛[2] | 106 | 23.00S | 15.00 E |
| Muḥammad, Ra's ➤ | 109 | 27.44N | 34.15 E | Namibe | 106 | 15.10S | 12.09 E |
| Mühlviertel ➛[1] | 90 | 48.25N | 14.10 E | Namibia □[1] | 106 | 22.00S | 17.00 E |
| Mukden | | | | Nampa | 138 | 43.32N | 116.33W |
| → Shenyang | 114 | 41.48N | 123.27 E | Namp'o | 114 | 38.45N | 125.23 E |
| Mulatupo | 130 | 8.57N | 77.45W | Nampula | 106 | 15.07S | 39.15 E |
| Mulhacén ⋀ | 94 | 37.03N | 3.19W | Namsos | 89 | 64.29N | 11.30 E |
| Mulhouse | 92 | 47.45N | 7.20 E | Nanchang | 114 | 28.41N | 115.53 E |
| Mull, Island of ॥ | 88 | 56.27N | 6.00W | Nanchong | 114 | 30.48N | 106.04 E |
| Multān | 110 | 30.11N | 71.29 E | Nancy | 92 | 48.41N | 6.12 E |
| München (Munich) | 90 | 48.08N | 11.34 E | Nanda Devi ⋀ | 112 | 30.23N | 79.59 E |
| Munhango | 106 | 12.12S | 18.42 E | Nānga Parbat ⋀ | 112 | 35.15N | 74.36 E |
| Munich | | | | Nanjing (Nanking) | 114 | 32.03N | 118.47 E |
| → München | 90 | 48.08N | 11.34 E | Nanling ⋌ | 114 | 25.00N | 112.00 E |
| Münster | 90 | 51.57N | 7.37 E | Nanning | 114 | 22.48N | 108.20 E |
| Munster □[9] | 88 | 52.25N | 8.20W | Nansei-shotō (Ryukyu | | | |
| Muqdisho | 108 | 2.01N | 45.20 E | Islands) ॥ | 114 | 26.30N | 128.00 E |
| Mura (Mur) ≊ | 90 | 46.18N | 16.53 E | Nantes | 92 | 47.13N | 1.33W |
| Murcia | 94 | 37.59N | 1.07W | Nantong | 114 | 32.02N | 120.53 E |
| Murcia □[9] | 94 | 38.30N | 1.45W | Nantucket Island ॥ | 140 | 41.16N | 70.03W |
| Mureş (Maros) ≊ | 90 | 46.15N | 20.13 E | Nanuque | 132 | 17.50S | 40.21W |
| Murfreesboro | 138 | 35.50N | 86.23W | Napanee | 140 | 44.15N | 76.57W |
| Murmansk | 86 | 68.58N | 33.05 E | Napier | 126 | 39.29S | 176.55 E |
| Murom | 100 | 55.34N | 42.02 E | Naples | | | |
| Muroran | 116a | 42.18N | 140.59 E | → Napoli | 96 | 40.51N | 14.17 E |
| Murray ≊ | 124 | 35.22S | 139.22 E | Napo ≊ | 132 | 3.20S | 72.40W |
| Murraysburg | 106 | 31.58S | 23.47 E | Napoleon | 140 | 41.23N | 84.07W |
| Murrumbidgee ≊ | 124 | 34.43S | 143.12 E | Napoli (Naples) | 96 | 40.51N | 14.17 E |
| Murupara | 126 | 38.28S | 176.42 E | Nara | 116 | 34.41N | 135.50 E |
| Mürzzuschlag | 90 | 47.36N | 15.41 E | Narathiwat | 120 | 6.26N | 101.50 E |
| Mūsā, Jabal (Mount | | | | Nārāyanganj | 112 | 23.37N | 90.30 E |
| Sinai) ⋀ | 109 | 28.32N | 33.59 E | Narbonne | 92 | 43.11N | 3.00 E |
| Musala ⋀ | 98 | 42.11N | 23.34 E | Narew ≊ | 90 | 52.26N | 20.42 E |

| Name | Page No. | Lat. | Long. |
|------|----------|------|-------|
| Narmada ≏ | 112 | 21.38 N | 72.36 E |
| Narodnaja, Gora ᴧ | 102 | 65.04 N | 60.09 E |
| Narva | 100 | 59.23 N | 28.12 E |
| Narvik | 89 | 68.26 N | 17.25 E |
| Nashua | 140 | 42.45 N | 71.28 W |
| Nashville | 138 | 36.09 N | 86.47 W |
| Nāsik | 111 | 19.59 N | 73.48 E |
| Nassau | 130 | 25.05 N | 77.21 W |
| Nasser, Lake ᴇ¹ | 108 | 22.40 N | 32.00 E |
| Natal | 132 | 5.47 S | 35.13 W |
| Natchez | 138 | 31.33 N | 91.24 W |
| Natchitoches | 128 | 31.45 N | 93.05 W |
| Natuna Besar ᴵ | 120 | 4.00 N | 108.15 E |
| Naumburg | 90 | 51.09 N | 11.48 E |
| Nausori | 127c | 18.02 S | 175.32 E |
| Navojoa | 128 | 27.06 N | 109.26 W |
| Nawābganj | 112 | 24.36 N | 88.17 E |
| Nawābshāh | 112 | 26.15 N | 68.25 E |
| Náxos ᴵ | 98 | 37.02 N | 25.35 E |
| Nazaré | 135 | 13.02 S | 39.00 W |
| Nazca | 132 | 14.50 S | 74.57 W |
| Naze | 117b | 28.23 N | 129.30 E |
| Nazilli | 98 | 37.55 N | 28.21 E |
| N'Djamena (Fort-Lamy) | 104 | 12.07 N | 15.03 E |
| Ndola | 106 | 12.58 S | 28.38 E |
| Néa Páfos (Paphos) | 109 | 34.45 N | 32.25 E |
| Near Islands ᴵᴵ | 144 | 52.40 N | 173.30 E |
| Nebraska □³ | 138 | 41.30 N | 100.00 W |
| Nechí | 130 | 8.07 N | 74.46 W |
| Neepawa | 136 | 50.13 N | 99.29 W |
| Negele | 108 | 5.20 N | 39.36 E |
| Negombo | 111 | 7.13 N | 79.50 E |
| Negra, Punta ≻ | 132 | 6.06 S | 81.09 W |
| Negro ≏, Arg. | 134 | 41.02 S | 62.47 W |
| Negro ≏, S.A. | 132 | 3.08 S | 59.55 W |
| Negros ᴵ | 118 | 10.00 N | 123.00 E |
| Nei Monggol Zizhiqu (Inner Mongolia) □⁴ | 114 | 43.00 N | 115.00 E |
| Neisse ≏ | 90 | 52.04 N | 14.46 E |
| Neiva | 132 | 2.56 N | 75.18 W |
| Nelson, B.C., Can. | 136 | 49.29 N | 117.17 W |
| Nelson, N.Z. | 126 | 41.17 S | 173.17 E |
| Neman (Nemunas) ≏ | 100 | 55.18 N | 21.23 E |
| Nemunas (Neman) ≏ | 100 | 55.18 N | 21.23 E |
| Nemuro | 116a | 43.20 N | 145.35 E |
| Nemuro Strait ᴜ | 116a | 44.00 N | 145.20 E |
| Nenana | 144 | 64.34 N | 149.07 W |
| Nepal □¹ | 110 | 28.00 N | 84.00 E |
| Nerastro, Sarīr ◆² | 104 | 24.20 N | 20.37 E |
| Ness, Loch ᴇ | 88 | 57.15 N | 4.30 W |
| Netherlands □¹ | 86 | 52.15 N | 5.30 E |
| Netherlands Antilles □² | 130 | 12.15 N | 69.00 W |
| Neubrandenburg | 90 | 53.33 N | 13.15 E |
| Neuchâtel, Lac de ᴇ | 92 | 46.52 N | 6.50 E |
| Neumünster | 90 | 54.04 N | 9.59 E |
| Neunkirchen | 90 | 49.20 N | 7.10 E |
| Neusiedler See ᴇ | 96 | 47.50 N | 16.46 E |
| Neustrelitz | 90 | 53.21 N | 13.04 E |
| Nevada □³ | 138 | 39.00 N | 117.00 W |
| Nevada, Sierra ⫪ | 142 | 38.00 N | 119.15 W |
| Nevers | 92 | 47.00 N | 3.09 E |
| Nevinnomyssk | 86 | 44.38 N | 41.56 E |
| Nevis, Ben ᴧ | 88 | 56.48 N | 5.01 W |
| New Amsterdam | 132 | 6.15 N | 57.31 W |
| Newark, N.J., U.S. | 140 | 40.44 N | 74.10 W |
| Newark, Oh., U.S. | 140 | 40.04 N | 82.24 W |
| New Bedford | 140 | 41.38 N | 70.56 W |
| New Braunfels | 128 | 29.42 N | 98.07 W |
| New Brunswick | 140 | 40.29 N | 74.27 W |
| New Brunswick □⁴ | 136 | 46.30 N | 66.15 W |
| Newburgh | 140 | 41.30 N | 74.00 W |
| New Caledonia □² | 127b | 21.30 S | 165.30 E |
| Newcastle, Austl. | 122 | 32.56 S | 151.46 E |
| Newcastle, N.B., Can. | 136 | 47.00 N | 65.34 W |
| New Castle, Pa., U.S. | 140 | 41.00 N | 80.20 W |
| Newcastle upon Tyne | 88 | 54.59 N | 1.35 W |

| Name | Page No. | Lat. | Long. |
|------|----------|------|-------|
| Newcastle Waters | 122 | 17.24 S | 133.24 E |
| New Delhi | 112 | 28.36 N | 77.12 E |
| Newfoundland □⁴ | 136 | 52.00 N | 56.00 W |
| Newfoundland ᴵ | 136 | 48.30 N | 56.00 W |
| New Georgia ᴵ | 127a | 8.15 S | 157.30 E |
| New Georgia Group ᴵᴵ | 127a | 8.30 S | 157.20 E |
| New Glasgow | 136 | 45.35 N | 62.39 W |
| New Guinea ᴵ | 118 | 5.00 S | 140.00 E |
| New Hampshire □³ | 138 | 43.35 N | 71.40 W |
| New Haven | 140 | 41.18 N | 72.56 W |
| New Hebrides → Vanuatu □¹ | 127b | 16.00 S | 167.00 E |
| New Jersey □³ | 138 | 40.15 N | 74.30 W |
| New Liskeard | 136 | 47.30 N | 79.40 W |
| New London | 140 | 41.21 N | 72.07 W |
| Newmarket | 140 | 43.04 N | 70.56 W |
| New Martinsville | 140 | 39.38 N | 80.51 W |
| New Mexico □³ | 138 | 34.30 N | 106.00 W |
| New Orleans | 138 | 29.57 N | 90.04 W |
| New Philadelphia | 140 | 40.30 N | 81.27 W |
| New Plymouth | 126 | 39.04 S | 174.05 E |
| Newport, Wales, U.K. | 88 | 51.35 N | 3.00 W |
| Newport, R.I., U.S. | 140 | 41.29 N | 71.18 W |
| Newport, Vt., U.S. | 140 | 44.56 N | 72.12 W |
| Newport News | 138 | 36.58 N | 76.25 W |
| New Providence ᴵ | 130 | 25.02 N | 77.24 W |
| Newry | 88 | 54.11 N | 6.20 W |
| New South Wales □³ | 122 | 33.00 S | 146.00 E |
| Newton Stewart | 88 | 54.57 N | 4.29 W |
| Newtownards | 88 | 54.36 N | 5.41 W |
| New York | 140 | 40.43 N | 74.01 W |
| New York □³ | 138 | 43.00 N | 75.00 W |
| New Zealand □¹ | 126 | 41.00 S | 174.00 E |
| Nezahualcóyotl, Presa ᴇ¹ | 128 | 17.10 N | 93.40 W |
| Nguigmi | 104 | 14.15 N | 13.07 E |
| Nha-trang | 120 | 12.15 N | 109.11 E |
| Niagara Falls, On., Can. | 136 | 43.06 N | 79.04 W |
| Niagara Falls, N.Y., U.S. | 140 | 43.05 N | 79.03 W |
| Niamey | 104 | 13.31 N | 2.07 E |
| Nias, Pulau ᴵ | 120 | 1.05 N | 97.35 E |
| Nicaragua □¹ | 130 | 13.00 N | 85.00 W |
| Nicaragua, Lago de ᴇ | 130 | 11.30 N | 85.30 W |
| Nice | 92 | 43.42 N | 7.15 E |
| Nicholasville | 140 | 37.52 N | 84.34 W |
| Nicobar Islands ᴵᴵ | 120 | 8.00 N | 93.30 E |
| Nicosia | 109 | 35.10 N | 33.22 E |
| Nicoya, Península de ≻¹ | 130 | 10.00 N | 85.25 W |
| Nienburg | 90 | 52.38 N | 9.13 E |
| Niger □¹ | 104 | 16.00 N | 8.00 E |
| Niger ≏ | 104 | 5.33 N | 6.33 E |
| Nigeria □¹ | 104 | 10.00 N | 8.00 E |
| Niigata | 116 | 37.55 N | 139.03 E |
| Niihama | 116 | 33.58 N | 133.16 E |
| Niihau ᴵ | 143 | 21.55 N | 160.10 W |
| Niitsu | 116 | 37.48 N | 139.07 E |
| Nijmegen | 90 | 51.50 N | 5.50 E |
| Nikkō | 116 | 36.45 N | 139.37 E |
| Nikolajev | 86 | 46.58 N | 32.00 E |
| Nile (Nahr an-Nīl) ≏ | 104 | 30.10 N | 31.06 E |
| Nimba, Mont ᴧ | 104 | 7.37 N | 8.25 W |
| Nîmes | 92 | 43.50 N | 4.21 E |
| Nine Degree Channel ᴜ | 111 | 9.00 N | 73.00 E |
| Ningbo | 114 | 29.52 N | 121.31 E |
| Niort | 92 | 46.19 N | 0.27 W |
| Nipigon, Lake ᴇ | 136 | 49.50 N | 88.30 W |
| Nipissing, Lake ᴇ | 140 | 46.17 N | 80.00 W |
| Niš | 98 | 43.19 N | 21.54 E |
| Niterói | 132 | 22.53 S | 43.07 W |
| Nitra | 90 | 48.20 N | 18.05 E |
| Nivelles | 90 | 50.36 N | 4.20 E |
| Nižn'aja Tunguska ≏ | 102 | 65.48 N | 88.04 E |
| Nižneudinsk | 102 | 54.54 N | 99.03 E |

| Name | Page No. | Lat. | Long. |
|---|---|---|---|
| Okazaki | 116 | 34.57N | 137.10 E |
| Okeechobee, Lake ◉ | 138 | 26.55N | 80.45W |
| Okhotsk, Sea of | | | |
| (Ochotskoje More) | | | |
| ▼ ² | 102 | 53.00N | 150.00 E |
| Oki-guntō II | 116 | 36.15N | 133.15 E |
| Okinawa-jima I | 117b | 26.30N | 128.00 E |
| Oklahoma □ ³ | 138 | 35.30N | 98.00W |
| Oklahoma City | 138 | 35.28N | 97.30W |
| Oksskolten ᴧ | 89 | 65.59N | 14.15 E |
| Okt'abr'skoj | | | |
| Revol'ucii, Ostrov I | 102 | 79.30N | 97.00 E |
| Öland I | 89 | 56.45N | 16.38 E |
| Olcott | 140 | 43.20N | 78.42W |
| Old Bahama Channel | | | |
| ᴻ | 130 | 22.30N | 78.50W |
| Old Crow | 136 | 67.35N | 139.50W |
| Oldenburg | 90 | 53.08N | 8.13 E |
| Old Forge | 140 | 43.42N | 74.58W |
| Old Town | 140 | 44.56N | 68.38W |
| Olean | 140 | 42.04N | 78.25W |
| Oléron, Île d' I | 92 | 45.56N | 1.15W |
| Olimarao I ¹ | 118 | 7.41N | 145.52 E |
| Ólimbos ᴧ, Cyp. | 109 | 34.56N | 32.52 E |
| Ólimbos ᴧ, Grc. | 98 | 40.05N | 22.21 E |
| Olímpia | 135 | 20.44S | 48.54W |
| Olinda | 132 | 8.01S | 34.51W |
| Oliveira | 135 | 20.41S | 44.49W |
| Ollagüe | 134 | 21.14S | 68.16W |
| Olmos | 132 | 5.59S | 79.46W |
| Olomouc | 90 | 49.36N | 17.16 E |
| Olsztyn (Allenstein) | 90 | 53.48N | 20.29 E |
| Olt ≃ | 98 | 43.43N | 24.51 E |
| Olympia | 138 | 47.02N | 122.53W |
| Olympus, Mount ᴧ | 138 | 47.48N | 123.43W |
| Olympus, Mount | | | |
| → Ólimbos ᴧ | 98 | 40.05N | 22.21 E |
| Omagh | 88 | 54.36N | 7.18W |
| Omaha | 138 | 41.15N | 95.56W |
| Oman □ ¹ | 108 | 22.00N | 58.00 E |
| Oman, Gulf of c | 108 | 24.30N | 58.30 E |
| Omarama | 126 | 44.29S | 169.58 E |
| Ometepe, Isla de I | 130 | 11.30N | 85.35W |
| Ōmiya | 116 | 35.54N | 139.38 E |
| Omsk | 102 | 55.00N | 73.24 E |
| Ōmuta | 116 | 33.02N | 130.27 E |
| Ondangua | 106 | 17.55S | 16.00 E |
| Oneida | 140 | 43.05N | 75.39W |
| Oneida Lake ◉ | 140 | 43.13N | 76.00W |
| Oneonta | 140 | 42.27N | 75.03W |
| Onslow | 122 | 21.39S | 115.06 E |
| Ontario | 138 | 44.01N | 116.57W |
| Ontario □ ⁴ | 136 | 51.00N | 85.00W |
| Ontario, Lake ◉ | 138 | 43.45N | 78.00W |
| Ooldea | 122 | 30.27S | 131.50 E |
| Oostende (Ostende) | 90 | 51.13N | 2.55 E |
| Opava | 90 | 49.56N | 17.54 E |
| Opelousas | 128 | 30.32N | 92.04W |
| Opole (Oppeln) | 90 | 50.41N | 17.55 E |
| Opotiki | 126 | 38.00S | 177.17 E |
| Opunake | 126 | 39.27S | 173.51 E |
| Oradea | 98 | 47.03N | 21.57 E |
| Orange, Austl. | 122 | 33.17S | 149.06 E |
| Orange, Tx., U.S. | 128 | 30.05N | 93.44W |
| Orange, Va., U.S. | 140 | 38.14N | 78.06W |
| Orange (Oranje) ≃ | 106 | 28.41S | 16.28 E |
| Orange Walk | 130 | 18.06N | 88.33W |
| Oranjestad | 130 | 12.33N | 70.06W |
| Orchon ≃ | 114 | 50.21N | 106.05 E |
| Örebro | 89 | 59.17N | 15.13 E |
| Orechovo-Zujevo | 100 | 55.49N | 38.59 E |
| Oregon □ ³ | 138 | 44.00N | 121.00W |
| Orenburg | 86 | 51.54N | 55.06 E |
| Orense | 94 | 42.20N | 7.51W |
| Oriental, Cordillera ⱪ | 132 | 11.00S | 74.00W |
| Orillia | 140 | 44.37N | 79.25W |
| Orinoco ≃ | 132 | 8.37N | 62.15W |

| Name | Page No. | Lat. | Long. |
|---|---|---|---|
| Orissa □ ³ | 111 | 20.00N | 84.00 E |
| Orizaba, Pico de ᴧ ¹ | 128 | 19.01N | 97.16W |
| Orkney Islands II | 88 | 59.00N | 3.00W |
| Orlando | 138 | 28.32N | 81.22W |
| Orléanais □ ⁹ | 92 | 47.50N | 2.00 E |
| Orléans | 92 | 47.55N | 1.54 E |
| Örnsköldsvik | 89 | 63.18N | 18.43 E |
| Orohena, Mont ᴧ | 127d | 17.37S | 149.28W |
| Or'ol | 100 | 52.59N | 36.05 E |
| Oroville | 142 | 39.30N | 121.33W |
| Orša | 100 | 54.30N | 30.24 E |
| Orsk | 86 | 51.12N | 58.34 E |
| Orūmīyeh | 86 | 37.33N | 45.04 E |
| Oruro | 132 | 17.59S | 67.09W |
| Osa, Península de ⱦ ¹ | 130 | 8.34N | 83.31W |
| Ōsaka | 116 | 34.40N | 135.30 E |
| Osăm ≃ | 98 | 43.42N | 24.51 E |
| Oscoda | 140 | 44.26N | 83.20W |
| Oshawa | 136 | 43.54N | 78.51W |
| Oshkosh | 138 | 44.01N | 88.32W |
| Oshogbo | 104 | 7.47N | 4.34 E |
| Osijek | 98 | 45.33N | 18.41 E |
| Oslo | 89 | 59.55N | 10.45 E |
| Osmaniye | 109 | 37.05N | 36.14 E |
| Osnabrück | 90 | 52.16N | 8.02 E |
| Osorno | 134 | 40.34S | 73.09W |
| Ossa, Mount ᴧ | 122 | 41.54S | 146.01 E |
| Östersund | 89 | 63.11N | 14.39 E |
| Ostfriesische Inseln II | 90 | 53.44N | 7.25 E |
| Ostrava | 90 | 49.50N | 18.17 E |
| Ostrov | 90 | 50.17N | 12.57 E |
| Ostrowiec | | | |
| Świętokrzyski | 90 | 50.57N | 21.23 E |
| Ostrów Wielkopolski | 90 | 51.39N | 17.49 E |
| Ōsumi-kaikyō ᴻ | 116 | 31.00N | 131.00 E |
| Oswego | 140 | 43.27N | 76.30W |
| Otaru | 116a | 43.13N | 141.00 E |
| Otra ≃ | 89 | 58.09N | 8.00 E |
| Otranto, Strait of ≃ ¹ | 98 | 40.00N | 19.00 E |
| Ötscher ᴧ | 90 | 47.52N | 15.12 E |
| Ōtsu | 116 | 35.00N | 135.52 E |
| Ottawa | 140 | 45.25N | 75.42W |
| Ottawa ≃ | 136 | 45.20N | 73.58W |
| Ouagadougou | 104 | 12.22N | 1.31W |
| Ouahigouya | 104 | 13.35N | 2.25W |
| Ouarane ᴧ ¹ | 104 | 21.00N | 10.30W |
| Oubangui (Ubangi) ≃ | 104 | 1.15N | 17.50 E |
| Ouessant, Île d' I | 92 | 48.28N | 5.05W |
| Oujda | 104 | 34.41N | 1.45W |
| Oulu | 89 | 65.01N | 25.28 E |
| Oulujärvi ◉ | 89 | 64.20N | 27.15 E |
| Ourinhos | 135 | 22.59S | 49.52W |
| Ouro Prêto | 135 | 20.23S | 43.30W |
| Ovalle | 134 | 30.36S | 71.12W |
| Ovamboland □ ⁹ | 106 | 17.45S | 16.30 E |
| Overton | 142 | 36.32N | 114.26W |
| Oviedo | 94 | 43.22N | 5.50W |
| Owens Lake ◉ | 142 | 36.25N | 117.56W |
| Owen Sound | 136 | 44.34N | 80.56W |
| Owen Stanley Range ⱪ | 122 | 9.20S | 147.55 E |
| Owenton | 140 | 38.32N | 84.50W |
| Owosso | 140 | 42.59N | 84.10W |
| Owyhee ≃ | 142 | 43.46N | 117.02W |
| Oxford | 88 | 51.46N | 1.15W |
| Oxnard | 142 | 34.11N | 119.10W |
| Ozark Plateau ᴧ ¹ | 138 | 36.30N | 92.30W |
| Ozarks, Lake of the ◉ ¹ | 138 | 38.10N | 92.50W |
| Ózd | 90 | 48.14N | 20.18 E |

**P**

| | | | |
|---|---|---|---|
| Paarl | 106 | 33.45S | 18.56 E |
| Paauilo | 143 | 20.02N | 155.22W |
| Pābna | 112 | 24.00N | 89.15 E |
| Pacasmayo | 132 | 7.24S | 79.34W |
| Pachuca [de Soto] | 128 | 20.07N | 98.44W |

| Name | Page No. | Lat. | Long. |
|---|---|---|---|
| Peterborough, On., Can. | 136 | 44.18N | 78.19W |
| Peterborough, Eng., U.K. | 88 | 52.35N | 0.15W |
| Petersburg | 144 | 56.49N | 132.57W |
| Petoskey | 140 | 45.22N | 84.57W |
| Petrič | 98 | 41.24N | 23.13 E |
| Petrolina | 132 | 9.24S | 40.30W |
| Petropavlovsk | 102 | 54.54N | 69.06 E |
| Petropavlovsk-Kamčatskij | 102 | 53.01N | 158.39 E |
| Petrópolis | 132 | 22.31S | 43.10W |
| Petroşani | 98 | 45.25N | 23.22 E |
| Petrozavodsk | 86 | 61.47N | 34.20 E |
| Pforzheim | 90 | 48.54N | 8.42 E |
| Phan-rang | 120 | 11.34N | 108.59 E |
| Phan-thiet | 120 | 10.56N | 108.06 E |
| Phet Buri | 120 | 13.06N | 99.57 E |
| Philadelphia | 140 | 39.57N | 75.09W |
| Philippi | 140 | 39.09N | 80.02W |
| Philippines □[1] | 118 | 13.00N | 122.00 E |
| Philippine Sea ☞[2] | 82 | 20.00N | 135.00 E |
| Philipsburg | 140 | 40.53N | 78.13W |
| Phitsanulok | 120 | 16.50N | 100.15 E |
| Phnum Pénh | 120 | 11.33N | 104.55 E |
| Phoenix | 138 | 33.26N | 112.04W |
| Phôngsali | 120 | 21.41N | 102.06 E |
| Phra Nakhon Si Ayutthaya | 120 | 14.21N | 100.33 E |
| Phuket | 120 | 7.53N | 98.24 E |
| Phu-vinh | 120 | 9.56N | 106.20 E |
| Piacenza | 96 | 45.01N | 9.40 E |
| Piatra-Neamţ | 98 | 46.56N | 26.22 E |
| Picardie □[9] | 92 | 50.00N | 3.30 E |
| Pickford | 140 | 46.09N | 84.21W |
| Pidurutalagala ∧ | 111 | 7.00N | 80.46 E |
| Piedras Negras, Guat. | 130 | 17.11N | 91.15W |
| Piedras Negras, Mex. | 128 | 28.42N | 100.31W |
| Pieksämäki | 89 | 62.18N | 27.08 E |
| Pielinen ☺ | 89 | 63.15N | 29.40 E |
| Pierre | 138 | 44.22N | 100.21W |
| Pietermaritzburg | 106 | 29.37S | 30.16 E |
| Pietersburg | 106 | 23.54S | 29.25 E |
| Pietrosu, Vîrful ∧, Rom. | 98 | 47.08N | 25.11 E |
| Pietrosu, Vîrful ∧, Rom. | 98 | 47.36N | 24.38 E |
| Pikes Peak ∧ | 138 | 38.51N | 105.03W |
| Piła (Schneidemühl) | 90 | 53.10N | 16.44 E |
| Pilica ≗ | 90 | 51.52N | 21.17 E |
| Pinang → George Town | 120 | 5.25N | 100.20 E |
| Pinar del Río | 130 | 22.25N | 83.42W |
| Píndhos óros ⋌ | 98 | 39.49N | 21.14 E |
| Pine Bluff | 138 | 34.13N | 92.00W |
| Pins, Île des I | 127b | 22.37S | 167.30 E |
| Pinsk | 100 | 52.07N | 26.04 E |
| Piombino | 96 | 42.55N | 10.32 E |
| Piotrków Trybunalski | 90 | 51.25N | 19.42 E |
| Pipmouacane, Réservoir ☺[1] | 136 | 49.35N | 70.30W |
| Piqua | 140 | 40.08N | 84.14W |
| Piracicaba | 135 | 22.43S | 47.38W |
| Piraiévs (Piraeus) | 98 | 37.57N | 23.38 E |
| Piraju | 135 | 23.12S | 49.23W |
| Pirapora | 135 | 17.21S | 44.56W |
| Pirmasens | 90 | 49.12N | 7.36 E |
| Pisa | 96 | 43.43N | 10.23 E |
| Pisco | 132 | 13.42S | 76.13W |
| Pisticci | 96 | 40.23N | 16.34 E |
| Piteå | 89 | 65.20N | 21.30 E |
| Piteşti | 98 | 44.52N | 24.52 E |
| Pittsburgh | 140 | 40.26N | 79.59W |
| Pittsfield | 140 | 42.27N | 73.14W |
| Piura | 132 | 5.12S | 80.38W |
| Placetas | 130 | 22.19N | 79.40W |
| Planeta Rica | 130 | 8.25N | 75.36W |

| Name | Page No. | Lat. | Long. |
|---|---|---|---|
| Plata, Río de la ⊂[1] | 134 | 35.00S | 57.00W |
| Platte ≗ | 138 | 39.16N | 94.50W |
| Plattsburgh | 140 | 44.41N | 73.27W |
| Plauen | 90 | 50.30N | 12.08 E |
| Plenty, Bay of ⊂ | 126 | 37.40S | 177.00 E |
| Plétipi, Lac ☺ | 136 | 51.44N | 70.06W |
| Pleven | 98 | 43.25N | 24.37 E |
| Płock | 90 | 52.33N | 19.43 E |
| Ploieşti | 98 | 44.56N | 26.02 E |
| Plovdiv | 98 | 42.09N | 24.45 E |
| Plymouth, Eng., U.K. | 88 | 50.23N | 4.10W |
| Plymouth, Ma., U.S. | 140 | 41.57N | 70.40W |
| Plzeň | 90 | 49.45N | 13.23 E |
| Po ≗ | 96 | 44.57N | 12.04 E |
| Pobeda, Gora ∧ | 102 | 65.12N | 146.12 E |
| Pocatello | 138 | 42.52N | 112.26W |
| Poços de Caldas | 135 | 21.48S | 46.34W |
| Podlasie ◆[1] | 90 | 52.30N | 23.00 E |
| Podol'sk | 100 | 55.26N | 37.33 E |
| Podor | 104 | 16.40N | 14.57W |
| Pofadder | 106 | 29.10S | 19.22 E |
| Poiana Ruşcăi, Munţii ⋌ | 98 | 45.41N | 22.30 E |
| Pointe-à-Pitre | 130 | 16.14N | 61.32W |
| Pointe-Noire | 106 | 4.48S | 11.51 E |
| Point Pleasant | 140 | 40.04N | 74.04W |
| Point Reyes National Seashore ◆ | 142 | 38.00N | 122.58W |
| Poitiers | 92 | 46.35N | 0.20 E |
| Poland □[1] | 86 | 52.00N | 19.00 E |
| Polevskoj | 86 | 56.26N | 60.11 E |
| Poltava | 86 | 49.35N | 34.34 E |
| Poltimore | 140 | 45.47N | 75.43W |
| Polynesia ‖ | 82 | 4.00S | 156.00W |
| Pomerania □[9] | 90 | 54.00N | 16.00 E |
| Pomeranian Bay ⊂ | 90 | 54.00N | 14.15 E |
| Ponca City | 138 | 36.42N | 97.05W |
| Ponce | 130 | 18.01N | 66.37W |
| Pondicherry □[8] | 111 | 11.56N | 79.50 E |
| Ponta Grossa | 134 | 25.05S | 50.09W |
| Pontchartrain, Lake ☺ | 128 | 30.10N | 90.10W |
| Ponte Nova | 135 | 20.24S | 42.54W |
| Pontevedra | 94 | 42.26N | 8.38W |
| Pontiac | 140 | 42.38N | 83.17W |
| Pontianak | 118 | 0.02S | 109.20 E |
| Poopó, Lago ☺ | 132 | 18.45S | 67.07W |
| Popayán | 132 | 2.27N | 76.36W |
| Poplar Bluff | 138 | 36.45N | 90.23W |
| Popocatépetl, Volcán ∧[1] | 128 | 19.02N | 98.38W |
| Popomanaseu, Mount ∧ | 122 | 9.42S | 160.04 E |
| Poprad | 90 | 49.03N | 20.18 E |
| Pordenone | 96 | 45.57N | 12.39 E |
| Pori | 89 | 61.29N | 21.47 E |
| Porlamar | 130 | 10.57N | 63.51W |
| Poronajsk | 102 | 49.14N | 143.04 E |
| Portadown | 88 | 54.26N | 6.27W |
| Portage | 140 | 42.12N | 85.34W |
| Port Allegany | 140 | 41.48N | 78.16W |
| Port Arthur | 138 | 29.53N | 93.55W |
| Port Augusta | 122 | 32.30S | 137.46 E |
| Port-au-Prince | 130 | 18.32N | 72.20W |
| Port Austin | 140 | 44.02N | 82.59W |
| Port Blair | 120 | 11.40N | 92.45 E |
| Port Clyde | 140 | 43.55N | 69.15W |
| Port Elgin | 140 | 44.26N | 81.24W |
| Port Elizabeth | 106 | 33.58S | 25.40 E |
| Port Ellen | 88 | 55.39N | 6.12W |
| Porterville | 142 | 36.03N | 119.00W |
| Port-Gentil | 106 | 0.43S | 8.47 E |
| Port Harcourt | 104 | 4.43N | 7.05 E |
| Port Hedland | 122 | 20.19S | 118.34 E |
| Port Henry | 140 | 44.02N | 73.27W |
| Port Huron | 140 | 42.58N | 82.25W |
| Portland, Austl. | 122 | 38.21S | 141.36 E |
| Portland, Me., U.S. | 140 | 43.39N | 70.15W |

| Name | Page No. | Lat. | Long. |
|------|----------|------|-------|
| Portland, Or., U.S. | 138 | 45.31N | 122.40W |
| Port Lavaca | 128 | 28.36N | 96.37W |
| Port Lincoln | 122 | 34.44S | 135.52 E |
| Port Louis | 106 | 20.10S | 57.30 E |
| Port Macquarie | 122 | 31.26S | 152.55 E |
| Port Moresby | 122 | 9.30S | 147.10 E |
| Port Nolloth | 106 | 29.17S | 16.51 E |
| Porto | 94 | 41.11N | 8.36W |
| Pôrto Alegre | 134 | 30.04S | 51.11W |
| Porto Amboim | 106 | 10.44S | 13.44 E |
| Portobelo | 130 | 9.33N | 79.39W |
| Port of Spain | 130 | 10.39N | 61.31W |
| Porto-Novo | 104 | 6.29N | 2.37 E |
| Port Orford | 142 | 42.44N | 124.29W |
| Porto-Vecchio | 96 | 41.35N | 9.16 E |
| Pôrto Velho | 132 | 8.46S | 63.54W |
| Port Pirie | 122 | 33.11S | 138.01 E |
| Port Said |  |  |  |
| → Bûr Sa'ïd | 104 | 31.16N | 32.18 E |
| Port Shepstone | 106 | 30.46S | 30.22 E |
| Portsmouth, Eng., U.K. | 88 | 50.48N | 1.05W |
| Portsmouth, N.H., U.S. | 140 | 43.04N | 70.45W |
| Portsmouth, Oh., U.S. | 140 | 38.43N | 82.59W |
| Porttipahdan tekojärvi ⊜[1] | 89 | 68.08N | 26.40 E |
| Portugal □[1] | 86 | 39.30N | 8.00W |
| Portugalete | 94 | 43.19N | 3.01W |
| Posadas | 134 | 27.23S | 55.53W |
| Potenza | 96 | 40.38N | 15.49 E |
| Potgietersrus | 106 | 24.15S | 28.55 E |
| Potomac ≃ | 140 | 38.00N | 76.18W |
| Potosí | 132 | 19.35S | 65.45W |
| Potsdam | 90 | 52.24N | 13.04 E |
| Poughkeepsie | 140 | 41.42N | 73.55W |
| Poume | 127b | 20.14S | 164.02 E |
| Pouso Alegre | 135 | 22.13S | 45.56W |
| Poûthĭsăt | 120 | 12.32N | 103.55 E |
| Povungnituk | 136 | 60.02N | 77.10W |
| Powassan | 140 | 46.05N | 79.22W |
| Powell, Lake ⊜[1] | 138 | 37.25N | 110.45W |
| Poza Rica de Hidalgo | 128 | 20.33N | 97.27W |
| Poznań | 90 | 52.25N | 16.55 E |
| Prague |  |  |  |
| → Praha | 90 | 50.05N | 14.26 E |
| Praha (Prague) | 90 | 50.05N | 14.26 E |
| Preparis North Channel ⋃ | 120 | 15.27N | 94.05 E |
| Preparis South Channel ⋃ | 120 | 14.40N | 94.00 E |
| Presidente Epitácio | 135 | 21.46S | 52.06W |
| Presidente Prudente | 132 | 22.07S | 51.22W |
| Presidio | 128 | 29.33N | 104.22W |
| Prešov | 90 | 49.00N | 21.15 E |
| Prespa, Lake ⊜ | 98 | 40.55N | 21.00 E |
| Presque Isle | 138 | 46.40N | 68.00W |
| Preston, Eng., U.K. | 88 | 53.46N | 2.42W |
| Preston, Id., U.S. | 138 | 42.05N | 111.52W |
| Pretoria | 106 | 25.45S | 28.10 E |
| Prey Vêng | 120 | 11.29N | 105.19 E |
| Přibram | 90 | 49.42N | 14.01 E |
| Prievidza | 90 | 48.47N | 18.37 E |
| Prilep | 98 | 41.20N | 21.33 E |
| Prince Albert | 136 | 53.12N | 105.46W |
| Prince Edward Island □[4] | 136 | 46.20N | 63.20W |
| Prince George | 136 | 53.55N | 122.45W |
| Prince of Wales Island I, N.T., Can. | 136 | 72.40N | 99.00W |
| Prince of Wales Island I, Ak., U.S. | 144 | 55.47N | 132.50W |
| Prince Rupert | 136 | 54.19N | 130.19W |
| Princeton | 140 | 40.20N | 74.39W |
| Prinzapolca | 130 | 13.24N | 83.34W |
| Priština | 98 | 42.39N | 21.10 E |
| Prizren | 98 | 42.12N | 20.44 E |

| Name | Page No. | Lat. | Long. |
|------|----------|------|-------|
| Proctor | 140 | 43.39N | 73.02W |
| Prokopjevsk | 102 | 53.53N | 86.45 E |
| Prome (Pyè) | 120 | 18.49N | 95.13 E |
| Prostĕjov | 90 | 49.29N | 17.07 E |
| Provence □[9] | 92 | 44.00N | 6.00 E |
| Providence | 140 | 41.49N | 71.24W |
| Providence, Cape ⊁ | 126 | 46.01S | 166.28 E |
| Provincetown | 140 | 42.03N | 70.10W |
| Provo | 138 | 40.14N | 111.39W |
| Prudhoe Bay ⊂ | 144 | 70.20N | 148.20W |
| Pruszków | 90 | 52.11N | 20.48 E |
| Prut ≃ | 98 | 45.30N | 28.12 E |
| Przemyśl | 90 | 49.47N | 22.47 E |
| Pskov | 100 | 57.50N | 28.20 E |
| Puapua | 127e | 13.34S | 172.09W |
| Pucallpa | 132 | 8.23S | 74.32W |
| Pudukkottai | 111 | 10.23N | 78.49 E |
| Puebla [de Zaragoza] | 128 | 19.03N | 98.12W |
| Pueblo | 138 | 38.15N | 104.36W |
| Puerto Aisén | 134 | 45.24S | 72.42W |
| Puerto Armuelles | 130 | 8.17N | 82.52W |
| Puerto Asís | 132 | 0.30N | 76.31W |
| Puerto Barrios | 130 | 15.43N | 88.36W |
| Puerto Berrío | 132 | 6.29N | 74.24W |
| Puerto Cabello | 130 | 10.28N | 68.01W |
| Puerto Cabezas | 130 | 14.02N | 83.23W |
| Puerto Carreño | 132 | 6.12N | 67.22W |
| Puerto Casado | 134 | 22.20S | 57.55W |
| Puerto Cortés, C.R. | 130 | 8.58N | 83.32W |
| Puerto Cortés, Hond. | 130 | 15.48N | 87.56W |
| Puerto Cumarebo | 130 | 11.29N | 69.21W |
| Puerto de Nutrias | 132 | 8.05N | 69.18W |
| Puerto Deseado | 134 | 47.45S | 65.54W |
| Puerto la Cruz | 132 | 10.13N | 64.38W |
| Puerto Leguízamo | 132 | 0.12S | 74.46W |
| Puertollano | 94 | 38.41N | 4.07W |
| Puerto Lobos | 134 | 42.00S | 65.06W |
| Puerto Madryn | 134 | 42.46S | 65.03W |
| Puerto Maldonado | 132 | 12.36S | 69.11W |
| Puerto Montt | 134 | 41.28S | 72.57W |
| Puerto Natales | 134 | 51.44S | 72.31W |
| Puerto Rico □[2] | 130 | 18.15N | 66.30W |
| Puerto Vallarta | 128 | 20.37N | 105.15W |
| Pula | 96 | 44.52N | 13.50 E |
| Pulaski | 140 | 43.34N | 76.07W |
| Puławy | 90 | 51.25N | 21.57 E |
| Pune (Poona) | 111 | 18.32N | 73.52 E |
| Punjab □[3] | 112 | 31.00N | 75.30 E |
| Puno | 132 | 15.50S | 70.02W |
| Punta Arenas | 134 | 53.09S | 70.55W |
| Puntarenas | 130 | 9.58N | 84.50W |
| Punto Fijo | 132 | 11.42N | 70.13W |
| Puri | 112 | 19.48N | 85.51 E |
| Purnea | 112 | 25.47N | 87.31 E |
| Purus (Purús) ≃ | 132 | 3.42S | 61.28W |
| Pusan | 114 | 35.06N | 129.03 E |
| Puto | 127a | 5.41S | 154.43 E |
| Putumayo (Içá) ≃ | 132 | 3.07S | 67.58W |
| Puy de Sancy ∧ | 92 | 45.32N | 2.49 E |
| Pyinmana | 120 | 19.44N | 96.13 E |
| P'yŏngyang | 114 | 39.01N | 125.45 E |
| Pyramid Lake ⊜ | 142 | 40.00N | 119.35W |
| Pyrenees ⋌ | 94 | 42.40N | 1.00 E |
| Pyu | 120 | 18.29N | 96.26 E |

**Q**

| Name | Page No. | Lat. | Long. |
|------|----------|------|-------|
| Qacentina | 104 | 36.22N | 6.37 E |
| Qaidam Pendi ≊[1] | 114 | 37.00N | 95.00 E |
| Qalāt | 112 | 32.07N | 66.54 E |
| Qamar, Ghubbat al- ⊂ | 108 | 16.00N | 52.30 E |
| Qandahār | 112 | 31.32N | 65.30 E |
| Qatar □[1] | 108 | 25.00N | 51.10 E |
| Qinā | 109 | 26.10N | 32.43 E |
| Qingdao (Tsingtao) | 114 | 36.06N | 120.19 E |
| Qinhuangdao | 114 | 39.56N | 119.36 E |

| Name | Page No. | Lat. | Long. |
|---|---|---|---|
| Qiqihar | 114 | 47.19N | 123.55 E |
| Qom | 108 | 34.39N | 50.54 E |
| Quanzhou | 114 | 24.54N | 118.35 E |
| Quartzsite | 142 | 33.39N | 114.13W |
| Québec | 136 | 46.49N | 71.14W |
| Quebec (Québec) □⁴ | 136 | 52.00N | 72.00W |
| Quedlinburg | 90 | 51.48N | 11.09 E |
| Queen Charlotte Islands ❙❙ | 136 | 53.00N | 132.00W |
| Queen Charlotte Sound ⨆ | 136 | 51.30N | 129.30W |
| Queen Maud Land ➔¹ | 85 | 72.30S | 12.00 E |
| Queen Maud Mountains ⩘ | 85 | 86.00S | 160.00W |
| Queensland □³ | 122 | 22.00S | 145.00 E |
| Queenstown, N.Z. | 126 | 45.02S | 168.40 E |
| Queenstown, S. Afr. | 106 | 31.52S | 26.52 E |
| Quelimane | 106 | 17.53S | 36.51 E |
| Querétaro | 128 | 20.36N | 100.23W |
| Quetta | 112 | 30.12N | 67.00 E |
| Quezon City | 118 | 14.38N | 121.00 E |
| Quibdó | 132 | 5.42N | 76.40W |
| Quilpie | 122 | 26.37S | 144.15 E |
| Quimper | 92 | 48.00N | 4.06W |
| Quincemil | 132 | 13.16S | 70.38W |
| Qui-nhon | 120 | 13.46N | 109.14 E |
| Quiros, Cape ➤ | 127b | 14.55S | 167.01 E |
| Quito | 132 | 0.13S | 78.30W |
| Qūș | 109 | 25.55N | 32.45 E |

**R**

| Name | Page No. | Lat. | Long. |
|---|---|---|---|
| Rabat (Victoria), Malta | 96 | 36.02N | 14.14 E |
| Rabat, Mor. | 104 | 34.02N | 6.51W |
| Rach-gia | 120 | 10.01N | 105.05 E |
| Racibórz (Ratibor) | 90 | 50.06N | 18.13 E |
| Radom | 90 | 51.25N | 21.10 E |
| Radomsko | 90 | 51.05N | 19.25 E |
| Raetihi | 126 | 39.26S | 175.17 E |
| Rafaela | 134 | 31.16S | 61.29W |
| Rafah | 109 | 31.18N | 34.15 E |
| Ragusa | 96 | 36.55N | 14.44 E |
| Rahīmyār Khān | 112 | 28.25N | 70.18 E |
| Raiatea ⊘ | 127d | 16.50S | 151.25W |
| Rāichūr | 111 | 16.12N | 77.22 E |
| Raipur | 112 | 21.14N | 81.38 E |
| Rājahmundry | 111 | 16.59N | 81.47 E |
| Rajang ≏ | 118 | 2.04N | 111.12 E |
| Rājapālaiyam | 111 | 9.27N | 77.34 E |
| Rājasthān □⁴ | 112 | 27.00N | 74.00 E |
| Rajčichinsk | 102 | 49.46N | 129.25 E |
| Rājkot | 112 | 22.18N | 70.47 E |
| Raleigh | 138 | 35.46N | 78.38W |
| Rama | 130 | 12.09N | 84.15W |
| Ramm, Jabal ⋀ | 109 | 29.35N | 35.24 E |
| Rāmpur | 112 | 28.49N | 79.02 E |
| Ramree Island ❙ | 120 | 19.06N | 93.48 E |
| Ramu ≏ | 118 | 5.00S | 144.40 E |
| Rancagua | 134 | 34.10S | 70.45W |
| Ränchī | 112 | 23.21N | 85.20 E |
| Randers | 89 | 56.28N | 10.03 E |
| Randolph | 140 | 43.55N | 72.39W |
| Rangeley | 140 | 44.57N | 70.38W |
| Rangitikei ≏ | 126 | 40.18S | 175.14 E |
| Rangoon (Yangon) | 120 | 16.47N | 96.10 E |
| Rangpur | 112 | 25.45N | 89.15 E |
| Rankin Inlet | 136 | 62.45N | 92.10W |
| Rann of Kutch ≌ | 112 | 24.00N | 70.00 E |
| Rantauprapat | 120 | 2.06N | 99.50 E |
| Rapid City | 138 | 44.04N | 103.13W |
| Ras Dashan Terara ⋀ | 108 | 13.10N | 38.26 E |
| Rasht | 86 | 37.16N | 49.36 E |
| Rat Islands ❙❙ | 144 | 52.00N | 178.00 E |
| Ratlām | 112 | 23.19N | 75.04 E |
| Rauma | 89 | 61.08N | 21.30 E |
| Ravena | 140 | 42.28N | 73.49W |

| Name | Page No. | Lat. | Long. |
|---|---|---|---|
| Ravenna | 96 | 44.25N | 12.12 E |
| Ravensburg | 90 | 47.47N | 9.37 E |
| Ravenshoe | 122 | 17.37S | 145.29 E |
| Ravensthorpe | 122 | 33.35S | 120.02 E |
| Rāwalpindi | 112 | 33.36N | 73.04 E |
| Rawson | 134 | 43.18S | 65.06W |
| Raz, Pointe du ➤ | 92 | 48.02N | 4.44W |
| R'azan' | 100 | 54.38N | 39.44 E |
| Razgrad | 98 | 43.32N | 26.31 E |
| Ré, Île de ❙ | 92 | 46.12N | 1.25W |
| Reading, Eng., U.K. | 88 | 51.28N | 0.59W |
| Reading, Pa., U.S. | 140 | 40.20N | 75.55W |
| Real, Cordillera ⩘ | 132 | 19.00S | 66.30W |
| Realicó | 134 | 35.02S | 64.15W |
| Recherche, Cape ➤ | 127a | 10.11S | 161.19 E |
| Recife | 132 | 8.03S | 34.54W |
| Recklinghausen | 90 | 51.36N | 7.13 E |
| Red (Hong-ha) (Yuanjiang) ≏, Asia | 120 | 20.17N | 106.34 E |
| Red ≏, U.S. | 138 | 31.00N | 91.40W |
| Red Deer | 136 | 52.16N | 113.48W |
| Redding | 142 | 40.35N | 122.23W |
| Red Lake | 136 | 51.03N | 93.49W |
| Red Sea ⟶² | 108 | 20.00N | 38.00 E |
| Reed City | 140 | 43.52N | 85.30W |
| Reefton | 126 | 42.07S | 171.52 E |
| Regensburg | 90 | 49.01N | 12.06 E |
| Reggio di Calabria | 96 | 38.07N | 15.39 E |
| Reggio nell'Emilia | 96 | 44.43N | 10.36 E |
| Regina | 136 | 50.25N | 104.39W |
| Rehoboth Beach | 140 | 38.43N | 75.04W |
| Reḥovot | 109 | 31.54N | 34.49 E |
| Reims | 92 | 49.15N | 4.02 E |
| Remada | 104 | 32.19N | 10.24 E |
| Rendsburg | 90 | 54.18N | 9.40 E |
| Renfrew | 140 | 45.28N | 76.41W |
| Rennes | 92 | 48.05N | 1.41W |
| Reno | 142 | 39.31N | 119.48W |
| Reschenpass )( | 92 | 46.50N | 10.30 E |
| Resistencia | 134 | 27.27S | 58.59W |
| Reșița | 98 | 45.17N | 21.53 E |
| Réthimnon | 98 | 35.22N | 24.29 E |
| Reunion □² | 106 | 21.06S | 55.36 E |
| Reus | 94 | 41.09N | 1.07 E |
| Reutlingen | 90 | 48.29N | 9.11 E |
| Revelstoke | 136 | 50.59N | 118.12W |
| Revillagigedo, Islas ❙❙ | 128 | 19.00N | 111.30W |
| Rewa | 112 | 24.32N | 81.18 E |
| Rewāri | 112 | 28.11N | 76.37 E |
| Rey, Isla del ❙ | 130 | 8.22N | 78.55W |
| Reyes | 132 | 14.19S | 67.23W |
| Reykjavík | 86 | 64.09N | 21.51W |
| Reynosa | 128 | 26.07N | 98.18W |
| Rhaetian Alps ⩘ | 92 | 46.30N | 10.00 E |
| Rheine | 90 | 52.17N | 7.26 E |
| Rhein → Rhine ≏ | 90 | 51.52N | 6.02 E |
| Rhine (Rhein) (Rhin) ≏ | 90 | 51.52N | 6.02 E |
| Rhinelander | 138 | 45.38N | 89.24W |
| Rhode Island □³ | 138 | 41.40N | 71.30W |
| Rhodes → Ródhos ❙ | 98 | 36.10N | 28.00 E |
| Rhodope Mountains ⩘ | 98 | 41.30N | 24.30 E |
| Rhône ≏ | 92 | 43.20N | 4.50 E |
| Riau, Kepulauan ❙❙ | 120 | 1.00N | 104.30 E |
| Ribeirão Prêto | 132 | 21.10S | 47.48W |
| Riberalta | 132 | 10.59S | 66.06W |
| Richfield, Id., U.S. | 142 | 43.02N | 114.09W |
| Richfield, Ut., U.S. | 138 | 38.46N | 112.05W |
| Richmond, In., U.S. | 140 | 39.49N | 84.53W |
| Richmond, Ky., U.S. | 140 | 37.44N | 84.17W |
| Richmond, Va., U.S. | 138 | 37.33N | 77.27W |
| Richwood | 140 | 38.13N | 80.32W |
| Riesa | 90 | 51.18N | 13.17 E |
| Rieti | 96 | 42.24N | 12.51 E |
| Rif ⩘ | 94 | 35.00N | 4.00W |

| Name | Page No. | Lat. | Long. |
|---|---|---|---|
| Rift Valley **V** | 106 | 3.00S | 29.00 E |
| Riga | 100 | 56.57N | 24.06 E |
| Riga, Gulf of **c** | 100 | 57.30N | 23.35 E |
| Rigestán **◆**[1] | 110 | 31.00N | 65.00 E |
| Rijeka | 96 | 45.20N | 14.27 E |
| Rimini | 96 | 44.04N | 12.34 E |
| Ringgold Isles **II** | 127c | 16.15S | 179.25 W |
| Ringvassøya **I** | 89 | 69.55N | 19.15 E |
| Riobamba | 132 | 1.40S | 78.38 W |
| Rio Branco | 132 | 9.58S | 67.48 W |
| Río Cuarto | 134 | 33.08S | 64.21 W |
| Rio de Janeiro | 132 | 22.54S | 43.14 W |
| Río Gallegos | 134 | 51.38S | 69.13 W |
| Río Grande, Arg. | 134 | 53.47S | 67.42 W |
| Rio Grande, Braz. | 134 | 32.02S | 52.05 W |
| Ríohacha | 132 | 11.33N | 72.55 W |
| Río Hato | 130 | 8.23N | 80.10 W |
| Río Mayo | 134 | 45.41S | 70.16 W |
| Rio Verde | 135 | 17.43S | 50.56 W |
| Ripley | 140 | 38.49N | 81.42 W |
| Ritter, Mount **A** | 142 | 37.42N | 119.12 W |
| Rivas | 130 | 11.26N | 85.50 W |
| Rivera | 134 | 30.54S | 55.31 W |
| Riverhead | 140 | 40.55N | 72.39 W |
| Riverina **◆**[1] | 124 | 35.30S | 145.30 E |
| Riverside | 142 | 33.57N | 117.23 W |
| Riyadh | | | |
| → Ar-Riyād | 108 | 24.38N | 46.43 E |
| Rizzuto, Capo **➤** | 96 | 38.54N | 17.06 E |
| Roanne | 92 | 46.02N | 4.04 E |
| Roanoke | 138 | 37.16N | 79.56 W |
| Roberts Peak **A** | 136 | 52.57N | 120.32 W |
| Roberval | 136 | 48.31N | 72.13 W |
| Roboré | 132 | 18.20S | 59.45 W |
| Rocha | 134 | 34.29S | 54.20 W |
| Rochefort | 92 | 45.57N | 0.58 W |
| Rochester, Mn., U.S. | 138 | 44.01N | 92.28 W |
| Rochester, N.H., U.S. | 140 | 43.18N | 70.58 W |
| Rochester, N.Y., U.S. | 140 | 43.09N | 77.36 W |
| Rockefeller Plateau **↗**[1] | 85 | 80.00S | 135.00 W |
| Rockford, Il., U.S. | 138 | 42.16N | 89.05 W |
| Rockford, Mi., U.S. | 140 | 43.07N | 85.33 W |
| Rockhampton | 122 | 23.23S | 150.31 E |
| Rock Island | 138 | 41.30N | 90.34 W |
| Rockland | 140 | 44.06N | 69.06 W |
| Rock Springs | 138 | 41.35N | 109.12 W |
| Rockville | 140 | 39.05N | 77.09 W |
| Rocky Mountains **↗** | 82 | 48.00N | 116.00 W |
| Rodez | 92 | 44.21N | 2.35 E |
| Ródhos (Rhodes) | 98 | 36.26N | 28.13 E |
| Ródhos **I** | 98 | 36.10N | 28.00 E |
| Roebourne | 122 | 20.47S | 117.09 E |
| Roeselare | 90 | 50.57N | 3.08 E |
| Rogue **≃** | 142 | 42.26N | 124.25 W |
| Rohtak | 112 | 28.54N | 76.34 E |
| Roma (Rome) | 96 | 41.54N | 12.29 E |
| Roman | 98 | 46.55N | 26.56 E |
| Romania **▫**[1] | 86 | 46.00N | 25.30 E |
| Romans [-sur-Isère] | 92 | 45.03N | 5.03 E |
| Rome, Ga., U.S. | 138 | 34.15N | 85.09 W |
| Rome, N.Y., U.S. | 140 | 43.12N | 75.27 W |
| Romeo | 140 | 42.48N | 83.00 W |
| Rome | | | |
| → Roma | 96 | 41.54N | 12.29 E |
| Roncador, Serra do **↗**[1] | 132 | 12.00S | 52.00 W |
| Ron-ma, Mui **➤** | 120 | 18.07N | 106.22 E |
| Ronne Ice Shelf **▨** | 85 | 78.30S | 61.00 W |
| Roosevelt Island **I** | 85 | 79.30S | 162.00 W |
| Roraima, Mount **A** | 132 | 5.12N | 60.44 W |
| Rosario | 134 | 32.57S | 60.40 W |
| Roscommon | 88 | 53.38N | 8.11 W |
| Roseau | 130 | 15.18N | 61.24 W |
| Roseburg | 142 | 43.13N | 123.20 W |
| Rosenheim | 90 | 47.51N | 12.07 E |
| Ross Ice Shelf **▨** | 85 | 81.30S | 175.00 W |
| Rosslare | 88 | 52.17N | 6.23 W |
| Ross Sea **ᴛ**[2] | 85 | 76.00S | 175.00 W |

| Name | Page No. | Lat. | Long. |
|---|---|---|---|
| Rostock | 90 | 54.05N | 12.07 E |
| Rostov-na-Donu | 86 | 47.14N | 39.42 E |
| Roswell | 138 | 33.23N | 104.31 W |
| Rotorua | 126 | 38.09S | 176.15 E |
| Rotterdam | 90 | 51.55N | 4.28 E |
| Roubaix | 92 | 50.42N | 3.10 E |
| Rouen | 92 | 49.26N | 1.05 E |
| Rouyn-Noranda | 136 | 48.15N | 79.01 W |
| Rovaniemi | 89 | 66.34N | 25.48 E |
| Rovno | 86 | 50.37N | 26.15 E |
| Royan | 92 | 45.37N | 1.01 W |
| Ruapehu **A** | 126 | 39.17S | 175.34 E |
| Rubcovsk | 102 | 51.33N | 81.10 E |
| Ruby | 144 | 64.44N | 155.30 W |
| Ruby Lake **≅** | 142 | 40.10N | 115.30 W |
| Rudolf, Lake **⊜** | 108 | 3.30N | 36.00 E |
| Rügen **I** | 90 | 54.25N | 13.24 E |
| Rukwa, Lake **⊜** | 106 | 8.00S | 32.25 E |
| Rump Mountain **A** | 140 | 45.12N | 71.04 W |
| Rupert | 142 | 42.37N | 113.40 W |
| Ruse | 98 | 43.50N | 25.57 E |
| Rüsselsheim | 90 | 50.00N | 8.25 E |
| Russia **▫**[1] | 86 | 60.00N | 100.00 E |
| Rutland | 140 | 43.36N | 72.58 W |
| Ruvuma (Rovuma) **≃** | 106 | 10.29S | 40.28 E |
| Rwanda **▫**[1] | 106 | 2.30S | 30.00 E |
| Rybinsk | 100 | 58.03N | 38.52 E |
| Rybinskoje | | | |
| Vodochranilišče **⊜**[1] | 100 | 58.30N | 38.25 E |
| Rysy **A** | 90 | 49.12N | 20.04 E |
| Ryukyu Islands | | | |
| → Nansei-shotō **II** | 114 | 26.30N | 128.00 E |
| Rzeszów | 90 | 50.03N | 22.00 E |

## S

| | | | |
|---|---|---|---|
| Saarbrücken | 90 | 49.14N | 6.59 E |
| Saaremaa **I** | 100 | 58.25N | 22.30 E |
| Sab, Tônlé **⊜** | 120 | 13.00N | 104.00 E |
| Sabinas Hidalgo | 128 | 26.30N | 100.10 W |
| Sabine **≃** | 128 | 30.00N | 93.45 W |
| Sable, Île de **I** | 122 | 19.15S | 159.56 E |
| Sachalin, Ostrov | | | |
| (Sakhalin) **I** | 102 | 51.00N | 143.00 E |
| Šachty | 86 | 47.42N | 40.13 E |
| Sacramento | 142 | 38.34N | 121.29 W |
| Sacramento **≃** | 142 | 38.03N | 121.56 W |
| Sacramento Valley **V** | 142 | 39.15N | 122.00 W |
| Sado **I** | 116 | 38.00N | 138.25 E |
| Saga | 116 | 33.15N | 130.18 E |
| Sagami-nada **c** | 116 | 35.00N | 139.30 E |
| Sāgar | 112 | 23.50N | 78.45 E |
| Saginaw | 140 | 43.25N | 83.56 W |
| Saginaw Bay **c** | 140 | 43.50N | 83.40 W |
| Sagua de Tánamo | 130 | 20.35N | 75.14 W |
| Sagua la Grande | 130 | 22.49N | 80.05 W |
| Saguaro National | | | |
| Monument **◆** | 128 | 32.12N | 110.38 W |
| Sagunto | 94 | 39.41N | 0.16 W |
| Sahara **◆**[2] | 104 | 26.00N | 13.00 E |
| Sahāranpur | 112 | 29.58N | 77.33 E |
| Saidpur | 112 | 25.47N | 88.54 E |
| Sai-gon | | | |
| → Thanh-pho Ho | | | |
| Chi Minh | 120 | 10.45N | 106.40 E |
| Saint Anthony | 136 | 51.22N | 55.35 W |
| Saint Augustine | 138 | 29.53N | 81.18 W |
| Saint-Augustin- | | | |
| Saguenay | 136 | 51.14N | 58.39 W |
| Saint-Brieuc | 92 | 48.31N | 2.47 W |
| Saint Catharines | 140 | 43.10N | 79.15 W |
| Saint-Chamond | 92 | 45.28N | 4.30 E |
| Saint Christopher | | | |
| (Saint Kitts) **I** | 130 | 17.20N | 62.45 W |
| Saint Clair | 140 | 42.48N | 82.29 W |
| Saint Croix **I** | 130 | 17.45N | 64.45 W |

| Name | Page No. | Lat. | Long. |
|------|----------|------|-------|
| Saint-Denis, Fr. | 92 | 48.56N | 2.22 E |
| Saint-Denis, Reu. | 106 | 20.52S | 55.28 E |
| Saint-Dizier | 92 | 48.38N | 4.57 E |
| Saint Elias, Mount ∧ | 144 | 60.18N | 140.55W |
| Saint-Étienne | 92 | 45.26N | 4.24 E |
| Saint George | 122 | 28.02S | 148.35 E |
| Saint George's | 130 | 12.03N | 61.45W |
| Saint George's Bay c | 136 | 48.20N | 59.00W |
| Saint George's Channel ⊔ | 88 | 52.00N | 6.00W |
| Saint Helier | 92 | 49.12N | 2.37W |
| Saint-Hyacinthe | 140 | 45.38N | 72.57W |
| Saint James | 140 | 45.45N | 85.30W |
| Saint James, Cape ⊁ | 136 | 51.56N | 131.01W |
| Saint-Jean | 140 | 45.19N | 73.16W |
| Saint-Jérôme | 140 | 45.46N | 74.00W |
| Saint John | 136 | 45.16N | 66.03W |
| Saint John, Cape ⊁ | 136 | 50.00N | 55.32W |
| Saint John's | 136 | 47.34N | 52.43W |
| Saint Johnsbury | 140 | 44.25N | 72.00W |
| Saint Joseph | 138 | 39.46N | 94.50W |
| Saint Joseph, Lake ⊜ | 136 | 51.05N | 90.35W |
| Saint-Jovite | 140 | 46.07N | 74.36W |
| Saint Kilda I | 88 | 57.49N | 8.36W |
| Saint Kitts and Nevis □¹ | 130 | 17.20N | 62.45W |
| Saint Kitts → Saint Christopher I | 130 | 17.20N | 62.45W |
| Saint Lawrence ≃ | 136 | 49.30N | 67.00W |
| Saint Lawrence, Gulf of c | 136 | 48.00N | 62.00W |
| Saint Lawrence Island I | 144 | 63.30N | 170.30W |
| Saint-Lô | 92 | 49.07N | 1.05W |
| Saint-Louis, Sen. | 104 | 16.02N | 16.30W |
| Saint Louis, Mo., U.S. | 138 | 38.37N | 90.11W |
| Saint Lucia □¹ | 130 | 13.53N | 60.58W |
| Saint-Malo | 92 | 48.39N | 2.01W |
| Saint-Malo, Golfe de c | 92 | 48.45N | 2.00W |
| Sainte-Marie, Cap ⊁ | 106 | 25.36S | 45.08 E |
| Saint Marys | 140 | 41.25N | 78.33W |
| Saint-Nazaire | 92 | 47.17N | 2.12W |
| Saint Paul | 138 | 44.57N | 93.05W |
| Saint Peter Port | 92 | 49.27N | 2.32W |
| Saint Petersburg | 138 | 27.46N | 82.40W |
| Saint Petersburg → Sankt-Peterburg | 100 | 59.55N | 30.15 E |
| Saint Pierre and Miquelon □² | 136 | 46.55N | 56.10W |
| Saint-Quentin | 92 | 49.51N | 3.17 E |
| Saintes | 92 | 45.45N | 0.52W |
| Saint Thomas | 140 | 42.47N | 81.12W |
| Saint Vincent, Gulf c | 124 | 35.00S | 138.05 E |
| Saint Vincent and the Grenadines □¹ | 130 | 13.15N | 61.12W |
| Saipan I | 118 | 15.12N | 145.45 E |
| Sairecábur, Cerro ∧ | 132 | 22.43S | 67.54W |
| Saito | 116 | 32.06N | 131.24 E |
| Sajama, Nevado ∧ | 132 | 18.06S | 68.54W |
| Sakai | 116 | 34.35N | 135.28 E |
| Sakata | 116 | 38.55N | 139.50 E |
| Sakau | 127b | 16.49S | 168.24 E |
| Sakhalin → Sachalin, Ostrov I | 102 | 51.00N | 143.00 E |
| Saku | 116 | 36.09N | 138.26 E |
| Sakurai | 116 | 34.30N | 135.51 E |
| Salamanca | 94 | 40.58N | 5.39W |
| Saldanha | 106 | 33.00S | 17.56 E |
| Salem, Ma., U.S. | 140 | 42.31N | 70.53W |
| Salem, Oh., U.S. | 140 | 40.54N | 80.51W |
| Salem, Or., U.S. | 138 | 44.56N | 123.02W |
| Salerno | 96 | 40.41N | 14.47 E |
| Salgótarján | 90 | 48.07N | 19.48 E |
| Salihli | 98 | 38.29N | 28.09 E |
| Salinas | 142 | 36.40N | 121.39W |
| Salinas ≃ | 142 | 36.45N | 121.48W |
| Salisbury, Eng., U.K. | 88 | 51.05N | 1.48W |
| Salisbury, Md., U.S. | 140 | 38.21N | 75.35W |
| Salmon River Mountains ⋊ | 138 | 44.45N | 115.00W |
| Salonika → Thessaloníki | 98 | 40.38N | 22.56 E |
| Sal'sk | 86 | 46.28N | 41.33 E |
| Salta | 134 | 24.47S | 65.25W |
| Saltillo | 128 | 25.25N | 101.00W |
| Salt Lake City | 138 | 40.45N | 111.53W |
| Salto | 134 | 31.23S | 57.58W |
| Salton Sea ⊜ | 142 | 33.19N | 115.50W |
| Salvador | 132 | 12.59S | 38.31W |
| Salween (Nu) ≃ | 120 | 16.31N | 97.37 E |
| Salyersville | 140 | 37.45N | 83.04W |
| Salzburg | 90 | 47.48N | 13.02 E |
| Salzgitter | 90 | 52.10N | 10.25 E |
| Samar I | 118 | 12.00N | 125.00 E |
| Samara | 86 | 53.12N | 50.09 E |
| Samarinda | 118 | 0.30S | 117.09 E |
| Samarkand | 110 | 39.40N | 66.48 E |
| Sambalpur | 112 | 21.27N | 83.58 E |
| Samoa Islands II | 127e | 14.00S | 171.00W |
| Sámos I | 98 | 37.48N | 26.44 E |
| Samothráki (Samothrace) I | 98 | 40.30N | 25.32 E |
| Sam Rayburn Reservoir ⊜¹ | 138 | 31.27N | 94.37W |
| Samsun | 86 | 41.17N | 36.20 E |
| Samui, Ko I | 120 | 9.30N | 100.00 E |
| Samut Prakan | 120 | 13.36N | 100.36 E |
| San ≃ | 90 | 50.45N | 21.51 E |
| San'ā' | 108 | 15.23N | 44.12 E |
| San Agustin, Cape ⊁ | 118 | 6.16N | 126.11 E |
| San Andrés | 130 | 12.35N | 81.42W |
| San Andrés, Isla de I | 130 | 12.32N | 81.42W |
| San Angelo | 138 | 31.27N | 100.26W |
| San Antonio | 138 | 29.25N | 98.29W |
| San Antonio, Cabo ⊁ | 130 | 21.52N | 84.57W |
| San Antonio Oeste | 134 | 40.44S | 64.56W |
| San Benedetto del Tronto | 96 | 42.57N | 13.53 E |
| San Benito | 130 | 16.55N | 89.54W |
| San Bernardino | 142 | 34.07N | 117.18W |
| San Bernardino Mountains ⋊ | 142 | 34.10N | 117.00W |
| San Blas, Cape ⊁ | 138 | 29.40N | 85.22W |
| San Carlos | 130 | 11.07N | 84.47W |
| San Carlos de Bariloche | 134 | 41.09S | 71.18W |
| San Carlos del Zulia | 130 | 9.01N | 71.55W |
| San Carlos de Río Negro | 132 | 1.55N | 67.04W |
| San Clemente | 142 | 33.25N | 117.36W |
| San Clemente Island I | 142 | 32.54N | 118.29W |
| San Cristóbal | 132 | 7.46N | 72.14W |
| San Cristóbal I | 127a | 10.36S | 161.45 E |
| Sancti-Spíritus | 130 | 21.56N | 79.27W |
| Sandakan | 118 | 5.50N | 118.07 E |
| Sandia | 132 | 14.17S | 69.26W |
| San Diego | 142 | 32.42N | 117.09W |
| Sandnes | 89 | 58.51N | 5.44 E |
| Sandusky, Mi., U.S. | 140 | 43.25N | 82.49W |
| Sandusky, Oh., U.S. | 140 | 41.26N | 82.42W |
| Sandviken | 89 | 60.37N | 16.46 E |
| Sandy Hook | 140 | 38.05N | 83.07W |
| Sandy Lake ⊜ | 136 | 53.00N | 93.07W |
| San Felipe | 130 | 10.20N | 68.44W |
| San Fernando, Spain | 94 | 36.28N | 6.12W |
| San Fernando, Trin. | 130 | 10.17N | 61.28W |
| San Fernando de Apure | 132 | 7.54N | 67.28W |
| San Fernando de Atabapo | 132 | 4.03N | 67.42W |
| Sanford | 140 | 43.26N | 70.46W |
| San Francisco | 142 | 37.46N | 122.25W |
| San Francisco de Macorís | 130 | 19.18N | 70.15W |

| Name | Page No. | Lat. | Long. |
|---|---|---|---|
| San Gabriel Mountains ⋏ | 142 | 34.20N | 118.00W |
| Sāngli | 111 | 16.52N | 74.34 E |
| San Gottardo, Passo del ⋊ | 92 | 46.33N | 8.34 E |
| San Jacinto | 130 | 9.50N | 75.08W |
| San Joaquin ≃ | 142 | 38.03N | 121.50W |
| San Joaquin Valley ⋁ | 142 | 36.50N | 120.10W |
| San Jorge, Golfo ⊂ | 134 | 46.00S | 67.00W |
| San José, C.R. | 130 | 9.56N | 84.05W |
| San Jose, Ca., U.S. | 142 | 37.20N | 121.53W |
| San José de Chiquitos | 132 | 17.51S | 60.47W |
| San José de Guanipa | 130 | 8.54N | 64.09W |
| San José del Guaviare | 132 | 2.35N | 72.38W |
| San Juan, Arg. | 134 | 31.32S | 68.31W |
| San Juan, P.R. | 130 | 18.28N | 66.07W |
| San Juan ≃ | 130 | 10.56N | 83.42W |
| San Juan del Norte | 130 | 10.55N | 83.42W |
| San Juan de los Cayos | 130 | 11.10N | 68.25W |
| San Juan de los Morros | 130 | 9.55N | 67.21W |
| San Julián | 134 | 49.18S | 67.43W |
| San Justo | 134 | 30.47S | 60.35W |
| Sankt Gallen | 92 | 47.25N | 9.23 E |
| Sankt Moritz | 92 | 46.30N | 9.50 E |
| Sankt-Peterburg (Saint Petersburg) | 100 | 59.55N | 30.15 E |
| Sankt Pölten | 90 | 48.12N | 15.37 E |
| San Lucas, Cabo ⋗ | 128 | 22.52N | 109.53W |
| San Luis, Guat. | 130 | 16.14N | 89.27W |
| San Luis, Ven. | 130 | 11.07N | 69.42W |
| San Luis Obispo | 142 | 35.16N | 120.39W |
| San Luis Potosí | 128 | 22.09N | 100.59W |
| San Luis Río Colorado | 128 | 32.29N | 114.48W |
| San Marcos | 128 | 29.52N | 97.56W |
| San Marino | 96 | 43.55N | 12.28 E |
| San Marino ◻[1] | 86 | 43.56N | 12.25 E |
| San Mateo, Ca., U.S. | 142 | 37.33N | 122.19W |
| San Mateo, Ven. | 130 | 9.45N | 64.33W |
| San Miguel | 130 | 13.29N | 88.11W |
| San Miguel de Tucumán | 134 | 26.49S | 65.13W |
| San Nicolas Island I | 142 | 33.15N | 119.31W |
| San Onofre | 130 | 9.44N | 75.32W |
| San Pedro, Punta ⋗ | 134 | 25.30S | 70.38W |
| San Pedro de las Colonias | 128 | 25.45N | 102.59W |
| San Pedro de Macorís | 130 | 18.27N | 69.18W |
| San Pedro Sula | 130 | 15.27N | 88.02W |
| San Rafael, Arg. | 134 | 34.36S | 68.20W |
| San Rafael, Mex. | 128 | 25.01N | 100.33W |
| San Remo | 96 | 43.49N | 7.46 E |
| San Salvador | 130 | 13.41N | 89.17W |
| San Salvador de Jujuy | 134 | 24.11S | 65.18W |
| San Sebastián | 94 | 43.19N | 1.59W |
| San Severo | 96 | 41.41N | 15.23 E |
| Santa Ana, Bol. | 132 | 15.31S | 67.30W |
| Santa Ana, Hond. | 130 | 13.59N | 89.34W |
| Santa Ana, Ca., U.S. | 142 | 33.44N | 117.52W |
| Santa Barbara | 142 | 34.25N | 119.42W |
| Santa Barbara Channel ∐ | 142 | 34.15N | 119.55W |
| Santa Catalina, Gulf of ⊂ | 142 | 33.20N | 117.45W |
| Santa Clara, Cuba | 130 | 22.24N | 79.58W |
| Santa Clara, Ca., U.S. | 142 | 37.20N | 121.56W |
| Santa Cruz, Bol. | 132 | 17.48S | 63.10W |
| Santa Cruz, Ca., U.S. | 142 | 36.58N | 122.01W |
| Santa Cruz de Tenerife | 104 | 28.27N | 16.14W |
| Santa Cruz Island I | 142 | 34.01N | 119.45W |
| Santa Fe, Arg. | 134 | 31.38S | 60.42W |
| Santa Fe, N.M., U.S. | 138 | 35.41N | 105.56W |
| Santa Fe de Bogotá | 132 | 4.36N | 74.05W |
| Santa Isabel I | 127a | 8.00S | 159.00 E |
| Santa Lucia Range ⋏ | 142 | 36.00N | 121.20W |
| Santa Maria, Braz. | 134 | 29.41S | 53.48W |
| Santa Maria, Ca., U.S. | 142 | 34.57N | 120.26W |
| Santa Maria, Cabo de ⋗ | 106 | 13.25S | 12.32 E |
| Santa María Island I | 127b | 14.15S | 167.30 E |
| Santa Marta | 132 | 11.15N | 74.13W |
| Santana do Livramento | 134 | 30.53S | 55.31W |
| Santander | 94 | 43.28N | 3.48W |
| Santarém | 132 | 2.26S | 54.42W |
| Santa Rosa, Arg. | 134 | 36.37S | 64.17W |
| Santa Rosa, Arg. | 134 | 32.20S | 65.12W |
| Santa Rosa, Ca., U.S. | 142 | 38.26N | 122.42W |
| Santa Rosa Island I | 142 | 33.58N | 120.06W |
| Santiago | 134 | 33.27S | 70.40W |
| Santiago de Compostela | 94 | 42.53N | 8.33W |
| Santiago de Cuba | 130 | 20.01N | 75.49W |
| Santiago del Estero | 134 | 27.47S | 64.16W |
| Santiago [de los Caballeros] | 130 | 19.27N | 70.42W |
| Santo André | 135 | 23.40S | 46.31W |
| Santo Ângelo | 134 | 28.18S | 54.16W |
| Santo Antônio de Jesus | 135 | 12.58S | 39.16W |
| Santo Domingo | 130 | 18.28N | 69.54W |
| Santos | 132 | 23.57S | 46.20W |
| San Valentín, Cerro ⋀ | 134 | 46.36S | 73.20W |
| San Vicente | 130 | 13.38N | 88.48W |
| San Vicente de Baracaldo | 94 | 43.18N | 2.59W |
| San Vito, Capo ⋗ | 96 | 38.11N | 12.43 E |
| São Carlos | 135 | 22.01S | 47.54W |
| São Francisco ≃ | 132 | 10.30S | 36.24W |
| São José do Rio Prêto | 132 | 20.48S | 49.23W |
| São José dos Campos | 135 | 23.11S | 45.53W |
| São Leopoldo | 134 | 29.46S | 51.09W |
| São Luís | 132 | 2.31S | 44.16W |
| São Mateus | 132 | 18.44S | 39.51W |
| Saône ≃ | 90 | 46.05N | 4.45 E |
| São Paulo | 132 | 23.32S | 46.37W |
| São Roque, Cabo de ⋗ | 132 | 5.29S | 35.16W |
| São Sebastião, Ilha de I | 135 | 23.50S | 45.18W |
| São Sebastião, Ponta ⋗ | 106 | 22.07S | 35.30 E |
| São Tomé | 106 | 0.20N | 6.44 E |
| São Tomé, Cabo de ⋗ | 135 | 21.59S | 40.59W |
| Sao Tome and Principe ◻[1] | 106 | 1.00N | 7.00 E |
| São Vicente, Cabo de ⋗ | 94 | 37.01N | 9.00W |
| Sapitwa ⋀ | 106 | 15.57S | 35.36 E |
| Sapporo | 116a | 43.03N | 141.21 E |
| Sarajevo | 98 | 43.52N | 18.25 E |
| Saransk | 86 | 54.11N | 45.11 E |
| Sarapul | 86 | 56.28N | 53.48 E |
| Sarasota | 138 | 27.20N | 82.31W |
| Saratoga Springs | 140 | 43.04N | 73.47W |
| Saratov | 86 | 51.34N | 46.02 E |
| Sardegna (Sardinia) I | 96 | 40.00N | 9.00 E |
| Sargodha | 112 | 32.05N | 72.40 E |
| Sarh | 104 | 9.09N | 18.23 E |
| Sarmiento | 134 | 45.36S | 69.05W |
| Sarnia | 136 | 42.58N | 82.23W |
| Saronikós Kólpos ⊂ | 98 | 37.54N | 23.12 E |
| Sarthe ≃ | 92 | 47.30N | 0.32W |
| Sasamungga | 127a | 7.02S | 156.47 E |
| Sasebo | 116 | 33.10N | 129.43 E |
| Saskatchewan ◻[4] | 136 | 54.00N | 105.00W |
| Saskatoon | 136 | 52.07N | 106.38W |
| Sassandra ≃ | 104 | 4.58N | 6.05W |
| Sassari | 96 | 40.44N | 8.33 E |
| Sātāra | 111 | 17.41N | 73.59 E |
| Satawa | 127e | 13.28S | 172.40W |
| Satna | 112 | 24.35N | 80.50 E |
| Satsunan-shotō II | 117b | 29.00N | 130.00 E |
| Satu Mare | 98 | 47.48N | 22.53 E |
| Saudi Arabia ◻[1] | 108 | 25.00N | 45.00 E |
| Sauerland ⬥[1] | 90 | 51.10N | 8.00 E |
| Saugerties | 140 | 42.04N | 73.57W |
| Sault Sainte Marie, On., Can. | 136 | 46.31N | 84.20W |

| Name | Page No. | Lat. | Long. |
|---|---|---|---|
| Spanish North Africa □² | 94 | 35.53N | 5.19W |
| Spanish Town | 130 | 17.59N | 76.57W |
| Sparks | 142 | 39.32N | 119.45W |
| Spárti (Sparta) | 98 | 37.05N | 22.27 E |
| Spassk-Dal'nij | 102 | 44.37N | 132.48 E |
| Spencer Gulf c | 124 | 34.00S | 137.00 E |
| Speyer | 90 | 49.19N | 8.26 E |
| Split | 96 | 43.31N | 16.27 E |
| Spokane | 138 | 47.39N | 117.25W |
| Spoleto | 96 | 42.44N | 12.44 E |
| Springbok | 106 | 29.43S | 17.55 E |
| Springdale | 136 | 49.30N | 56.04W |
| Springfield, Il., U.S. | 138 | 39.48N | 89.38W |
| Springfield, Ma., U.S. | 140 | 42.06N | 72.35W |
| Springfield, Mo., U.S. | 138 | 37.12N | 93.17W |
| Springfield, Oh., U.S. | 140 | 39.55N | 83.48W |
| Springfontein | 106 | 30.19S | 25.36 E |
| Springhill | 136 | 45.39N | 64.03W |
| Springs | 106 | 26.13S | 28.25 E |
| Spruce Knob ∧ | 140 | 38.42N | 79.32W |
| Squillace, Golfo di c | 96 | 38.50N | 16.50 E |
| Srednesibirskoje Ploskogorje ⚹¹ | 102 | 65.00N | 105.00 E |
| Sri Lanka □¹ | 110 | 7.00N | 81.00 E |
| Sri Lanka I | 111 | 7.00N | 81.00 E |
| Srinagar | 112 | 34.05N | 74.49 E |
| Stade | 90 | 53.36N | 9.28 E |
| Stafford | 88 | 52.48N | 2.07W |
| Stalingrad → Volgograd | 86 | 48.44N | 44.25 E |
| Stamford | 140 | 41.03N | 73.32W |
| Standish | 140 | 43.58N | 83.57W |
| Stanke Dimitrov | 98 | 42.16N | 23.07 E |
| Stanley Falls → Boyoma Falls ⌣ | 106 | 0.15N | 25.30 E |
| Stanovoje Nagorje (Stanovoy Mountains) ⚹ | 102 | 56.00N | 114.00 E |
| Stanton | 140 | 37.50N | 83.51W |
| Starachowice | 90 | 51.03N | 21.04 E |
| Staraja Russa | 100 | 58.00N | 31.23 E |
| Stara Planina (Balkan Mountains) ⚹ | 98 | 43.15N | 25.00 E |
| Stara Zagora | 98 | 42.25N | 25.38 E |
| Starogard Gdański | 90 | 53.59N | 18.33 E |
| State College | 140 | 40.47N | 77.51W |
| Staunton | 140 | 38.08N | 79.04W |
| Stavanger | 89 | 58.58N | 5.45 E |
| Stavropol' | 86 | 45.02N | 41.59 E |
| Steinkjer | 89 | 64.01N | 11.30 E |
| Stelvio, Passo dello )( | 92 | 46.32N | 10.27 E |
| Stendal | 90 | 52.36N | 11.51 E |
| Stepanakert | 86 | 39.49N | 46.44 E |
| Sterling | 138 | 40.37N | 103.12W |
| Sterlitamak | 86 | 53.37N | 55.58 E |
| Steubenville | 140 | 40.22N | 80.38W |
| Stewart | 136 | 55.56N | 129.59W |
| Stewart Island I | 126 | 47.00S | 167.50 E |
| Steyr | 90 | 48.03N | 14.25 E |
| Stockerau | 90 | 48.23N | 16.13 E |
| Stockholm | 89 | 59.20N | 18.03 E |
| Stockton | 142 | 37.57N | 121.17W |
| Stoke-on-Trent | 88 | 53.00N | 2.10W |
| Stowe | 140 | 44.27N | 72.41W |
| Stralsund | 90 | 54.19N | 13.05 E |
| Strasbourg | 92 | 48.35N | 7.45 E |
| Strasburg | 140 | 38.59N | 78.21W |
| Stratford | 140 | 43.22N | 80.57W |
| Stratford-upon-Avon | 88 | 52.12N | 1.41W |
| Stratton | 140 | 45.08N | 70.26W |
| Straubing | 90 | 48.53N | 12.34 E |
| Struma (Strimón) ≈ | 98 | 40.47N | 23.51 E |
| Sturgis | 140 | 41.47N | 85.25W |
| Stuttgart | 90 | 48.46N | 9.11 E |
| Subotica | 98 | 46.06N | 19.39 E |
| Suceava | 98 | 47.39N | 26.19 E |
| Suchumi | 86 | 43.01N | 41.02 E |
| Sucre | 132 | 19.02S | 65.17W |
| Sudan □¹ | 104 | 15.00N | 30.00 E |
| Sudan ➤¹ | 104 | 10.00N | 20.00 E |
| Sudbury | 136 | 46.30N | 81.00W |
| Sukkur | 112 | 27.42N | 68.52 E |
| Sula, Kepulauan II | 118 | 1.52S | 125.22 E |
| Sulaimān Range ⚹ | 112 | 30.30N | 70.10 E |
| Sulawesi (Celebes) I | 118 | 2.00S | 121.00 E |
| Sullana | 132 | 4.53S | 80.41W |
| Sulmona | 96 | 42.03N | 13.55 E |
| Sulu Archipelago II | 118 | 6.00N | 121.00 E |
| Sulu Sea ⊤² | 118 | 8.00N | 120.00 E |
| Sumatera (Sumatra) I | 118 | 0.05S | 102.00 E |
| Sumba I | 118 | 10.00S | 120.00 E |
| Sumbawa I | 118 | 8.40S | 118.00 E |
| Šumen | 98 | 43.16N | 26.55 E |
| Summit Lake | 136 | 54.17N | 122.38W |
| Sumoto | 116 | 34.21N | 134.54 E |
| Sumy | 86 | 50.55N | 34.45 E |
| Sunbury | 140 | 40.51N | 76.47W |
| Sunderland | 88 | 54.55N | 1.23W |
| Sundsvall | 89 | 62.23N | 17.18 E |
| Sunnyvale | 142 | 37.22N | 122.02W |
| Superior, Lake ⊜ | 138 | 48.00N | 88.00W |
| Suqutrā (Socotra) I | 108 | 12.30N | 54.00 E |
| Şūr (Tyre) | 109 | 33.16N | 35.11 E |
| Surabaya | 118 | 7.15S | 112.45 E |
| Surakarta | 118 | 7.35S | 110.50 E |
| Surat | 112 | 21.10N | 72.50 E |
| Surat Thani (Ban Don) | 120 | 9.08N | 99.19 E |
| Surendranagar | 112 | 22.42N | 71.41 E |
| Suretamati, Mount ∧ | 127b | 13.47S | 167.29 E |
| Surgut | 102 | 61.14N | 73.20 E |
| Suriname □¹ | 132 | 4.00N | 56.00W |
| Surt | 104 | 31.12N | 16.35 E |
| Surt, Khalīj c | 104 | 31.30N | 18.00 E |
| Surud Ad ∧ | 108 | 10.41N | 47.18 E |
| Susquehanna ≈ | 140 | 39.33N | 76.05W |
| Sutlej (Satluj) (Langchuhe) ≈ | 112 | 29.23N | 71.02 E |
| Suva | 127c | 18.08S | 178.25 E |
| Suwa | 116 | 36.02N | 138.08 E |
| Suways, Khalīj as- (Gulf of Suez) c | 109 | 29.00N | 32.50 E |
| Suways, Qanāt as- (Suez Canal) ≊ | 109 | 29.55N | 32.33 E |
| Suzhou | 114 | 31.18N | 120.37 E |
| Svartenhuk ➤¹ | 136 | 71.55N | 55.00W |
| Svinecea ∧ | 98 | 44.48N | 22.09 E |
| Svobodnyj | 102 | 51.24N | 128.08 E |
| Swan River | 136 | 52.06N | 101.16W |
| Swansea | 88 | 51.38N | 3.57W |
| Swaziland □¹ | 106 | 26.30S | 31.30 E |
| Sweden □¹ | 86 | 62.00N | 15.00 E |
| Sweetwater | 138 | 32.28N | 100.24W |
| Swellendam | 106 | 34.02S | 20.26 E |
| Świdnica (Schweidnitz) | 90 | 50.51N | 16.29 E |
| Świnoujście (Swinemünde) | 90 | 53.53N | 14.14 E |
| Switzerland □¹ | 86 | 47.00N | 8.00 E |
| Sydney | 122 | 33.52S | 151.13 E |
| Syktyvkar | 86 | 61.40N | 50.46 E |
| Sylhet | 112 | 24.54N | 91.52 E |
| Syracuse | 140 | 43.02N | 76.08W |
| Syria □¹ | 109 | 35.00N | 38.00 E |
| Syzran' | 86 | 53.09N | 48.27 E |
| Szczecin (Stettin) | 90 | 53.24N | 14.32 E |
| Szczecinek (Neustettin) | 90 | 53.43N | 16.42 E |
| Szeged | 90 | 46.15N | 20.09 E |
| Székesfehérvár | 90 | 47.12N | 18.25 E |
| Szolnok | 90 | 47.10N | 20.12 E |
| Szombathely | 90 | 47.14N | 16.38 E |

| Name | Page No. | Lat. | Long. |
|---|---|---|---|
| Toulouse | 92 | 43.36N | 1.26 E |
| Toungoo | 120 | 18.56N | 96.26 E |
| Tours | 92 | 47.23N | 0.41 E |
| Townsville | 122 | 19.16S | 146.48 E |
| Toyama | 116 | 36.41N | 137.13 E |
| Toyohashi | 116 | 34.46N | 137.23 E |
| Toyota | 116 | 35.05N | 137.09 E |
| Tracy | 142 | 37.44N | 121.25W |
| Tralee | 88 | 52.16N | 9.42 W |
| Trancas | 134 | 26.13S | 65.17W |
| Transkei □ 9 | 106 | 31.20S | 29.00 E |
| Transylvania □ 9 | 98 | 46.30N | 24.00 E |
| Transylvanian Alps |  |  |  |
| → Carpaţii |  |  |  |
| Meridionali ⋏ | 98 | 45.30N | 24.15 E |
| Trapani | 96 | 38.01N | 12.31 E |
| Traverse City | 140 | 44.45N | 85.37W |
| Treinta y Tres | 134 | 33.14S | 54.23W |
| Trelew | 134 | 43.15S | 65.18W |
| Tremblant, Mont ⋀ | 140 | 46.16N | 74.35W |
| Trenčín | 90 | 48.54N | 18.04 E |
| Trento | 96 | 46.04N | 11.08 E |
| Trenton, On., Can. | 140 | 44.06N | 77.35W |
| Trenton, N.J., U.S. | 140 | 40.13N | 74.44W |
| Tres Arroyos | 134 | 38.23S | 60.17W |
| Três Corações | 135 | 21.42S | 45.16W |
| Três Lagoas | 135 | 20.48S | 51.43W |
| Três Pontas | 135 | 21.22S | 45.31W |
| Tres Puntas, Cabo ≻ | 134 | 47.06S | 65.53W |
| Treviso | 96 | 45.40N | 12.15 E |
| Trichūr | 111 | 10.31N | 76.13 E |
| Trier | 90 | 49.45N | 6.38 E |
| Trieste | 96 | 45.40N | 13.46 E |
| Triglav ⋀ | 96 | 46.23N | 13.50 E |
| Tríkala | 98 | 39.34N | 21.46 E |
| Trincomalee | 111 | 8.34N | 81.14 E |
| Trinidad, Bol. | 132 | 14.47S | 64.47W |
| Trinidad, Co., U.S. | 138 | 37.10N | 104.30W |
| Trinidad I | 130 | 10.30N | 61.15W |
| Trinidad and Tobago |  |  |  |
| □ 1 | 130 | 11.00N | 61.00W |
| Trípolis | 98 | 37.31N | 22.21 E |
| Tripoli |  |  |  |
| → Ţarābulus, Leb. | 109 | 34.26N | 35.51 E |
| Tripoli |  |  |  |
| → Ţarābulus, Libya | 104 | 32.54N | 13.11 E |
| Tripura □ 4 | 112 | 24.00N | 92.00 E |
| Trivandrum | 111 | 8.29N | 76.55 E |
| Trnava | 90 | 48.23N | 17.35 E |
| Trobriand Islands II | 122 | 8.35S | 151.05 E |
| Trois-Rivières | 140 | 46.21N | 72.33W |
| Tromelin I | 106 | 15.52S | 54.25 E |
| Tromsø | 89 | 69.40N | 18.58 E |
| Trondheim | 89 | 63.25N | 10.25 E |
| Trondheimsfjorden ⊂ 2 | 89 | 63.39N | 10.49 E |
| Troy, N.Y., U.S. | 140 | 42.43N | 73.41W |
| Troy, Oh., U.S. | 140 | 40.02N | 84.12W |
| Troyes | 92 | 48.18N | 4.05 E |
| Truckee ≏ | 142 | 39.51N | 119.24W |
| Trujillo, Peru | 132 | 8.07S | 79.02W |
| Trujillo, Ven. | 130 | 9.22N | 70.26W |
| Trutnov | 90 | 50.34N | 15.55 E |
| Tsingtao |  |  |  |
| → Qingdao | 114 | 36.06N | 120.19 E |
| Tsu | 116 | 34.43N | 136.31 E |
| Tsuchiura | 116 | 36.05N | 140.12 E |
| Tsugaru-kaikyō ⊔ | 116 | 41.35N | 141.00 E |
| Tsumeb | 106 | 19.13S | 17.42 E |
| Tsuruga | 116 | 35.39N | 136.04 E |
| Tsuruoka | 116 | 38.44N | 139.50 E |
| Tsuyama | 116 | 35.03N | 134.00 E |
| Tual | 118 | 5.40S | 132.45 E |
| Tubarão | 134 | 28.30S | 49.01W |
| Tübingen | 90 | 48.31N | 9.02 E |
| Tucson | 138 | 32.13N | 110.55W |
| Tucumcari | 138 | 35.10N | 103.43W |
| Tucupita | 130 | 9.04N | 62.03W |
| Tudmur (Palmyra) | 109 | 34.33N | 38.17 E |
| Tuktoyaktuk | 136 | 69.27N | 133.02W |
| Tula | 100 | 54.12N | 37.37 E |
| Tulancingo | 128 | 20.05N | 98.22W |
| Tulare | 142 | 36.12N | 119.20W |
| Tulcán | 132 | 0.48N | 77.43W |
| Tulcea | 98 | 45.11N | 28.48 E |
| Tulsa | 138 | 36.09N | 95.59W |
| Tulun | 102 | 54.35N | 100.33 E |
| Tumaco | 132 | 1.49N | 78.46W |
| Tumbes | 132 | 3.34S | 80.28W |
| T'umen' | 102 | 57.09N | 65.32 E |
| Tumeremo | 132 | 7.18N | 61.30W |
| Tumuc-Humac |  |  |  |
| Mountains ⋏ | 132 | 2.20N | 55.00W |
| Tundža (Tunca) ≏ | 98 | 41.40N | 26.34 E |
| Tunis | 104 | 36.48N | 10.11 E |
| Tunisia □ 1 | 104 | 34.00N | 9.00 E |
| Tunja | 132 | 5.31N | 73.22W |
| Tuolumne ≏ | 142 | 37.36N | 121.10W |
| Tupã | 135 | 21.56S | 50.30W |
| Tupaciguara | 135 | 18.35S | 48.42W |
| Tupelo | 138 | 34.15N | 88.42W |
| Tupper Lake | 140 | 44.13N | 74.29W |
| Turbo | 132 | 8.06N | 76.43W |
| Turda | 98 | 46.34N | 23.47 E |
| Turgutlu | 98 | 38.30N | 27.43 E |
| Turin |  |  |  |
| → Torino | 96 | 45.03N | 7.40 E |
| Turkey □ 1 | 86 | 39.00N | 35.00 E |
| Turkmenistan □ 1 | 86 | 40.00N | 60.00 E |
| Turks and Caicos |  |  |  |
| Islands □ 2 | 130 | 21.45N | 71.35W |
| Turks Islands II | 130 | 21.24N | 71.07W |
| Turku (Åbo) | 89 | 60.27N | 22.17 E |
| Turquino, Pico ⋀ | 130 | 19.59N | 76.50W |
| Turuchansk | 102 | 65.49N | 87.59 E |
| Tuscaloosa | 138 | 33.12N | 87.34W |
| Tuticorin | 111 | 8.47N | 78.08 E |
| Tutuila I | 127e | 14.18S | 170.42W |
| Tuxpan de Rodríguez |  |  |  |
| Cano | 128 | 20.57N | 97.24W |
| Tuxtla Gutiérrez | 128 | 16.45N | 93.07W |
| Tuzla | 96 | 44.32N | 18.41 E |
| Tver' | 100 | 56.52N | 35.55 E |
| Twin Falls | 138 | 42.33N | 114.27W |
| Tyler | 138 | 32.21N | 95.18W |
| Tyrrhenian Sea (Mare |  |  |  |
| Tirreno) ⊤ 2 | 96 | 40.00N | 12.00 E |
| **U** |  |  |  |
| Ubá | 135 | 21.07S | 42.56W |
| Ubangi (Oubangui) ≏ | 104 | 1.15N | 17.50 E |
| Ube | 116 | 33.56N | 131.15 E |
| Úbeda | 94 | 38.01N | 3.22W |
| Uberaba | 132 | 19.45S | 47.55W |
| Uberlândia | 132 | 18.56S | 48.18W |
| Ubon Ratchathani | 120 | 15.14N | 104.54 E |
| Ucayali ≏ | 132 | 4.30S | 73.27W |
| Uchta | 102 | 63.33N | 53.38 E |
| Udaipur | 112 | 24.35N | 73.41 E |
| Uddevalla | 89 | 58.21N | 11.55 E |
| Udine | 96 | 46.03N | 13.14 E |
| Udon Thani | 120 | 17.26N | 102.46 E |
| Ueda | 116 | 36.24N | 138.16 E |
| Ufa | 86 | 54.44N | 55.56 E |
| Uganda □ 1 | 106 | 1.00N | 32.00 E |
| Uitenhage | 106 | 33.40S | 25.28 E |
| Ujiji | 106 | 4.55S | 29.41 E |
| Ujung Pandang |  |  |  |
| (Makasar) | 118 | 5.07S | 119.24 E |
| Ukiah | 142 | 39.09N | 123.12W |
| Ukraine □ 1 | 86 | 49.00N | 32.00 E |
| Ulaanbaatar | 114 | 47.55N | 106.53 E |

| Name | Page No. | Lat. | Long. |
|---|---|---|---|
| Wanaka | 126 | 44.42S | 169.09 E |
| Wanganui | 126 | 39.56S | 175.03 E |
| Wanxian | 114 | 30.52N | 108.22 E |
| Warangal | 111 | 18.00N | 79.35 E |
| Wargla | 104 | 31.59N | 5.25 E |
| Warner Mountains ⋩ | 142 | 41.40N | 120.20 W |
| Warren, Mi., U.S. | 140 | 42.28N | 83.01 W |
| Warren, Oh., U.S. | 140 | 41.14N | 80.49 W |
| Warren, Pa., U.S. | 140 | 41.50N | 79.08 W |
| Warrenton | 140 | 38.42N | 77.47 W |
| Warrnambool | 122 | 38.23S | 142.29 E |
| Warsaw, Ky., U.S. | 140 | 38.47N | 84.54 W |
| Warsaw, Va., U.S. | 140 | 37.57N | 76.45 W |
| Warsaw → Warszawa | 90 | 52.15N | 21.00 E |
| Warszawa (Warsaw) | 90 | 52.15N | 21.00 E |
| Washington, D.C., U.S. | 140 | 38.53N | 77.02 W |
| Washington, Pa., U.S. | 140 | 40.10N | 80.14 W |
| Washington □³ | 138 | 47.30N | 120.30 W |
| Washington, Mount ⋀ | 140 | 44.15N | 71.15 W |
| Washington Court House | 140 | 39.32N | 83.26 W |
| Waspán | 130 | 14.44N | 83.58 W |
| Waterbury | 140 | 41.33N | 73.02 W |
| Waterford | 88 | 52.15N | 7.06 W |
| Waterloo, On., Can. | 140 | 43.28N | 80.31 W |
| Waterloo, Ia., U.S. | 138 | 42.29N | 92.20 W |
| Watertown, N.Y., U.S. | 140 | 43.58N | 75.54 W |
| Watertown, S.D., U.S. | 136 | 44.53N | 97.06 W |
| Waterville | 140 | 44.33N | 69.37 W |
| Watrous | 136 | 51.40N | 105.28 W |
| Watson Lake | 136 | 60.07N | 128.48 W |
| Wāw | 104 | 7.42N | 28.00 E |
| Wawa | 136 | 47.59N | 84.47 W |
| Waycross | 138 | 31.12N | 82.21 W |
| Waynesboro, Pa., U.S. | 140 | 39.45N | 77.34 W |
| Waynesboro, Va., U.S. | 140 | 38.04N | 78.53 W |
| Weatherford | 128 | 32.45N | 97.47 W |
| Webster Springs | 140 | 38.28N | 80.24 W |
| Weddell Sea ⊤² | 85 | 72.00S | 45.00 W |
| Weiden in der Oberpfalz | 90 | 49.41N | 12.10 E |
| Weifang | 114 | 36.42N | 19.04 E |
| Weirton | 140 | 40.25N | 80.35 W |
| Welkom | 106 | 27.59S | 26.45 E |
| Wellington | 126 | 41.18S | 174.47 E |
| Wellington, Isla ⵊ | 134 | 49.20S | 74.40 W |
| Wells | 142 | 41.06N | 114.57 W |
| Wellsford | 126 | 36.17S | 174.31 E |
| Wellston | 140 | 39.07N | 82.31 W |
| Wels | 90 | 48.10N | 14.02 E |
| Wendover | 142 | 40.44N | 114.02 W |
| Wenzhou | 114 | 28.01N | 120.39 E |
| West Bengal □³ | 112 | 24.00N | 88.00 E |
| Westerly | 140 | 41.22N | 71.49 W |
| Western Australia □³ | 122 | 25.00S | 122.00 E |
| Western Ghāts ⋩ | 111 | 14.00N | 75.00 E |
| Western Sahara □² | 104 | 24.30N | 13.00 W |
| Western Samoa □¹ | 127e | 13.55S | 172.00 W |
| Westerville | 140 | 40.07N | 82.55 W |
| West Falkland ⵊ | 134 | 51.50S | 60.00 W |
| Westfield | 140 | 42.19N | 79.34 W |
| West Indies ⵊⵊ | 130 | 19.00N | 70.00 W |
| West Liberty | 140 | 37.55N | 83.15 W |
| Westminster | 140 | 39.34N | 76.59 W |
| West Palm Beach | 138 | 26.42N | 80.03 W |
| Westport | 126 | 41.45S | 171.36 E |
| West Virginia □³ | 138 | 38.45N | 80.30 W |
| Wetaskiwin | 136 | 52.58N | 113.22 W |
| Wexford | 88 | 52.20N | 6.27 W |
| Weymouth | 88 | 50.36N | 2.28 W |
| Whangarei | 126 | 35.43S | 174.19 E |
| Whataroa | 126 | 43.17S | 170.25 E |
| Wheeler Peak ⋀, Nv., U.S. | 142 | 38.59N | 114.19 W |
| Wheeler Peak ⋀, N.M., U.S. | 138 | 36.34N | 105.25 W |
| Wheeling | 140 | 40.03N | 80.43 W |
| Whitehaven | 88 | 54.33N | 3.35 W |
| Whitehorse | 136 | 60.43N | 135.03 W |
| White Mountains ⋩ | 140 | 44.10N | 71.35 W |
| White Nile (Al-Baḥr al-Abyaḍ) ⩲ | 108 | 15.38N | 32.31 E |
| White Plains | 140 | 41.02N | 73.45 W |
| White Sands National Monument ⧫ | 128 | 32.48N | 106.20 W |
| White Volta (Volta Blanche) ⩲ | 104 | 9.10N | 1.15 W |
| Whitney, Mount ⋀ | 142 | 36.35N | 118.18 W |
| Whyalla | 124 | 33.02S | 137.35 E |
| Wichita | 138 | 37.41N | 97.20 W |
| Wichita Falls | 138 | 33.54N | 98.29 W |
| Wielkopolska ⬥¹ | 90 | 51.50N | 17.20 E |
| Wien (Vienna) | 90 | 48.13N | 16.20 E |
| Wiener Neustadt | 90 | 47.49N | 16.15 E |
| Wieprz ⩲ | 90 | 51.34N | 21.49 E |
| Wieprz-Krzna, Kanał ≊ | 90 | 51.56N | 22.56 E |
| Wiesbaden | 90 | 50.05N | 8.14 E |
| Wilhelm, Mount ⋀ | 118 | 5.45S | 145.05 E |
| Wilhelmshaven | 90 | 53.31N | 8.08 E |
| Wilkes-Barre | 140 | 41.14N | 75.52 W |
| Wilkes Land ⬥¹ | 85 | 69.00S | 120.00 E |
| Willard | 140 | 41.03N | 82.44 W |
| Willemstad | 130 | 12.06N | 68.56 W |
| Williams Lake | 136 | 52.08N | 122.09 W |
| Williamsport | 140 | 41.14N | 76.59 W |
| Williston | 138 | 48.08N | 103.38 W |
| Wilmington, De., U.S. | 140 | 39.44N | 75.32 W |
| Wilmington, N.C., U.S. | 138 | 34.13N | 77.56 W |
| Wiluna | 122 | 26.36S | 120.13 E |
| Winchester, In., U.S. | 140 | 40.10N | 84.58 W |
| Winchester, Va., U.S. | 140 | 39.11N | 78.10 W |
| Windhoek | 106 | 22.34S | 17.06 E |
| Windsor, N.S., Can. | 136 | 44.59N | 64.08 W |
| Windsor, On., Can. | 136 | 42.18N | 83.01 W |
| Windsor, P.Q., Can. | 140 | 45.34N | 72.00 W |
| Windsor, Eng., U.K. | 88 | 51.29N | 0.38 W |
| Windward Islands ⵊⵊ | 130 | 13.00N | 61.00 W |
| Windward Passage ⵘ | 138 | 20.00N | 73.50 W |
| Winisk | 136 | 55.15N | 85.12 W |
| Winisk Lake ⬵ | 136 | 52.55N | 87.22 W |
| Winnemucca | 142 | 40.58N | 117.44 W |
| Winnfield | 128 | 31.55N | 92.38 W |
| Winnipeg | 136 | 49.53N | 97.09 W |
| Winnipeg, Lake ⬵ | 136 | 52.00N | 97.00 W |
| Winnipesaukee, Lake ⬵ | 140 | 43.35N | 71.20 W |
| Winslow | 140 | 44.32N | 69.37 W |
| Winston-Salem | 138 | 36.05N | 80.14 W |
| Winterport | 140 | 44.38N | 68.51 W |
| Winton, Austl. | 122 | 22.23S | 143.02 E |
| Winton, N.Z. | 126 | 46.09S | 168.20 E |
| Wisconsin □³ | 138 | 44.45N | 89.30 W |
| Wisła ⩲ | 90 | 54.22N | 18.55 E |
| Wismar, Ger. | 90 | 53.53N | 11.28 E |
| Wismar, Guy. | 132 | 6.00N | 58.18 W |
| Wittenberg | 90 | 51.52N | 12.39 E |
| Wittenberge | 90 | 53.00N | 11.44 E |
| Woleai ⵊ¹ | 118 | 7.21N | 143.52 E |
| Wolfsberg | 90 | 46.51N | 14.51 E |
| Wolfsburg | 90 | 52.25N | 10.47 E |
| Wollongong | 124 | 34.25S | 150.54 E |
| Wŏnsan | 114 | 39.09N | 127.25 E |
| Woodbridge | 140 | 38.39N | 77.15 W |
| Woodland | 142 | 38.40N | 121.46 W |
| Woodlark Island ⵊ | 122 | 9.05S | 152.50 E |
| Woods, Lake of the ⬵ | 138 | 49.15N | 94.45 W |
| Woodstock | 140 | 43.08N | 80.45 W |
| Woodsville | 140 | 44.09N | 72.02 W |
| Woodville | 126 | 40.20S | 175.52 E |
| Woomera | 122 | 31.31S | 137.10 E |
| Woonsocket | 140 | 42.00N | 71.30 W |

| Name | Page No. | Lat. | Long. | Name | Page No. | Lat. | Long. |
|------|----------|------|-------|------|----------|------|-------|
| Zgierz | 90 | 51.52N | 19.25 E | Znojmo | 90 | 48.52N | 16.02 E |
| Zhangjiakou | 114 | 40.50N | 114.53 E | Zomba | 106 | 15.23S | 35.18 E |
| Zhangzhou | 114 | 24.33N | 117.39 E | Zudañez | 132 | 19.06S | 64.44 W |
| Zhanjiang | 114 | 21.16N | 110.28 E | Zugspitze ⋀ | 90 | 47.25N | 10.59 E |
| Zhengzhou | 114 | 34.48N | 113.39 E | Zuiderzee | | | |
| Zhuzhou | 114 | 27.50N | 113.09 E | → IJsselmeer ▼ [2] | 90 | 52.45N | 5.25 E |
| Zigong | 114 | 29.24N | 104.47 E | Zululand □ [9] | 106 | 28.10S | 32.00 E |
| Ziguinchor | 104 | 12.35N | 16.16 W | Zunyi | 114 | 27.39N | 106.57 E |
| Žilina | 90 | 49.14N | 18.46 E | Zürich | 92 | 47.23N | 8.32 E |
| Zimbabwe □ [1] | 106 | 20.00S | 30.00 E | Zvolen | 90 | 48.35N | 19.08 E |
| Žitomir | 86 | 50.16N | 28.40 E | Zwettl | 90 | 48.37N | 15.10 E |
| Zlín | 90 | 49.13N | 17.41 E | Zwickau | 90 | 50.44N | 12.29 E |
| Žlobin | 100 | 52.54N | 30.03 E | Zwolle | 90 | 52.30N | 6.05 E |

# World Flags

Afghanistan

Albania

Algeria

Andorra

Angola

Antigua and Barbuda

Argentina

Armenia

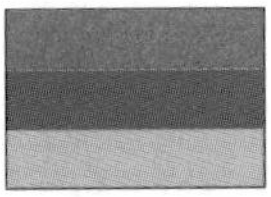

Australia

Austria

Azerbaijan

Bahamas

Bahrain

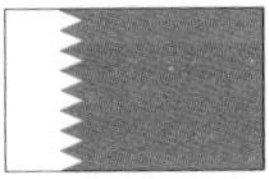

Bangladesh

Barbados

Belarus

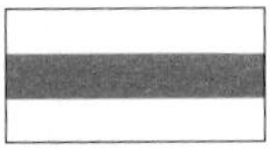

Belgium

Belize

Benin

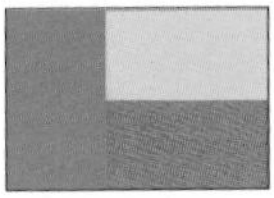

Bhutan

Bolivia

Bosnia and Hercegovina

Botswana

Brazil

Brunei

Bulgaria

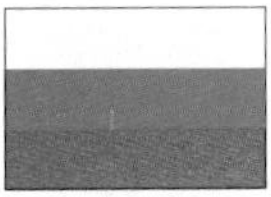

Burkina Faso

Burma (Myanmar)

Burundi

Cambodia

Cameroon

Canada

Cape Verde

Central African Republic

Chad

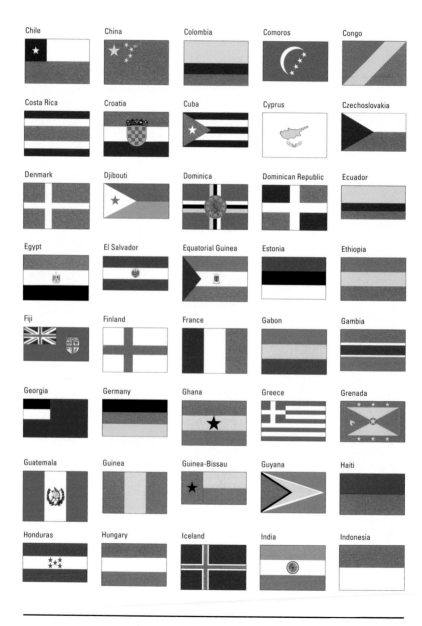

Chile

China

Colombia

Comoros

Congo

Costa Rica

Croatia

Cuba

Cyprus

Czechoslovakia

Denmark

Djibouti

Dominica

Dominican Republic

Ecuador

Egypt

El Salvador

Equatorial Guinea

Estonia

Ethiopia

Fiji

Finland

France

Gabon

Gambia

Georgia

Germany

Ghana

Greece

Grenada

Guatemala

Guinea

Guinea-Bissau

Guyana

Haiti

Honduras

Hungary

Iceland

India

Indonesia

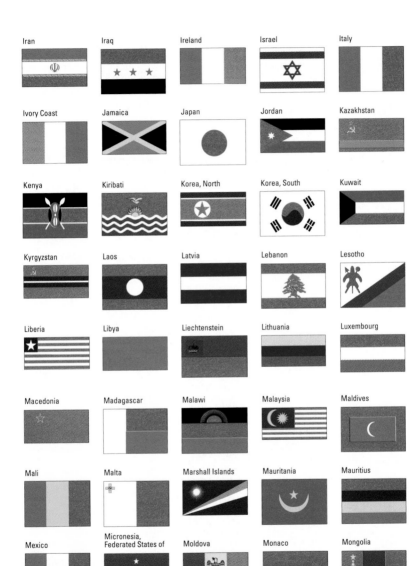

| Iran | Iraq | Ireland | Israel | Italy |

| Ivory Coast | Jamaica | Japan | Jordan | Kazakhstan |

| Kenya | Kiribati | Korea, North | Korea, South | Kuwait |

| Kyrgyzstan | Laos | Latvia | Lebanon | Lesotho |

| Liberia | Libya | Liechtenstein | Lithuania | Luxembourg |

| Macedonia | Madagascar | Malawi | Malaysia | Maldives |

| Mali | Malta | Marshall Islands | Mauritania | Mauritius |

| Mexico | Micronesia, Federated States of | Moldova | Monaco | Mongolia |

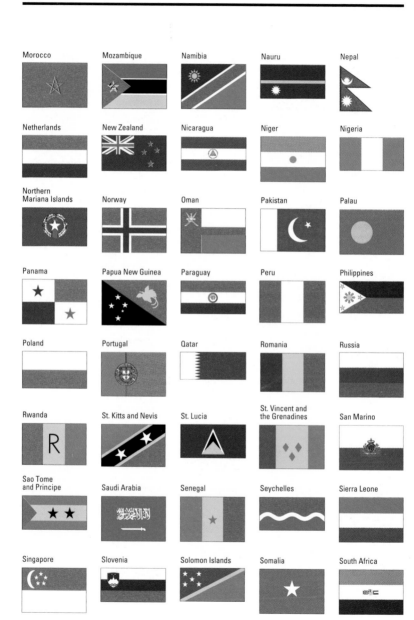

Morocco

Mozambique

Namibia

Nauru

Nepal

Netherlands

New Zealand

Nicaragua

Niger

Nigeria

Northern
Mariana Islands

Norway

Oman

Pakistan

Palau

Panama

Papua New Guinea

Paraguay

Peru

Philippines

Poland

Portugal

Qatar

Romania

Russia

Rwanda

St. Kitts and Nevis

St. Lucia

St. Vincent and
the Grenadines

San Marino

Sao Tome
and Principe

Saudi Arabia

Senegal

Seychelles

Sierra Leone

Singapore

Slovenia

Solomon Islands

Somalia

South Africa

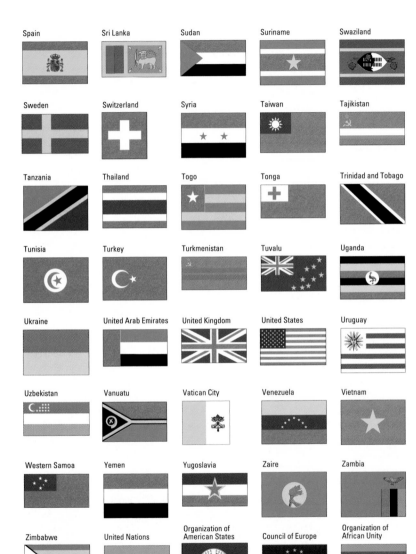

| Spain | Sri Lanka | Sudan | Suriname | Swaziland |
|---|---|---|---|---|
| Sweden | Switzerland | Syria | Taiwan | Tajikistan |
| Tanzania | Thailand | Togo | Tonga | Trinidad and Tobago |
| Tunisia | Turkey | Turkmenistan | Tuvalu | Uganda |
| Ukraine | United Arab Emirates | United Kingdom | United States | Uruguay |
| Uzbekistan | Vanuatu | Vatican City | Venezuela | Vietnam |
| Western Samoa | Yemen | Yugoslavia | Zaire | Zambia |
| Zimbabwe | United Nations | Organization of American States | Council of Europe | Organization of African Unity |

# Country Profiles

## Afghanistan (Afghānestān)

**Location:** Southern Asia, landlocked
**Area:** 251,826 mi² (652,225 km²)
**Population:** 16,880,000 (Urban: 22%)
**Literacy:** 29%
**Capital:** Kabōl, 1,424,400
**Government:** Republic
**Languages:** Dari, Pashto, Uzbek, Turkmen
**Ethnic Groups:** Pathan 50%, Tajik 25%, Uzbek 9%, Hazara 9%
**Religions:** Sunni Muslim 74%, Shiite Muslim 15%
**Currency:** Afghani

## Albania (Shqipëria)

**Location:** Southeastern Europe
**Area:** 11,100 mi² (28,748 km²)
**Population:** 3,352,000 (Urban: 35%)
**Literacy:** 72%
**Capital:** Tiranë, 238,100
**Government:** Republic
**Languages:** Albanian, Greek
**Ethnic Groups:** Albanian (Illyrian) 96%
**Religions:** Muslim 20%, Christian 5%
**Currency:** Lek
**Tel. Area Code:** 355

## Algeria (Djazaïr)

**Location:** Northern Africa
**Area:** 919,595 mi² (2,381,741 km²)
**Population:** 26,360,000 (Urban: 45%)
**Literacy:** 50%
**Capital:** Algier, 1,507,241
**Government:** Provisional military government
**Languages:** Arabic, Berber dialects, French
**Ethnic Groups:** Arab-Berber 99%
**Religions:** Sunni Muslim 99%, Christian and Jewish
**Currency:** Dinar
**Tel. Area Code:** 213

## Angola

**Location:** Southern Africa
**Area:** 481,354 mi² (1,246,700 km²)
**Population:** 10,425,000 (Urban: 28%)
**Literacy:** 42%
**Capital:** Luanda, 1,459,900
**Government:** Republic
**Languages:** Portuguese, indigenous
**Ethnic Groups:** Ovimbundu 37%, Mbundu 25%, Kongo 13%, mulatto 2%, European 1%
**Religions:** Animist 47%, Roman Catholic 38%, other Christian 15%
**Currency:** Kwanza

## Antigua and Barbuda

**Location:** Caribbean islands
**Area:** 171 mi² (443 km²)
**Population:** 64,000 (Urban: 32%)
**Literacy:** 89%
**Capital:** St. John's, 24,359
**Government:** Parliamentary state
**Languages:** English, local dialects
**Ethnic Groups:** Black
**Religions:** Anglican, Protestant, Roman Catholic
**Currency:** East Caribbean dollar
**Tel. Area Code:** 809

## Argentina

**Location:** Southern South America
**Area:** 1,073,400 mi² (2,780,092 km²)
**Population:** 32,860,000 (Urban: 86%)
**Literacy:** 95%
**Capital:** Buenos Aires, 2,922,829
**Government:** Republic
**Languages:** Spanish, English, Italian, German, French
**Ethnic Groups:** White 85%, mestizo, Amerindian, and others 15%
**Religions:** Roman Catholic 90%, Jewish 2%, Protestant 2%
**Currency:** Peso
**Tel. Area Code:** 54

## Armenia (Hayastan)

**Location:** Southwestern Asia, landlocked
**Area:** 11,506 mi² (29,800 km²)
**Population:** 3,360,000 (Urban: 68%)
**Literacy:** 99%

**Capital:** Jerevan, 1,199,000
**Government:** Republic
**Languages:** Armenian, Azerbaijani, Russian
**Ethnic Groups:** Armenian 93%, Azeri 3%, Russian 2%
**Religions:** Armenian orthodox
**Currency:** Ruble

## Australia

**Location:** Continent between South Pacific and Indian oceans
**Area:** 2,966,155 mi$^2$ (7,682,300 km$^2$)
**Population:** 17,420,000 (Urban: 86%)
**Literacy:** 100%
**Capital:** Canberra, 247,194
**Government:** Parliamentary state
**Languages:** English, indigenous
**Ethnic Groups:** European 95%, Asian 4%, Aboriginal and other 1%
**Religions:** Anglican 24%, Roman Catholic 26%, other Christian 23%
**Currency:** Dollar
**Tel. Area Code:** 61

## Austria (Österreich)

**Location:** Central Europe, landlocked
**Area:** 32,377 mi$^2$ (83,855 km$^2$)
**Population:** 7,681,000 (Urban: 58%)
**Literacy:** 99%
**Capital:** Wien (Vienna), 1,482,800
**Government:** Republic
**Languages:** German
**Ethnic Groups:** German 99%
**Religions:** Roman Catholic 85%, Protestant 6%
**Currency:** Schilling
**Tel. Area Code:** 43

## Azerbaijan (Azerbajdžan)

**Location:** Southwestern Asia, landlocked
**Area:** 33,436 mi$^2$ (86,600 km$^2$)
**Population:** 7,170,000 (Urban: 54%)
**Literacy:** 98%
**Capital:** Baku, 1,080,500
**Government:** Republic
**Languages:** Azerbaijani, Russian, Armenian
**Ethnic Groups:** Azeri 83%, Armenian 6%, Russian 6%
**Religions:** Muslim, Christian
**Currency:** Ruble

## Bahamas

**Location:** Caribbean islands
**Area:** 5,382 mi$^2$ (13,939 km$^2$)
**Population:** 260,000 (Urban: 59%)
**Literacy:** 90%
**Capital:** Nassau, 141,000
**Government:** Parliamentary state
**Languages:** English, Creole
**Ethnic Groups:** Black 85%, white 15%
**Religions:** Baptist 29%, Anglican 23%, Roman Catholic 22%
**Currency:** Dollar
**Tel. Area Code:** 809

## Bahrain (Al-Bahrayn)

**Location:** Southwestern Asian islands (in Persian Gulf)
**Area:** 267 mi$^2$ (691 km$^2$)
**Population:** 546,000 (Urban: 83%)
**Literacy:** 77%
**Capital:** Al-Manāmah (Manama), 115,054
**Government:** Monarchy
**Languages:** Arabic, English, Farsi, Urdu
**Ethnic Groups:** Bahraini 63%, Asian 13%, other Arab 10%
**Religions:** Shiite Muslim 70%, Sunni Muslim 30%
**Currency:** Dinar
**Tel. Area Code:** 973

## Bangladesh

**Location:** Southern Asia
**Area:** 55,598 mi$^2$ (143,998 km$^2$)
**Population:** 118,000,000 (Urban: 14%)
**Literacy:** 35%
**Capital:** Dhaka, 2,365,695
**Government:** Islamic republic
**Languages:** Bangla, English
**Ethnic Groups:** Bengali 98%
**Religions:** Muslim 83%, Hindu 16%
**Currency:** Taka
**Tel. Area Code:** 880

## Barbados

**Location:** Caribbean island
**Area:** 166 mi$^2$ (430 km$^2$)
**Population:** 257,000 (Urban: 45%)
**Literacy:** 99%
**Capital:** Bridgetown, 7,466
**Government:** Parliamentary state
**Languages:** English
**Ethnic Groups:** Black 92%, white 3%, mixed 3%, East Indian 1%

**Religions:** Anglican 40%, Pentecostal 8%,
Methodist 7%, Roman Catholic 4%
**Currency:** Dollar
**Tel. Area Code:** 809

## Belarus (Byelarus')

**Location:** Eastern Europe, landlocked
**Area:** 80,155 mi$^2$ (207,600 km$^2$)
**Population:** 10,390,000 (Urban: 65%)
**Literacy:** 99%
**Capital:** Minsk, 1,633,600
**Government:** Republic
**Languages:** Belorussian, Russian
**Ethnic Groups:** Belorussian 78%,
Russian 13%, Polish 4%
**Religions:** Eastern Orthodox, Roman
Catholic
**Currency:** Ruble

## Belgium (Belgique, België)

**Location:** Western Europe
**Area:** 11,783 mi$^2$ (30,518 km$^2$)
**Population:** 9,932,000 (Urban: 97%)
**Literacy:** 99%
**Capital:** Bruxelles (Brussels), 136,920
**Government:** Constitutional monarchy
**Languages:** Dutch (Flemish), French,
German
**Ethnic Groups:** Fleming 55%, Walloon 33%,
mixed and others 12%
**Religions:** Roman Catholic 75%
**Currency:** Franc
**Tel. Area Code:** 32

## Belize

**Location:** Central America
**Area:** 8,866 mi$^2$ (22,963 km$^2$)
**Population:** 232,000 (Urban: 52%)
**Literacy:** 91%
**Capital:** Belmopan, 5,256
**Government:** Parliamentary state
**Languages:** English, Spanish, Garifuna,
Mayan
**Ethnic Groups:** Creole 40%, mestizo 33%,
Amerindian 16%
**Religions:** Roman Catholic 62%,
Anglican 12%, Methodist 6%,
Mennonite 4%
**Currency:** Dollar
**Tel. Area Code:** 501

## Benin (Bénin)

**Location:** Western Africa
**Area:** 43,475 mi$^2$ (112,600 km$^2$)
**Population:** 4,914,000 (Urban: 42%)
**Literacy:** 23%
**Capital:** Porto-Novo (designated), 164,000;
Cotonou (de facto), 478,000
**Government:** Republic
**Languages:** French, Fon, Adja, indigenous
**Ethnic Groups:** Fon 39%, Yoruba 12%,
Adja 10%, others
**Religions:** Fetishism 70%, Muslim 15%,
Christian 15%
**Currency:** CFA franc
**Tel. Area Code:** 229

## Bhutan (Druk-Yul)

**Location:** Southern Asia, landlocked
**Area:** 17,954 mi$^2$ (46,500 km$^2$)
**Population:** 1,614,000 (Urban: 5%)
**Capital:** Thimphu, 12,000
**Government:** Monarchy (Indian protection)
**Languages:** Dzongkha, Tibetan and
Nepalese dialects
**Ethnic Groups:** Bhotia 60%, Nepalese 25%,
indigenous 15%
**Religions:** Buddhist 75%, Hindu 25%
**Currency:** Ngultrum, Indian rupee
**Tel. Area Code:** 975

## Bolivia

**Location:** Central South America,
landlocked
**Area:** 424,165 mi$^2$ (1,098,581 km$^2$)
**Population:** 7,243,000 (Urban: 51%)
**Literacy:** 78%
**Capital:** La Paz (seat of government),
1,125,600; Sucre (seat of judiciary),
101,400
**Government:** Republic
**Languages:** Aymara, Quechua, Spanish
**Ethnic Groups:** Quechua 30%, Aymara 25%,
mixed 25-30%, European 5-15%
**Religions:** Roman Catholic 95%, Methodist
and other Protestant
**Currency:** Boliviano
**Tel. Area Code:** 591

## Bosnia and Hercegovina (Bosna i Hercegovina)

**Location:** Eastern Europe
**Area:** 19,741 mi$^2$ (51,129 km$^2$)
**Population:** 4,519,000 (Urban: 36%)
**Literacy:** 86%

**Capital:** Sarajevo, 341,200
**Government:** Republic
**Languages:** Serb, Croat, Albanian
**Ethnic Groups:** Bosnian, Serbian, Croatian
**Religions:** Serbian Orthodox, Muslim,
Roman Catholic
**Currency:** Yugoslavian dinar

## Botswana

**Location:** Southern Africa, landlocked
**Area:** 224,711 mi² (582,000 km²)
**Population:** 1,345,000 (Urban: 24%)
**Literacy:** 23%
**Capital:** Gaborone, 133,791
**Government:** Republic
**Languages:** English, Tswana
**Ethnic Groups:** Tswana 95%; Kalanga,
Baswara, and Kgalagadi 4%; white 1%
**Religions:** Tribal religionist 50%, Roman
Catholic and other Christian 50%
**Currency:** Pula
**Tel. Area Code:** 267

## Brazil (Brasil)

**Location:** Eastern South America
**Area:** 3,286,488 mi² (8,511,965 km²)
**Population:** 156,750,000 (Urban: 77%)
**Literacy:** 81%
**Capital:** Brasília, 1,567,709
**Government:** Republic
**Languages:** Portuguese, Spanish, English,
French
**Ethnic Groups:** White 55%, mixed 38%,
black 6%
**Religions:** Roman Catholic 96%
**Currency:** Cruzeiro
**Tel. Area Code:** 55

## Brunei

**Location:** Southeastern Asia (island of
Borneo)
**Area:** 2,226 mi² (5,765 km²)
**Population:** 411,000 (Urban: 58%)
**Literacy:** 78%
**Capital:** Bandar Seri Begawan, 22,777
**Government:** Monarchy
**Languages:** Malay, English, Chinese
**Ethnic Groups:** Malay 65%, Chinese 20%,
indigenous 8%, Tamil 3%
**Religions:** Muslim 63%, Buddhist 14%,
Roman Catholic and other Christian 10%
**Currency:** Dollar
**Tel. Area Code:** 673

## Bulgaria (Bâlgarija)

**Location:** Eastern Europe
**Area:** 42,823 mi² (110,912 km²)
**Population:** 8,902,000 (Urban: 70%)
**Literacy:** 93%
**Capital:** Sofija (Sofia), 1,136,875
**Government:** Republic
**Languages:** Bulgarian
**Ethnic Groups:** Bulgarian (Slavic) 85%,
Turkish 9%, Gypsy 3%, Macedonian 3%
**Religions:** Bulgarian Orthodox, Muslim
**Currency:** Lev
**Tel. Area Code:** 359

## Burkina Faso

**Location:** Western Africa, landlocked
**Area:** 105,869 mi² (274,200 km²)
**Population:** 9,510,000 (Urban: 9%)
**Literacy:** 18%
**Capital:** Ouagadougou, 441,514
**Government:** Provisional military
government
**Languages:** French, indigenous
**Ethnic Groups:** Mossi 30%, Fulani, Lobi,
Malinke, Bobo, Senufo, Gurunsi, others
**Religions:** Animist 65%, Muslim 25%,
Roman Catholic and other Christian
**Currency:** CFA franc

## Burma (Myanmar)

**Location:** Southeastern Asia
**Area:** 261,228 mi² (676,577 km²)
**Population:** 42,615,000 (Urban: 25%)
**Literacy:** 81%
**Capital:** Rangoon (Yangon), 2,705,039
**Government:** Provisional military
government
**Languages:** Burmese, indigenous
**Ethnic Groups:** Bamar (Burmese) 69%,
Shan 9%, Kayin 6%, Rakhine 5%
**Religions:** Buddhist 89%, Muslim 4%,
Christian 5%
**Currency:** Kyat

## Burundi

**Location:** Eastern Africa, landlocked
**Area:** 10,745 mi² (27,830 km²)
**Population:** 5,924,000 (Urban: 7%)
**Literacy:** 50%
**Capital:** Bujumbura, 226,628
**Government:** Republic
**Languages:** French, Kirundi, Swahili
**Ethnic Groups:** Hutu 85%, Tutsi 14%,
Twa 1%

**Religions:** Roman Catholic 62%,
Animist 32%, Protestant 5%, Muslim 1%
**Currency:** Franc

## Cambodia (Kâmpŭchéa)

**Location:** Southeastern Asia
**Area:** 69,898 mi$^2$ (181,035 km$^2$)
**Population:** 8,543,000 (Urban: 12%)
**Literacy:** 35%
**Capital:** Phnum Pénh (Phnom Penh),
477,874
**Government:** Socialist republic
**Languages:** Khmer, French
**Ethnic Groups:** Khmer 90%, Chinese 5%
**Religions:** Buddhist 95%, Animist, Muslim
**Currency:** Riel

## Cameroon (Cameroun)

**Location:** Central Africa
**Area:** 183,569 mi$^2$ (475,442 km$^2$)
**Population:** 11,550,000 (Urban: 49%)
**Literacy:** 54%
**Capital:** Yaoundé, 653,670
**Government:** Republic
**Languages:** English, French, indigenous
**Ethnic Groups:** Cameroon Highlander 31%,
Equatorial Bantu 19%, Kirdi 11%,
Fulani 10%
**Religions:** Animist 51%, Christian 33%,
Muslim 16%
**Currency:** CFA franc
**Tel. Area Code:** 237

## Canada

**Location:** Northern North America
**Area:** 3,849,674 mi$^2$ (9,970,610 km$^2$)
**Population:** 26,985,000 (Urban: 76%)
**Literacy:** 99%
**Capital:** Ottawa, 300,763
**Government:** Parliamentary state
**Languages:** English, French
**Ethnic Groups:** British origin 40%, French
origin 27%, other European 23%, native
Canadian 2%
**Religions:** Roman Catholic 47%, United
Church 16%, Anglican 10%, other
Christian
**Currency:** Dollar
**Tel. Area Code:** $

## Cape Verde (Cabo Verde)

**Location:** Western African islands
**Area:** 1,557 mi$^2$ (4,033 km$^2$)
**Population:** 393,000 (Urban: 52%)
**Literacy:** 66%
**Capital:** Praia, 61,797
**Government:** Republic
**Languages:** Portuguese, Crioulo
**Ethnic Groups:** Creole (mulatto) 71%,
African 28%, European 1%
**Religions:** Roman Catholic, Nazarene and
other Protestant
**Currency:** Escudo
**Tel. Area Code:** 238

## Central African Republic (République centrafricaine)

**Location:** Central Africa, landlocked
**Area:** 240,535 mi$^2$ (622,984 km$^2$)
**Population:** 2,990,000 (Urban: 47%)
**Literacy:** 27%
**Capital:** Bangui, 473,817
**Government:** Republic
**Languages:** French, Sango, Arabic,
indigenous
**Ethnic Groups:** Baya 34%, Banda 27%,
Mandja 21%, Sara 10%
**Religions:** Protestant 25%, Roman
Catholic 25%, Animist 24%, Muslim 15%
**Currency:** CFA franc

## Chad (Tchad)

**Location:** Central Africa, landlocked
**Area:** 495,755 mi$^2$ (1,284,000 km$^2$)
**Population:** 5,178,000 (Urban: 33%)
**Literacy:** 30%
**Capital:** N'Djamena, 500,000
**Government:** Republic
**Languages:** Arabic, French, indigenous
**Ethnic Groups:** Sara and other African,
Arab
**Religions:** Muslim 44%, Christian 33%,
Animist 23%
**Currency:** CFA franc

## Chile

**Location:** Southern South America
**Area:** 292,135 mi$^2$ (756,626 km$^2$)
**Population:** 13,395,000 (Urban: 86%)
**Literacy:** 93%
**Capital:** Santiago, 232,667
**Government:** Republic
**Languages:** Spanish

**Ethnic Groups:** White and mestizo 95%,
Amerindian 3%
**Religions:** Roman Catholic 89%, Pentecostal
and other Protestant 11%
**Currency:** Peso
**Tel. Area Code:** 56

## China (Zhongguo)

**Location:** Eastern Asia
**Area:** 3,689,631 mi$^2$ (9,556,100 km$^2$)
**Population:** 1,181,580,000 (Urban: 21%)
**Literacy:** 73%
**Capital:** Beijing (Peking), 6,710,000
**Government:** Socialist republic
**Languages:** Chinese dialects
**Ethnic Groups:** Han Chinese 93%, Zhuang,
Hui, Uygur, Yi, Miao, Manchu, Tibetan,
others
**Religions:** Confucian, Taoist, Buddhist,
Muslim
**Currency:** Yuan
**Tel. Area Code:** 86

## Colombia

**Location:** Northern South America
**Area:** 440,831 mi$^2$ (1,141,748 km$^2$)
**Population:** 33,170,000 (Urban: 70%)
**Literacy:** 87%
**Capital:** Santa Fe de Bogotá, 3,982,941
**Government:** Republic
**Languages:** Spanish
**Ethnic Groups:** Mestizo 58%, white 20%,
mulatto 14%, black 4%
**Religions:** Roman Catholic 95%
**Currency:** Peso
**Tel. Area Code:** 57

## Comoros (Al-Qumur, Comores)

**Location:** Southeastern African islands
**Area:** 863 mi$^2$ (2,235 km$^2$)
**Population:** 484,000 (Urban: 28%)
**Literacy:** 48%
**Capital:** Moroni, 23,432
**Government:** Islamic republic
**Languages:** Arabic, French, Shaafi Islam
(Swahili), Malagasy
**Ethnic Groups:** African-Arab descent
(Antalote, Cafre, Makua, Oimatsaha,
Sakalava)
**Religions:** Sunni Muslim 86%, Roman
Catholic 14%
**Currency:** Franc

## Congo

**Location:** Central Africa
**Area:** 132,047 mi$^2$ (342,000 km$^2$)
**Population:** 2,344,000 (Urban: 42%)
**Literacy:** 57%
**Capital:** Brazzaville, 585,812
**Government:** Socialist republic
**Languages:** French, Lingala, Kikongo,
indigenous
**Ethnic Groups:** Kongo 48%, Sangho 20%,
Bateke 17%, Mbochis 12%
**Religions:** Christian 50%, Animist 48%,
Muslim 2%
**Currency:** CFA franc
**Tel. Area Code:** 242

## Costa Rica

**Location:** Central America
**Area:** 19,730 mi$^2$ (51,100 km$^2$)
**Population:** 3,151,000 (Urban: 54%)
**Literacy:** 93%
**Capital:** San José, 278,600
**Government:** Republic
**Languages:** Spanish
**Ethnic Groups:** White and mestizo 96%,
black 3%, Amerindian 1%
**Religions:** Roman Catholic 95%
**Currency:** Colon
**Tel. Area Code:** 506

## Croatia (Hrvatska)

**Location:** Eastern Europe
**Area:** 21,829 mi$^2$ (56,538 km$^2$)
**Population:** 1,989,000 (Urban: 51%)
**Literacy:** 92%
**Capital:** Zagreb, 697,925
**Government:** Republic
**Languages:** Croatian, Serbian
**Ethnic Groups:** Croatian, Serbian
**Religions:** Roman Catholic
**Currency:** Yugoslavian dinar

## Cuba

**Location:** Caribbean island
**Area:** 42,804 mi$^2$ (110,861 km$^2$)
**Population:** 10,785,000 (Urban: 75%)
**Literacy:** 94%
**Capital:** La Habana (Havana), 2,119,059
**Government:** Socialist republic
**Languages:** Spanish
**Ethnic Groups:** White 66%, mixed 22%,
black 12%

**Religions:** Roman Catholic, Pentecostal,
Baptist
**Currency:** Peso

## Cyprus (Kípros, Kıbrıs)

**Location:** Southern part of the island of
Cyprus
**Area:** 2,276 mi$^2$ (5,896 km$^2$)
**Population:** 713,000 (Urban: 53%)
**Literacy:** 90%
**Capital:** Nicosia (Levkosía), 48,221
**Government:** Republic
**Languages:** Greek, English
**Ethnic Groups:** Greek
**Religions:** Greek Orthodox
**Currency:** Pound
**Tel. Area Code:** 357

## Czechoslovakia (Československo)

**Location:** Eastern Europe, landlocked
**Area:** 49,382 mi$^2$ (127,899 km$^2$)
**Population:** 15,755,000 (Urban: 69%)
**Literacy:** 99%
**Capital:** Prague (Praha), 1,215,656
**Government:** Republic
**Languages:** Czech, Slovak, Hungarian
**Ethnic Groups:** Czech 64%, Slovak 31%,
Hungarian 4%
**Religions:** Roman Catholic 77%,
Protestant 20%, Orthodox 2%
**Currency:** Koruna
**Tel. Area Code:** 42

## Denmark (Danmark)

**Location:** Northern Europe
**Area:** 16,638 mi$^2$ (43,093 km$^2$)
**Population:** 5,154,000 (Urban: 86%)
**Literacy:** 99%
**Capital:** København (Copenhagen), 466,723
**Government:** Constitutional monarchy
**Languages:** Danish
**Ethnic Groups:** Danish (Scandinavian),
German
**Religions:** Lutheran 90%
**Currency:** Krone
**Tel. Area Code:** 45

## Djibouti

**Location:** Eastern Africa
**Area:** 8,958 mi$^2$ (23,200 km$^2$)
**Population:** 351,000 (Urban: 81%)
**Literacy:** 48%

**Capital:** Djibouti, 120,000
**Government:** Republic
**Languages:** French, Somali, Afar, Arabic
**Ethnic Groups:** Somali (Issa) 60%, Afar 35%
**Religions:** Muslim 94%, Christian 6%
**Currency:** Franc

## Dominica

**Location:** Caribbean island
**Area:** 305 mi$^2$ (790 km$^2$)
**Population:** 87,000 (Urban: 27%)
**Literacy:** 94%
**Capital:** Roseau, 9,348
**Government:** Republic
**Languages:** English, French
**Ethnic Groups:** Black 91%, mixed 6%, West
Indian 2%
**Religions:** Roman Catholic 77%,
Methodist 5%, Pentecostal 3%
**Currency:** East Caribbean dollar
**Tel. Area Code:** 809

## Dominican Republic (República Dominicana)

**Location:** Caribbean island (eastern
Hispaniola)
**Area:** 18,704 mi$^2$ (48,442 km$^2$)
**Population:** 8,124,000 (Urban: 60%)
**Literacy:** 83%
**Capital:** Santo Domingo, 2,411,900
**Government:** Republic
**Languages:** Spanish
**Ethnic Groups:** Mulatto 73%, white 16%,
black 11%
**Religions:** Roman Catholic 95%
**Currency:** Peso
**Tel. Area Code:** 809

## Ecuador

**Location:** Western South America
**Area:** 109,484 mi$^2$ (283,561 km$^2$)
**Population:** 10,880,000 (Urban: 57%)
**Literacy:** 86%
**Capital:** Quito, 1,094,318
**Government:** Republic
**Languages:** Spanish, Quechua, indigenous
**Ethnic Groups:** Mestizo 65%,
Amerindian 25%, white 7%, black 10%
**Religions:** Roman Catholic 95%
**Currency:** Sucre
**Tel. Area Code:** 593

## Egypt (Misr)

**Location:** Northeastern Africa
**Area:** 386,662 mi² (1,001,449 km²)
**Population:** 55,105,000 (Urban: 49%)
**Literacy:** 48%
**Capital:** Al-Qāhirah, 6,052,836
**Government:** Socialist republic
**Languages:** Arabic
**Ethnic Groups:** Egyptian (Eastern Hamitic) 90%
**Religions:** Muslim 94%, Coptic Christian and others 6%
**Currency:** Pound
**Tel. Area Code:** 20

## El Salvador

**Location:** Central America
**Area:** 8,124 mi² (21,041 km²)
**Population:** 5,473,000 (Urban: 44%)
**Literacy:** 73%
**Capital:** San Salvador, 462,652
**Government:** Republic
**Languages:** Spanish, Nahua
**Ethnic Groups:** Mestizo 89%, Amerindian 10%, white 1%
**Religions:** Roman Catholic 97%
**Currency:** Colon
**Tel. Area Code:** 503

## Equatorial Guinea (Guinea Ecuatorial)

**Location:** Central Africa
**Area:** 10,831 mi² (28,051 km²)
**Population:** 384,000 (Urban: 65%)
**Literacy:** 50%
**Capital:** Malabo, 31,630
**Government:** Republic
**Languages:** Spanish, indigenous, English
**Ethnic Groups:** Fang 80%, Bubi 15%
**Religions:** Roman Catholic 83%, other Christian, tribal religionist
**Currency:** CFA franc

## Estonia (Eesti)

**Location:** Eastern Europe
**Area:** 17,413 mi² (45,100 km²)
**Population:** 1,606,000 (Urban: 72%)
**Literacy:** 99%
**Capital:** Tallinn, 481,500
**Government:** Republic
**Languages:** Estonian, Russian
**Ethnic Groups:** Estonian 62%, Russian 30%, Ukrainian 3%
**Religions:** Lutheran
**Currency:** Ruble

## Ethiopia (Ītyop'iya)

**Location:** Eastern Africa
**Area:** 483,123 mi² (1,251,282 km²)
**Population:** 54,040,000 (Urban: 13%)
**Literacy:** 62%
**Capital:** Adis Abeba (Addis Ababa), 1,686,300
**Government:** Socialist republic
**Languages:** Amharic, Tigrinya, Orominga, Arabic
**Ethnic Groups:** Oromo (Galla) 40%, Amhara and Tigrean 32%, Sidamo 9%, Shankella 6%, Somali 6%
**Religions:** Muslim 45%, Ethiopian Orthodox 35%, Animist 15%
**Currency:** Birr
**Tel. Area Code:** 251

## Fiji (Viti)

**Location:** South Pacific islands
**Area:** 7,078 mi² (18,333 km²)
**Population:** 747,000 (Urban: 44%)
**Literacy:** 86%
**Capital:** Suva, 69,665
**Government:** Republic
**Languages:** English, Fijian, Hindustani
**Ethnic Groups:** Indian 49%, Fijian 46%
**Religions:** Methodist and other Christian 53%, Hindu 38%, Muslim 8%
**Currency:** Dollar
**Tel. Area Code:** 679

## Finland (Suomi)

**Location:** Northern Europe
**Area:** 130,559 mi² (338,145 km²)
**Population:** 5,001,000 (Urban: 68%)
**Literacy:** 100%
**Capital:** Helsinki, 489,965
**Government:** Republic
**Languages:** Finnish, Swedish
**Ethnic Groups:** Finnish (mixed Scandinavian and Baltic), Swedish, Lappic, Gypsy, Tatar
**Religions:** Jehova's Witness, Free Church, Adventist, Confessional Lutheran
**Currency:** Markka
**Tel. Area Code:** 358

## France

**Location:** Western Europe
**Area:** 211,208 mi$^2$ (547,026 km$^2$)
**Population:** 57,010,000 (Urban: 74%)
**Literacy:** 99%
**Capital:** Paris, 2,152,423
**Government:** Republic
**Languages:** French
**Ethnic Groups:** French (mixed Celtic, Latin, and Teutonic)
**Religions:** Roman Catholic 90%, Protestant 2%, Jewish 1%, Muslim 1%
**Currency:** Franc
**Tel. Area Code:** 33

## French Guiana (Guyane)

**Location:** Northeastern South America
**Area:** 35,135 mi$^2$ (91,000 km$^2$)
**Population:** 104,000 (Urban: 75%)
**Literacy:** 82%
**Capital:** Cayenne, 38,091
**Government:** Overseas department (France)
**Languages:** French
**Ethnic Groups:** Black or mulatto 66%; white 12%; East Indian, Chinese, and Amerindian 12%
**Religions:** Roman Catholic
**Currency:** French franc
**Tel. Area Code:** 594

## French Polynesia (Polynésie française)

**Location:** South Pacific islands
**Area:** 1,544 mi$^2$ (4,000 km$^2$)
**Population:** 198,000 (Urban: 65%)
**Literacy:** 98%
**Capital:** Papeete, 23,555
**Government:** Overseas territory (France)
**Languages:** French, Tahitian, Chinese
**Ethnic Groups:** Polynesian 69%, European 12%, Chinese 10%
**Religions:** Evangelical and other Protestant 55%, Roman Catholic 32%
**Currency:** CFP franc
**Tel. Area Code:** 689

## Gabon

**Location:** Central Africa
**Area:** 103,347 mi$^2$ (267,667 km$^2$)
**Population:** 1,088,000 (Urban: 46%)
**Literacy:** 61%
**Capital:** Libreville, 235,700
**Government:** Republic
**Languages:** French, Fang, indigenous
**Ethnic Groups:** Fang, Eshira, Bapounou, Teke
**Religions:** Roman Catholic and other Christian 55-75%, Fetishism, Muslim
**Currency:** CFA franc
**Tel. Area Code:** 241

## Gambia

**Location:** Western Africa
**Area:** 4,127 mi$^2$ (10,689 km$^2$)
**Population:** 889,000 (Urban: 23%)
**Literacy:** 27%
**Capital:** Banjul, 44,188
**Government:** Republic
**Languages:** English, Malinke, Wolof, Fula, indigenous
**Ethnic Groups:** Malinke 40%, Fulani 19%, Wolof 15%, Jola 10%, Serahuli 8%
**Religions:** Muslim 90%, Christian 9%, tribal religionist 1%
**Currency:** Dalasi
**Tel. Area Code:** 220

## Georgia (Sakartvelo)

**Location:** Southwestern Asia
**Area:** 26,911 mi$^2$ (69,700 km$^2$)
**Population:** 5,550,000 (Urban: 56%)
**Literacy:** 99%
**Capital:** Tbilisi, 1,279,000
**Government:** Provisional military government
**Languages:** Georgian, Russian, Armenian
**Ethnic Groups:** Georgian 70%, Armenian 8%, Russian 6%
**Religions:** Christian
**Currency:** Ruble

## Germany (Deutschland)

**Location:** Northern Europe
**Area:** 137,822 mi$^2$ (356,955 km$^2$)
**Population:** 79,710,000 (Urban: 84%)
**Literacy:** 99%
**Capital:** Berlin (designated), 3,409,737; Bonn (de facto), 287,117
**Government:** Republic
**Languages:** German
**Ethnic Groups:** German (Teutonic)
**Religions:** Evangelical and other Protestant 45%, Roman Catholic 37%
**Currency:** Mark
**Tel. Area Code:** 49

## Ghana

**Location:** Western Africa
**Area:** 92,098 mi$^2$ (238,533 km$^2$)
**Population:** 15,865,000 (Urban: 33%)
**Literacy:** 60%
**Capital:** Accra, 949,113
**Government:** Provisional military government
**Languages:** English, Akan, indigenous
**Ethnic Groups:** Akan 44%, Moshi-Dagomba 16%, Ewe 13%, Ga 8%
**Religions:** Tribal religionist 38%, Muslim 30%, Christian 24%
**Currency:** Cedi

## Greece (Ellás)

**Location:** Southeastern Europe
**Area:** 50,962 mi$^2$ (131,990 km$^2$)
**Population:** 10,285,000 (Urban: 63%)
**Literacy:** 93%
**Capital:** Athínai (Athens), 748,110
**Government:** Republic
**Languages:** Greek
**Ethnic Groups:** Greek 98%, Turkish 1%
**Religions:** Greek Orthodox 98%, Muslim 1%
**Currency:** Drachma
**Tel. Area Code:** 30

## Greenland (Kalaallit Nunaat, Grønland)

**Location:** North Atlantic island
**Area:** 840,004 mi$^2$ (2,175,600 km$^2$)
**Population:** 57,000 (Urban: 78%)
**Capital:** Godthåb, 12,217
**Government:** Self-governing territory (Danish protection)
**Languages:** Danish, Greenlandic, Inuit dialects
**Ethnic Groups:** Greenlander (Inuit and native-born whites) 86%, Danish 14%
**Religions:** Lutheran
**Currency:** Danish krone
**Tel. Area Code:** 299

## Grenada

**Location:** Caribbean island
**Area:** 133 mi$^2$ (344 km$^2$)
**Population:** 98,000 (Urban: 15%)
**Literacy:** 98%
**Capital:** St. George's, 4,788
**Government:** Parliamentary state
**Languages:** English, French
**Ethnic Groups:** Black 82%, mixed 13%, East Indian 3%

**Religions:** Roman Catholic 59%, Anglican 17%, Seventh Day Adventist 6%
**Currency:** East Caribbean dollar
**Tel. Area Code:** 809

## Guatemala

**Location:** Central America
**Area:** 42,042 mi$^2$ (108,889 km$^2$)
**Population:** 9,386,000 (Urban: 42%)
**Literacy:** 55%
**Capital:** Guatemala, 1,057,210
**Government:** Republic
**Languages:** Spanish, indigenous
**Ethnic Groups:** Ladino (mestizo and westernized Maya) 56%, Maya 44%
**Religions:** Roman Catholic, Protestant, tribal religionist
**Currency:** Quetzal
**Tel. Area Code:** 502

## Guinea (Guinée)

**Location:** Western Africa
**Area:** 94,926 mi$^2$ (245,857 km$^2$)
**Population:** 7,553,000 (Urban: 26%)
**Literacy:** 24%
**Capital:** Conakry, 800,000
**Government:** Provisional military government
**Languages:** French, indigenous
**Ethnic Groups:** Fulani, Malinke, Susu, others
**Religions:** Muslim 85%, Christian 10%, Animist 5%
**Currency:** Franc

## Guinea-Bissau (Guiné-Bissau)

**Location:** Western Africa
**Area:** 13,948 mi$^2$ (36,125 km$^2$)
**Population:** 1,036,000 (Urban: 31%)
**Literacy:** 36%
**Capital:** Bissau, 125,000
**Government:** Republic
**Languages:** Portuguese, Crioulo, indigenous
**Ethnic Groups:** Balanta 30%, Fulani 20%, Manjaca 14%, Malinke 13%, Papel 7%
**Religions:** Tribal religionist 65%, Muslim 30%, Christian 5%
**Currency:** Peso

## Guyana

**Location:** Northeastern South America
**Area:** 83,000 mi$^2$ (214,969 km$^2$)
**Population:** 748,000 (Urban: 35%)

Literacy: 95%
Capital: Georgetown, 78,500
Government: Republic
Languages: English, indigenous
Ethnic Groups: East Indian 51%, black 30%,
   mixed 11%, Amerindian 5%
Religions: Anglican and other
   Christian 57%, Hindu 33%, Muslim 9%
Currency: Dollar
Tel. Area Code: 592

## Haiti (Haïti)

Location: Caribbean island (western
   Hispaniola)
Area: 10,714 mi² (27,750 km²)
Population: 6,361,000 (Urban: 30%)
Literacy: 53%
Capital: Port-au-Prince, 797,000
Government: Provisional military
   government
Languages: Creole, French
Ethnic Groups: Black 95%, mulatto and
   white 5%
Religions: Roman Catholic 80%,
   Baptist 10%, Pentecostal 4%
Currency: Gourde
Tel. Area Code: 509

## Honduras

Location: Central America
Area: 43,277 mi² (112,088 km²)
Population: 5,342,000 (Urban: 44%)
Literacy: 73%
Capital: Tegucigalpa, 551,606
Government: Republic
Languages: Spanish, indigenous
Ethnic Groups: Mestizo 90%,
   Amerindian 7%, black 2%, white 1%
Religions: Roman Catholic 97%
Currency: Lempira
Tel. Area Code: 504

## Hong Kong (Xianggang)

Location: Eastern Asia (islands and
   mainland area on China's southeastern
   coast)
Area: 414 mi² (1,072 km²)
Population: 5,874,000 (Urban: 93%)
Literacy: 77%
Capital: Victoria (Hong Kong), 1,250,993
Government: Chinese territory under British
   administration
Languages: Chinese (Cantonese), English
Ethnic Groups: Chinese 95%

Religions: Buddhist and Taoist 90%,
   Christian 10%
Currency: Dollar
Tel. Area Code: 852

## Hungary (Magyarország)

Location: Eastern Europe, landlocked
Area: 35,920 mi² (93,033 km²)
Population: 10,555,000 (Urban: 60%)
Literacy: 99%
Capital: Budapest, 2,018,035
Government: Republic
Languages: Hungarian
Ethnic Groups: Hungarian (Magyar) 99%
Religions: Roman Catholic 68%,
   Calvinist 20%, Lutheran 5%
Currency: Forint
Tel. Area Code: 36

## Iceland (Ísland)

Location: North Atlantic island
Area: 39,769 mi² (103,000 km²)
Population: 261,000 (Urban: 91%)
Literacy: 100%
Capital: Reykjavík, 97,569
Government: Republic
Languages: Icelandic
Ethnic Groups: Icelander (mixed Norwegian
   and Celtic)
Religions: Lutheran 95%, other Christian 3%
Currency: Krona
Tel. Area Code: 354

## India (Bharat)

Location: Southern Asia
Area: 1,237,062 mi² (3,203,975 km²)
Population: 874,150,000 (Urban: 28%)
Literacy: 48%
Capital: New Delhi, 294,149
Government: Republic
Languages: English, Hindi, Telugu, Bengali,
   indigenous
Ethnic Groups: Indo-Aryan 72%,
   Dravidian 25%, Mongoloid and other 3%
Religions: Hindu 80%, Muslim 11%,
   Christian 2%, Sikh 2%
Currency: Rupee
Tel. Area Code: 91

## Indonesia

Location: Southeastern Asian islands
Area: 752,410 mi² (1,948,732 km²)
Population: 195,300,000 (Urban: 29%)

Literacy: 77%
Capital: Jakarta, 9,200,000
Government: Republic
Languages: Indonesian, Javanese,
 Sundanese, Madurese, other indigenous
Ethnic Groups: Javanese 45%,
 Sundanese 14%, Madurese 8%, coastal
 Malay 8%
Religions: Muslim 87%, Protestant 7%,
 Catholic 3%, Hindu 2%
Currency: Rupiah
Tel. Area Code: 62

## Iran (Īrān)

Location: Southwestern Asia
Area: 632,457 mi$^2$ (1,638,057 km$^2$)
Population: 60,000,000 (Urban: 55%)
Literacy: 54%
Capital: Tehrān, 6,042,584
Government: Islamic republic
Languages: Farsi, Turkish, Kurdish, Arabic,
 English, French
Ethnic Groups: Persian 63%, Turkish 18%,
 other Iranian 13%, Kurdish 3%
Religions: Shiite Muslim 93%, Sunni
 Muslim 5%
Currency: Rial
Tel. Area Code: 98

## Iraq (Al-'Īrāq)

Location: Southwestern Asia
Area: 169,235 mi$^2$ (438,317 km$^2$)
Population: 19,915,000 (Urban: 74%)
Literacy: 60%
Capital: Baghdād, 3,841,268
Government: Republic
Languages: Arabic, Kurdish, Assyrian,
 Armenian
Ethnic Groups: Arab 75%-80%; Kurdish 15-
 20%; Turkoman, Assyrian, or other 5%
Religions: Shiite Muslim 60-65%, Sunni
 Muslim 32-37%, Christian and others 3%
Currency: Dinar

## Ireland (Éire)

Location: Northwestern European island
 (five-sixths of island of Ireland)
Area: 27,137 mi$^2$ (70,285 km$^2$)
Population: 3,484,000 (Urban: 59%)
Literacy: 98%
Capital: Dublin, 502,749
Government: Republic
Languages: English, Irish Gaelic
Ethnic Groups: Irish (Celtic), English

Religions: Roman Catholic 93%, Church of
 Ireland 3%
Currency: Pound (punt)
Tel. Area Code: 353

## Israel (Yisra'el, Isrā'īl)

Location: Southwestern Asia
Area: 8,019 mi$^2$ (20,770 km$^2$)
Population: 4,393,000 (Urban: 92%)
Literacy: 92%
Capital: Yerushalayim (Jerusalem), 524,500
Government: Republic
Languages: Hebrew, Arabic, Yiddish
Ethnic Groups: Jewish 83%, Arab and
 others 17%
Religions: Jewish 82%, Muslim 14%,
 Christian 2%, Druze 2%
Currency: Shekel
Tel. Area Code: 972

## Italy (Italia)

Location: Southern Europe
Area: 116,324 mi$^2$ (301,277 km$^2$)
Population: 57,830,000 (Urban: 69%)
Literacy: 97%
Capital: Roma (Rome), 2,815,457
Government: Republic
Languages: Italian
Ethnic Groups: Italian (Latin)
Religions: Roman Catholic 99%
Currency: Lira
Tel. Area Code: 39

## Ivory Coast (Côte d'Ivoire)

Location: Western Africa
Area: 124,518 mi$^2$ (322,500 km$^2$)
Population: 13,240,000 (Urban: 47%)
Literacy: 54%
Capital: Abidjan (de facto), 1,950,000;
 Yamoussoukro (future), 80,000
Government: Republic
Languages: French, indigenous
Ethnic Groups: Baule 23%, Bete 18%,
 Senoufou 15%, Malinke 11%, other
 African
Religions: Animist 63%, Muslim 25%,
 Christian 12%
Currency: CFA franc
Tel. Area Code: 255

## Jamaica

Location: Caribbean island
Area: 4,244 mi$^2$ (10,991 km$^2$)

**Population:** 2,501,000 (Urban: 52%)
**Literacy:** 98%
**Capital:** Kingston, 646,400
**Government:** Parliamentary state
**Languages:** English, Creole
**Ethnic Groups:** Black 75%, mixed 13%, East Indian 1%
**Religions:** Church of God and other Protestant, Anglican, Roman Catholic
**Currency:** Dollar
**Tel. Area Code:** 809

## Japan (Nihon)

**Location:** Eastern Asian islands
**Area:** 145,870 mi$^2$ (377,801 km$^2$)
**Population:** 124,270,000 (Urban: 77%)
**Literacy:** 99%
**Capital:** Tōkyō, 8,163,127
**Government:** Constitutional monarchy
**Languages:** Japanese
**Ethnic Groups:** Japanese 99%, Korean
**Religions:** Buddhist and Shinto
**Currency:** Yen
**Tel. Area Code:** 81

## Jordan (Al-Urdun)

**Location:** Southwestern Asia
**Area:** 35,135 mi$^2$ (91,000 km$^2$)
**Population:** 3,485,000 (Urban: 68%)
**Literacy:** 80%
**Capital:** 'Ammān, 936,300
**Government:** Constitutional monarchy
**Languages:** Arabic
**Ethnic Groups:** Arab 98%, Circassian 1%, Armenian 1%
**Religions:** Sunni Muslim 95%, Christian 5%
**Currency:** Dinar
**Tel. Area Code:** 962

## Kazakhstan

**Location:** Central Asia, landlocked
**Area:** 1,049,156 mi$^2$ (2,717,300 km$^2$)
**Population:** 16,880,000 (Urban: 57%)
**Literacy:** 98%
**Capital:** Alma-Ata, 1,156,200
**Government:** Republic
**Languages:** Kazakh, Russian, German, Ukrainian
**Ethnic Groups:** Kazakh 40%, Russian 38%, German 6%
**Religions:** Muslim
**Currency:** Ruble

## Kenya

**Location:** Eastern Africa
**Area:** 224,961 mi$^2$ (582,646 km$^2$)
**Population:** 25,695,000 (Urban: 24%)
**Literacy:** 69%
**Capital:** Nairobi, 1,505,000
**Government:** Republic
**Languages:** English, Swahili, indigenous
**Ethnic Groups:** Kikuyu 21%, Luhya 14%, Luo 13%, Kamba 11%, Kalenjin 11%, Kisii 6 %, Meru 5%
**Religions:** Protestant 38%, Roman Catholic 28%, Animist 26%, Muslim 6%
**Currency:** Shilling
**Tel. Area Code:** 254

## Kiribati

**Location:** Central Pacific islands
**Area:** 313 mi$^2$ (811 km$^2$)
**Population:** 72,000 (Urban: 36%)
**Capital:** Bairiki, 2,226
**Government:** Republic
**Languages:** English, Gilbertese
**Ethnic Groups:** Kiribatian (Micronesian) 98%
**Religions:** Roman Catholic 53%, Congregationalist 39%, Bahai 2%
**Currency:** Australian dollar

## Korea, North (Chosŏn-minjujuŭi-inmīn-konghwaguk)

**Location:** Eastern Asia
**Area:** 46,540 mi$^2$ (120,538 km$^2$)
**Population:** 22,250,000 (Urban: 67%)
**Capital:** P'yŏngyang, 1,283,000
**Government:** Socialist republic
**Languages:** Korean
**Ethnic Groups:** Korean 100%
**Religions:** Shamanist, Chondoist, Buddhist
**Currency:** Won

## Korea, South (Taehan-min'guk)

**Location:** Eastern Asia
**Area:** 38,230 mi$^2$ (99,016 km$^2$)
**Population:** 43,305,000 (Urban: 72%)
**Literacy:** 96%
**Capital:** Sŏul (Seoul), 10,627,790
**Government:** Republic
**Languages:** Korean
**Ethnic Groups:** Korean
**Religions:** Buddhist 20%, Roman Catholic 16%, Protestant 5%, Confucian 1%

**Currency:** Won
**Tel. Area Code:** 82

## Kuwait (Al-Kuwayt)

**Location:** Southwestern Asia
**Area:** 6,880 mi$^2$ (17,818 km$^2$)
**Population:** 2,244,000 (Urban: 96%)
**Literacy:** 74%
**Capital:** Al-Kuwayt (Kuwait), 44,335
**Government:** Constitutional monarchy
**Languages:** Arabic, English
**Ethnic Groups:** Kuwaiti 40%, other
Arab 39%, Southern Asian 9%, Iranian 4%
**Religions:** Sunni Muslim 45%, Shiite
Muslim 30%, Christian 6%
**Currency:** Dinar
**Tel. Area Code:** 965

## Kyrgyzstan

**Location:** Central Asia, landlocked
**Area:** 76,641 mi$^2$ (198,500 km$^2$)
**Population:** 4,385,000 (Urban: 38%)
**Literacy:** 97%
**Capital:** Biškek (Frunze), 631,300
**Government:** Republic
**Languages:** Kirghiz, Russian, Uzbek
**Ethnic Groups:** Kirghiz 52%, Russian 21%,
Uzbek 13%
**Religions:** Muslim
**Currency:** Ruble

## Laos (Lao)

**Location:** Southeastern Asia, landlocked
**Area:** 91,429 mi$^2$ (236,800 km$^2$)
**Population:** 4,158,000 (Urban: 19%)
**Literacy:** 84%
**Capital:** Viangchan (Vientiane), 377,409
**Government:** Socialist republic
**Languages:** Lao, French, Thai, indigenous
**Ethnic Groups:** Lao 50%; Thai 20%;
Phoutheung 15%; Miao, Hmong, Yao, and
others 15%
**Religions:** Buddhist 85%, Animist and
others 15%
**Currency:** Kip

## Latvia (Latvija)

**Location:** Eastern Europe
**Area:** 24,595 mi$^2$ (63,700 km$^2$)
**Population:** 2,737,000 (Urban: 71%)
**Literacy:** 99%
**Capital:** Rīga, 910,200
**Government:** Republic

**Languages:** Latvian, Russian
**Ethnic Groups:** Latvian 52%, Russian 34%,
Belorussian 5%
**Religions:** Roman Catholic, Lutheran
**Currency:** Ruble

## Lebanon (Lubnān)

**Location:** Southwestern Asia
**Area:** 4,015 mi$^2$ (10,400 km$^2$)
**Population:** 3,409,000 (Urban: 84%)
**Literacy:** 80%
**Capital:** Bayrūt (Beirut), 509,000
**Government:** Republic
**Languages:** Arabic, French, Armenian,
English
**Ethnic Groups:** Arab 93%, Armenian 6%
**Religions:** Muslim 75%, Christian 25%,
Jewish
**Currency:** Pound

## Lesotho

**Location:** Southern Africa, landlocked
**Area:** 11,720 mi$^2$ (30,355 km$^2$)
**Population:** 1,824,000 (Urban: 20%)
**Literacy:** 59%
**Capital:** Maseru, 109,382
**Government:** Constitutional monarchy
**Languages:** English, Sesotho, Zulu, Xhosa
**Ethnic Groups:** Sotho 99%
**Religions:** Roman Catholic and other
Christian 80%, tribal religionist 20%
**Currency:** Loti
**Tel. Area Code:** 266

## Liberia

**Location:** Western Africa
**Area:** 38,250 mi$^2$ (99,067 km$^2$)
**Population:** 2,776,000 (Urban: 44%)
**Literacy:** 40%
**Capital:** Monrovia, 465,000
**Government:** Republic
**Languages:** English, indigenous
**Ethnic Groups:** Indigenous black 95%,
descendants of freed American slaves 5%
**Religions:** Animist 70%, Muslim 20%,
Christian 10%
**Currency:** Dollar
**Tel. Area Code:** 231

## Libya (Lībiyā)

**Location:** Northern Africa
**Area:** 679,362 mi$^2$ (1,759,540 km$^2$)
**Population:** 4,416,000 (Urban: 70%)

Literacy: 64%
Capital: Ṭarābulus (Tripoli), 591,062
Government: Socialist republic
Languages: Arabic
Ethnic Groups: Arab-Berber 97%
Religions: Sunni Muslim 97%
Currency: Dinar
Tel. Area Code: 218

## Liechtenstein

Location: Central Europe, landlocked
Area: 62 mi² (160 km²)
Population: 28,000 (Urban: 26%)
Literacy: 100%
Capital: Vaduz, 4,874
Government: Constitutional monarchy
Languages: German
Ethnic Groups: Liechtensteiner (Alemannic)
66%, Swiss 15%, Austrian 7%, German 4%
Religions: Roman Catholic 85%,
Protestant 9%
Currency: Swiss franc
Tel. Area Code: 41

## Lithuania (Lietuva)

Location: Eastern Europe
Area: 25,174 mi² (65,200 km²)
Population: 3,767,000 (Urban: 68%)
Literacy: 99%
Capital: Vilnius, 582,000
Government: Republic
Languages: Lithuanian, Russian, Polish
Ethnic Groups: Lithuanian 80%,
Russian 9%, Polish 7%
Religions: Roman Catholic
Currency: Ruble

## Luxembourg (Lezebuurg)

Location: Western Europe, landlocked
Area: 998 mi² (2,586 km²)
Population: 390,000 (Urban: 84%)
Literacy: 100%
Capital: Luxembourg, 75,622
Government: Constitutional monarchy
Languages: French, Luxembourgish,
German
Ethnic Groups: Luxembourger (mixed
Celtic, French, and German)
Religions: Roman Catholic 97%, Jewish and
Protestant 3%
Currency: Franc
Tel. Area Code: 352

## Macao (Macau)

Location: Eastern Asia (islands and
peninsula off China's southeastern coast)
Area: 6.6 mi² (17 km²)
Population: 448,000 (Urban: 99%)
Literacy: 90%
Capital: Macau, 429,000
Government: Chinese territory under
Portuguese administration
Languages: Portuguese, Chinese (Cantonese)
Ethnic Groups: Chinese 95%, Portuguese 3%
Religions: Buddhist 45%, Roman
Catholic 16%, other Christian 3%
Currency: Pataca
Tel. Area Code: 853

## Macedonia (Makedonija)

Location: Eastern Europe
Area: 9,928 mi² (25,713 km²)
Population: 2,120,000 (Urban: 54%)
Literacy: 89%
Capital: Skopje, 444,900
Government: Republic
Languages: Macedonian, Albanian
Ethnic Groups: Macedonian, Albanian
Religions: Orthodox, Muslim
Currency: Yugoslavian dinar

## Madagascar (Madagasikara)

Location: Southeastern African island
Area: 226,658 mi² (587,041 km²)
Population: 12,380,000 (Urban: 25%)
Literacy: 80%
Capital: Antananarivo, 1,250,000
Government: Republic
Languages: Malagasy, French
Ethnic Groups: Merina 15%,
Betsimisaraka 9%, Betsileo 7%,
Tsimihety 4%, Antaisaka 4%, other tribes
Religions: Animist 52%, Christian 41%,
Muslim 7%
Currency: Franc

## Malawi (Malaŵi)

Location: Southern Africa, landlocked
Area: 45,747 mi² (118,484 km²)
Population: 9,523,000 (Urban: 15%)
Literacy: 22%
Capital: Lilongwe, 233,973
Government: Republic
Languages: Chichewa, English, Tombuka
Ethnic Groups: Chewa, Nyanja, Tumbuka,
Yao, Lomwe, others

**Religions:** Protestant 55%, Roman
Catholic 20%, Muslim 20%
**Currency:** Kwacha
**Tel. Area Code:** 265

# Malaysia
**Location:** Southeastern Asia (includes part
of the island of Borneo)
**Area:** 129,251 mi$^2$ (334,758 km$^2$)
**Population:** 18,200,000 (Urban: 42%)
**Literacy:** 78%
**Capital:** Kuala Lumpur, 919,610
**Government:** Constitutional monarchy
**Languages:** Malay, Chinese dialects,
English, Tamil
**Ethnic Groups:** Malay and other
indigenous 61%, Chinese 30%, Indian 8%
**Religions:** Muslim 53%, Buddhist 17%,
Chinese religions 12%, Hindu 7%
**Currency:** Ringgit
**Tel. Area Code:** 60

# Maldives
**Location:** Indian Ocean islands
**Area:** 115 mi$^2$ (298 km$^2$)
**Population:** 230,000 (Urban: 21%)
**Literacy:** 92%
**Capital:** Male, 46,334
**Government:** Republic
**Languages:** Divehi
**Ethnic Groups:** Maldivian (mixed Sinhalese,
Dravidian, Arab, and black)
**Religions:** Sunni Muslim
**Currency:** Rufiyaa

# Mali
**Location:** Western Africa, landlocked
**Area:** 478,767 mi$^2$ (1,240,000 km$^2$)
**Population:** 8,438,000 (Urban: 19%)
**Literacy:** 32%
**Capital:** Bamako, 658,275
**Government:** Republic
**Languages:** French, Bambara, indigenous
**Ethnic Groups:** Malinke 50%, Fulani 17%,
Voltaic 12%, Songhai 6%
**Religions:** Sunni Muslim 90%, Animist 9%,
Christian 1%
**Currency:** CFA franc

# Malta
**Location:** Mediterranean island
**Area:** 122 mi$^2$ (316 km$^2$)
**Population:** 357,000 (Urban: 87%)

**Literacy:** 84%
**Capital:** Valletta, 9,199
**Government:** Republic
**Languages:** English, Maltese
**Ethnic Groups:** Maltese (mixed Arab,
Sicilian, Norman, Spanish, Italian, and
English)
**Religions:** Roman Catholic 98%
**Currency:** Lira
**Tel. Area Code:** 356

# Mauritania (Mūrītāniyā, Mauritanie)
**Location:** Western Africa
**Area:** 395,956 mi$^2$ (1,025,520 km$^2$)
**Population:** 2,028,000 (Urban: 42%)
**Literacy:** 34%
**Capital:** Nouakchott, 285,000
**Government:** Provisional military
government
**Languages:** Arabic, French, indigenous
**Ethnic Groups:** Mixed Moor and black 40%,
Moor 30%, black 30%
**Religions:** Sunni Muslim 100%
**Currency:** Ouguiya
**Tel. Area Code:** 222

# Mauritius
**Location:** Indian Ocean island
**Area:** 788 mi$^2$ (2,040 km$^2$)
**Population:** 1,085,000 (Urban: 42%)
**Literacy:** 61%
**Capital:** Port Louis, 141,870
**Government:** Parliamentary state
**Languages:** English, Creole, Bhojpuri, Hindi
**Ethnic Groups:** Indo-Mauritian 68%,
Creole 27%, Sino-Mauritian 3%, Franco-
Mauritian 2%
**Religions:** Hindu 31%, Muslim 13%,
Sanatanist 10%
**Currency:** Rupee

# Mexico (México)
**Location:** Southern North America
**Area:** 756,066 mi$^2$ (1,958,201 km$^2$)
**Population:** 91,000,000 (Urban: 73%)
**Literacy:** 87%
**Capital:** Ciudad de México (Mexico City),
8,831,079
**Government:** Republic
**Languages:** Spanish, indigenous
**Ethnic Groups:** Mestizo 60%,
Amerindian 30%, white 9%
**Religions:** Roman Catholic 97%,
Protestant 3%

Currency: Peso
Tel. Area Code: 52

## Moldova

Location: Eastern Europe, landlocked
Area: 13,012 mi$^2$ (33,700 km$^2$)
Population: 4,440,000 (Urban: 47%)
Literacy: 99%
Capital: Kišinev, 676,700
Government: Republic
Languages: Romanian (Moldovan), Russian, Ukrainian
Ethnic Groups: Moldovan 64%, Ukrainian 14%, Russian 13%
Currency: Ruble

## Monaco

Location: Southern Europe (on the southeastern coast of France)
Area: 0.7 mi$^2$ (1.9 km$^2$)
Population: 30,000 (Urban: 100%)
Capital: Monaco, 30,000
Government: Constitutional monarchy
Languages: French, English, Italian, Monegasque
Ethnic Groups: French 47%, Monegasque 17%, Italian 16%, English 4%, Belgian 2 %, Swiss 1%
Religions: Roman Catholic 95%
Currency: French franc
Tel. Area Code: 33

## Mongolia (Mongol Uls)

Location: Central Asia, landlocked
Area: 604,829 mi$^2$ (1,566,500 km$^2$)
Population: 2,278,000 (Urban: 51%)
Literacy: 90%
Capital: Ulaanbaatar (Ulan Bator), 548,400
Government: Socialist republic
Languages: Khalkha Mongol, Kazakh, Russian, Chinese
Ethnic Groups: Mongol 90%, Kazakh 4%, Chinese 2%, Russian 2%
Religions: Shamanic, Tibetan Buddhist, Muslim
Currency: Tughrik

## Morocco (Al-Magrib)

Location: Northwestern Africa
Area: 172,414 mi$^2$ (446,550 km$^2$)
Population: 26,470,000 (Urban: 49%)
Literacy: 50%
Capital: Rabat, 518,616

Government: Constitutional monarchy
Languages: Arabic, Berber dialects, French
Ethnic Groups: Arab-Berber 99%
Religions: Sunni Muslim 99%
Currency: Dirham
Tel. Area Code: 212

## Mozambique (Moçambique)

Location: Southern Africa
Area: 308,642 mi$^2$ (799,380 km$^2$)
Population: 15,460,000 (Urban: 27%)
Literacy: 33%
Capital: Maputo, 1,069,727
Government: Republic
Languages: Portuguese, indigenous
Ethnic Groups: Makua, Lomwe, Thonga, others
Religions: Tribal religionist 60%, Roman Catholic and other Christian 30%, Muslim
Currency: Metical
Tel. Area Code: 258

## Namibia

Location: Southern Africa
Area: 317,818 mi$^2$ (823,144 km$^2$)
Population: 1,548,000 (Urban: 57%)
Literacy: 38%
Capital: Windhoek, 114,500
Government: Republic
Languages: Afrikaans, English, German, indigenous
Ethnic Groups: Ovambo 49%, Kavango 9%, Damara 8%, Herero 7%, white 7%, mixed 7 %
Religions: Lutheran and other Protestant, Roman Catholic, Animist
Currency: South African rand
Tel. Area Code: 264

## Nepal (Nepāl)

Location: Southern Asia, landlocked
Area: 56,827 mi$^2$ (147,181 km$^2$)
Population: 19,845,000 (Urban: 10%)
Literacy: 26%
Capital: Kāṭmāṇḍāu (Kathmandu), 235,160
Government: Constitutional monarchy
Languages: Nepali, Maithali, Bhojpuri, other indigenous
Ethnic Groups: Newar, Indian, Tibetan, Gurung, Magar, Tamang, Bhotia, others
Religions: Hindu 90%, Buddhist 5%, Muslim 3%

Currency: Rupee
Tel. Area Code: 977

## Netherlands (Nederland)

Location: Western Europe
Area: 16,133 mi$^2$ (41,785 km$^2$)
Population: 15,065,000 (Urban: 89%)
Literacy: 99%
Capital: Amsterdam (designated), 702,686;
The Hague (seat of government), 444,256
Government: Constitutional monarchy
Languages: Dutch
Ethnic Groups: Dutch (mixed Scandinavian,
French, and Celtic) 99%, Indonesian and
others 1%
Religions: Roman Catholic 36%, Dutch
Reformed 19%, Calvinist 8%
Currency: Guilder
Tel. Area Code: 31

## New Caledonia (Nouvelle-Calédonie)

Location: South Pacific islands
Area: 7,358 mi$^2$ (19,058 km$^2$)
Population: 174,000 (Urban: 81%)
Literacy: 91%
Capital: Nouméa, 65,110
Government: Overseas territory (France)
Languages: French, Malay-Polynesian
languages
Ethnic Groups: Melanesian 43%,
French 37%, Wallisian 8%, Polynesian 4%,
Indonesian 4 %, Vietnamese 2%
Religions: Roman Catholic 60%,
Protestant 30%
Currency: CFP franc
Tel. Area Code: 687

## New Zealand

Location: South Pacific islands
Area: 103,519 mi$^2$ (268,112 km$^2$)
Population: 3,463,000 (Urban: 84%)
Literacy: 99%
Capital: Wellington, 137,495
Government: Parliamentary state
Languages: English, Maori
Ethnic Groups: European origin 86%,
Maori 9%, Samoan and other Pacific
islander 3%
Religions: Anglican 24%, Presbyterian 18%,
Roman Catholic 15%, Methodist 5%
Currency: Dollar
Tel. Area Code: 64

## Nicaragua

Location: Central America
Area: 50,054 mi$^2$ (129,640 km$^2$)
Population: 3,805,000 (Urban: 60%)
Literacy: 57%
Capital: Managua, 682,000
Government: Republic
Languages: Spanish, English, indigenous
Ethnic Groups: Mestizo 69%, white 17%,
black 9%, Amerindian 5%
Religions: Roman Catholic 95%
Currency: Cordoba
Tel. Area Code: 505

## Niger

Location: Western Africa, landlocked
Area: 489,191 mi$^2$ (1,267,000 km$^2$)
Population: 8,113,000 (Urban: 20%)
Literacy: 28%
Capital: Niamey, 398,265
Government: Provisional military
government
Languages: French, Hausa, Djerma,
indigenous
Ethnic Groups: Hausa 56%, Djerma 22%,
Fulani 9%, Taurge 8%, Beriberi 4%
Religions: Muslim 80%, Animist and
Christian 20%
Currency: CFA franc
Tel. Area Code: 227

## Nigeria

Location: Western Africa
Area: 356,669 mi$^2$ (923,768 km$^2$)
Population: 124,300,000 (Urban: 35%)
Literacy: 51%
Capital: Lagos (de facto), 1,213,000; Abuja
(future)
Government: Provisional military
government
Languages: English, Hausa, Fulani, Yoruba,
Ibo, indigenous
Ethnic Groups: Hausa, Fulani, Yoruba, Ibo,
others
Religions: Muslim 50%, Christian 40%,
Animist 10%
Currency: Naira
Tel. Area Code: 234

## Norway (Norge)

Location: Northern Europe
Area: 149,412 mi$^2$ (386,975 km$^2$)
Population: 4,286,000 (Urban: 74%)
Literacy: 99%

**Capital:** Oslo, 452,415
**Government:** Constitutional monarchy
**Languages:** Norwegian, Lapp
**Ethnic Groups:** Norwegian (Scandinavian), Lappic
**Religions:** Lutheran 94%, other Protestant and Roman Catholic 4%
**Currency:** Krone
**Tel. Area Code:** 47

## Oman ('Umān)

**Location:** Southwestern Asia
**Area:** 82,030 mi$^2$ (212,457 km$^2$)
**Population:** 1,562,000 (Urban: 11%)
**Capital:** Muscat, 30,000
**Government:** Monarchy
**Languages:** Arabic, English, Baluchi, Urdu, Indian dialects
**Ethnic Groups:** Arab, Baluchi, Zanzibari, Indian
**Religions:** Ibadite Muslim 75%, Sunni Muslim, Shiite Muslim, Hindu
**Currency:** Rial
**Tel. Area Code:** 968

## Pakistan (Pākistān)

**Location:** Southern Asia
**Area:** 339,732 mi$^2$ (879,902 km$^2$)
**Population:** 119,000,000 (Urban: 32%)
**Literacy:** 35%
**Capital:** Islāmābād, 204,364
**Government:** Islamic republic
**Languages:** English, Urdu, Punjabi, Pashto, Sindhi, Saraiki
**Ethnic Groups:** Punjabi, Sindhi, Pathan, Baluchi
**Religions:** Sunni Muslim 77%, Shiite Muslim 20%, Christian 1%, Hindu 1%
**Currency:** Rupee
**Tel. Area Code:** 92

## Panama (Panamá)

**Location:** Central America
**Area:** 29,157 mi$^2$ (75,517 km$^2$)
**Population:** 2,503,000 (Urban: 55%)
**Literacy:** 88%
**Capital:** Panamá, 411,549
**Government:** Republic
**Languages:** Spanish, English, indigenous
**Ethnic Groups:** Mestizo 70%, West Indian 14%, white 10%, Amerindian 6%
**Religions:** Roman Catholic 93%, Protestant 6%

**Currency:** Balboa
**Tel. Area Code:** 507

## Papua New Guinea

**Location:** South Pacific islands
**Area:** 178,704 mi$^2$ (462,840 km$^2$)
**Population:** 3,960,000 (Urban: 16%)
**Literacy:** 52%
**Capital:** Port Moresby, 193,242
**Government:** Parliamentary state
**Languages:** English, Motu, Pidgin, indigenous
**Ethnic Groups:** Melanesian, Papuan, Negrito, Micronesian, Polynesian
**Religions:** Roman Catholic 35%, Lutheran 26%, United Church 13%, Evangelical 9%
**Currency:** Kina
**Tel. Area Code:** 675

## Paraguay

**Location:** Central South America, landlocked
**Area:** 157,048 mi$^2$ (406,752 km$^2$)
**Population:** 4,871,000 (Urban: 48%)
**Literacy:** 90%
**Capital:** Asunción, 477,100
**Government:** Republic
**Languages:** Spanish, Guarani
**Ethnic Groups:** Mestizo 95%, white and Amerindian 5%
**Religions:** Roman Catholic 90%, Mennonite and other Protestant
**Currency:** Guarani
**Tel. Area Code:** 595

## Peru (Perú)

**Location:** Western South America
**Area:** 496,225 mi$^2$ (1,285,216 km$^2$)
**Population:** 22,585,000 (Urban: 70%)
**Literacy:** 85%
**Capital:** Lima, 371,122
**Government:** Republic
**Languages:** Quechua, Spanish, Aymara
**Ethnic Groups:** Amerindian 45%, mestizo 37%, white 15%
**Religions:** Roman Catholic 89%, Protestant 5%
**Currency:** Inti
**Tel. Area Code:** 51

## Philippines (Pilipinas)

**Location:** Southeastern Asian islands
**Area:** 115,831 mi$^2$ (300,000 km$^2$)
**Population:** 62,380,000 (Urban: 42%)
**Literacy:** 90%
**Capital:** Manila, 1,587,000
**Government:** Republic
**Languages:** English, Pilipino, Tagalog
**Ethnic Groups:** Christian Malay 92%, Muslim Malay 4%, Chinese 2%
**Religions:** Roman Catholic 83%, Protestant 9%, Muslim 5%, Buddhist and others 3%
**Currency:** Peso
**Tel. Area Code:** 63

## Poland (Polska)

**Location:** Eastern Europe
**Area:** 120,728 mi$^2$ (312,683 km$^2$)
**Population:** 37,840,000 (Urban: 63%)
**Literacy:** 99%
**Capital:** Warszawa (Warsaw), 1,655,700
**Government:** Republic
**Languages:** Polish
**Ethnic Groups:** Polish (mixed Slavic and Teutonic) 99%, Ukrainian, Byelorussian
**Religions:** Roman Catholic 95%
**Currency:** Zloty
**Tel. Area Code:** 48

## Portugal

**Location:** Southwestern Europe
**Area:** 35,516 mi$^2$ (91,985 km$^2$)
**Population:** 10,410,000 (Urban: 33%)
**Literacy:** 85%
**Capital:** Lisbon, 807,167
**Government:** Republic
**Languages:** Portuguese
**Ethnic Groups:** Portuguese (Mediterranean), black
**Religions:** Roman Catholic 81%, Protestant 1%
**Currency:** Escudo
**Tel. Area Code:** 351

## Puerto Rico

**Location:** Caribbean island
**Area:** 3,515 mi$^2$ (9,104 km$^2$)
**Population:** 3,528,000 (Urban: 74%)
**Literacy:** 89%
**Capital:** San Juan, 426,832
**Government:** Commonwealth (U.S. protection)
**Languages:** Spanish
**Ethnic Groups:** Puerto Rican (mixed Spanish and black)
**Religions:** Roman Catholic 85%
**Currency:** U.S. dollar

## Qatar

**Location:** Southwestern Asia
**Area:** 4,416 mi$^2$ (11,437 km$^2$)
**Population:** 532,000 (Urban: 90%)
**Literacy:** 76%
**Capital:** Ad-Dawḥah (Doha), 217,294
**Government:** Monarchy
**Languages:** Arabic, English
**Ethnic Groups:** Arab 40%, Pakistani 18%, Indian 18%, Iranian 10%
**Religions:** Muslim 95%
**Currency:** Riyal
**Tel. Area Code:** 974

## Romania (România)

**Location:** Eastern Europe
**Area:** 91,699 mi$^2$ (237,500 km$^2$)
**Population:** 23,465,000 (Urban: 50%)
**Literacy:** 96%
**Capital:** Bucureşti (Bucharest), 2,036,894
**Government:** Republic
**Languages:** Romanian, Hungarian, German
**Ethnic Groups:** Romanian (mixed Latin, Thracian, Slavic, and Celtic) 89%, Hungarian 8%, German 2%
**Religions:** Romanian Orthodox 80%, Roman Catholic 6%
**Currency:** Leu
**Tel. Area Code:** 40

## Russia (Rossija)

**Location:** Eastern Europe and Northern Asia
**Area:** 6,592,849 mi$^2$ (17,075,400 km$^2$)
**Population:** 150,505,000 (Urban: 74%)
**Literacy:** 99%
**Capital:** Moskva (Moscow), 8,801,500
**Government:** Republic
**Languages:** Russian, Tatar, Ukrainian
**Ethnic Groups:** Russian 82%, Tatar 4%, Ukrainian 3%
**Religions:** Russian Orthodox
**Currency:** Ruble

## Rwanda

**Location:** Eastern Africa, landlocked
**Area:** 10,169 mi$^2$ (26,338 km$^2$)
**Population:** 8,053,000 (Urban: 8%)

Literacy: 50%
Capital: Kigali, 181,600
Government: Provisional military government
Languages: French, Kinyarwanda
Ethnic Groups: Hutu 89%, Tutsi 10%, Twa
Religions: Roman Catholic 52%, Protestant 21%, Animist 9%
Currency: Franc

## St. Kitts and Nevis

Location: Caribbean islands
Area: 104 mi$^2$ (269 km$^2$)
Population: 42,000 (Urban: 49%)
Literacy: 98%
Capital: Basseterre, 14,725
Government: Parliamentary state
Languages: English
Ethnic Groups: Black 94%, mixed 3%, white 1%
Religions: Anglican 33%, Methodist 29%, Moravian 9%, Roman Catholic 7%
Currency: East Caribbean dollar
Tel. Area Code: 809

## St. Lucia

Location: Caribbean island
Area: 238 mi$^2$ (616 km$^2$)
Population: 155,000 (Urban: 46%)
Literacy: 67%
Capital: Castries, 53,933
Government: Parliamentary state
Languages: English, French
Ethnic Groups: Black 87%, mixed 9%, East Indian 3%
Religions: Roman Catholic 86%, Seventh Day Adventist 4%, Anglican 3%
Currency: East Caribbean dollar
Tel. Area Code: 809

## St. Vincent and the Grenadines

Location: Caribbean islands
Area: 150 mi$^2$ (388 km$^2$)
Population: 115,000 (Urban: 21%)
Literacy: 96%
Capital: Kingstown, 19,028
Government: Parliamentary state
Languages: English, French
Ethnic Groups: Black 82%, mixed 14%, East Indian 2%, white 1%
Religions: Anglican 42%, Methodist 21%, Roman Catholic 12%, Baptist 6%
Currency: East Caribbean dollar
Tel. Area Code: 809

## Sao Tome and Principe (São Tomé e Príncipe)

Location: Western African islands
Area: 372 mi$^2$ (964 km$^2$)
Population: 130,000 (Urban: 42%)
Literacy: 57%
Capital: São Tomé, 17,380
Government: Republic
Languages: Portuguese, Fang
Ethnic Groups: Black, mixed black and Portuguese, Portuguese
Religions: Roman Catholic, African Protestant, Seventh Day Adventist
Currency: Dobra

## Saudi Arabia (Al-'Arabīyah as-Su'ūdīyah)

Location: Southwestern Asia
Area: 830,000 mi$^2$ (2,149,690 km$^2$)
Population: 16,690,000 (Urban: 77%)
Literacy: 62%
Capital: Ar-Riyāḍ (Riyadh), 1,250,000
Government: Monarchy
Languages: Arabic
Ethnic Groups: Arab 90%, Afro-Asian 10%
Religions: Muslim 100%
Currency: Riyal
Tel. Area Code: 966

## Senegal (Sénégal)

Location: Western Africa
Area: 75,951 mi$^2$ (196,712 km$^2$)
Population: 7,569,000 (Urban: 38%)
Literacy: 38%
Capital: Dakar, 1,490,450
Government: Republic
Languages: French, Wolof, Fulani, Serer, indigenous
Ethnic Groups: Wolof 44%, Fulani 23%, Serer 15%, Diola 6%, Malinke 5%
Religions: Muslim 94%, Christian 5%
Currency: CFA franc
Tel. Area Code: 221

## Seychelles

Location: Indian Ocean islands
Area: 175 mi$^2$ (453 km$^2$)
Population: 69,000 (Urban: 59%)
Literacy: 58%
Capital: Victoria, 23,000
Government: Republic
Languages: English, French, Creole

**Ethnic Groups:** Seychellois (mixed Asian, African, and European)
**Religions:** Roman Catholic 90%, Anglican 8%
**Currency:** Rupee

## Sierra Leone

**Location:** Western Africa
**Area:** 27,925 mi$^2$ (72,325 km$^2$)
**Population:** 4,330,000 (Urban: 32%)
**Literacy:** 21%
**Capital:** Freetown, 469,776
**Government:** Republic
**Languages:** English, Krio, indigenous
**Ethnic Groups:** Temne 30%, Mende 30%, Creole 2%, other African
**Religions:** Muslim 30%, Animist 30%, Christian 10%
**Currency:** Leone

## Singapore

**Location:** Southeastern Asian island
**Area:** 246 mi$^2$ (636 km$^2$)
**Population:** 3,062,000 (Urban: 100%)
**Literacy:** 88%
**Capital:** Singapore, 3,062,000
**Government:** Republic
**Languages:** Chinese (Mandarin), English, Malay, Tamil
**Ethnic Groups:** Chinese 76%, Malay 15%, Indian 6%
**Religions:** Taoist 29%, Buddhist 27%, Muslim 16%, Christian 10%, Hindu 4%
**Currency:** Dollar
**Tel. Area Code:** 65

## Slovenia (Slovenija)

**Location:** Eastern Europe
**Area:** 7,819 mi$^2$ (20,251 km$^2$)
**Population:** 4,800,000 (Urban: 49%)
**Literacy:** 99%
**Capital:** Ljubljana, 233,200
**Government:** Republic
**Languages:** Slovene
**Ethnic Groups:** Slovene, Italian, Hungarian
**Religions:** Roman Catholic
**Currency:** Tolar, Yugoslavian dinar

## Solomon Islands

**Location:** South Pacific islands
**Area:** 10,954 mi$^2$ (28,370 km$^2$)
**Population:** 353,000 (Urban: 11%)
**Capital:** Honiara, 30,413

**Government:** Parliamentary state
**Languages:** English, Malay-Polynesian languages
**Ethnic Groups:** Melanesian 93%, Polynesian 4%, Micronesian 2%
**Religions:** Church of Melanesia 34%, Roman Catholic 19%, South Sea Evangelical 17%
**Currency:** Dollar
**Tel. Area Code:** 677

## Somalia (Soomaaliya)

**Location:** Eastern Africa
**Area:** 246,201 mi$^2$ (637,657 km$^2$)
**Population:** 6,823,000 (Urban: 36%)
**Literacy:** 24%
**Capital:** Mogadishu, 600,000
**Government:** Provisional military government
**Languages:** Arabic, Somali, English, Italian
**Ethnic Groups:** Somali 85%
**Religions:** Sunni Muslim
**Currency:** Shilling

## South Africa (Suid-Afrika)

**Location:** Southern Africa
**Area:** 433,680 mi$^2$ (1,123,226 km$^2$)
**Population:** 36,765,000 (Urban: 59%)
**Literacy:** 76%
**Capital:** Pretoria (administrative), 443,059; Cape Town (legislative), 776,617; Bloemfontein (judicial), 104,381
**Government:** Republic
**Languages:** Afrikaans, English, Xhosa, Zulu, Swazi, other indigenous
**Ethnic Groups:** Black 70%, white 16%, mulatto (coloured) 10%, Indian 3%
**Religions:** Black Independent 19%, Dutch Reformed 14%, Roman Catholic 10%
**Currency:** Rand
**Tel. Area Code:** 27

## Spain (España)

**Location:** Southwestern Europe
**Area:** 194,885 mi$^2$ (504,750 km$^2$)
**Population:** 39,465,000 (Urban: 78%)
**Literacy:** 95%
**Capital:** Madrid, 3,102,846
**Government:** Constitutional monarchy
**Languages:** Spanish (Castilian), Catalan, Galician, Basque
**Ethnic Groups:** Spanish (mixed Mediterranean and Teutonic)
**Religions:** Roman Catholic 99%

Currency: Peseta
Tel. Area Code: 34

## Sri Lanka

Location: Southern Asian island
Area: 24,962 mi$^2$ (64,652 km$^2$)
Population: 17,530,000 (Urban: 21%)
Literacy: 87%
Capital: Colombo (de facto), 683,000; Sri
Jayawardenapura (future), 104,000
Government: Socialist republic
Languages: English, Sinhala, Tamil
Ethnic Groups: Sinhalese 74%, Ceylon
Tamil 10%, Ceylon Moor 7%, Indian
Tamil 6%
Religions: Buddhist 69%, Hindu 15%,
Muslim 8%, Christian 7%
Currency: Rupee
Tel. Area Code: 94

## Sudan (As-Sūdān)

Location: Eastern Africa
Area: 967,500 mi$^2$ (2,505,813 km$^2$)
Population: 27,630,000 (Urban: 22%)
Literacy: 27%
Capital: Al-Kharṭūm (Khartoum), 476,218
Government: Provisional military
government
Languages: Arabic, indigenous, English
Ethnic Groups: Black 52%, Arab 39%,
Beja 6%
Religions: Sunni Muslim 70%,
indigenous 20%, Christian 5%
Currency: Pound

## Suriname

Location: Northeastern South America
Area: 63,251 mi$^2$ (163,820 km$^2$)
Population: 405,000 (Urban: 48%)
Literacy: 95%
Capital: Paramaribo, 241,000
Government: Republic
Languages: Dutch, Sranan Tongo, English,
Hindustani, Javanese
Ethnic Groups: East Indian 37%,
Creole 31%, Javanese 15%, black 10%,
Amerindian 3 %, Chinese 2%
Religions: Hindu 27%, Protestant 25%,
Roman Catholic 23%, Muslim 20%
Currency: Guilder
Tel. Area Code: 597

## Swaziland

Location: Southern Africa, landlocked
Area: 6,704 mi$^2$ (17,364 km$^2$)
Population: 875,000 (Urban: 33%)
Literacy: 64%
Capital: Mbabane (de facto), 38,290;
Lobamba (future)
Government: Monarchy
Languages: English, siSwati
Ethnic Groups: Swazi 95%, European 2%,
Zulu 1%
Religions: African Protestant and other
Christian 57%, tribal religionist 43%
Currency: Lilangeni
Tel. Area Code: 268

## Sweden (Sverige)

Location: Northern Europe
Area: 173,732 mi$^2$ (449,964 km$^2$)
Population: 8,581,000 (Urban: 84%)
Literacy: 99%
Capital: Stockholm, 674,452
Government: Constitutional monarchy
Languages: Swedish
Ethnic Groups: Swedish (Scandinavian)
92%, Finnish, Lappic
Religions: Lutheran (Church of Sweden)
94%, Roman Catholic 2%
Currency: Krona
Tel. Area Code: 46

## Switzerland (Schweiz, Suisse, Svizzera)

Location: Central Europe, landlocked
Area: 15,943 mi$^2$ (41,293 km$^2$)
Population: 6,804,000 (Urban: 60%)
Literacy: 99%
Capital: Bern, 134,393
Government: Republic
Languages: German, French, Italian,
Romansch
Ethnic Groups: German 65%, French 18%,
Italian 10%, Romansch 1%
Religions: Roman Catholic 48%,
Protestant 44%
Currency: Franc
Tel. Area Code: 41

## Syria (Sūrīyah)

Location: Southwestern Asia
Area: 71,498 mi$^2$ (185,180 km$^2$)
Population: 13,210,000 (Urban: 52%)
Literacy: 64%
Capital: Dimashq (Damascus), 1,326,000
Government: Socialist republic

**Languages:** Arabic, Kurdish, Armenian,
Aramaic, Circassian
**Ethnic Groups:** Arab 90%, Kurdish,
Armenian, and others 10%
**Religions:** Sunni Muslim 74%, other
Muslim 16%, Christian 10%
**Currency:** Pound
**Tel. Area Code:** 963

## Taiwan (T'aiwan)

**Location:** Eastern Asian island
**Area:** 13,900 mi$^2$ (36,002 km$^2$)
**Population:** 20,785,000 (Urban: 66%)
**Literacy:** 91%
**Capital:** T'aipei, 2,719,659
**Government:** Republic
**Languages:** Chinese dialects
**Ethnic Groups:** Taiwanese 84%,
Chinese 14%, aborigine 2%
**Religions:** Buddhist, Confucian, and
Taoist 93%, Christian 5%
**Currency:** Dollar
**Tel. Area Code:** 886

## Tajikistan

**Location:** Central Asia, landlocked
**Area:** 55,251 mi$^2$ (143,100 km$^2$)
**Population:** 5,210,000 (Urban: 33%)
**Literacy:** 96%
**Capital:** Dušanbe, 582,400
**Government:** Republic
**Languages:** Tajik, Uzbek, Russian
**Ethnic Groups:** Tajik 62%, Uzbek 24%,
Russian 8%
**Religions:** Muslim
**Currency:** Ruble

## Tanzania

**Location:** Eastern Africa
**Area:** 364,900 mi$^2$ (945,087 km$^2$)
**Population:** 27,325,000 (Urban: 33%)
**Literacy:** 46%
**Capital:** Dar es Salaam (de facto),
1,300,000; Dodoma (future), 54,000
**Government:** Republic
**Languages:** English, Swahili, indigenous
**Ethnic Groups:** African 99%
**Religions:** Animist 35%, Muslim 35%,
Christian 30%
**Currency:** Shilling
**Tel. Area Code:** 255

## Thailand (Prathet Thai)

**Location:** Southeastern Asia
**Area:** 198,115 mi$^2$ (513,115 km$^2$)
**Population:** 57,200,000 (Urban: 23%)
**Literacy:** 93%
**Capital:** Krung Thep (Bangkok), 5,845,152
**Government:** Constitutional monarchy
**Languages:** Thai, indigenous
**Ethnic Groups:** Thai 84%, Chinese 12%
**Religions:** Buddhist 98%, Muslim 1%
**Currency:** Baht
**Tel. Area Code:** 66

## Togo

**Location:** Western Africa
**Area:** 21,925 mi$^2$ (56,785 km$^2$)
**Population:** 3,880,000 (Urban: 26%)
**Literacy:** 43%
**Capital:** Lomé, 500,000
**Government:** Provisional military
government
**Languages:** French, indigenous
**Ethnic Groups:** Ewe, Mina, Kabye, others
**Religions:** Animist 70%, Christian 20%,
Muslim 10%
**Currency:** CFA franc
**Tel. Area Code:** 228

## Tonga

**Location:** South Pacific islands
**Area:** 290 mi$^2$ (750 km$^2$)
**Population:** 103,000 (Urban: 21%)
**Literacy:** 100%
**Capital:** Nuku'alofa, 21,265
**Government:** Constitutional monarchy
**Languages:** Tongan, English
**Ethnic Groups:** Tongan (Polynesian) 98%
**Religions:** Methodist 47%, Roman
Catholic 16%, Free Church 14%, Church
of Tonga 9%
**Currency:** Pa'anga

## Trinidad and Tobago

**Location:** Caribbean islands
**Area:** 1,980 mi$^2$ (5,128 km$^2$)
**Population:** 1,293,000 (Urban: 69%)
**Literacy:** 95%
**Capital:** Port of Spain, 50,878
**Government:** Republic
**Languages:** English, Hindi, French, Spanish
**Ethnic Groups:** Black 41%, East Indian 41%,
mixed 16%, white 1%
**Religions:** Roman Catholic 33%, Anglican
and other Protestant 29%, Hindu 25%

**Currency:** Dollar
**Tel. Area Code:** 809

## Tunisia (Tunisie, Tunis)

**Location:** Northern Africa
**Area:** 63,170 mi$^2$ (163,610 km$^2$)
**Population:** 8,367,000 (Urban: 54%)
**Literacy:** 65%
**Capital:** Tunis, 596,654
**Government:** Republic
**Languages:** Arabic, French
**Ethnic Groups:** Arab 98%, European 1%
**Religions:** Muslim 98%, Christian 1%
**Currency:** Dinar
**Tel. Area Code:** 216

## Turkey (Türkiye)

**Location:** Southeastern Europe and southwestern Asia
**Area:** 300,948 mi$^2$ (779,452 km$^2$)
**Population:** 58,850,000 (Urban: 48%)
**Literacy:** 81%
**Capital:** Ankara, 2,559,471
**Government:** Republic
**Languages:** Turkish, Kurdish, Arabic
**Ethnic Groups:** Turkish 85%, Kurdish 12%
**Religions:** Muslim 98%
**Currency:** Lira
**Tel. Area Code:** 90

## Turkmenistan

**Location:** Central Asia, landlocked
**Area:** 188,456 mi$^2$ (488,100 km$^2$)
**Population:** 3,615,000 (Urban: 45%)
**Literacy:** 97%
**Capital:** Ašhabad, 412,200
**Government:** Republic
**Languages:** Turkmen, Russian, Uzbek, Kazakh
**Ethnic Groups:** Turkmen 72%, Russian 9%, Uzbek 9%
**Religions:** Muslim
**Currency:** Ruble

## Uganda

**Location:** Eastern Africa, landlocked
**Area:** 93,104 mi$^2$ (241,139 km$^2$)
**Population:** 18,485,000 (Urban: 10%)
**Literacy:** 48%
**Capital:** Kampala, 773,463
**Government:** Republic
**Languages:** English, Luganda, Swahili, indigenous
**Ethnic Groups:** Ganda, Nkole, Gisu, Soga, Turkana, Chiga, Lango, Acholi
**Religions:** Roman Catholic 33%, Protestant 33%, Muslim 16%, Animist
**Currency:** Shilling
**Tel. Area Code:** 256

## Ukraine (Ukrayina)

**Location:** Eastern Europe
**Area:** 233,090 mi$^2$ (603,700 km$^2$)
**Population:** 52,800,000 (Urban: 67%)
**Literacy:** 97%
**Capital:** Kijev (Kiev), 2,635,000
**Government:** Republic
**Languages:** Ukrainian, Russian
**Ethnic Groups:** Ukrainian 73%, Russian 22%
**Religions:** Eastern Orthodox, Roman Catholic
**Currency:** Ruble, hryvnia

## United Arab Emirates (Al-Imārāt al-'Arabīyah al-Muttahidah)

**Location:** Southwestern Asia
**Area:** 32,278 mi$^2$ (83,600 km$^2$)
**Population:** 2,459,000 (Urban: 78%)
**Literacy:** 68%
**Capital:** Abū Ẓaby (Abu Dhabi), 242,975
**Government:** Federation of monarchs
**Languages:** Arabic, English, Farsi, Hindi, Urdu
**Ethnic Groups:** South Asian 50%, native Emirian 19%, other Arab 23%
**Religions:** Muslim 89%, Christian 6%
**Currency:** Dirham
**Tel. Area Code:** 971

## United Kingdom

**Location:** Northwestern European islands
**Area:** 94,248 mi$^2$ (244,100 km$^2$)
**Population:** 57,630,000 (Urban: 93%)
**Literacy:** 99%
**Capital:** London, 6,574,009
**Government:** Constitutional monarchy
**Languages:** English, Welsh, Gaelic
**Ethnic Groups:** English 82%, Scottish 10%, Irish 2%, Welsh 2%
**Religions:** Anglican 45%, Roman Catholic 9%, Presbyterian 3%, Methodist 1%
**Currency:** Pound sterling
**Tel. Area Code:** 44

## United States

**Location:** Central North America
**Area:** 3,787,425 mi² (9,809,431 km²)
**Population:** 253,510,000 (Urban: 74%)
**Literacy:** 97%
**Capital:** Washington, 606,900
**Government:** Republic
**Languages:** English, Spanish
**Ethnic Groups:** White 85%, black 12%
**Religions:** Baptist and other Protestant 56%, Roman Catholic 28%, Jewish 2%
**Currency:** Dollar

## Uruguay

**Location:** Eastern South America
**Area:** 68,500 mi² (177,414 km²)
**Population:** 3,130,000 (Urban: 86%)
**Literacy:** 96%
**Capital:** Montevideo, 1,251,647
**Government:** Republic
**Languages:** Spanish
**Ethnic Groups:** White 88%, mestizo 8%, black 4%
**Religions:** Roman Catholic 66%, Protestant 2%, Jewish 2%
**Currency:** Peso
**Tel. Area Code:** 598

## Uzbekistan (Ŭzbekiston)

**Location:** Central Asia, landlocked
**Area:** 172,742 mi² (447,400 km²)
**Population:** 20,325,000 (Urban: 41%)
**Literacy:** 97%
**Capital:** Taškent, 2,113,300
**Government:** Republic
**Languages:** Uzbek, Russian, Kazakh, Tajik, Tatar
**Ethnic Groups:** Uzbek 71%, Russian 8%, Tajik 5%
**Religions:** Muslim
**Currency:** Ruble

## Vanuatu

**Location:** South Pacific islands
**Area:** 4,707 mi² (12,190 km²)
**Population:** 153,000 (Urban: 30%)
**Literacy:** 53%
**Capital:** Port-Vila, 18,905
**Government:** Republic
**Languages:** Bislama, English, French
**Ethnic Groups:** Ni-Vanuatu 92%, European 2%, other Pacific Islander 2%

**Religions:** Presbyterian 37%, Anglican 15%, Roman Catholic 15%, other Protestant
**Currency:** Vatu

## Vatican City (Città del Vaticano)

**Location:** Southern Europe, landlocked (within the city of Rome, Italy)
**Area:** 0.2 mi² (0.4 km²)
**Population:** 800 (Urban: 100%)
**Literacy:** 100%
**Capital:** Città del Vaticano, 800
**Government:** Ecclesiastical city-state
**Languages:** Italian, Latin
**Ethnic Groups:** Italian, Swiss
**Religions:** Roman Catholic
**Currency:** Lira
**Tel. Area Code:** 39

## Venezuela

**Location:** Northern South America
**Area:** 352,145 mi² (912,050 km²)
**Population:** 20,430,000 (Urban: 91%)
**Literacy:** 85%
**Capital:** Caracas, 1,816,901
**Government:** Republic
**Languages:** Spanish, indigenous
**Ethnic Groups:** Mestizo 67%, white 21%, black 10%, Indian 2%
**Religions:** Roman Catholic 96%, Protestant 2%
**Currency:** Bolivar
**Tel. Area Code:** 58

## Vietnam (Viet Nam)

**Location:** Southeastern Asia
**Area:** 128,066 mi² (331,689 km²)
**Population:** 68,310,000 (Urban: 22%)
**Literacy:** 88%
**Capital:** Ha Noi, 905,939
**Government:** Socialist republic
**Languages:** Vietnamese, French, Chinese, English, Khmer, indigenous
**Ethnic Groups:** Kinh 87%, Hao 2%, Tay 2%
**Religions:** Buddhist, Chondoist, Roman Catholic, Animist, Muslim, Confucian
**Currency:** Dong

## Western Samoa (Samoa i Sisifo)

**Location:** South Pacific islands
**Area:** 1,093 mi² (2,831 km²)
**Population:** 192,000 (Urban: 23%)
**Literacy:** 98%
**Capital:** Apia, 33,170

**Government:** Constitutional monarchy
**Languages:** English, Samoan
**Ethnic Groups:** Samoan, mixed European and Polynesian
**Religions:** Congregational 50%, Roman Catholic 22%, Methodist 16%, Mormon 8%
**Currency:** Tala

## Yemen (Al-Yaman)

**Location:** Southwestern Asia
**Area:** 205,356 mi² (531,869 km²)
**Population:** 11,825,000 (Urban: 24%)
**Literacy:** 38%
**Capital:** Ṣan'ā', 427,150
**Government:** Republic
**Languages:** Arabic
**Ethnic Groups:** Arab, Afro-Arab
**Religions:** Muslim, Christian, Hindu
**Currency:** Dinar and Riyal
**Tel. Area Code:** 967

## Yugoslavia (Jugoslavija)

**Location:** Eastern Europe
**Area:** 39,449 mi² (102,173 km²)
**Population:** 10,622,000 (Urban: 50%)
**Literacy:** 90%
**Capital:** Beograd (Belgrade), 1,130,000
**Government:** Socialist republic
**Languages:** Serbian, Montenegrin, Albanian, Macedonian, Bulgarian, Hungarian
**Ethnic Groups:** Serbian, Montenegrin, Albanian, Macedonian, Bulgarian, Hungarian
**Religions:** Eastern Orthodox, Muslim, Roman Catholic, Protestant
**Currency:** Dinar
**Tel. Area Code:** 38

## Zaire

**Location:** Central Africa
**Area:** 905,446 mi² (2,345,095 km²)
**Population:** 38,475,000 (Urban: 40%)

**Literacy:** 72%
**Capital:** Kinshasa, 3,000,000
**Government:** Republic
**Languages:** French, Kikongo, Lingala, Swahili, Tshiluba
**Ethnic Groups:** Kongo, Luba, Mongo, Mangbetu-Azande, others
**Religions:** Roman Catholic 50%, Protestant 20%, Kimbanguist 10%, Muslim 10%
**Currency:** Zaire
**Tel. Area Code:** 243

## Zambia

**Location:** Southern Africa, landlocked
**Area:** 290,586 mi² (752,614 km²)
**Population:** 8,201,000 (Urban: 56%)
**Literacy:** 73%
**Capital:** Lusaka, 921,000
**Government:** Republic
**Languages:** English, Tonga, Lozi, other indigenous
**Ethnic Groups:** African 99%, European 1%
**Religions:** Christian 70%, tribal religionist 29%, Muslim and Hindu 1%
**Currency:** Kwacha
**Tel. Area Code:** 260

## Zimbabwe

**Location:** Southern Africa, landlocked
**Area:** 150,873 mi² (390,759 km²)
**Population:** 9,748,000 (Urban: 28%)
**Literacy:** 67%
**Capital:** Harare, 681,000
**Government:** Republic
**Languages:** English, ChiShona, SiNdebele
**Ethnic Groups:** Shona 71%, Ndebele 16%, white 1%
**Religions:** Animist, Roman Catholic, Apostolic and other Protestant
**Currency:** Dollar
**Tel. Area Code:** 263